Contents

Preface   5
Acknowledgements   6

1 **Organisations**   7
   What is an organisation?   7
   Why organise?   8
   Coordinating the specialist roles   9
   Organisational structures   16
   The growing organisation   21
   • Assignments   34

2 **How to be a better communicator**   41
   The importance of communication   41
   How and why organisations communicate
      internally   44
   Business-related communication   47
   Communicating a culture   51
   Relationship to structures   52
   Communication theory   55
   Skill-based approaches   57
   Redundancy and entropy   66
   Barriers to effective communication   69
   7-point plan for improved communication   74
   • Assignments   75

3 **The paperwork**   81
   The business letter   81
   Applying for a job   97
   The summary   101
   Telex   103
   The memorandum   103
   Writing reports   107
   Oral reports   122
   Forms and questionnaires   123
   • Assignments   129

4 **Dealing with people**   137
   The personnel department   137
   Person-to-person communicating   140
   Non-verbal communication   143
   Influencing other people   154
   Make them like you   156
   Summary and checklist for giving instructions   157
   I heard it on the grapevine   157
   Job interviews   159
   Appraisal interviews   162
   Counselling interviews   164
   • Assignments   168

5 **Wiring up the office**   174
   New technology?   174
   Systems   175
   Inputs   178
   Communication   180
   Storage   184
   Process   188

Outputs   191
Control   198
The office of tomorrow   199
● Assignments   201

6   **Winning the argument   210**

Putting your case   210
Spotting the flaws   218
Bringing our information alive   224
Giving presentations   234
Promoting an image   239
Meeting the media   242
● Assignments   247

7   **Working with others   257**

Communicating in groups   257
Working together   258
Group processes   259
Roles in groups   261
Group norms and cohesiveness   263
The group in the organisation   265
Group leadership   268
Trade unions and employers' organisations   271
Conflict in organisations   272
Meetings   275
Paperwork in meetings   281
● Assignments   288

8   **Getting the best from people   294**

Who's best for the job?   294
Advertising vacant posts   296
The interview   300
Promoting efficiency: management services   302
Improving job satisfaction   309
Motivation   311
Occupational psychology   314
How managers see themselves   318
Functions of the manager   321
● Assignments   323

9   **More about organisations   332**

How organisations grow   332
Some causes and effects of growth   336
Organisations in crisis   337
Relocating the growing organisation   338
Reorganising the office   341
Designing an office layout   343
From the pre-industrial office to the electronic
    office   345
Health and safety at work   347
Change in the commercial environment   353
The vanishing office   357
● Assignments   360

Index   365

Peopie in organisations

Dm Robinson

Page

Fella

Hutchinson

London   Melbourne   Auckland Johannesburg

Hutchinson Education

An imprint of Century Hutchinson Ltd
62–65 Chandos Place, London WC2N 4NW

Century Hutchinson Australia Pty Ltd
PO Box 496, 16–22 Church Street, Hawthorn,
Victoria 3122, Australia

Century Hutchinson New Zealand Ltd
PO Box 40-086, Glenfield, Auckland 10, New Zealand

Century Hutchinson South Africa (Pty) Ltd
PO Box 337, Bergvlei, 2012 South Africa

First published 1988
© Don Robinson, Stephen Page and Barbara Fella 1988

Typeset in 11 on 13 pt Palatino by
H. Charlesworth & Co. Ltd
254 Deighton Road, Huddersfield

Design by Heather Richards

Printed in Great Britain by
Butler & Tanner Ltd, Frome and London

British Library Cataloguing in Publication Data

Robinson, D.
  People in organizations.
  1. Organization
  I. Title   II. Page, S.   III. Fella, B.
  302.3′5′024658   HM131

ISBN 0–09–173152–6

Preface

This book has been written to help you meet all the requirements of the BTEC National double-core unit *People in Organisations* and, indeed, many other courses which also require an understanding of organisational structures and the ways in which people and information systems function within them.

People in Organisations is not intended to be studied as a single subject in the same way that you may have studied subjects for school examinations. Instead, it has been identified by BTEC as being part of an integrated course, involving the study of a number of complementary units containing a range of key themes common to all units of the course. The three themes are:

- Money
- Technology
- Change

These themes have been taken into account in the preparation of this book, and realistic business contexts have been used wherever possible to allow these themes to permeate naturally both the teaching and the learning strategies employed.

We have employed a conventional format of headed chapters, with **activities** integrated into the text, and longer **assignments** at the end of each chapter. This makes it very useful as either a class text in conjunction with tuition at college or for independent study. Care has been taken to ensure that the book is equally helpful whether you are a full- or part-time student, and allowances have been made for the fact that experience of the workplace and of study skills will differ between readers. Full use should be made of the index at the back of the book.

A glance at the contents page will confirm that the book follows closely the sequence of objectives specified by BTEC. However, this does not mean that topics cannot be studied in a different order where this is more convenient. To help you, each chapter contains cross references wherever a topic is dealt with elsewhere in the book. Generally, the level of difficulty posed by some activities and assignments increases as the book progresses, reflecting BTEC's philosophy that the first year of the course 'will focus on the skills and knowledge needed … in order to operate effectively within the work organisation' while the second year is expected to be 'directed towards the more complex needs of individuals and groups in the organisation'.

As you may know, the philosophy of BTEC courses is that students learn best when they experience things for themselves. For this reason, the activities and assignments are important parts of the book. The activities are to help you to understand points made as the text unfolds, and the assignments are to help to reinforce your knowledge and skills by applying and extending them within real-life contexts for which some preliminary work may be necessary. In all cases, there are opportunities to develop and explore the core skill elements defined by BTEC. Because of this, college lecturers may safely use these assignments for assessment purposes. Students following the course on their own will need to make contact with other students in order to provide experience of working in a group. If these conditions are met, this book will provide you with a reliable guide to the labyrinth of the organisation and of the ways in which people behave within it.

Acknowledgements

We would like to thank all our friends and teaching colleagues who have helped us with their contributions and advice. We are also grateful to the following for permission to reproduce copyright material.

Apple Computer (UK) Ltd
Association of Professional, Executive, Clerical and Computer Staff (APEX)
DGR Barratt
Birmingham City Council
Cadbury-Schweppes
Fontana
Gold Spot Division
Health Education Council
HMSO
The Independent
Lyons Tetley Limited
Management Today
Midland Bank Plc
The Observer
Office Secretary
Pan Books
Penguin Books Ltd
Personnel Management
Rover Group
Woodland Trust
Works Management

1

Organisations

What is an organisation?

Organisations are everywhere and their influence on our lives is far-reaching. For example, where are you reading this book? At home? If so, 'home' is probably the base for the organisation you know as your family. It may not seem very organised; nonetheless it possesses the principal characteristic of an organisation, for it is a group of people cooperating to achieve some purpose — in your case we hope it provides some physical comforts and a sense of security.

Perhaps you are reading this book at college. Your college is yet another type of organisation, but it still possesses the characteristic of groups of people cooperating with each other to achieve the common purpose of providing a satisfactory education for you and other students. Or, maybe, you are reading the book in a library. This, too, is an organisation where staff perform a variety of tasks from ordering, cataloguing, and shelving new books and magazines, to recording loans made to borrowers. In other words, it is an organisation whose function is to ensure that the resources which you and others require are readily available.

These are all examples of organisations to which you may belong: your family, a college of further education and a library. However, most people belong to dozens of organisations during their lives.

ACTIVITY

Make a list of all the organisations of which you are, or were, a member. You may head your list with: 1 Family, 2 College, 3 Library.

You will have found your list to be quite extensive and you may wish to extend it even further when you compare it with the lists of others. Most people have had a job at some time in their lives, even if only a part-time one, and, with the exception of self-employed people, they will have been working for an organisation. Indeed, this experience is what most people think of when they begin the study of organisations. So working for a company or a public undertaking is a very common way of experiencing organisations, and it is one to which we shall return many times in the course of this book.

The workplace is only one of many places where we experience organisations. Some of you may have been a patient in hospital. A hospital is a particularly vivid example of how organisations affect and influence people. As a patient, you can expect to be prodded and probed, your nakedness exposed to all and sundry, your body cut open, stitched up, and smothered in plaster, with tubes stuck in your mouth and elsewhere. You will be subjected to a remarkable degree of control under a strict daily regime which you dare not challenge. As one patient in Peter Nichols' play, *The National Health*, wryly comments 'They wake you up to give you a sleeping pill here'.

In your list, you may have said that you are a member of a church or religious group, or of a political party or pressure group, and you probably accept that your attitudes and behaviour have been influenced in one way or another by your membership. Some of you will have recorded membership of recreational groups: of choirs, youth clubs, works' social clubs and sports clubs. Although these are usually voluntary groupings, they are still organisations in which groups of people cooperate for a common purpose.

An analysis of team sports is a particularly helpful way of understanding organisations and provides a useful introduction to organisational theory. Team sports obviously require the collaboration of the players; they are highly competitive (most organisations compete with each other); their success rate can be monitored easily (do they win or lose?); and many are involved in big business, run on a commercial footing, with professional players earning a living by selling their skills, even if only for a relatively short period in their early adult life.

Why organise?

Look at this press cutting which reports the signing of Gary Lineker by Barcelona:

Barcelona goes for bust

World Cup hero Gary Lineker has signed for Spanish giants Barcelona in a £3 million deal that will make him a virtual millionaire overnight.

Barcelona officials emerged from several hours of talks in London to reveal the Everton and England striker was committing himself to a six-year contract.

They declined to confirm the fee, but the deal is expected to be worth £3 million to Everton.

Lineker, one of world football's hottest properties after capping his Footballer of the Year season by becoming the six-goal top scorer in the World Cup, was due to complete the formalities today.

Lineker, 25, came face-to-face with Barcelona manager Terry Venables while working as a BBC panellist during Sunday's TV coverage of the World Cup final.

Both parties remained tight-lipped on the move, but Barcelona director Jose Luis Nunez junior was already working behind the scenes to complete the deal before Lineker marries on Saturday.

Everton's windfall from the Lineker sale is good news for Leicester, his former club. A clause laid down by the tribunal who fixed his £800,000 fee from Filbert Street to Goodison Park 12 months ago stated that Leicester should receive part of the profits if Everton sold him within two years.

▲ *Based on Everton FC press release*

Why does the Spanish club want to buy this particular player? Obviously for his ability to score goals and not for his ability as a goalkeeper, or because he can tackle opponents, or for his passing ability. It is principally because he is a 'striker'. In other words, he is expected to fulfil a very specialised role in any team he plays for, namely to put the finishing touch to a scoring move.

You will probably be familiar with the idea of playing in a given position from your school games lessons: soccer, hockey, netball, cricket and rugby football all contain elements of this concept. Associated with the various positions on the field are a range of appropriate skills, and the idea is that by playing regularly in a particular position a player is given the chance to develop specialised skills by regular practice. Specialisation by function, as this is known, has other advantages. When a player is injured, he or she can be replaced by another player with similar skills, with minimal disruption to the team's performance. As well as this, players come to know what to expect of each other, which considerably advances group cooperation, and this in turn may determine the difference between a winning and a losing team performance.

Now apply this idea of specialisation by function in an organisation that you know fairly well. If you have a job, this is the best place to start. If not, try applying it to a hospital or to some other similar public institution, like a college.

Although it is not possible to discuss the full range of specialisms that are present in any particular organisation, we can briefly look at just two: a hospital and a college. In a hospital, besides all the administrative, laboratory and cleaning staff, there is a broad division between those who diagnose illness and prescribe treatment (the doctors) and those who administer it and care for patients round the clock (the nurses). And within these two groups are further hierarchies, so woe-betide the patient who confuses a distinguished consultant for a junior houseman or who muddles up Sister with a student nurse. Alternatively, if you jotted down the specialisms to be found in a college, you will have distinguished between the lecturers, the administrative, cleaning and technician staff. Though teaching is a skill, it too has its specialisms, and a lecturer in accountancy will be unwilling to take a class in, say, human biology. Similarly, a lecturer in a subject with a declining demand is unlikely to be able to switch to teaching within a growth area, for example from classics to information processing. This illustrates one disadvantage of specialisation. It can create problems in an organisation when a key staff member is sick or absent, or when an industry is experiencing rapid technological change. However, it is a price most organisations are willing to pay because of its greater benefits.

Coordinating the specialist roles

If each individual member of a group of specialists is performing his or her own functions well, the group as a whole may still not be successful. If we reconsider the example of a football team for a moment, we can see this very clearly. There have been many examples of clubs that have bought established players, often at great expense, and yet have failed to achieve the success that might have been expected from so talented a group of players. One reason for failure might be because individual players have been unable to play together successfully.

A solution adopted by clubs to stimulate cooperation has been to put one person in actual charge of the team during the game: the team captain. However, even more important than the captain is the off-stage figure of the team manager, who devises tactics and motivates the players. The captain is usually an experienced player who leads by example. The manager may be a former player, but he or she must lead by inspiration and by calculated judgement, and have the ability to deliver the success that players and fans want.

This relationship between manager and captain and between captain and players can be expressed diagrammatically.

Team Manager
|
Team Captain
/ | \
Rest of players

▲ *Relationships within a team*

Such diagrams have their limitations. For example, the manager will not only contact players through the intermediary figure of the captain, but will also communicate directly with individual players. However, the chart does indicate the formal structure of authority within a sports club, and for that reason it is useful.

However, for a professional sports club, the playing of matches is only one of a number of functions undertaken. In an average British Football League Club, a structure like the one shown below may exist.

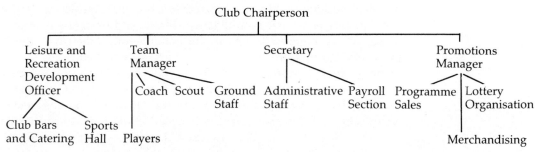

▲ *The structure of a professional football league club showing vertical structuring by function*

What is noticeable here is that a great deal more than just training and playing goes on at a professional football ground. Indeed, it is questionable whether football managers, who are often former players, are equipped with the many skills the club as a whole may need. The usual strategy adopted to cope with this problem is to divide up the workforce into sections, based on the individual's function in the organisation, and this is known as the **vertical** division of an organisation, because the lines of division run through the organisation from top to bottom.

Another example, this time based on a subsidiary of the National Bus Company, is shown below. It again shows the diversity of functions that exist in even a relatively small organisation providing only a limited product or service range.

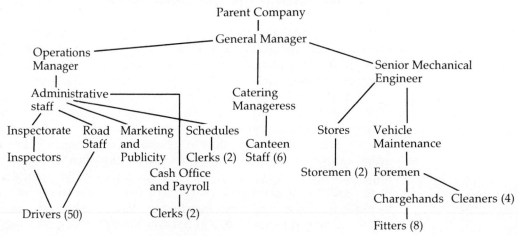

▲ *The organisation of a small bus company*

It is likely that you will have drawn a 'family tree' diagram that looks like this:

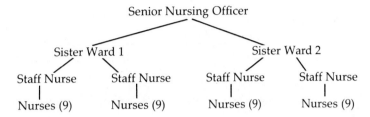

▲ *The organisation of nursing staff in a small District General Hospital*

There are other ways of representing organisational structures and we shall consider some of these later, but there is no doubt that this vertical type is more usual and more helpful in understanding the nature of organisations that have a *hierarchical* structure.

Do you remember what we said about the nature of organisations at the beginning of this chapter? We claimed that organisations are groups of people cooperating to achieve a purpose. But this does not mean that cooperators all have to be of equal status. Consider the family as an example. Scientific study has pointed to countless examples of families where either the mother or the father plays the dominant role in exercising authority over their children, while at the same time willingly accepting responsibility for their welfare. It is interesting that many people in authority in hierarchical organisations like to talk about their company or their department as being 'one big happy family' and see themselves, most being men, as father figures. Yet, just as parents can never rely on children to behave in exactly the way they should behave, so people in organisations cannot be relied upon to comply exactly with the demands of the organisation. That at least is the conclusion of Etzioni, a distinguished American sociologist and writer on the subject of organisations. His views are reflected in this fragment of conversation between two shop workers who are discussing their supervisor's holiday.

Sue: 'I'll be glad when she's on holiday. Then we might get a bit of peace. I'm really looking forward to next week.'

Michelle: 'Yeah, that's right, me too. She's always chasing after us. I'm gonna take it easy and enjoy myself.'

Unlike most families, organisations like to have a formal structure or a hierarchy of authority. According to Etzioni, workers need to have job descriptions for each specialism, laid down procedures for doing things, and above all supervision within a chain of command. We shall discuss in more detail the topic of employee needs in Chapter 8.

This means that most organisations may not only be represented as a 'family tree' showing the functional differences between individuals and groups, but they can also be represented as a pyramid, which has the advantage of showing the *power structure* within an institution at a glance. An example of such a pyramid is given at the top of page 12.

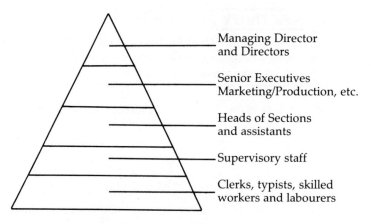

▲ *An organisational pyramid of a private sector company*

At the top is the Managing Director of the company; at the bottom are the production staff or operatives; and in the middle the managers and supervisors. The pyramid shape suggests a 'tall' organisation containing several layers of 'bosses' whose individual level of authority or power increases in relation to the distance from the base of the pyramid. However, within each layer, particularly within the bottom two layers, the relationship between supervisors and their subordinates can vary from firm to firm and from department to department. One useful model we can use employs what are called 'spans of control', which simply means the number of staff each supervisor is directly in charge of. Obviously the number of staff a person has to supervise will have an important bearing not only on production targets, but in terms of departmental communication and personal relationships. We will look at just two types of 'spans of control', although both types can exist within the same organisation.

- Small span of control within a tall organisational structure
- Large span of control within a flat organisational structure

When an organisation employs a small span of control at supervisory level, this means that each supervisor is directly responsible for only a small number of staff. In the following example, each supervisor is responsible for three operatives:

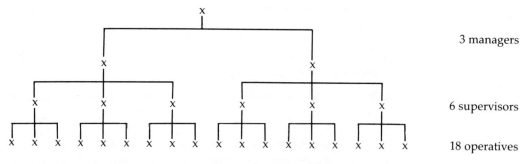

▲ *Tall organisational structure — small span of control*

Within this organisation it should be easy for each supervisor to maintain group control and develop closer human ties, providing the supervisor has the right kind of personal qualities and skills. On the other hand, because there are more intervening layers of management, communication both up and down the management line will take a little longer than in the following example of the 'flat' structure.

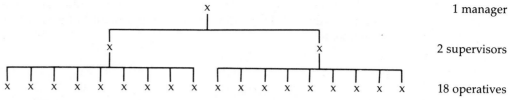

x	1 manager
x x	2 supervisors
x x x x x x x x x x x x x x x x x x	18 operatives

▲ *Flat organisational structure — large span of control*

Flat structures are also cheaper because money is saved on supervisors' wages. However, they are usually only appropriate where large numbers of employees are performing routinely similar tasks. When task differences between small groups of workers are more marked, it is sensible to adopt the tall structure to avoid imposing impossible burdens of coordination and supervision upon a single supervisor. So while a flat structure might be appropriate for a telephone exchange, a tall structure might be preferred for a complex department like Finance.

ACTIVITY

Read these snatches of conversation and answer the following questions.

Pattie: Hullo! Where have you been sticking your fingers then?

George: (holding up a bandaged finger) In that stupid photocopier. Why didn't someone tell me it's bust? I've torn one of my nails off.

Pattie: Ooooh! That's Emma's job. She's the supervisor. She should have stuck a notice on it. She doesn't seem to have time to do anything these days since her job's been expanded. She's been put in charge of the payroll section, you know.

George: Yes … (thinking) … things have changed here. It's difficult to find a supervisor these days. I wonder how much time is wasted chasing about trying to get a decision made? … My finger doesn't half throb.

1 (a) Suggest what kind of supervisory changes have occurred in this office.

   (b) With reference to the passage where appropriate, explore the possible effects of large and small spans of supervisory control in relation to:
      — output and labour costs;
      — interpersonal communication and problem solving;
      — safety factors.
   You may draw on examples from your own place of work if you wish.

2 Explain which type of management structure, tall or flat, would be most suitable in the following situations:
      — the night shift at a photographic processing laboratory;
      — a comprehensive school;
      — a large retail department store.

Whether tall or flat or any other combination of what are called 'T' charts, these structures illustrate what is known as the **Scalar** principle. This says that all employees must know where they stand, with a clear unbroken chain of command running from the top to the bottom of the organisation. Supporters of traditional structures such as these argue that clear-cut line relationships between subordinates and their superiors, represented in these diagrams by unbroken lines, are important both for efficiency and good decision-making. Under these circumstances, staff know to whom they have a *responsibility* (i.e., to the person immediately above them in the management line) and over whom they have *authority* (i.e., over those below them).

However, not all working relationships can be represented like this because people work not only with those in their own department but also with people from different departments.

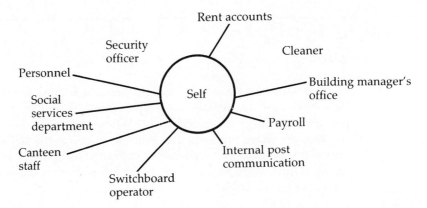

▲ *Some organisational contacts across departments for clerk in Housing Allocation Section of a local authority*

Look back at the organisational structures we have considered so far. None of them shows any cross-departmental communication, unless we assume it travels up one branch of the management line to the top, before crossing to another department; in other words, by following *line relationshps* between people. Clearly, this seldom occurs. However, horizontal communication between different departments is vital for large organisations, and is a frequent event. None the less such informal communication may exist with no-one being able to exercise any control over anyone else, except by mutual agreement. These relationships are not shown, therefore, on any diagram of an organisation's structure.

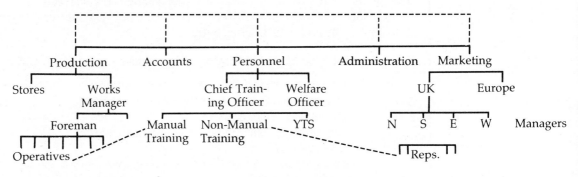

▲ *Line and staff relationships in a manufacturing company*

However, another category of relationship, does exist. Examples are shown on the diagram above using broken lines, and are known as *staff relationships*. In this case the Personnel Department (which has its own line management) can be seen acting as a specialist department, operating on behalf of *all* other departments in the provision of training courses.

These staff relationships are not a substitute for line management, but complement it. So, a sales representative's area manager will direct and control him in his day-to-day work, but it is the Training Section which will organise courses in selling skills or product knowledge. However, Training has no authority to direct a representative to attend such a course; it can only suggest or recommend such action, and leave the final decision to the line manager.

You will find another example of such staff relationships incorporated in the structure diagram of a traditional shire county Police Force later in this chapter. In the case of the Police, however, there is a special problem that lower ranking officers in specialist branches (e.g. CID) may resent the legitimate exercise of authority by senior officers in the non-specialist uniform branch. For example, a detective constable, though technically of lower rank, may find it difficult to take orders from a sergeant in uniform.

ACTIVITY

Consider the following situation:

The missing drawings

Helen, a junior designer, is working in the drawing office when the phone rings. It is a call from the Marketing Manager who says that after lunch he is going to pop out to see the buyer for one of the firm's most valued customers. He asks whether he could 'borrow' a set of drawings to take with him to show the buyer, who is very interested in the new product line due to be launched in the autumn. There is no-one else in the office, but Helen knows that her own boss, the chief designer, is not keen on drawings being taken away as some details have to be finalised. However, as the request comes from the Marketing Manager, she agrees.

When she returns from lunch she finds her colleagues searching the office and her boss fuming. One set of drawings for the new product line seems to be missing. When Helen explains that the company may win a big order because of what she's done, she gets a vicious dressing-down from her boss. Angrily she accuses him of doing a similar thing only last week. He retorts that what a boss can do is different from what an assistant can do. She says the rules should be the same for everybody. He says, finally, that she ought not to say any more and get on with her work.

1 In organisational terms, what do you think has happened here?

2 What advice would you offer to prevent a similar situation in the future?

To summarise, we have said that organisations have the following characteristics.

- Shared objectives
- Departmental structures
- Hierarchies

Hierarchies also provide the framework on which career structures are built. Career structures themselves allow individuals to climb the promotion ladder. The promotion ladder, in turn, reflects the value that organisations place on success. The higher up one climbs, so the rewards increase. In order to attract the most able to apply for these lofty positions, organisations are obliged to offer the most attractive inducements possible. Although these inducements are usually linked directly with the organisation itself, in some jobs there may be indirect financial rewards. Before you start the next activity you might like to discuss the indirect financial advantages of being:

- a Member of Parliament
- a BBC chat-show presenter
- a buyer

ACTIVITY

What inducements are offered to employees to progress to more senior or powerful positions within an organisation? Try to give examples from an organisation that you know.

How many of these points did you make?

- More money — promotion invariably means a higher rate of pay, although it may mean loss of potential overtime payment.

- More status — the very structure of the company may allow the promoted person to gain authority 'over' former colleagues.

- Better conditions — a bigger desk, perhaps an office set apart from others, and possibly protection from unwelcome intrusion by a personal assistant called a secretary.

- The opportunity to regulate one's own work — if necessary by passing less desirable work to subordinates.

- Different work — the job may consist of high-status tasks, such as being taken out to lunch by sales representatives and dealing with important customers.

- Unofficial flexibility over hours — the emphasis shifts towards 'doing the job effectively', rather than 'attending the office for X hours a week'.

You probably thought of several others. The point is that most hierarchical organisations set out to make promotion as attractive as possible in order to ensure that staff continue to be motivated well after their initial enthusiasm for the company or the job has worn off. Indeed, the perks have also to offset the disadvantages of climbing the hierarchical ladder. The major change is that the further an employee goes up the ladder, the more responsibility he/she has to accept for work over which he/she may have little real control. General Eisenhower's claim that he had a sign on his desk, when he was President of the USA, which read 'The Buck Stops Here' is an example of this principle. In other words, as individuals get promoted their success or failure becomes more reliant on the success or failure of subordinates.

Once again, professional sport provides a graphic example of this burden of responsibility. Consider how frequently managers of ailing football clubs risk sudden dismissal when the team is doing badly. Even if the fault lies elsewhere, it is usually 'the boss' who draws the hostility of the fans and the attention of the directors, who may fire him.

Organisational structures

It is now time to consider the ways in which the structures of organisations vary. There are several reasons for this.

- Organisations vary in size.
- Some organisations perform few, others many, functions.
- Organisations produce different things: some manufacture goods, others provide services.
- Organisations may operate on one site, others on several.
- Organisations may work a 9 to 5 day, others work all round the clock.
- Organisations operate in different markets: some markets are stable (primary education), others are volatile (car and computer sales).
- Organisations tend to respond to the latest fashion and trends in management theory.

ACTIVITY

Suggest an example for each of the different types of organisations contained in the previous list. Can you think of any further reasons why the structures of organisations might vary?

Underlying all these factors is the belief that the way an organisation is structured will influence that organisation's success. Managers seeking to get the best from their workforces will review systems to look for refinements to improve output and efficiency. Such changes may be triggered by internal factors, such as delays, or by external factors, such as restructuring by a major competitor. The type of organisational structure adopted will influence not only the person applying for a job, but more obviously the lives of those who actually work there. Let us look more closely at the relationship between structure and its influence upon employees.

The size of organisations

Size (i.e., number of employees) is the most important factor in influencing the way a business is likely to be organised. The organisational objectives, in turn, not only determine the type of management structure, but also have important consequences for each individual employee. Perhaps the most telling way of illustrating the effects of size on both the nature of the organisation and the individual is by comparing the experiences of people who work for the two extreme types of organisation: very small and very large.

The first task is to make a few notes about your own place of work. On the left in the following list there are seven characteristics that are considered to be important features of organisations. On the right, each characteristic has been reinterpreted in the form of questions that should help you with your notemaking. If you are a full-time student these questions could be used to compile a questionnaire with which to conduct a survey with employed students. But first you will have to think about what exactly is meant by the terms 'small', 'medium' and 'large' in describing organisations.

How would you describe the size of your employing organisation?

Large ____ Medium ____ Small ____

Characteristics	Questions to consider
1 Awareness of structure	How far are you aware of the structure of your organisation? (other sections, departments, promotions, etc.) How were you made aware of it: group induction, staff handbook, casual conversations, etc? How much do you know about your organisation's management structures and staff gradings?
2 Frequency of written internal communication	What sorts of written communication do you experience? How much time do you spend on internal communication? What percentage of written communication is relevant to you?
3 Separation of function and task demarcation lines	Do you experience a strict division of labour? Do you tend to do the same kinds of jobs in the same place? Is your salary and grading linked with your job title?
4 Number and nature of groups and subgroups within the organisation	Generally speaking, do the staff get on well together regardless of status? How many, and what sorts of small-group cliques can you identify? How vigorously do these groups resist 'outsiders'?
5 Differences between intention and actuality	Do all departments and sections actually do what they are supposed to do? Is everybody convinced of the value of their work? Does any person or group take 'advantage' of the organisation?
6 Extent to which parts of the organisation are self-regulating	How often is your work effort assessed? How easy is it to cover up mistakes or continue with bad habits? Is there an obvious relationship between being good at the job and 'getting on'?
7 Management styles	How accessible is the boss? How accessible is your supervisor? What kinds of 'barriers' exist to prevent easy access to your bosses? In value-for-money terms, how does your contribution compare with the supervisory staffs' contribution?

You can now form into discussion groups and compare notes. Here is a record of a few comments made by a student working for an electrical equipment manufacturer (Brenda) and a student from a hairdressing salon (Biff).

	Brenda's comments (big organisation)	Biff's comments (small organisations)
1	People at my place see themselves as cogs in a wheel — all aware of being part of a larger whole. We find this because we're obviously taken on to do a pre-determined job in a way that somebody else lays down. We were given loads of papers to read at induction and we were told lots about the organisation — but I've forgotten most of it.	Although I began as a trainee, I've gradually taken on more and more responsibility. Although Mario is still 'the boss', he isn't very heavy-handed about it. We talk things over and try to work them out between us. I don't remember anything about induction. I just turned up on the first day, got introduced, and started work.
2	My desk will probably have two or three memos on it when I get in tomorrow. Nothing important, I bet. We know most of the stuff already — either that or it's not really relevant. Then if something important does turn up, it is often ignored because we're always being bombarded with paper.	Mario's never written a memo in his life! If any problem crops up, everyone knows about it in a short time, so what's the point of memos? There aren't many secrets in the salon. If Mario sees something he doesn't like, he'll come over at once.
3	Definitely! Everybody has their own work to do, and doesn't want to be lumbered with anyone else's. It's becoming a problem for management. Mind you, it's even worse on the shop floor. Sometimes jobs stand unfinished for ages because the specialist fitter is tied up or off sick.	Everybody has little jobs they have to do — like the trainees have to shampoo nearly all the customers' hair. Mario likes to do all the rich women and he never lets anyone else do the books. But if anyone's off sick, we all just get stuck in and the jobs get done.
4	Most people are fairly friendly, but there's friendly and friendly — if you know what I mean. I mean the top bosses are nice and smiling, but they don't mean it, and if they are busy, they'll just ignore us completely. I try to be nice to the cleaners, but we've not got much in common. The place is so big it's not possible to be friendly with everyone. I often meet staff I've never even seen before.	Now that I think about it, the two trainees we've got at the moment — they're a bit cliquish. Always giggling and talking about the fellas who come into the salon or wait at the bus stop outside. Mario likes to rub shoulders with the other shop owners on the parade. But apart from that I don't think there are any internal divisions to speak of. We're either all happy or all miserable together.
5	It depends. Some sections seem so strict. I wouldn't want to work there. Other sections are very sloppy. I work in audit — sometimes the figures we have to work on are riddled with mistakes. No-one ever seems to get pulled up about it. But if yours truly does anything wrong, that's a different story. But this woman in our section, always off sick, although there's nothing wrong with her — but she gets away with it.	Mario says we've got to send every customer away feeling happier than when they walked in. Apart from that, there isn't a stack of rules. Mario just gives you a lot of dirty looks, say if you're late. If we make a real mess of someone's hair, he'll come over and make suggestions or gradually take over. He might give us a bit of a lecture when the customer's gone. Even when he's not there, we still behave ourselves. It's what the customers expect.

6   A few years ago we started having assessment interviews with Mrs Pearman. But to be honest, we don't do much self-assessment. People are always moaning about the time we take to do audits, but we always make excuses to justify delays rather than try to find out what caused them. It's very difficult to understand why some people get promoted and others don't. They must be good at interviewing!

Mario's brilliant. We all try to live up to his standards, not very easy some of the time. It's a very public job, too, as there aren't any cubicles or anywhere you can hide your mistakes from others. Also it's very competitive — lots of other salons — so we're pretty receptive to new ideas, I think. There's no real opportunities for promotion. Getting on usually in this game means leaving and setting up your own business.

7   I've never seen Sir Hector. Not in the flesh. I've seen his Roller in the executive car park though. Our supervisor, Mrs Rathbone, has a desk in one corner that she's surrounded with potted plants to make out it's a separate office, but nobody's fooled. She hates to be called 'Mave', so some of us call her that just to get her back up. I reckon I could do her job actually.

Mario's in every day, except Thursdays in term time, when he does this part-time lecturing job at the college. You know he's the boss, of course. He's got a little office at the back, which we can only go in when he wants to see us. But he's very friendly and approachable. There's no way I can compete — he's a genius. But I could do the paperwork better.

┌ ACTIVITY ┐

Describe the characteristics of large and small organisations that are likely to have important consequences for an individual employee. You may quote from Brenda's and Biff's comments and draw on your own experiences to illustrate your answer.

Although it is impossible to predict exactly what your group will have said in discussion, given the variety of management styles that organisations employ, it will be surprising if you have not mentioned some of the differences noted by Brenda and Biff about large and small organisations. For example, employees in large organisations are usually more aware of the existence and effects of structure because it is important to them and their work. Matters such as promotion, regrading, trade union wage claims, moving office, discussion about where so-and-so works are the bread and butter of office chatter, and endless private conversations may take place over the internal telephone system.

Equally important is the greater need for written communication in larger organisations. It is not the fact that in small organisations everyone can be told face-to-face about things relatively easily which avoids the need for flurries of paper. As growth occurs, people begin to form subgroups — departments, sections, project teams, interest groups — and loyalty to the organisation as a whole becomes overtaken by loyalty to the subgroup. As a result, big companies resort not only to memos and notices, but to house magazines, electronic mailings, posters and briefing meetings, to inform their dispersed and sectionalised staff about important items of company news.

You may also have commented on the tricky subject of 'unofficial' conduct within the organisation. People are sometimes unwilling to confess to bending the rules, so perhaps the members of your group seem rather virtuous! However, in large companies staff tend to be more conscious of official and unofficial conduct because the sheer size or complexity of the organisation has forced management constantly to remind staff about what they can and cannot do. In small companies, like a hairdressers, there are simply fewer formal rules and regulations from which staff can deviate. Therefore, it is not possible to get told off for clocking someone in because there is no clocking-in system. On the other hand, it is difficult to cover up mistakes because there are no mountains of paper to hide behind. Unofficial conduct is not always damaging to an organisation. Sometimes it is a response to a changing set of circumstances, which later forces a change in official procedure. For instance, the introduction of 'flexible working hours' followed management pressure that workers should arrive punctually and not leave early. But dental appointments, the demands of children, bad weather and difficulties with public transport meant that rules were frequently breached. Finally, many organisations introduced 'flexitime' so that such 'unofficial' conduct could be accommodated within the system.

The extent to which official procedures develop in large organisations can best be illustrated by the highly controlled drill of the soldier. Although some companies require employees to behave creatively, the army sergeant uses the drill routine to repress the desire of the individual soldier to think himself different from any other soldier. This is because in battle conditions, orders have to be obeyed to the letter and there is no room for independent action — at least, not for the common soldier. Following orders is more important than the exercise of individual responsibility. Similar attitudes can be found in large civilian organisations where the call for standardised procedure is normal, and even encouraged at the expense of personal initiative, and the phrase 'I'm only doing my job' is employed as an escape route. Similarly the phrase 'it's more than my job's worth' is usually a tactical device used by staff who have decided that what the customer wants is in conflict with what the organisation approves.

Because such procedural controls discourage staff from thinking for themselves, a recurring trend in management techniques in large organisations has been to try and remove the unhelpful aspects of these procedures by transferring decision-making processes to the lowest possible level, thus encouraging individual initiative. In other words, large organisations are seeking to recapture the self-regulating characteristics of small organisations that they lost in the process of growth.

Lastly, you were asked to think about the remoteness of the 'boss'. Some of you may work in firms so big that you never meet or even see the Chairperson or the Managing Director. As a substitute, a photograph and perhaps a supporting message will appear from time to time in the house magazine. This 'distancing' has the effect of shoring up the authority of those in senior positions by making them remote; perhaps they even occupy an office high-up in the building, with access controlled (i.e., restricted) by a secretary in an anteroom. Even in small firms a certain sense of remoteness may be engendered by the 'boss', and older employees may notice that he/she becomes a little less approachable as the business expands and prospers.

ACTIVITY

These extracts are taken from real-life advertisements.

1 Describe briefly the management structures likely to be found in these two organisations. On what basis did you arrive at your decision?

2 In what respect are the jobs likely to be
   (a) similar
   (b) different
   in terms of professional responsibilities and personal relationship with management?

3 What techniques have been used (perhaps unconsciously) by the advertisers to communicate their differing organisational structures and demands?

SECRETARIAL CHALLENGE

We're looking for an experienced, unflappable secretary to work for a team of dynamic advertising managers.

Ours is an exciting environment, where the work is varied and fast moving, calling for a high level of organisational ability, initiative and adaptability.

You'll also need to demonstrate very accurate typing skills, including audio, together with a good telephone manner and the confidence to utilise our modern communications equipment to the full.

So, if you have enough experience and 'go' to rise to the challenge, we'll reward you well — and in addition you'll have all the benefits that go with working for a very friendly and successful city firm.

Please apply in writing to:

The growing organisation

Few organisations start large, but many find a need to increase their production and take on extra staff, even if this was not their original intention.

ACTIVITY

Ken, a painter and decorator who works from home, describes himself as a one-man business. However, he actually has to perform quite a number of functions, in addition to rubbing down or stripping and applying paints or hanging paper. What else would you include in his working day?

?   ?

?   ?

?   ?

Preparing, painting and decorating

Purchasing materials

In fact, he has many functions, and you could have listed any of the following:

Day-to-day book-keeping

Transport

Preparing accounts and tax returns

Preparing, painting and decorating

Jobbing repairs (e.g. replacing rotten woodwork, retiling bathrooms)

Taking telephone enquiries

Advertising

Estimating

Correspondence

Purchasing materials and maintaining equipment

Advice on design/decor

Ken finds he has so many jobs to do, that he can't manage all of them by himself. So his wife, Mary, takes the telephone calls, types letters and estimates for customers and helps keep the books. For professional advice, particularly about tax, he engages an accountant. Additionally, one of his friends, Graham, helps out with jobbing repairs, or when Ken gets a job too big to manage on his own.

ACTIVITY

From time to time Ken's accountant suggests he should take on extra people and increase his turnover. So far, Ken has resisted. What reasons might Ken have for not taking on extra staff? Here are some clues:

▲ *Come on lads! Let's have another hand. Ken's gotta pay us, whatever the weather.*

▲ *Well, how were we to know which way up to hang the paper, Ken?*

▲ *I dunno! I never seem to get out on site anymore.*

The badge maker

Betty decided to invest her £1000 redundancy pay in a badge-making machine. This device consisted of a hand-operated press that clamped together the metal and plastic picture discs. Betty's main interest was graphic design, and she created a number of one-off badges with different pictures and messages on them. She would then wear them when she went out and sell them to anyone who showed an interest. At 50p a badge, when the components cost only 5p, this seemed set to be a profitable business.

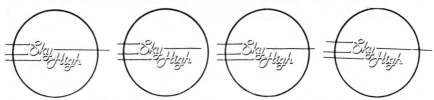

After a few weeks, a friend who had a band asked Betty to make 200 badges which could be sold to fans. Betty was excited at getting an order of this size and started work with enthusiasm. This soon waned. The badge press could produce a maximum of 100 an hour, assuming it did not clog or jam (which it frequently did!). The work gave Betty an aching back and shoulder, and was extremely boring. She had dropped her price to 20p a badge for the bulk order, and with components, design materials and printing costing 12p, this seemed to be a hard way of earning £16. When the local school requested 1000 badges for their annual fete, Betty wondered whether her muscles could stand it, and also when she was going to find time to go out looking for new customers or create new designs.

Fortunately, her friend Eric then offered to help. Eric was a body builder who spent all day in a gym pumping iron. He was not very bright, and was quite happy doing a repetitive job providing it built up his muscles. He took over all production, freeing Betty for the work she did best.

Eventually Betty ran out of orders from her immediate circle. It was clear that new markets must be found if the business was to survive. However, she found it difficult to get out looking for customers while the design and preparation of existing orders took up most of the day, and if she waited until her order book was empty, there was no money coming in. Then Steve — whose own business selling personalised T-shirts had failed for the same reason — offered to use his wide network of contacts in the entertainment and retail fields to find new badge customers. He spent every day travelling round collecting orders and delivering badges. It was Steve who suggested that Betty could call her business *First Impressions*.

The three of them worked flat out, and every night Steve would return to base with his pockets bulging with money. Some would be seized back for petrol, Eric would take some to buy new badge components and Betty would take the rest for printing and art materials. And there would be nothing left! Although the three were working to capacity, and turnover was increasing, there didn't seem to be any corresponding rise in profits. They were not even able to pay themselves a wage. Then Helen came to their rescue. Shocked at the lack of records, she insisted on opening a bank account, on recording all income and expenditure, and on pricing each order with regard to labour as well as material costs. As an accountant, she paid for herself within a few weeks.

Betty's next problem was not apparent for several months. Then past customers started to ask for repeat orders. But where was the original design? Letters and telephone calls making enquiries or asking for quotes kept arriving. Who would deal with them? It was clear that an administrator/secretary was needed to set up job files for each enquiry, to process correspondence in and out, and generally to ensure the other four specialists were able to concentrate their attentions on their own jobs.

The one-person business had grown to appreciate the need for the four major functions which exist in ALL business organisations:

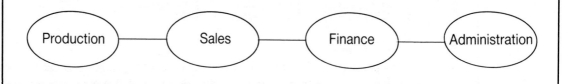

The previous story illustrates several points.

- Each person has a limited number of hours in his or her day and the business may demand more.
- Each person has limited skills
- Each person has specific aptitudes and skills and is most productively employed using them and not others.

However, it also reveals the problems that emerge through growth.

- There are increased costs, e.g., in wages, stock, transport and premises.
- There is a need to trust others and to delegate to them.
- There is the creation of the new job of managing-the-work-of-others. This may prove to be as difficult and time-consuming as the original work that was delegated.

One of the first decisions of the growing organisation that is taking on new staff is to decide how to divide up the work.

Jane Payne is the proprietor of Jane's Jeans, a retail business selling jeans, T-shirts and casual wear for young people. She employs 26 people. She wants to review the current structure of her organisation to see whether she will need to take on more staff before opening another shop.

1 From the following information, construct an organisation chart.

Job title	Number of employees
Sales assistants	12
Store manager	1
Senior sales persons	4
Wages clerk	1
Clerical assistant	1
Supervisors	4
Buyer	1
Cleaner	1
Accountant/Administration manager	1

2 Describe the role and provide a brief job description for each of the following staff. (You are advised to do some research into these jobs before you begin.)

- Supervisor
- Buyer
- Store manager

3 *Jane's Jeans* decides to launch its own brand label. They plan to promote the brand by using, amongst other media, a give-away badge. When you contact the badge-makers *First Impressions*, they suggest that you draw out a couple of alternative design ideas on 7 cm circles.

The influence of size on organisational structure can now be summarised in the following developmental chart, which shows the changing characteristics of a manufacturing company as it expands. (Based on Hunt's *Managing People at Work* — Pan Books.)

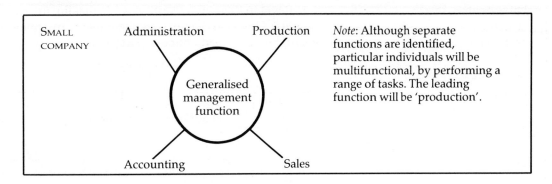

SMALL COMPANY — Administration, Production, Generalised management function, Accounting, Sales

Note: Although separate functions are identified, particular individuals will be multifunctional, by performing a range of tasks. The leading function will be 'production'.

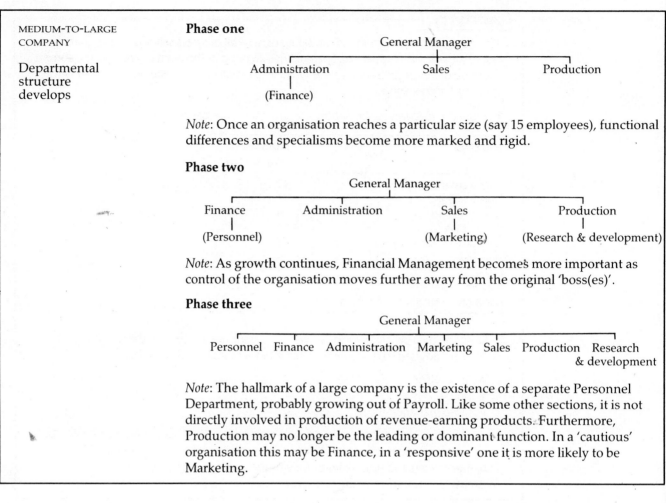

MEDIUM-TO-LARGE
COMPANY

Departmental
structure
develops

Phase one

General Manager

Administration — Sales — Production

(Finance)

Note: Once an organisation reaches a particular size (say 15 employees), functional differences and specialisms become more marked and rigid.

Phase two

General Manager

Finance — Administration — Sales — Production

(Personnel) — (Marketing) — (Research & development)

Note: As growth continues, Financial Management becomes more important as control of the organisation moves further away from the original 'boss(es)'.

Phase three

General Manager

Personnel Finance Administration Marketing Sales Production Research & development

Note: The hallmark of a large company is the existence of a separate Personnel Department, probably growing out of Payroll. Like some other sections, it is not directly involved in production of revenue-earning products. Furthermore, Production may no longer be the leading or dominant function. In a 'cautious' organisation this may be Finance, in a 'responsive' one it is more likely to be Marketing.

VERY LARGE
COMPANY TO
CONGLOMERATE

Divisional
structure
employed

Head Office
structure

Divisional
structures
replicate
those at Head
Office

Note: One way in which companies respond to successful penetration of their markets by competitors is to buy them out. Another is to diversify into new products and new markets. When either occurs, a common response to the structural difficulties that ensue is to adopt a divisional structure. This permits the divisions to develop their own identity, while making the success of their activities easy to monitor. However, it may lead to conflict between local (i.e., divisional management) and the Head Office departments.

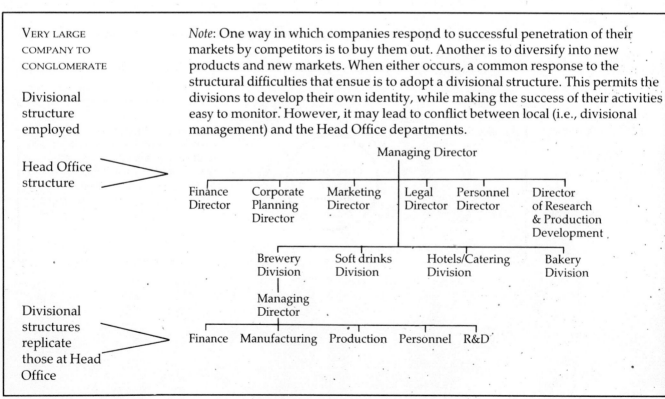

Managing Director

Finance Director — Corporate Planning Director — Marketing Director — Legal Director — Personnel Director — Director of Research & Production Development

Brewery Division — Soft drinks Division — Hotels/Catering Division — Bakery Division

Managing Director

Finance Manufacturing Production Personnel R&D

- You can see that at its inception, a small company will probably have no functional structure at all. This is not because specialist functions do not exist or are not recognised, but because they are usually distributed on an informal basis, with staff, particularly if they are founders and partners, performing a whole range of functions as the need arises.

- As growth occurs, informal arrangements gradually become formalised, so that the organisation can benefit from specialisation. As a result, structures emerge. The structure shown for **Phase one** will probably emerge when employees number about 15 or so.

- If growth continues, it becomes less easy for those who started the company to ensure financial control of their business. If they have used the services of an external accountant, they may have to take up more and more of his time. Perhaps the company will employ a debt collection agency to chase up bad debts, or perhaps the need for internal auditing to increase efficiency or identify such things as pilfering will call for a specialist employee to oversee the financial management of the business. If none of the founders is a specialist, a new department called Finance will come into being.

- As expansion continues, new functional specialisms begin to press for adequate time, resources and recognition. By **Phase three** the maturing company has added a separate Research and Development Department (to keep one step ahead of the opposition), a Marketing Department (to keep two steps ahead of the competition), and probably a Personnel Department (to coordinate training, recruit and select new employees and to keep an eye on morale).

The founders probably stare in bewilderment at the structure that results. It is so different from when they started. Looking along the **Phase three** line, they count seven departmental heads (eight with the General Manager) and only one of them is directly concerned with making what they actually sell. Quite understandably, during time of cut-back, it is the most recently established departments which are the most likely candidates for pruning. However, this is not to say that the function is discarded, merely performed in another way. For example, Birmingham City Football Club has recently franchised a number of functions which were formerly performed on an 'in-house' basis. These include promotions, catering, match programmes and car parking. In local councils, too, it is common to see cuts in the numbers of workers and managers because some council functions have been put out to tender. Alternatively, some part of the salary bill may be saved by merging departments — perhaps by reverting to an earlier phase in the organisation's growth.

┌─ **ACTIVITY** ───

You work for Hendon Bicycle Company. In organisational terms they have reached **Phase three**, with seven departmental heads under a General Manager. Unfortunately, they are going through a serious crisis, with outdated products, poor sales, promising or successful staff being poached by rivals, and poor morale among those who remain. It has been decided to 'slim down' the present structure by saving at least two Head of Departments' salaries. In your class or group, stage a debate in which each departmental head and Managing Director (to be played by members of the group) makes a short statement in defence of his/her post, and argues for his/her department to remain a separate entity. Other group members may cross-examine speakers, before a vote is taken and the victims chosen. Obviously this activity requires some preliminary research into the general functions of each department.

Differences in organisational output

Variations in output may also influence structure. So far we have seen how specialist functions create departments, but structures may also be set up around a particular product, service, process or even items of equipment. For example, when computers were first introduced they were so expensive and space-consuming that specialist departments were set up to service the functional departments which could not afford an installation of their own.

It is also very common in manufacturing to find that the production function may be structured around individual products or product groups, with perhaps a few service or equipment-based sections remaining the direct responsibility of the Production Manager. Such a departure from traditional organisations is illustrated in the following diagrams. Diagram (a) represents traditional structuring by function, the so-called 'process-based' structure, while (b) shows how the structure changes when it becomes 'product' based.

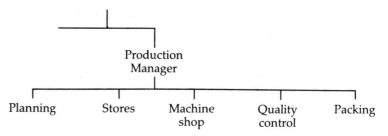

▲ *(a) Production organisation: 'process-based' organisation*

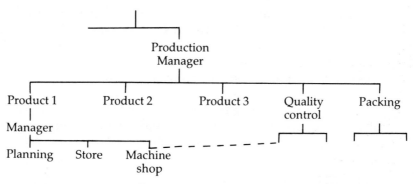

▲ *(b) Production organisation: 'product-based' organisation*

In the diagram showing the product-based structure, it can be seen that there is an absence of a 'career structure' for some specialists in each product group. One way round this problem is to establish some sort of *matrix* structure, which we will discuss on page 31.

A further refinement in some organisations occurs when there is a limited number of very important customers. Under these circumstances it may be necessary to structure the organisation so that selected employees 'specialise' in the needs of one, or just a few, customer(s). A good example of this is the Account Executive in an advertising agency who looks after the interests of particular clients.

▼ *Customer-based organisation (Advertising Agency)*

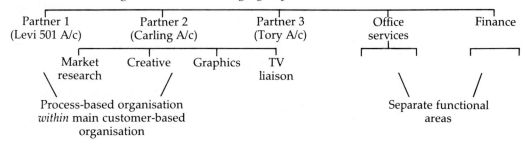

The influence of time and place on structure

We no longer have to work 16 or even 12 hours a day as was common in Victorian factories and mines, but many organisations need to operate a 16- or 24-hour day. This has led to the development of the double and treble 8-hour working shift. This shift system has been adopted, with minor variations, in a number of enterprises, for example in mining industries, photographic processing laboratories, the police force, and so on. Such *time-based* systems create difficulties in supervision and coordination, which need to be accommodated in a modified management structure.

Several locations may also mean a further level of authority within a structure. Regional tiers of management may be found in the Health Service, in many companies involved in sales and servicing, in banks and building societies. The police force, which is organised on a county and regional basis, is divided into divisions and subdivisions. It is therefore interesting to study the structure of a typical force because it shows the influence of the three factors we have considered: function, time and place.

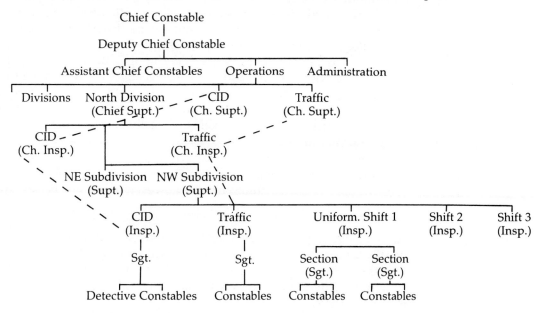

▲ *Operating structure: traditional Shire County Police Force*

ACTIVITY

Look carefully at the diagram and try these questions.

1 How are police forces organised: (a) on an area basis, (b) on a time basis, (c) by functional specialism? Explain your answer.

2 Identify the staff who have responsibility for coordination on the basis of: (a) operational area, (b) time of day, (c) specialist function.

3 Find the Traffic Inspector in the North West Subdivision. To whom does he/she have line responsibility? What is his/her relationship with the Chief Inspector (Traffic) at Divisional HQ?

4 This diagram is a simplification because it does not include all the functions or methods used by the police — for example, dog handlers, or members of specialist squads such as the Drug Squad. Nonetheless, it does help us to understand some of the problems that might exist for the police in liaison and coordination. Suggest some problems that you would expect to find.

The effects of external influences

No organisation is isolated from external pressure. Even the most bureaucratic organisations (e.g., central government departments and large companies with a dominant market share) are affected by what goes on beyond their boundaries. However, those organisations likely to be most responsive to a changing environment are those which are most obviously in competition with others.

Once again, sport provides a graphic example. Until 1957 England considered itself the finest footballing country in the world. So it came as something of a culture shock when the visiting Hungarian team trounced the home side 6 goals to 3 at Wembley in that year. Suddenly English clubs had to review their playing strategies and implement team formations that found favour in Europe and South America. A disturbing external influence (i.e., losing to superior teams) resulted in structural change in positional play on the pitch.

For most organisations, the principal external influence is the market. Sometimes the importance of particular customers is so great that the organisational structure is fashioned around them. This is often the case with advertising agencies where internal structures are based upon the accounts of particular clients. On the other hand, if competitors are moving in to reduce market share (as with the British motor vehicle industry) or if a firm's market share is declining because of changing taste or technical progress (as with the demand for some beers, e.g., the change to lager), the first response of any organisation is likely to be to raise the marketing function in importance, either by improving the publicity of the product (and hence its sales) or by seeking new markets in which to sell either existing or totally new products. The next step is to think about reorganisation.

One type of reorganisation we have already discussed is the change to a divisional structure. Can you remember why such structures are likely to evolve? Check back if you are not sure. Structural change, however, need not be so far-reaching as this. Consider the circumstances in which an existing client calls for a major innovation in a product or service which the organisation supplies. At first, each department responds, but finds difficulty in coordinating their response with those of other departments. This usually leads to the development of a **hybrid structure**. In other words, in order to cope with the problem, a new temporary structure is imposed over the existing departmental structure. There are two basic variants of hybrid structures: the project team and the matrix structure.

Project teams

Project teams come in many forms. They may be called by that name, although they are often called **working parties** to begin with. Later, if the project team approach has been successful, it may replace the functional department structure under the supervision of **product managers**. This point has already been mentioned on page 28.

In an organisation opting to use the project team approach, it will be normal to appoint a project manager and to give him or her a clear set of objectives to be achieved within a defined period of time, and then to appoint a team, either nominated from existing departments or by internal application and interview. However, their appointment to the team does not mean they have parted company with their former departments as they will still be responsible to their old line manager as well as to the new project manager.

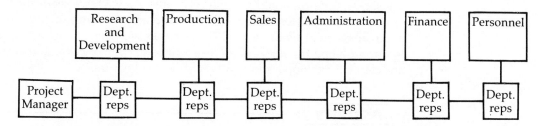

▲ *A project team structure*

ACTIVITY

Can you suggest the problems that membership of a project team would pose for the employee concerned and for the department he/she has just left?

Matrix structures

Where project teams provide short-term solutions to the organisation's problems, the functional departments continue to exercise control over the employee. However, when the organisation believes that this form of integrative structure is of lasting value, a true matrix structure may be introduced. It is called a matrix because it is represented on paper as a grid. The grid has two axes which represent the twin loyalties of each employee: one to the departmental structure, the other to the integrated group in which they are involved. Such matrices are known as **routine matrices** because they are relatively long-lived.

If you are studying at a college you may like to ask your lecturer whether there is a matrix structure at the college. A lecturer may be a member of the Business Studies Department, but the courses on offer may require lecturers from more than one department. Therefore the two axes on the matrix of a college are first the departments (organised on the basis of subjects) and second the qualifications for which courses are offered.

	Multi-subject courses, organised by Course Coordinator	DEPARTMENTS (5 Heads)				
		Science	Business Studies	Electrical Engineering	General Studies	Art and Design
Students enrol for	GCE 'A' Level	*	*	*	*	*
	Pre-Vocational		*	*		*
	Recreation/Leisure		*		*	*
	Sound and Video	*		*	*	*
	Women's Studies	*	*	*	*	*

* Indicates courses on offer in that particular area of study

▲ *Example of a simplified matrix structure at a College of Further Education*

A word of warning. Do not get muddled up between the two axes of the matrix and the horizontal and vertical divisions of organisations that we dealt with earlier. The matrix is a method of achieving integration across the functional departments which keep their own horizontal and vertical characteristics.

The influence of fashion on organisational design

The project team and the matrix are currently undergoing a period of popularity. Before this, conventional wisdom preferred the more traditional structures, shaped by specialisation, time-span and geographical area. As we have seen, such organisations were expected to have clear chains of command and channels of communication: known as line management relationships. However, as we know, many acts of communication do not occur along the line, rather they run across the organisation between departments, and depend on cooperation and reciprocated favours.

From this chapter you should have gathered that there are a number of ways in which organisations can be structured. Unfortunately, there is no single organisational structure which is universally acceptable, so the design of organisations is very much at the discretion of those who manage them. Furthermore, the structures adopted are likely to undergo change as organisations add or discard functions, grow or shrink in size, or otherwise respond to external pressure. The impact of technological change upon organisations is likely to produce further refinements in structure, and these will be dealt with in Chapter 5.

You will also be aware by now that the organisation of the workplace has important consequences for us in the way we personally experience the activity called 'work'. The structures of organisations not only determine how many departments and bosses we have, but crucially influence the size of work teams, our working conditions, our personal relationships, and above all the way we communicate with each other. However, we must not fall into the trap of believing that 'big' always means 'impersonal' and 'small' always means 'friendly' when we talk of organisations. In ordinary human terms, working for a huge organisation might in practice mean working effectively with a small friendly team under an easy-going boss with whom one gets on well. Working in a small organisation can mean experiencing a deeply hostile and impersonal environment. Even so, there can be no doubt that we cannot understand human relationships properly unless we take into account the structure of organisations. We are now in a position to examine the nature of communication within organisations in more detail.

Car factory puts young in driving seat

NO ONE has told them, but most of the 11,500 hopefuls applying for the 250 assembly jobs at Nissan's new car plant in the North-east are wasting their time.

As the first recruits report to work at the £50 million factory in Washington, Tyne and Wear, it is clear that the much-vaunted project is providing little opportunity for the unemployed or the over-thirties.

The company is looking for workers who already have a job in industry, but are still young enough to be moulded into the Japanese production philosophy. What it fears above all is entrenched attitudes.

In the town centre, where the jobless rate of 22 per cent is twice the national average, Harry Townsend, Job Centre manager processes applications for the plant believing that all ages stand a chance. He says: 'Over-representing any particular groups would bring problems of its own.'

The reality is very different. So different, in fact, that Brian Carolin, 29-year-old Nissan personnel manager meets the charge of rampant ageism with the remark: 'We do have one manufacturing staff person in his mid or late thirties.'

Nissan is taking on workers each week as it gears up to build its first car for sale in the summer. There are high hopes that within three years it will provide nearly 3,000 jobs and produce 100,000 cars a year.

After a tour of the factory last week, it was clear that, at the age of 32, I would be too old to pass muster.

At 45, Peter Wickens, the leading British Nissan director, is about the oldest person on the premises.

Remarkable pains are being taken to make interviews objective. A candidate is interviewed by two supervisors and then again by two others who make a separate assessment. The key to employment is the applicant's willingness to co-operate fully within each group of about 20 workers who build the cars.

Then, at the end of five hours of interviews, a successful job seeker is personally handed a job offer letter by his supervisor — a first step to building loyalty.

Christopher Hindmarsh, 25, is typical of the new breed. Until last month, he was a fitter at a nearby shipyard where he says job security was 'nil.'

Kitted out in the Nissan overalls worn by staff at all levels, Mr Hindmarsh says: 'The company offer you a lot as long as you are prepared to do things in their way—which is efficient and organised.

'We have a sympathetic team leader and you feel free to suggest ideas. It's very refreshing compared with the shipyard management.'

The lure of Nissan is not just security and perks like private medical insurance, available to even the most junior employee.

The absence of decisions imposed from above is also a draw. Mr Wickens, who spent 10 years with Ford, says: 'Even at this stage our staff are saying they are treated with respect by management.'

The company's obsession is that the British-built Nissan Bluebirds should match, or better, the high quality of the cars imported from Japan. Responsibility for quality lies with each worker, not inspectors.

Mr Wickens says: 'You only get quality by getting commitment and by offering shopfloor workers responsibility. It's no use management mouthing platitudes and continuing to kick people around.'

If this consensus style of management is a benefit, the drawback is the intense pressure on the individual from his group. Only recruits who will bow to this are being selected. No worker will need to clock on. Equally, no one is under any illusions about what will be said about lateness.

SCENARIO

You are asked to read these extracts from an article 'Car factory puts young in the driving seat'. (Observer 13 April 1986)

TASK ONE / QUESTIONS

1 Briefly summarise the main message of the article.

2 Why do you think the company is interested in only recruiting young workers? Suggest a few advantages of this policy for the company.

3 What did the Job Centre manager mean when he said 'Over-representing any particular groups would bring problems of its own'? What problems are likely to arise in the present and future for: (a) the company, and (b) the workers?

4 What techniques have the organisation adopted to increase worker participation?

5 In what way is Nissan likely to be different from traditional car plants in terms of line management responsibilities and attitudes? Can you think of any important disadvantages for Nissan employees?

TASK TWO / MEMO FOR PERSONNEL

Draft a two-page memo to be sent to the Personnel Department of your company. In it you will suggest ways to improve efficiency through greater employee participation. These may well include changes in company policy and line management structures — possibly by introducing matrix or project team ideas — as well as specific proposals that could be put into effect quickly.

To Senior Trainee   From Training Officer

Induction of new Trainees

As you will have heard by now, the company is likely to be taking on a number of trainees straight from school this year. This is good news in view of the fact that these will be the first to be taken on for three years. One of the problems, of which you will be well aware, is that the company has not been very successful in keeping trainees, so I am keen to 'win them over' as soon as they arrive.

I also know from interviews with you that the process by which you were introduced to the company was not very well received. I am most anxious to avoid some of the problems that we had then, and for this reason I am requesting your suggestions for improvements to the process.

First, I would like all new trainees to receive a pamphlet shortly before they arrive, setting out the answers to the sort of questions they might be asking before they start work. It should not be too lengthy: about two sheets of A4 paper folded, at most.

Second, I think all new trainees should be given a two-day Induction Course. The purpose of this is to introduce school-leavers to the organisation, to give them a little self-confidence, and to help them 'settle in'.

As part of your in-house training programme, I should like each of you to design such a leaflet to give to our newcomers. To help you do this, I am enclosing a useful summary of the sort of things to include, which I have taken from the book you are using at college, *People in Organisations*, by Robinson, Fella and Page.

I have also photocopied some extracts from 'exit' interviews of trainees who have left companies in recent months. I think these may help you in deciding what sessions we ought to have in the Induction Course.

Finally, I would welcome any general suggestions about what we ought to do for these young people. In view of the comments you made to me about your own experiences, I am looking forward to some very practical and relevant submissions.

SCENARIO

Your organisation has decided to review its induction procedures. In the internal post you receive this letter from your office manager.

TASK ONE / THE PAMPHLET

Prepare a pamphlet in accordance with the instructions given in the letter. You will have to make decisions about what to put in and what to leave out, and some of the information will be drawn from material covered on the other units of the course. However, you must not include information just because it is 'easy' to get hold of. You are expected to plan, write, and produce an attractive layout to the point of 'camera-ready' artwork, before submitting a photocopy for assessment. Please consider the inclusion of diagrams, drawings, charts, etc. to illustrate your pamphlet, and you are allowed an additional colour (e.g. black + red). Documents one and two on pages 36/37 may be of assistance.

TASK TWO / PLANNING THE COURSE

Assuming two days are available, work out, in outline, a suitable programme for the induction of new employees. You may decide that the best way to do this is by dividing up the days into convenient time slots before adding the details. Remember that you are expected to produce an interesting and varied programme that is not all 'talk'.

Present your outline plan for submission along with your pamphlet. You will be joined by others to form a discussion group to help you with this as only one programme per group is required.

DOCUMENT ONE

Employer's guide for an Induction Programme

I am providing you with some general headings for your guidance. Although some of them are not relevant to our company, they should help you with your task.

Reception

What the employee should bring with him/her before starting work.
Whom he/she should meet.
Under what circumstances the reception should take place.
What he/she should be told about the size, function and structure of the company.

Conditions of employment

Hours of work, lunch and tea breaks, periods of notice.
Salary calculation, stoppages and method of payment.
Suggestions for effective 'budgeting' of wages.
Overtime and bonus schemes.
Pension and other schemes.
Holiday and sickness leave.
Medical certificates.
Absence through illness — procedures.
Welfare and recreation facilities.
Education and training — college attendance.
Trade union membership and employee/management consultation.
Other fringe benefits or perks.

Important locations

Cloakroom and lavatory facilities.
First Aid and medical facilities.
Entrances and exits.
Clocking in or signing in and out arrangements.
Canteen facilities.
Notice boards and publications for employees.
Layout of factory/office.

Special rules and regulations

Smoking.
Dress or special equipment.
Appropriate behaviour.
Security information.
Particular rules and regulations.

Safety and First Aid

Safety in general: lifts, legislation, special knowledge, protective clothing.
Fire precautions, drill, alarms and equipment.
Fire escapes and exits; fire doors.
First Aid and location of trained staff.
Hazardous materials and procedures.

DOCUMENT TWO

Statements made by young people in their exit interviews

Published in 'Management Review'

Below is a selection of extracts describing young workers' experiences of their early days at work.

A lot of people have told me that they didn't have a proper induction when they started work. I had two weeks altogether, and I can honestly say it was a waste of time. I've never been so bored in all my life. This old bloke kept giving us lectures on the history of the firm and introducing us to different staff, who then gave us more lectures. I can't remember anything they said. We were talked *at* every day for two weeks and shuffled round the place. We did watch a video about young people starting work and played a few games. In one game I was supposed to be a frog and someone else who was a worm had to convince me that she wasn't worth eating — that was a good laugh.

Clerical worker

My first big shock came when I got my first pay-packet. I really thought I'd be well off but it just wasn't true. I'd no idea about all the stoppages. I couldn't believe it when I saw all those columns of deductions like pensions, tax and insurance. To tell you the truth, I wish somebody would have explained all those things to me. I still don't know how income tax works. What's a code number for instance? I bet you half the population don't know what that is. I don't even know whether I've been paying too much tax. In fact, I had more money when I was a schoolgirl.

Catering trainee

You feel a real fool when you first start. I did anyway. Nobody would tell me anything. They were all too busy. I mean simple things like going to the lav — it took me ten minutes to find it — it could have been really embarrassing. When I first started I couldn't even find the entrance to the factory. Someone had sent me to the wrong place and when I asked for Mr Harris nobody knew what I was talking about. Later on I found that I should have brought my medical card with me, but I wasn't told. Then I discovered that there was no canteen and no-one told me where I could get anything to eat. I never did have anything to eat on that first day. It must have been the worst day of my life.

Factory worker

The day-release thing got me. To be honest with you I thought going to college would be easy. But after you get there at nine o'clock you don't leave until eight. Now if I was at work I'd be home at six. And you don't get paid any overtime. The company expects you to put in the hours. Also when you are at college you have plenty of work to do and you have to be just as punctual as you are at work. I've lost an hour's pay for being late for a class. You also find that you've got to do lots of homework. Now I knew most of this because I've got a good training officer. But some kids at college didn't really understand what was expected of them. Some of them got a big surprise when they were told they had to go to college. They thought they had left all that behind them when they left school.

Trainee electrician

SCENARIO

In preparation for the analysis of your own company, read the article on pages 39/40, 'Commercial approach proves its worth', published in *Works Management* (November 1981). This deals with two different approaches to the problem of making organisations more responsive to the needs of customers.

TASK ONE / QUESTIONS

Give brief answers to these questions.

1 State the names and business activities of the two companies mentioned in the article.

2 In your own words explain the nature of the problem each company was experiencing, and give a brief summary of how the problem was dealt with.

3 Explain, with reference to the article, whether or not the companies benefited in their business activities from greater consultation with the staff.

4 Which company, in your view, was forced to make the more radical change in management structure? Try to explain in what way the new structure was designed to change employee attitudes.

TASK TWO / MANAGEMENT STRUCTURES

1 Produce an organisational chart either for your own company or for one that you can find out about (i.e., your college or an organisation that a friend or relative works for).

2 State the total number employed by the company, its main business activities, and try to describe its overall organisational structure (i.e., departmental or matrix). Explain whether there has been any recent change in management techniques (e.g., introduction of working parties, project teams, department reorganisation).

3 Explain in detail the type of employees and specialist departments that have particular responsibilities for dealing with customers and relating customer requirements to other departments within the organisation.

TASK THREE / CUSTOMER RESPONSE

You are now to assess how responsive the organisation is to its customers' needs. In particular, whether the organisation's structure helps or hinders the customers in satisfying their needs. You could bear these questions in mind.

● What is the turn-round period for particular products or services?

● Do competing organisations have better turn-round periods than yours?

● Could turn-round times be improved? How?

● Does the organisation have a 'leading' function? Is the leading function an internal one (e.g., personnel) or is it more outward looking?

● How is the organisation structured? By functional specialisation or by product or client groups as in the case of Westland?

● Is there a form of 'matrix' structure in the place? Does it integrate employees any better than before its introduction?

● If no matrix exists, should one be introduced? How might it help to improve customer service?

Commercial approach proves its worth

Peter Chambers shows how two companies—and their line managers—have benefited from making production more market-sensitive

One of the commonest criticisms levelled at managers who have come up via the production/works route is that they have little understanding of and less sympathy with the commercial needs of the organisation. Conversely, many production people find it hard to get any co-operation from marketing when they want to improve production efficiency by rationalising products.

At any time, it can be instructive to look closely at companies of different sizes and in different industries that have managed to overcome these problems. We have been examining two contrasting organisations whose manufacturing executives show this vital breadth of vision and have an impact on the marketing side. In the process, we found, these companies have been able to tackle an issue which is particularly thorny at this time: achieving the level of stocks that best meets the powerful but conflicting demands of customers and cash flow.

In Hozelock Ltd, a 200-employee consumer products manufacturer, two of the key factors are regular informal contacts across functions and between different management levels; and the fact that the works manager has had extensive customer contact.

Westland Helicopters is quite a different case, though its target—responsiveness to customer demands—is the same. The company has over 7,000 employees and until less than two years ago it had a traditional functional management hierarchy which was perhaps appropriate for its purely military/governmental worldwide markets. A loss of £4.3 million in 1978, however, threatened the company's very existence: as a result it has branched out into the 'growth' civil markets and made production more responsive to commercial needs.

A closer look at Hozelock shows that it, too, could not survive without commercial sensitivity, which in this case has developed gradually over the years. The company's main product line is garden watering equipment such as hose connectors and sprinklers, in which it is the UK market leader and has a large share of the market in many of the 67 countries to which it exports. Sales are, of course, not only highly seasonal but also greatly influenced by the weather.

Hozelock copes with this in two ways. The first is by building up stocks of finished products before the start of each selling season. The other way is by providing a very rapid turnaround of production against orders, when the product quantities required are not all in stock. The company prides itself on being able to provide a two-week turnaround—on occasion, this includes getting in the raw plastics material and colourant in granule form, moulding the components, assembling the complete product and despatching it half-way round the world. With the aid of a computer, export orders are fed into a production programme within hours of their arrival. However, it's not often that a complete order has to be made from scratch, thanks to detailed planning and projection of demand. Needless to say, a tight rein is kept on suppliers' delivery and prices.

What are the implications for the way works manager Peter Fewell operates? "I look at the operation from the sales point of view," he says, "probably because in my early days with the company—I've been here 15 years—I often went overseas to talk to customers about what we could and could not do for them technically." Significantly, he has overall responsibility for product design, including packaging, as well as for industrial engineering and the production departments. His close working relationship with the chief executive is also crucial: his office is just a few steps away from that of managing director David Codling. They meet most days and work closely together on major projects—the latest is selection of the minicomputer system for production and stock control.

Economically meeting the needs of a wide range of customers can place a strain on production, but Hozelock meets the challenge head on: products are packaged in any of five different ways for different markets, and individual packs have product data and instructions printed in one of five languages. "In fact," says Fewell, "we spend as much on packaging as on any other area."

Being commercially-minded doesn't just mean doing everything the customer wants, though. Peter Fewell is constantly seeking ways of cutting production costs, for instance by automating parts of the assembly process.

The recent developments in their plastics clothes peg production shows what can be achieved. Originally the sales department insisted on a mix of three colours in each bag of pegs, but after complaints from production about the additional cost they tested consumer reaction in more detail and found that two colours would be acceptable. Then production engineering went to work and came up with a completely automated system whereby the injection machines feed two hoppers, one of each colour, and products are then fed through, mixed, automatically weighed, filled into printed polyethylene bags made on the spot, sealed and boxed. One operator now does the work that used to occupy five.

For Hozelock, the clothes pegs are one way of diversifying away from weather-sensitive markets. Another is the purchase last year of a range of pool equipment, such as underwater lights and fountains. Here production's main contribution so far has been in value analysis, making the products cheaper or more reliable. Long-term tests still under way suggest that with minor design modifications, polypropylene rather than the more expensive ABS plastic can be used in some components, and the underwater lights can in fact perform better without expensive sealed beam units.

Hozelock's adoption of commercial works management developed progressively in response to customer demand and the increasing emphasis on exports. Westland, on the other hand, was forced to attempt an instant transformation after its catastrophic plunge into losses in 1978. This was due largely to its poor responsiveness to market needs—the company had nothing to offer the 'civil' commercial helicopter market. To be successful in this area, Westland recognised it would have to make fundamental changes, improving cost and longevity of its products, and this could not be achieved with the existing structure. So, in 1979, Westland established a 'matrix' organisation (see below) of business/product groups, and support groups. Significantly, the functions such as engineering, manufacture, quality and 'materiel' (including production control, purchasing, stores etc), are termed 'support groups'. Under the old structure

Jack Bower was works director; now he is one of the main board directors with collective responsibility for all aspects of the business. He says the matrix means that "the production manager has to be sensitive and react to the needs of the business groups."

In order to learn about the new organisation all the managers involved—including foremen—attended a series of three-day meetings held off site. Corporate development staff bluntly outlined the problems the company had been facing, described its long-term objectives and discussed how they might be achieved. Each meeting was then divided into multi-disciplinary syndicates, with representatives from, say, production, personnel, engineering and buying. Then the participants examined the reasons for inadequate market penetration and devised their own plans for avoiding it in the future. The toughest part of the seminar came at the end, when they had to make a presentation to a panel of main board directors, who grilled them on their proposals. In general, the members agreed that the main reason for poor performance in the past had been inadequate market analysis, followed by poor timing, higher costs than anticipated, and then product defects.

The conference seems to have been successful: managers at all levels separately told me of the greater cross-fertilisation of ideas between people who previously had little to say to each other. They now feel qualified to suggest ways of overcoming the corporate weaknesses they have already discussed with senior

directors. A typical reaction comes from foreman Steve Parry: "We have tended to be very product orientated—to get helicopters out of the door, whatever the problems it caused to others—but now we're more aware of the commercial side." More co-operation between sales and production departments is beginning to overcome a longstanding problem: trimming the spares inventory—nearly half a million parts at the last count—without weakening customer service.

Just as important as the new structure, however, are the people who fill it. For example, the new customer service manager in the HM Government business group is an ex-production control manager and so is particularly qualified to deal with delivery problems.

Proof of the pudding: the new WG30 passenger-carrying helicopter will go into service with British Airways in early 1982; and Westland made an after-tax profit (historical accounting) of £9.6 million in 1979 and £13.5 million in 1980. A commercial approach to works management, then, can achieve a lot for the company—and for individual line managers' career prospects.

Westland's matrix organisation ensures production is sensitive to commercial needs.

Each group is headed by a divisional director; the inter-connections show how the various groups depend on each other

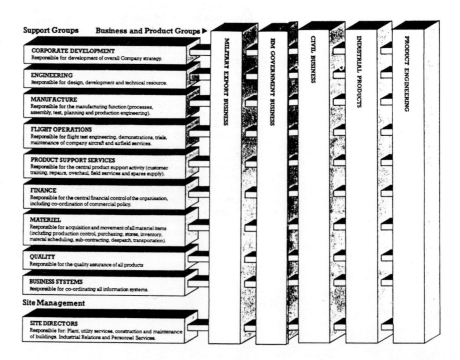

Support Groups   **Business and Product Groups ▶**

CORPORATE DEVELOPMENT
Responsible for development of overall Company strategy.

ENGINEERING
Responsible for design, development and technical resource.

MANUFACTURE
Responsible for the manufacturing function (processes, assembly, test, planning and production engineering).

FLIGHT OPERATIONS
Responsible for flight test engineering, demonstrations, trials, maintenance of company aircraft and airfield services.

PRODUCT SUPPORT SERVICES
Responsible for the central product support activity (customer training, repairs, overhaul, field services and spares supply).

FINANCE
Responsible for the central financial control of the organisation, including co-ordination of commercial policy.

MATERIEL
Responsible for acquisition and movement of all materiel items (including production control, purchasing, stores, inventory, material scheduling, sub-contracting, despatch, transportation).

QUALITY
Responsible for the quality assurance of all products

BUSINESS SYSTEMS
Responsible for co-ordinating all information systems.

Site Management

SITE DIRECTORS
Responsible for: Plant, utility services, construction and maintenance of buildings, Industrial Relations and Personnel Services.

MILITARY EXPORT BUSINESS · HM GOVERNMENT BUSINESS · CIVIL BUSINESS · INDUSTRIAL PRODUCTS · PRODUCT ENGINEERING

How to be a better communicator

This chapter sets out to explore a number of themes under the general heading of 'communicating'. In particular we shall consider:

- The crucial importance of communication in all our lives.

- The importance of communication to organisations in conducting their business, and in the creation of a work-based culture of shared values.

- How the structures of organisations (which we considered in the previous chapter) influence the way communication occurs.

- How an understanding of communication theory can help us to improve our own behaviour as a communicator and compensate for weaknesses in others.

- The twin notions of 'redundancy' and 'entropy' in communication.

- What it is that causes communication breakdown.

- Some simple guidelines to help get our message across.

The importance of communication

Imagine the scene. A quiet suburban street on a Sunday morning. In the garden of one house, Mr Shaw is doing some gardening. The front door of the house next door opens and out pops Mrs Green. She is going to church, as she does every Sunday. This conversation takes place.

Mrs Green: Hello.
Mr Shaw:　Hello there.
Mrs Green: Doing some gardening?
Mr Shaw:　That's right. You off to church?
Mrs Green: Uh-huh. (She nods) Just for a change. (They both laugh.) Still, mustn't be late.
Mr Shaw:　Don't let me keep you.
Mrs Green: 'Bye, then.
Mr Shaw:　'Bye, now.

Not the sort of stuff that keeps the readers of Frederick Forsyth or Catherine Cookson glued to the page. On the other hand, it equals for sheer stodginess many of the real-life exchanges between people that occur every day, in which all of us take part occasionally.

ACTIVITY

Jot down a few alternative answers to the questions 'Doing some gardening?' and 'You off to church?'.

No doubt some of your suggestions were quite unacceptable, if judged from the viewpoint that conversations should ideally seek to sustain rather than impair social harmony. As next-door neighbours, Mrs Green and Mr Shaw will probably be trying their best to maintain a friendly, but not intimate, relationship. To ignore each other would be to risk being thought of, at best, shy or retiring, and at worst, standoffish or ignorant. Mrs Green's question was obviously pointless as she could presumably see that Mr Shaw was gardening, and his counter-question was probably equally unnecessary. However, many conversations consist in their early stages of meaningless little pleasantries as people explore possible topics of conversation until they reach one which seems to grab their interest. This particular conversation did not really get off the ground.

So why did it take place at all? There are two principal reasons.

- People like to be liked. In practice it is impossible to know whether other people like us, unless there is evidence of this. If people we know ignore us, we will assume that they no longer like us or that they have come to dislike us (which is not quite the same).

- Trite exchanges, as in the previous example, keep open channels of communication for when they might be more useful. For example, a neighbour may be a helpful source of advice on house repairs or where to buy cheap petrol. He/she may even provide juicy bits of gossip. It is less likely that information like this will be forthcoming if one neighbour has snubbed another.

ACTIVITY

Discuss in your group the extent to which you all indulge in this form of conversation. How important do you consider similar conversations as an aid to encouraging healthy relationships, even with people with whom you have little in common? What attitudes and opinions do people have at work towards those who indulge in either too much or too little small talk?

When you were at school your teachers probably lectured you on the dangers of 'wasting time' in 'idle chatter', and perhaps at work you get the same message from your supervisor from time to time. Indeed, according to Dr W.P. Robinson, in his book, *Language and Social Behaviour*, one of the principal functions of language is to act as a substitute for less pleasant activities. For example, it is often easier to talk about catching the big fish than having actually to catch it. The same point could be made about communication in general. Television, for instance, must have done a great deal to ease the boredom of the elderly, the chronically disabled or those forced to endure long periods of unemployment, besides almost everyone else who enjoys nothing more than sinking silently into an armchair to watch TV after a day's work.

ACTIVITY

Analyse your own acts of communication so far today and explain what purposes they have served. Present them as a list under these headings:

Time of day   Communication act   Purpose of communication

Your answer may look something likes this:

Angela Baskerville / aged 22 years

Time of day	Communication act	Purpose of communication
7.05 am	Radio alarm. Mike Smith Show on Radio 1.	Wakes me up - makes the process a bit less unpleasant.
7.15	Kiss and cuddle with husband, Terry.	No comment !
7.35	Conversation with mother-in-law.	To find out what she had done with instant coffee.

7.55	Listen to weather forecast on TVam.	To decide what to wear today. Need to take brolly!
8.25	Spoke to bloke at bus stop.	To find out whether the bus had gone already — it had!
9.15	Spoke to lecturer.	To excuse late arrival at college
9.18	Whispered to Mandy in next seat.	Try to borrow pen.
9.19	Ask Claude in next but one seat.	Manage to borrow pen.

Angela's answers show that she uses communication for purposes we've discussed already. She sustains her relationship with her husband, keeps open the communication channel with her lecturer, and arguably uses the radio to soften the blow of having to get up to go to college (avoidance or delay of less pleasant activity) by taking her mind off it. However, she also uses it to obtain information (from the man at the bus stop), to obtain instant coffee (from her mother-in-law), and to persuade friends to lend her a pen (Mandy and Claude).

Your answers may have been more extensive — and more revealing. For example, did you say that you had bought a paper or a magazine? Newspapers and magazines are examples of communication serving as entertainment, as well as providing useful information (the TV guide). You may have said you were involved in an argument with someone, perhaps because you were in a bad mood, or because someone else was having a go at you. This suggests that communication also has a role to play in our emotional or psychological life. It enables us to express our innermost feelings and to fulfil emotional needs that may not be obvious to the casual observer.

Without communication it is difficult to see how cooperative ventures could be achieved. Returning to the example of sport which we used in Chapter 1, the signals that players give each other help them to anticipate their moves and passes and thus contribute to successful outcomes. So it is likely that many of you will have listed a consultation or a meeting during which collaboration or agreement to achieve an objective will have been reached. Some of you may have listed a flirtation or even a seduction. Communication is a vital part of the mating ritual of most animal species, but while for the lower animals the courtship displays are relatively straightforward, those for humans are fraught with difficulties and misunderstandings. It is unlikely, though not impossible, that pairings will come about without a form of introduction during which greater degrees of intimacy are negotiated.

Communication also serves a purpose to which few of us are likely to admit — even when we are conscious of it. You will certainly have some notion of the kind of person you are. You may perhaps consider yourself cheerful, generous, intelligent, loyal, caring, gifted or modest. Or less likely, clumsy, dull, miserly, careless, deprived or conceited. You will also have an idea of the way other people see you. Indeed, the two may be linked. Some people may enjoy feeding the expectations that others have of them. However, it is only through communication that we can establish what others think of us. The comments of other people, and their behaviour and attitudes towards us, help us to determine whether the image we have of ourselves, our **self-image**, is being projected accurately to the outside world. In other words, we need to be told by others from time to time that the image that we think we project is the one others perceive.

We can sum up the functions of communication in helping us to achieve basic human needs like this:

Needs	Examples of the role of communication
Physical	The provision of food, clothing and shelter from wealth created by the cooperative activity called work, in which communication plays a vital role.
Emotional	It creates and sustains human relationships and validates our self-image.
Physical and emotional	It initiates and sustains sexual relationships. It enables us to cooperate with others to achieve shared objectives. It provides amusement and entertainment.
Intellectual	It is a vehicle for information.

ACTIVITY

Wives are cheating for chat not sex

A lust for talk — not sex — causes women to cheat on their husbands, an American study shows.

The study supported other research that found the failure by spouses to communicate is a primary cause of marital problems, the the Ladies Home Journal magazine says in its September issue.

It also said that the search for new partners was not a result of the desire for more sex, but rather the need to communicate.

The study was headed by Lynn Atwater, an associate professor of sociology at Seton Hall University, New Jersey.

One researcher traced 100 couples who had been married for five years and found they spent only about 30 minutes a week talking with each other, the Journal said.

Journal readers surveyed by the magazine in 1983 found womens second biggest complaint about their marriages — after money fights — was, "We don't talk any more."

Family counsellors said the fast pace of life, as well as changes in lifestyles, as among the reasons why families do not talk as much as in the past.

Questions

1 Read the accompanying press cutting and discuss in groups the factors that might make families less talkative than they were in the past. (You may not agree with this point of view.)

2 What advice could be given to people whose marital breakdown is caused by faulty communication?

3 Does this have any implications for people at work? Explain.

▲ Source: *Express and Star*

How and why organisations communicate internally

We have already examined in Chapter 1 the implications of growth for organisations. It was argued that the challenge to keep people informed and to coordinate and monitor their activities demands procedures and structures of increasing formality in direct relationship to the organisation's size. Put simply, a hypermarket cannot function solely on a word-of-mouth communication channel adopted by a couple running a sweet shop. Broadly the information to be transmitted falls into two categories.

- Information necessary to sustain the business of the organisation.
- Information necessary to establish, sustain or refine the organisation's culture. (Culture is the prevailing set of attitudes or opinions within a firm.)

Similarly, the methods used to transmit information can be classified. This can be done according to their formality or informality. By formality we mean the extent to which the communication follows established procedures that can be said to be binding on the participants. It is therefore possible to map out a simple matrix on which communication activities can be plotted according to their purpose (business or culture) and their nature (formal or informal).

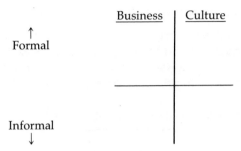

Two examples will show how this works.

The house magazine

The house magazine includes stories about how hard some people have worked and how generously the organisation has rewarded them. The intention is to boost morale and encourage other employees to behave likewise. The style, although printed, is cheerful and friendly — probably similar to that of tabloid newspapers. It therefore avoids the extremes of formality and informality, but as it is concerned mainly with transmitting values, it falls on the 'culture' side of the matrix.

House Magazine

Corridor conversation

Two colleagues pass in the corridor:

Sammy: Hello. Glad I caught you. Have you finished your department's absence returns yet? I want to get them on the computer — today if possible.

Rajindra: Oh, sorry! No, I haven't even started them yet. We've been so busy with Jill away, so …

Sammy: Okay. I'm getting some stick about this, but I suppose I can fob them off for a bit …

Rajindra: Look. I'll try to get them done … after lunch, perhaps.

Sammy: Oh, that'd be great. Before four o'clock anyway.

Rajindra: Okay, then. I'll bring them down before the tea trolley comes round.

Corridor conversation

Notice that this meeting is casual (nobody planned it), that the tone is fairly friendly (even though both sound a little resentful), and that they negotiate a solution, without anybody issuing an 'order' (which probably implies equality of status). However, the exchange is exclusively task-related and any values or attitudes transmitted are incidental. As this is a business-related activity, carried out informally, it falls in the lower left-hand side of the matrix.

ACTIVITY

Sketch a matrix in your notebook, and by entering the numbers 1 to 5, locate the following communication acts according to their purpose and degrees of formality.

1 Disciplinary interview resulting in the dismissal of an employee.
2 Entering new data on an organisation's computerised data base.
3 Telephone call to same-status employee to arrange a meeting.
4 Memo from the Managing Director seeking volunteers for redundancy and early retirement.
5 Memo from section head reminding staff about their persistent lateness.

Business or culture: formal or informal

It is not always easy to determine whether communication behaviour is directed exclusively towards facilitating business or reinforcing a culture. Usually there are elements of both. If you look again at the corridor conversation, both speakers seem to be tolerant about setting deadlines, so while the conversation relates to business activities, the way in which the problem is handled implies the existence of certain values and attitudes in the organisation.

Similarly, it is not easy to be certain about the formality of communication. A widely held view among communication teachers is that formality is determined by the medium employed to convey the information. If we are to write a message, we tend to take more care with our choice of words and use of grammar than we would in ordinary conversation. If you find this difficult to believe, then listen carefully to your next conversation — to the false starts, the incomplete utterances, the use of tone of voice to convey meaning, and even of non-words (e.g., er, ah, um). Nevertheless, it is possible to be very warm and intimate on paper, or cold and aloof in a personal interview, so the assumption about formality based simply on the medium employed must be treated with caution.

ACTIVITY

1 Collect any instructions or guidance notes issued by your own organisation about internal or external communication. These may give advice on how to answer the phone, to operate a machine, to write a memo, or to reply to a hostile letter or to deal with a difficult customer. Try to evaluate the success of these instructions based on your own and other employees' experiences.

2 Compare your own experiences, guidance notes and printed instructions with those of others in your group. Which instructions seem to be most successful in obtaining willing compliance? Why is this so?

3 Can you identify areas in your organisation where instructions or guidance are not issued, but ought to be? Can you identify existing instructions that most staff consider unsatisfactory? Explain why they are unsuccessful and make suggestions about their improvement.

In addition to routine acts of communication, there are a number of jobs in which the need for specialised or high-order communication skills is recognised. These jobs include:

- Sales
- Public relations
- Training and instruction of staff
- Personnel matters (counselling and interviewing)
- Supervision and management

ACTIVITY

In your notebook, describe the communication behaviour, specialised skills and personality traits which you think are desirable for the following specialisms.

Sales	Public relations	Training	Personnel	Supervision/ management

---

Business-related communication

In order to keep a business fed with information, a considerable amount of time, money and paperwork are involved.

ACTIVITY

Use this check-list to compare your own organisation's output with those of others in your group. Some spaces have been provided for you to add a few suggestions of your own.

Which of these media are used in your organisation?

Communication checklist

Ink-in the appropriate zero

	YES	NO
Written/printed		
Annual reports and accounts	0	0
One/five-year plans	0	0
Monthly/quarterly balance sheets	0	0
Stock/inventory checks	0	0
Status reports/print-outs	0	0
Accident reports	0	0
Order forms	0	0
Delivery notes	0	0
Questionnaires	0	0
Investigative reports	0	0
Memo/circulars	0	0
Notices/posters	0	0
Invoices	0	0
Suggestions of your own:		
_____	0	0
_____	0	0

Spoken		
Telephone	0	0
Face-to-face interview/selection	0	0
Face-to-face appraisal	0	0
Face-to-face disciplinary	0	0
Briefing meetings	0	0
Grapevine	0	0
Suggestions of your own:		
_____	0	0
_____	0	0

One problem for larger organisations is the sheer volume of paper in circulation. Paperwork is often seen as hindering the job, rather than as a vital component of the work itself, and one of the essential skills (usually learnt informally) for a new or newly transferred or promoted employee is to learn which communications are important and which are of secondary importance. Interestingly, a frequent complaint made by commerce and industry is that government overloads organisations with excessive paperwork, although it is doubtful whether many organisations keep their own house in order with their internally-produced paperwork. The following is an extract from *The Winning Streak*, in which Sir Kenneth Cork, one of Britain's best-known receivers and liquidators, speaks about paperwork:

Cork goes further: 'It used to be that there was a great shortage of paper in companies, in cash flows, profit forecasts and so on. People used to wait until the auditors turned up and then looked at the results with surprise … Now I think it is the opposite — it is a glut of paper, all printed in silly little dots that you can hardly read, on the computer.'

'When I go to a company to do an investigation, or to talk to the management, I ask them simple questions. 'What's your cash flow? When does it peak? What's your profit forecast? What's your turnover last week?' And all they do is press a ruddy button and in comes an accountant with a pile of papers a mile high. Then they shuffle them and they can't find the right one.'

'Nobody can think with a piece of paper. There's only one place you can think. A good businessman will answer all your questions out of his head.' All top management needs, he insists, is one sheet of paper.

Despite elaborate systems of paperwork, information can nonetheless be:

- Unintelligible to most readers
- Ignored
- Forgotten or misplaced
- Incomplete
- Inaccurate
- Irrelevant to recipients
- Misdirected or mistimed

It is a matter of touching faith that many managers believe that their memos will be read simply because they ought to be. Some managers still pin their words of wisdom on notice-boards, although photocopying facilities have vastly increased the number of documents being placed directly into the hands of employees. Although obviously more effective than the notice-board, some managers have seen the photocopier as a major saver of their own time, removing from them the obligation to read and edit incoming circulars for their staff. A common 'short-cut' has been to photocopy circulars and send copies to all staff, leaving them to sort out its implications. The photocopier — and more recently the dot-matrix printer — is something of a mixed blessing if it simply increases the number of unselected communications facing employees. It is probably unfair and certainly uneconomic to compel staff to read memos (usually by getting them to sign or initial a master copy) if in return the management does not operate a filter system to ensure that what staff are required to read and absorb is relevant.

ACTIVITY

1 At work, start a collection of forms, memos, circulars, letters and directives which will cross your desk, say over the next two months. When your collection is complete, grade them for relevance to:
(a) your own work and needs, and
(b) to the work of your section.
Place each of them under one of three headings:

Essential information   Desirable information   Unimportant information

If necessary, ask your section leader or department head on what basis memos are passed down the line or generated at his/her level.

2 Find out whether anybody monitors or records the material put out by your reprographics department each year, or calculates the amount of paper used by your computer-printers.

3 What changes in methods or procedures would you like to see introduced that would help to reduce paperwork in your department? Your ideas should be aimed at reducing unnecessary paperwork in a bid to improve communication.

So far we have considered the role of paper communication in directing and instructing employees. Another part of the 'business' function of communication is to provide information about the organisation's activities. Without such information, organisations cannot monitor their own performance nor plan for the future. To satisfy this need, **feedback loops** are established to feed information back to senior management.

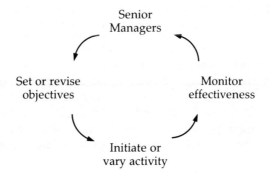

▲ *Feedback loops*

Monitoring takes many forms, including control and feedback checks on product lines, personnel performance and cash flows. Regular monitoring often takes place over a whole range of the organisation's activities, including those shown overleaf.

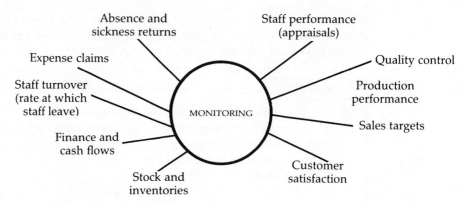

▲ *Monitoring performance*

However, it is not uncommon for these controls to become a meaningless exercise in some organisations, especially when statistics are ignored, misused, or presented in an unusable form. Some statistics are collected largely because they have always been collected, but they are not used for planning purposes, and no-one is monitoring their effectiveness. There are numerous instances of pointless form-filling. One example, from the bus industry, was the detailed information demanded on conductors' and drivers' waybills (records of cash received and numbers of passengers carried on journeys every day). Although the waybills had to be completed at fare stages, the company only broke down receipts by whole routes, and when more detailed information about levels of use and length of journeys was required, information was obtained by interviews carried out on the buses by staff recruited for that purpose.

ACTIVITY

Discuss in groups the kinds of information collection that seem to have little or no organisational value.

Clearly, the feedback of *some* information is indispensible to managers in the control of organisations, and it is an important cornerstone to success in achieving management objectives. Effective feedback systems ideally should have the following characteristics.

- They should be simple and relatively inexpensive to introduce.
- They should provide information that can easily be understood and used.
- They should be seen to be important and relevant to the section or department collecting the data — not because 'head office says we've got to'.
- They should be conducted regularly and promptly to emphasise their importance to the organisation and to the staff concerned.
- They should be designed to stimulate and motivate employees to improve performance.

Most feedback loops are internal. However, many companies also assess their standing with the public using customer satisfaction surveys. These are designed to find out whether companies are meeting customer expectations, and this gives them clues about how they should respond to changes in public taste. In the 1983 General Election, the Conservative Party, which achieved a landslide victory, employed computerised and telephone sampling techniques with key voting groups in marginal constituencies. This operation, known as 'Operation Fast Feedback', enabled the party to respond quickly to issues which were of concern to electors and to counteract the attractive policies or damaging attacks made by opponents. The operation fulfilled all the characteristics of an effective feedback loop, and respondents were either reached by phone or provided with reply-paid envelopes. Such was the success of this campaign that all the major political organisations are now busily involved in devising or updating their own feedback systems.

Communicating a culture

How would you describe the 'culture' of your own organisation? In other words, what attitudes and values are currently held by you and your co-workers? A 'culture' is the sum total of beliefs shared by employees: a sort of way of life that is particular to a workplace. Of course, employees will draw many of their attitudes from the wider society outside the organisation, but this does not mean that management should not attempt to establish desirable values and attitudes among staff, or that the attempt will necessarily be resisted by employees. Every organisation has its own culture. In managing the organisation it is necessary to manage the culture as well. Failure to manage effectively might encourage undesirable beliefs and behaviour that are damaging to the organisation. For example, it would not be in anyone's interests in the long term to create an unfavourable image of the company by providing a shoddy after-sales service. In order to avoid this, there are clear tasks for management to fulfil.

- Set a clear 'mission' to provide a sense of purpose for the organisation and its staff (if this is a socially acceptable mission, so much the better).
- Set clearly defined standards and encourage staff to reach and even exceed them.
- Ensure that staff feel involved in, and personally committed to, the objectives of the organisation.
- Keep staff informed about probable changes that will affect them.
- Lead by example: 'Do as I say, not as I do' styles of management are particularly unhelpful.

The methods that organisations use to encourage the most desirable culture include the ones displayed below.

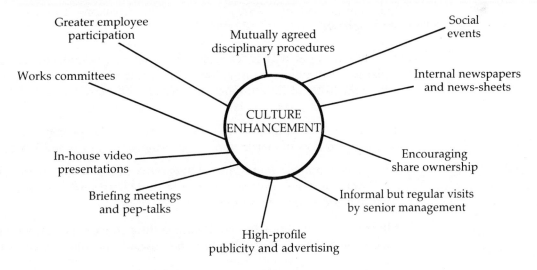

▲ *The promotion of culture within the organisation*

51

Also helpful in promoting a healthy organisational culture is an attractive public profile, as employees will be motivated by a desire to live up to a demanding public image. As advertising is one of the ways in which public opinion is shaped, improving employee morale within a healthier organisational culture can be a spin-off from a major advertising campaign. A similar effect may result from frequent favourable exposure in the mass media, although damaging criticism in the media may depress employees and generally tend to lower the organisation's morale.

ACTIVITY

In your group, try to arrive at a culture for your class at college. In particular:

1 What attitudes do you believe are shared towards:
  (a) personal study;
  (b) punctuality and attendance;
  (c) the relevance of the topics under study;
  (d) the need to meet assignment deadlines;
  (e) the importance of the qualification to employers;
  (f) the levels of difficulty in the tasks that are set;
  (g) the social facilities provided by the college;
  (h) one other factor of your choice.

2 Look at the five tasks it was suggested that management should fulfil in the promotion of a culture (page 50). Do you think your lecturers satisfy them? Discretely give as many details as you can.

3 Attempt a similar exercise for the organisation you now work for or have worked for in the past.

4 Do you think that the prevailing culture helped or hindered the standing and work of the organisation you described in the previous question? Explain.

Relationship to structures

The flow of information through organisations is usually understood as being a movement either up, down, or across structures. More information travels down through organisations than travels up, despite heroic efforts by managements in some companies to maintain a steady flow in both directions. The reasons for this imbalance are as follows.

- Communication that is 'owned' by high-status employees has a high-status value placed on it, unlike information held by low-status employees, which is mistakenly thought to be of little importance in organisational terms and therefore not sought regularly (except in a crisis).

- The need to coordinate and control the work of low-status employees stimulates the downward flow of instructions from management to subordinates.

- Employees may prefer to conceal their work from scrutiny, fearing hostile criticism, so information about progress will only be fed upwards when requested or when it exceeds the standards normally set.

- In some organisations the workplace culture condemns staff who try to curry favour with management, thus inhibiting the upward flow of ideas and suggestions.

The introduction of computerised data bases is beginning to challenge our ideas about the flow of information in organisations because computer networks are themselves communication systems, and access to information held by others is therefore easier. Notions about the status of information being related to the position of those who hold or disseminate it will become eroded, and as monitoring of organisational activity becomes easier, staff will be more used to regular scrutiny of their activities.

Electronic communication is also likely to undermine another feature of vertical communication: the tendency of information to pass up and down the line from one level to the next in the organisational structure. Although practices vary, it is generally felt that either line managers will have their position weakened if they are left out of the information chain, or that staff will be given contradictory instructions if several managers are simultaneously involved in the interpretation and transmission of identical information. The problems do not stop there, as these two short extracts show.

The memo

Mrs Brassington came into the office. 'Stop work a minute, Lulabelle', she said, smiling. 'I've got some good news for you. A memo has arrived this morning', she said, meaningfully, holding up the document.

'Oh! Is it about my transfer to the Senior Accountant's office?' Lulabelle asked.

'Why ... yes,' said Mrs Brassington, rather taken aback. 'How did you know?'

'Oh, I was talking to the Managing Director on Sunday up at the golf club — he and daddy are both members, you see. He promised me the job then — or as good as.'

'Well — then you don't really need me to tell you any more then, do you?' sneered Mrs Brassington. 'I hope you won't mind too much having to clear your desk before you go.'

Frank's dilemma

Frank Brown, a bus driver, was drinking tea in the canteen when the garage's Engineering Superintendent came in. 'On your break, Frank?' he asked. 'No, Mr Vaughan, I was spare driver this morning, but everyone turned up for their shift, so I wasn't needed.'

Mr Vaughan's weather-beaten face broke into a smile. 'Great! So, you're not doin' anything? Then I'd like you to help me out. I need someone to drive one of my lads over to Shrewsbury to collect a coach that broke down there on Saturday. I'd send two of my blokes, but we're a bit pushed. It's ok ... I'll tell your Traffic Superintendent where you've gone.'

A few minutes later, just as Mr Vaughan was about to return to the workshops, the canteen door opened, and the Traffic Superintendent, Brenda Moore, looked around the otherwise empty room. 'Seen my relief driver?' she asked.

'Frank Brown? Yes ... why?' asked Mr Vaughan, cautiously.

'We've just had a message that Winston Chambers has been taken ill at the wheel — it seems he's got a touch of the galloping habdabs again — and I'm going to need Frank to take a bus and finish his shift. Has he gone far?'

'Yes', Mr Vaughan said nervously. 'Shrewsbury.'

Although both extracts indicate how problems can occur if the line management system is not used for the transmission of information, a too rigid insistence on the use of lines for this purpose can mean that the advantages are bought at the price of excessively sluggish communication and a sense of remoteness between staff and senior levels of management. The first of these disadvantages is illustrated by the following procedure, which was used in a County police force in the 1970s.

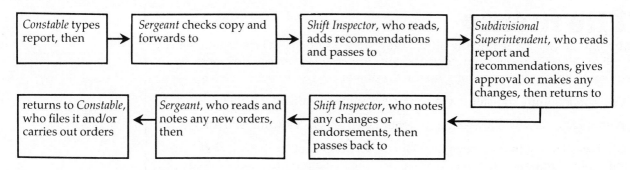

▲ *Based on Bunyard's Police Organisation*

As a result, where the organisational structure is a 'tall' one (see page 12), strict adherence to communication 'along the line' may lead to considerable delays, for which a price may have to be paid. For example, by the time action is taken, the burglar might have had time to cover his tracks. The second disadvantage, the remoteness of top managers caused by a lengthy communication chain, is one of the dangers that successful companies seem to guard against. This is the view taken by Goldsmith and Clutterbuck, in their book *The Winning Streak*, where they suggested that in successful organisations top management

- was highly visible, and
- provided a clear sense of purpose

while in less successful companies, top management was either remote or conducted itself in such an autocratic manner that when members visited offices and plant they were so formal that it seemed little more than a ritual inspection.

In successful companies senior executives identify strongly with the success of the organisation, and the way to make this clear to staff is through effective communication. In addition, a number of top executives who responded to the Goldsmith and Clutterbuck's questionnaire said how highly they valued the information that they got from informal talks with employees at the 'sharp end'. Of course, there is nothing new about this, but what Goldsmith and Clutterbuck have done is to suggest a link between open channels of communication and organisational success.

Structural complications

A further complication is the existence within organisations of trade union structures. In many organisations the role of informing and negotiating both with employees and employers about proposed innovations is usually handled by the local trade union officials. This practice heightens the feeling of remoteness between staff and top management, which may in turn lead union officials to reject or undermine new proposals in an attempt to demonstrate their skills in driving a hard bargain that is acceptable to their members. This has a further effect on the status of managers, who are often seen by employees as playing a largely hostile role in negotiating, in sharp contrast to the union's supportive role.

Communication across and between different departments is also a possible problem area for organisations. As we saw in Chapter 1, where there is a well-established departmental structure, liaison between departments is not an easy matter, unless we allow staff relationships to provide the means by which information flows across the organisation. Problems occur when staff see the performance of tasks 'for other departments' as some kind of favour 'because it's not for our section, is it?' Favours, of course, are not the same as obligations, so deadlines may be missed. Alternatively, interdepartmental resentments can lead to difficulties if for example one section argues that 'Accounts can wait for those figures, after the way Mrs Maguire spoke to our Angela last week'. Elimination of such attitudes can prove difficult if supervisors choose to hold these views in order to keep on good terms with their subordinates.

ACTIVITY

My job as a shop steward is to protect the interests of my members against the interests of the bosses. I accept that part of my role is to protect jobs even if this sometimes means that I have to take into account the needs of management — say by agreeing to some voluntary redundancies or to the introduction of new technology. But the simple fact is that workers and management are on different sides. So long as my members get £90 a week and the manager gets 20 grand a year and a lot of perks, they need to be protected against exploitation.

Bob Lewis,
Union Representative

As a manager I feel that I ought to have greater access to staff when it comes to negotiating their wages and conditions. Personally I find the activities of unions extremely disruptive. Last year we lost a big customer because we couldn't guarantee delivery schedules, mainly as a result of delays caused by long discussions I was drawn into with the union over manning levels. This idea that we're on different sides is ridiculous — I'm an employee too, and I stand to lose my job along with everybody else if the plug is pulled.

Malcolm Jones,
Manager

1 How common do you think these attitudes are in your own company? Which of the two attitudes is the closest to your own? What advice would you give to each of them that might help them to understand the other person's problems?
2 Can you suggest a few areas of management activity in your own organisation which are likely to be or have been resisted or modified by trade union intervention?
3 Can you think of any ways in which union intervention can be helpful to management objectives?

Communication theory

The study of communication is a relatively recent phenomenon which grew principally out of the study of electronic communication after the Second World War. In America the early pioneers in the field were keen to ensure that when people used their telephones — or when individuals and organisations addressed mass audiences on radio and television — they did so effectively. Such a view implies that communication is a fairly simple process which can be analysed and studied in the same sort of way as we learn music, and that the characteristics of effective communication (that is to say, successful) can be encouraged and copied. This approach forms the basis of much of the work done on Business Studies courses, and it is the basis of the approach used in this book. It is also a view that is commonly held in society as a whole — a point that you will be able to confirm for yourself. Have you ever heard people saying that some form of antisocial behaviour, for example leaving dogs in an unventilated car in hot weather, could be changed with an effective campaign of public information? Or that a long-running dispute between two sections at work is due to a 'breakdown in communication'?

Both arguments assume that by paying greater attention to the processes of communication, existing difficulties might be resolved — indeed, they might not have arisen in the first place. If only people were made to understand exactly what are the consequences of leaving their pets without fresh air (as dogs can't sweat, they need to pant fresh air to prevent overheating), and if only people from Accounts and Stores were just to sit down together and talk through their difficulties (they might discover that very little separates them). However, there are problems associated with this view, both in practical and theoretical terms. In practical terms, who would seriously suggest that just getting the warring sides together would solve the present problems besetting Northern Ireland and the Lebanon? Nor would a view of communication as a learning process that has gone wrong adequately explain the present divide in those communities. Instead, an alternative view of communication is needed, and this second approach is based on the assumption that communication involves the *creation of meanings*.

ACTIVITY

In one or two sentences, define and explain each of the following words. Then compare your definitions with the definitions of others in your group by reading them aloud.

homosexual	propaganda	communism
immigrant	freedom fighter	abortion
terrorist	strikes	vivisection
nuclear energy	literature	shop steward

This activity is likely to show that not only is there disagreement among English speakers as to the exact 'meaning' of well-known words, but that we also have certain attitudes about the concepts, objects or persons with which the word is associated. As an example, to identify someone as a terrorist is to imply disapproval, but to refer to the same individual as a freedom fighter indicates approval. Yet it is not clear what the difference is, except as a reflection of the attitude of the speaker or writer who uses these terms. To a President of the USA the 'Contras' are freedom fighters, to the Nicaraguan government the same people are terrorists. You might now like to discuss in your group the kinds of attitudes that were reflected in your word definitions for the previous activity, and also comment on the reasons why some of you found it necessary to change the tone of your voice when you were uttering certain words.

This second approach to the study of communication attempts to understand the characteristics of communication behaviour that are responsible for creating these meanings for us. It works on the principle that a great deal of what we call 'reality' is merely a convenient social construction that helps us to make sense of a complicated world. It is the sum total of learnt or conditioned responses to a selection of external stimuli. This can be most clearly understood if you think for a minute about some of the ideas or information that we absorb from the media. What do you really know about South Africa or the Soviet Union, or about politics, industrial relations or even sporting events? The honest answer will be 'what I've seen on TV or read in the papers'. As it is impossible personally to experience everything which is reported in our papers and news bulletins, so we rely almost completely on the media for information, and to a large degree on how we think about things.

Even on a day-to-day basis we depend on our friends, workmates and family to keep us up to date about events that have occurred outside our own experience, and though many events affect us directly, it is still possible that our attitudes may be changed by other people. The death of a near relative, for example, may be seen as a 'blessed release' if doctors and friends emphasise to us the suffering that our relative underwent. The process of transmitting attitudes and values as well as the information contained in messages is an important feature of communication and one that must not be ignored or underrated. It is directly linked with the role that communication plays in transmitting a culture. Since culture embraces many attitudes and beliefs, it is desirable for management to intervene in shaping the communication processes as a matter of policy in order to encourage attitudes that are helpful to the company.

ACTIVITY

1 Describe briefly your personal attitudes and feelings about:
   (a) arriving late for work;
   (b) opportunities for ethnic minorities at work;
   (c) petty pilfering ('borrowing' pens, paper, materials and tools for use at home);
   (d) people who don't work as hard as they should;
   (e) staff who are often absent.

2 How does management attempt to cultivate and communicate desirable attitudes in these particular areas?

3 Take some notes, and in groups discuss how the following might contribute to a person's attitudes:
   (a) religion
   (b) the family
   (c) the education system
   (d) the media
   (e) political ideas

Skill-based approaches

In the early part of your course you will spend some time studying the 'ways and means' in which organisations communicate, so it is helpful at this point to consider the work of what we might call the 'mechanistic' school of communication. The earliest writers in this field based their models on structures used in electrical circuitry, with which they were familiar. The terms 'transmitter' and 'receiver' were used to identify those who sent and those who received messages. Rather like this:

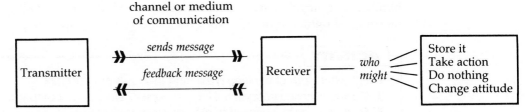

▲ *The mechanistic approach*

Possibly a more satisfactory way of understanding the mechanics of communication is by presenting the process in a circular form. This is because most communication is reciprocal in that one act leads to another in a seemingly never-ending sequence of stimulus and response, and the circle might be said to represent that continuity more effectively than a straight line. However, it is still a 'model' and as such reflects only shadows of what is an extremely complex process — not communication as it is, but as it might be.

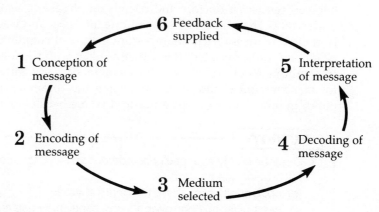

▲ *Communication as a process*

This division of communication into six stages is a little unreal in the experience of most people, and perhaps you are thinking 'surely I don't go through all this hundreds of times a day?' The point is that you probably do, though without being conscious of it, and in practice some of these stages overlap each other.

Let's examine this process, stage by stage.

1 Conception of message

You have an idea and you want to share it with someone else — but how? Obviously, by telling them what you have thought. You have now arrived at the first major difficulty, that of ensuring that the idea you have just experienced is conveyed to the person with whom you want to share it. Given that you find pure thought transference a little tricky (and if you don't, why are you bothering with this book?), your thought must be externalised. In other words, it must be expressed in a form that will be comprehensible to your friend, perhaps as a word, phrase, sentence or gesture.

For most of us, at least on some occasions, the conscious thinking process takes place in the form of language; that is, we think in 'words'. But many mental processes do not involve a thinking language, because if they did it would seriously reduce our chances of survival. When crossing a road, for example, an advancing car prompts a reflex action on the part of a careless pedestrian. If we stop to 'think' about what we should do we would be run over. So thought takes place at a level which does not necessarily need symbols like words, and if you are still not convinced, consider the number of times you have had a word 'on the tip of your tongue'. You know the meaning all right, but not the word used to express that meaning.

> ┌─ **ACTIVITY** ─┐
> 1 For what kinds of thinking is thinking-in-words most useful?
> 2 Do you ever find yourself talking to yourself? Under what circumstances?
> 3 Small children talk happily to themselves as they play. Why do you think adults grow out of it?
> 4 If ideas do exist in a form which does not require the use of words, whether internalised (thinking in words) or externalised (spoken, written, etc.), it is necessary to present them in a form that others will understand. Suggest a few of the ways in which thinking is communicated wordlessly.

2 Encoding of message

Symbols, for example words and drawings, cannot exist in isolation because they are meant to be shared with others and their significance and meaning mutually agreed. Since a symbol's relationship with its meaning is often obscure, this means that we have to learn, step by step, within our own unique culture, what these symbols stand for. Even when the symbol belongs to a group of similar symbols (as in a foreign language), or when the symbol imitates the real-life object it represents, the association of symbol and meaning can still be unclear. For example, it is believed that early man's attempt to communicate in writing involved the use of **pictograms**, which are drawings or pictures of the objects or events being described. So

might be understood as 'At dawn we went hunting and killed a deer'. As writing developed, more complex messages could be expressed in the form of **ideograms**, which are pictures conveying ideas as well as descriptions. And this is where our problems begin, if we try to interpret symbols without knowledge of ancient cultures. So a drawing of the sun might signify 'dawn', 'light' or 'heat', but also 'season', 'birth', 'sky-God' or 'war' (war was usually waged in the summer). Modern languages are, of course, written in **phonograms**, which are symbols representing vocal sounds that further extend our written vocabulary.

Using our own vocal sounds, in written English symbolised by only 26 letters of the alphabet, we are capable of producing an astonishing number of utterances, whose meaning can be extended almost without limit when combined with changes in vocal tones, facial expressions and gestures. As an experiment, get someone to repeat the sentence 'Lovely to see you' to create various meanings, and observe their facial expressions and tone of voice.

The mix-up

One day a taxi driver returned to the depot with the pride of the fleet — a brand new taxi, with an instrument panel that would not have been out of place in a jumbo jet. Angrily the driver shouted at the mechanic: 'This vehicle hasn't been filled up. It's a good job I'd only gone a short way when I noticed the fuel warning light was on — you'd have looked pretty silly if I'd run out of fuel on the motorway.'

The mechanic was indignant. He had only filled up half an hour before. 'Come and see for yourself', the driver said, and led him to the vehicle. Sure enough there was a warning light glowing on the console. Then the mechanic laughed. 'You idiot!' he said to the driver, and walked to the side of the taxi and shut the off-side passenger door. The console light went out. 'Oh!' said the driver, feeling rather foolish, 'I thought this little picture was a fuel pump'.

'A fuel pump?' joked the mechanic. 'Anybody with any sense can see it's a picture of a passenger door'.

This story illustrates how we use and misuse picture symbols (pictograms) in the late twentieth century. Symbols abound in our society, from road signs and traffic lights (why does red symbolise danger?) to sales logos and weather charts and signs. Ironically, the ancient pictograms seem to be having a new lease of life as computer software manufacturers struggle to create an electronic reality in children's games. If you think it unlikely that anybody could possibly be confused by symbols, try your hand at identifying a few of the following hazard warning signs. You should know them because they have been approved by the *Royal Society for the Prevention of Accidents* for use in all workplaces (solutions on page 74).

Symbols like these are used widely and offer considerable advantages over written or spoken communication. For example, organisations could not afford to employ staff to supervise potentially hazardous areas of the plant, warning staff about smoking or the need for protective clothing. Similarly, written messages might be ignored or misunderstood by employees with poor reading skills or by staff who cannot read English. After all, how would you cope if your home computer box carried the warning: QUESTO LATO IN SU PER NON DANNGGIARE I CONTENUTI? (English translation on page 74).

The main disadvantage of picture symbols is that they allow only simple messages to be transmitted. If a new hazard is identified, a new sign has to be drawn and a new meaning learned. Alternatively, a written or spoken warning could be given easily because of the greater range of symbols available in the form of words. Written and spoken language are examples of complex codes, while hazard warnings and traffic signs are examples of simple codes. The important thing to remember is that they are all codes with arbitrary meanings that need to be learned. For the communicator, the decision to be made at this stage is: 'Which code will most adequately convey my meaning?' It is important not to choose a code or set of symbols outside the experience of those for whom the message is intended.

3 Choosing the medium

Having chosen the code, the communicator has to decide *how* to send the message, which usually amounts to opening his or her mouth and letting the words spill out. In practice, there is little real choice because the code chosen (spoken language) may also determine the medium as well, for the medium is the means by which the message passes. Nonetheless, there are times when careful decisions have to be made about how a message is to be conveyed. It is very easy to upset people if we are careless about the media we choose to communicate with. If, on your way home tonight, you passed your bank and there was a big sign outside saying THIS WEEK'S TOP TEN OVERDRAFTS, with your name and address at number four (yes, folks, up six places from last week's number ten), you would be outraged at the breach of confidentiality this represented. On the other hand, you might secretly admire the bank's stunning tactics, although be furious that they should have picked on you.

There are many factors influencing the way that messages are sent. These include:

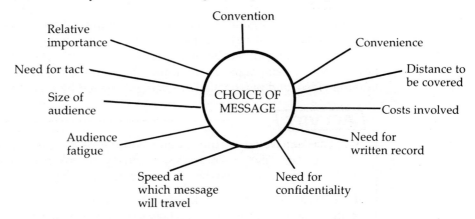

▲ *Factors determining choice of medium*

Although it is probably convenience that determines the medium chosen for most messages, another important factor is convention — by which we mean the action we take out of habit and custom. For example, how do we explain the torrent of greeting cards we exchange every year? At Christmas there is an orgy of card buying, writing, and posting, often to people with whom we have little or no contact throughout the year. Even the members of the same household will exchange cards, often affecting surprise and delight in the process. Another dismal convention (for some guests at least) are the speeches at wedding receptions, where relatives and friends make gushing remarks about the part each has played in the other's lives, spiced with naughty bits about what the lovely couple will be doing later that evening in preparation for the 'happy event'. Again, by convention, we are supposed to laugh, because laughing indicates not only our public approval of the match, but also because it is the expected behaviour appropriate to a particular social setting. In short, a great deal of communication is culturally determined.

ACTIVITY

1   What kinds of conventions exist in your organisation in the selection of the most appropriate channels of communication in the event of:
(a) retirement,
(b) births,
(c) marriage or engagements,
(d) birthdays,
(e) joining clubs or trade unions,
(f) sudden death,
(g) Christmas,
(h) joining the tea club/football pools syndicate?

2   Are there any conventions that you think 'go over the top' in the sense that they may actually impair the efficiency of the organisation? How would you go about getting rid of them if you were in charge? What medium/media of communication or tactics would you adopt if you wanted to persuade staff to desist?

Sometimes the decision about how to communicate a message involves sensitive matters of far-reaching importance. In such cases, there is rarely a wrong or right method, and what looks like a successful choice of medium and code might backfire. For instance, a duplicated note inserted in an employee's pay packet announcing imminent redundancy may satisfy legal requirements and may be administratively expedient, but may damage morale and do little to encourage loyalty among the employees who remain. Yet is there any 'good' way to communicate such information? How would you go about it?

Finally, many organisations now use a multi-media approach when they think that a single channel will not reach everyone they are aiming at, or if they feel that some channels are losing impact because audiences are getting bored about what they see and hear. A safety campaign, for example, might involve putting up posters, showing a training video, and personal advice being delivered by a safety officer.

┌ ACTIVITY ┤

What medium would you use to transmit the message in each of the following circumstances? Give details, and say whether you think there are any special tactics that might be helpful in getting the message across effectively.

1 Telling an employee at work about the sudden death of a close relative.
2 Instructing a new employee on how to operate the copier.
3 Telling your immediate superior of your feelings after being passed over for promotion.
4 Dealing with a subordinate who has arrived late for the third time in a fortnight.
5 Dealing with a subordinate who has been late on many occasions despite many verbal warnings.
6 Warning staff in your section that the toilets are to be closed for redecoration, and outlining alternative arrangements.
7 Informing a group of 20 employees that they are to be made redundant and their section closed down.
8 Informing all the staff at your Ealing plant that the plant is to be relocated in Wales, but that only 100 of the present 500 employees will be considered for transfer. The rest will be made redundant.

---

4 Decoding the message

Esoteric lexical items only serve to obfuscate the semantic content of transmissions, or to put it another way, difficult words only obscure the meaning of statements. The first version is deliberately off-putting and demonstrates that even when we write in English, it does not follow that it can be understood by an English reader, especially if the English used is sprinkled with words that are outside our everyday experience. In fact some words in the above sentence were drawn from the jargon of linguistics. **Jargon** is a term that describes particular words and phrases used by people who share a particular interest in some specialist field of activity, which is perfectly reasonable if it improves communication between experts. However, jargon is used for less worthwhile purposes when it is directed at the non-specialist, the person-in-the-street, thus forcing him to communicate on unequal terms. Faced with incomprehensible 'gobbledegook', and unable even to pronounce let alone understand some of the polysyllabic mouthfuls, we are driven first into silence and then into submission, thus allowing the specialist to determine the outcome of the exchange.

Since the purpose of effective communication is ideally to make clear and not to confuse, so it is important to make accurate guesses about the level of the linguistic skill a receiver might have. As a general rule, it is probably best to remember that almost anybody can read and understand the *Sun*, while others would not dream of reading *The Times* because they find it too difficult. If in doubt, what is to be communicated should be kept simple.

Check round your group to see if there is somebody who is learning to drive or about to take a driving test. If so, they will almost certainly have a copy of the *Highway Code*. (If not, make use of the following examples.) This activity will illustrate not only important points about communication, but improve their chances of passing the driving test. Before you begin to test them on their knowledge of road signs, divide and record on the chart, say, 15 selected signs in three groups of five, and test each individual randomly by one of the following methods.

GROUP A — by describing signs and asking examinees to identify them
GROUP B — by asking examinees to describe signs for particular purposes
GROUP C — by showing examinees signs and asking them to say what they mean.

TICK BOX

	ROAD SIGNS (brief description)	a	b	c	d	e
GROUP A	1					
	2					
	3					
	4					
	5					
GROUP B	6					
	7					
	8					
	9					
	10					
GROUP C	11					
	12					
	13					
	14					
	15					

KEY

a=excellent

b=good

c=average

d=fair

e=poor

1 Did the examinee perform better using one form of testing than another? Explain why this should be the case.

2 Did the examinee remember some signs more easily than others within the same group? Can *they* suggest an explanation for this?

3 Which of the three methods of delivery did you find the most satisfactory? Do you have an explanation?

4 Now conduct the test on a non-driver or on an experienced driver (the lecturer?). Analyse the results in a short informal report.

In theory, the best answers should have been given when the subjects were shown the actual sign and asked to give its meaning (Group C), largely because this is the way they are accustomed to seeing the sign. The poorest answers may have been given to the questions in Group B because of the absence of even a word description that can be pictured in the mind's eye. You might expect the most commonly occurring signs to be most easily identified. There are two conclusions to be drawn from this activity.

● Symbols have to be learned. If we don't understand the symbol we will not understand the message.

- It is not easy to switch from one code to another. For example, a sign that is widely known and recognised becomes more difficult to put across if switched to a spoken or written code.

5 Interpretation of message

Assuming that a receiver has decoded the message (i.e., roughly translated the symbols into meanings), there remains the problem of working out the transmitter's exact intention. How often have you heard this feeble but understandable excuse:

> I'm sorry I wasn't able to get to your meeting yesterday. I know that I'd agreed to come, but when you said it was on a Thursday, I thought you meant next Thursday because next Thursday is the third Thursday in the month, and we usually have our meetings then … don't we?

To begin with, there is the simple problem of ambiguity in which a statement appears to have at least two possible meanings. A great deal of humour is generated by double-meanings, such as the newspaper headline: *Strip clubs — Magistrates to Act on Indecent Shows*, or the memorial which was 'erected to the memory of Edwin Burke, drowned in the River Trent, 20th May 1897, by his sorrowing friends and relatives'. Much of this is deliberate, of course, as was the case of the song title *If I said you had a beautiful body, would you hold it against me?* Real meaning in these examples can easily be worked out, but when a document is of particular importance, then such lack of clarity cannot be excused. Those who draft laws, bye-laws and contracts have a duty to be precise, because what is actually published may later be the subject of court action.

ACTIVITY

A local authority is implementing its bye-laws governing access to public parks by dogs. The following were submitted for consideration as wording for a signpost. Which of the statements do you consider the most and the least ambiguous? Give reasons for your selection.

1 No dog will be admitted to the park without a lead.
2 All dogs must be kept on leads in the park.
3 No owner may bring a dog to this park unless it is on a lead.
4 Dogs not on a lead will not be admitted to this park.
5 Dog owners must ensure that dogs are on leads.
6 All dogs must be leashed and in control of a responsible adult in this park.

Another problem for communicators is in the interpretation of messages whose meaning seems clear, but where there are grounds for believing that the *real* meaning is hidden. What is the suspecting husband to make of the message that his wife is working late at the office and he must eat dinner alone? 'Why haven't I received a memo inviting me to a meeting with the boss when all the other section leaders have had one?' 'What exactly did the Marketing Director mean when she said that she was looking forward to introducing some new people to the section?' There are no simple answers and no clear-cut rules. All that the recipient can rely on, other than accepting the explicit content of the message, are clues in the behaviour of the transmitter, based on previous experience of their personal honesty, and by making judgements about motives that they might have for deceiving others.

6 Feedback supplied

The process has come full circle. We suggested earlier that communication is reciprocal. If it is not, it tends to dry up. The girl who writes letters to a soldier serving overseas may give up if there are no replies, and the employee who invites a new colleague to disclose a few personal details of his private life will prefer to talk to established colleagues if the newcomer chooses not to get involved.

Feedback, another term borrowed from electronics, is simply the reaction to an act of communication. (We used the term earlier when we talked about feedback loops enabling management to monitor efficiency, quality and progress in the organisation.) So when a joke is told, the anticipated feedback is laughter, and when an insult is hurled, a pained expression indicates that the taunt has struck home. Absence of feedback means that a speaker or writer can never be sure that what he is saying or writing is approved of or even being understood. Raised eyebrows on the part of the listener, for example, are enough to signal that a more detailed expansion is required on a point we have just made. A nod of the head means, perhaps, 'I agree' or 'Yes, I've got that'. A whole repertory of guttural explosions has been established to help us with feedback, including Er … Mmm … Eh … Yeah … Umm … Ugh.

Nonetheless, we are frequently lazy in the kind of feedback we require or supply. The mother who gives her son instructions about what to do and what not to do while out playing is only fooling herself that the child has taken anything in if it spent the time gazing furiously out of the window to where his/her friends are waiting. Similarly, we are often unwilling to admit that we haven't understood directions when we get lost in a strange place. We usually find ourselves saying: 'Thanks, I've got that', to a passer-by who has been kind enough to give us directions. Yet around the next corner we are lost again and asking the way from someone else. Admit it!

ACTIVITY

- A new member of staff is to be trained to use the franking machine, which is located in the office across the corridor. You can't leave your desk, so you explain how to use it. What sort of feedback should you expect, to save you from having to explain it all again in ten minutes, or worse still, from having to be forced to go and sort out the mess?

- A recently recruited office worker is finding difficulty in doing her job, and although nobody is being rude to her face, the feedback she gets leaves her in no doubt what people think.

   What form does this sort of feedback take in organisations?

   What effect is it likely to have on the new member of staff?

   If you were in charge, what would you do about it?

- You are to rearrange a meeting with your staff at the last minute because an important client is calling to see you. You decide to meet them earlier than intended. What feedback would you ask for to ensure that they all came on time?

Redundancy and entropy

To conclude our discussion on communication we would like to introduce you to the linked concepts of **redundancy** and **entropy**. These terms are used to describe the level of predictability in the content of what is being communicated. To explain this further, we need to present all the communication processes as a spectrum, with redundancy occupying one end and entropy the other.

Redundancy   Entropy

COMMUNICATION PROCESSES

Predictability   Unpredictability

▲ *Redundancy and entropy*

We use the term 'redundancy' to describe communication that seems predictable, and the term 'entropy' for communication that tends to be unpredictable. If we look at a newspaper story, it is fairly easy to separate out the redundant from the entropic.

Computer operator was 'the most boring person in the world'

A computer-obsessed operator bored his workmates to such a degree that he was asked to resign to stop his employer going bust, an industrial tribunal heard yesterday.

Despite repeated warnings, Bert Entwistle could not stop himself from interrupting his fellow workers to tell them about his latest computer obsession.

The problem reached crisis, the court heard, when the bespectacled Mr Entwistle, aged 22, of Sheply Road, Sheffield, prevented his company, Computergraphics, from finishing a vital rush job in time. This resulted in the customer cancelling all future orders.

According to the shift manager, Jill Davey, the delay was caused because staff had spent work-time hiding in the lavatories because they found Mr Entwistle 'the most boring person in the world'.

Mr Entwistle claimed unfair dismissal.

Jill Davey told the tribunal she had twice warned him about his obsessions, but he seemed unable to contain himself.

To begin with, the story is printed in English. As you can read and understand written English, the message form is a familiar one. Probably you read newspapers often, so you are also familiar with the style of language employed. Both the code and the content used (written English and newspaper report) are familiar, so to that extent they are predictable, and therefore the form of the message is, for you, redundant. The content of the report — the dismissal of a worker — is however much more unusual. We are accustomed to the idea of people being sacked for pilfering and poor timekeeping, but seldom because they are boring! The situation is novel and to that extent it is unpredictable. The content of the story is therefore entropic. However, once read, it ceases to be novel. It becomes predictable. From this we can see that notions of redundancy and entropy are not fixed; they are an assessment of our reactions to messages.

ACTIVITY

Analyse today's newspaper by drawing circles around what you judge to be entropic communication. Would you say that the photographs illustrating the news-stories are mainly entropic or redundant?

A great deal of communication is redundant. We don't listen to everything that is addressed to us because we know or think we know what the other person is going to say before they've said it. Also we often fail to pronounce all the syllables in words because they seem unnecessary, as our listeners can understand anyway. 'Good morning' and 'How do you do?' are examples of this. We usually finish up uttering something like 'Goomorin' or plain 'Mornin' and 'How do you do?' turns into a 'Howjudoo'. When reading, it is not necessary to register every detail of every word on the page, because if it were, nobody would progress beyond the pace they achieved in junior school. Instead, we anticipate what we are going to see and confirm or reject our guesses by glancing at the text. This explains the occasional experience of misreading a word or sentence and being forced to backtrack when the mistake is discovered.

PLEASE DO NOT
WALK ON THE
THE GRASS

The more familiar are the words and phrases, the more redundant is the print. It almost doesn't matter about the error in the previous warning sign because our understanding is complete. So important is the process of prediction in decoding messages, that many readers will still not have noticed that 'the' occurs twice. We simply 'construct' an acceptable version of words just as we construct complete images of what are in fact wildly incomplete images that we meet in cartoons and drawings. We find it easy to accept this woman, even though she has no feet and only half a face.

On the other hand, the more obscure or remote from our experiences is the language, the more entropic the text is to us. As a result, the guessing game becomes less certain and reading speed falls, and with false starts and delays, the motive to continue evaporates and the activity may even be abandoned.

The degree of redundancy of the message is not a measure of its uselessness. In communication, redundancy is not a critical term. Indeed, most of the successful forms of communication in our society are highly redundant. The *Sun* newspaper has established itself as the brand leader among tabloids for the endless repetition of topless women on page three. The subject matter is redundant and very predictable, but apparently retains enough entropy to maintain novelty value. Many instances of the value of redundancy in making communication accessible can be given. Popular music is highly predictable, and many performers repeat their particular style on record after record. Indeed, we would be disappointed if they didn't. Yet their rhythms and chords are drawn from a relatively narrow range and their lyrics are often about romantic love or lost love, written in rhyme to heighten predictability. But the most successful artists introduce just enough entropy to stay on top, while entropic (or unpredictable) music remains a cult taste, although for the cult followers the style eventually becomes redundant (predictable). Similarly, TV soap operas carry high levels of redundancy. Although settings may change, a remarkably limited range of plots and incidents, mostly concerned with people falling in and out of love, are played out by stock characters. The American TV soap of the sixties *Star Trek* displayed these characteristics in abundance, with the logical science officer Spock, the resourceful engineer Mr 'Scottie' Scott, the principled Doctor Macoy, and the gritty Captain Kirk battling every week against the odds to emerge victorious in the last gasp of each episode — just as the TV audience all knew they would. The entropy fed into each episode was the constant threat to inter-galactic civilisation.

It is worth noting that the most popular forms of communication are also the most redundant in form. Reading is considerably less popular than watching TV or video, and the telephone call is widely preferred as a means of keeping in touch to writing letters. This is because visual symbols and speech are more redundant than written symbols, and it is significant that high-circulation newspapers are those with considerable picture content. (The *Sun* sells over four million copies per day compared with the *Guardian*'s half million.) Even the so-called quality newspapers, such as *The Sunday Times*, have had colour supplements for years, which consist mainly of colourful illustrations and advertisements.

The entertainment media can bring considerable resources to bear in producing redundancy in acts of communication. A film director can convey a message, for example that the screen couple are 'in love', by what the actors are seen to do, by what they say, and by the use of musical soundtrack that uses symbolic values to reinforce an obvious story line. Daily papers will print mug-shots of well-known figures in their stories as a way of increasing the redundancy of the message.

In terms of communicating within organisations:

- Use forms and styles of communication which maximise redundancy.
- Repeat the message regularly but in slightly different ways, so that an element of entropy is retained.
- Redundancy and entropy are not fixed points. They are at opposite ends of the same spectrum, and what is redundant to you may not be so for everyone who works with you.

The advertisement on the right (slightly reduced) was published in *Woman's Own* in September 1985.

1 For the reader, under what circumstances would this advertisement be at its most entropic?

2 Which component in the advertisement has maximum entropy for its target audience?

3 Which particular features of the ad seek to maximise redundancy for that audience?

4 In TV commercials, what common techniques are adopted to further increase redundancy in the message?

MINT-COOL.
THE NEW MOUTH FRESHENER
BY GOLD SPOT.

Barriers to effective communication

Given the complexities involved in communicating, it is perhaps surprising that communication succeeds at all. Certainly, we should not be surprised when it goes wrong. Of course, the number of possible causes of communication breakdown are countless, but this unfortunately does not help us to anticipate, let alone avoid, such a possibility. Fortunately, it is possible to generalise about many of the causes of breakdown and to identify a number of typical barriers. Before we look at each of them in turn, we can present them together as shown below.

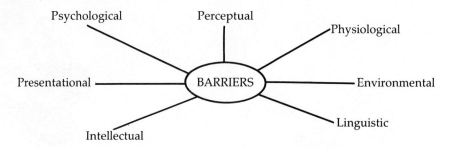

▲ *Barriers to communication*

Psychological

Our state of mind is highly influential in determining our performance when communicating. For example, someone who is worried about their marriage, or the health of somebody who means a lot to them, or who is upset about a problem at work, is likely to be either unresponsive or over-communicative. Similarly, a feeling of elation can make us insensitive to other people's feelings or render us unwilling to deal with trivial tasks. As employment itself is a source of debilitating worry to some employees, many big organisations have Personnel Departments that try to help with problems, to enable staff to concentrate on the tasks in hand. We take a closer look at the work of Personnel in Chapter 4.

Other states of mind that may impair communication are our personal prejudices. By prejudice we mean the tendency we all have to jump to premature conclusions before we have really thought about something. Everybody has prejudices — they are merely habitual ways of looking at people, events or ideas. If you don't think so, then try this activity.

ACTIVITY

What are your immediate reactions to:

Mrs Thatcher   Mr Kinnock   Dr Owen

Even if these politicians are no longer leaders of their parties, you will still know something about them, and 'knowing' them includes what you *feel* about them. You may instinctively like one of them, and instinctively dislike or loathe the other two. These are your prejudices, and as such, will influence what you think about the things that each one has to say. If you really despise a politician, then you are likely to be deeply hostile to anything they say — even when on the face of it, it sounds sensible. Maybe there is someone at work who is always boasting about their achievements, whose comments you therefore distrust. That again is a prejudice or a state of mind that influences the way you interpret what they might say to you. This leads us conveniently to the next barrier.

Perceptual

Look briefly at this illustration.
What do you see being communicated?

Ask your friends in the group whether their perception of the picture is the same as yours. The chances are that you will see either an old woman, looking down towards the left hand corner of the picture, or a woman in Edwardian dress, with gaze averted. She is much younger in appearance. The fact is that both perceptions are possible. The illustration is clearly designed to create this illusion. Yet both perceptions are equally correct and valid.

This exercise tells us that a symbol can be interpreted differently by different people, and that this interpretation will depend on their previous experience of the symbol. If you are British, it is likely but not certain that you will identify favourably with the Union Jack when you see it — but don't be surprised if people from other nations treat it differently. They may be hostile, and some may even treat it as a joke.

This is because people's experience of the Union Jack varies. This is an important factor in determining how we perceive symbols. However, within one culture or nation, it is often possible to be aware of a number of alternative perceptions, even if we do not think that they are all equally valid. Think about your perceptions of punks for a moment. Perhaps you are one, so you will perceive a punk's striking hair style and dress as a perfectly acceptable way of expressing one's individuality. Nonetheless, you will know that not everybody thinks like this, and that many people perceive the punk's appearance and dress, not just as a statement of individuality, but as a calculated snub towards the rest of society.

It is less likely that we will be aware of other perceptions, however, if we have not experienced them as part of our own culture. Argyle (1979) tells how westerners and Arabs have different assumptions about the amount of personal space that is appropriate between acquaintances at social gatherings. Arabs typically expect to stand closer to others than do westerners, who prefer to maintain a slightly greater gap, unless they want to express intimacy. So at social events at which the two cultures interact, both cultures misinterpret each other's communicative behaviour. Arabs believe westerners to be stand-offish, while westerners think the Arabs are too pushy. We explore more of this non-verbal communication in Chapter 4.

Physiological

Not all communication barriers are created in the mind. If you are suffering from piles or toothache (our condolences if you are), you will not be able to pay too much attention to this chapter. Similarly, poor eyesight and hearing can pose communication problems, although we may be unwilling to admit it and conceal our difficulties because of embarrassment or vanity.

Environmental

If somebody plays a transistor at full blast when we are trying to have a private conversation, we are likely to be distracted. Our environment possesses unlimited potential for distraction, particularly if we are not terribly interested in what we're reading or listening to. Holding a conversation with someone when another message is clamouring for our attention (e.g., TV programme, member of the opposite sex, ringing phone) can be a problem.

Many environmental distractions are found in the workplace. Are there draughts in your office? Is it too cold, hot or stuffy for the staff to be able to work comfortably? Is it too noisy to 'hear yourself think'? Is a neon strip light giving you a migraine? Such problems can depress morale and reduce concentration, which in turn may interfere with effective communication.

ACTIVITY

Consider your own workplace.

1 What distractions or discomforts can you think of?
2 In what way do they create communication problems?
3 How many of them could be cured simply, without spending a lot of money?

Linguistic

You will remember that earlier in this chapter we pointed out the dangers of expressing ourselves in an inappropriate code. Go back to page 59 if you have forgotten about this. We also asked you to review your organisation's information literature to see whether it was 'user-friendly'. In this context, it is worth noting that mistakes are still being made, as this clipping from the *Independent* newspaper shows (28 October 1986).

Clearer pill labels 'could save £300m'

ACCIDENTS would be avoided and the health service would save millions of pounds if labels on pill and medicine bottles were written in plainer English, it was claimed yesterday.

The Plain English Campaign is warning health ministers that up to £300m a year may be wasted because patients do not take their medicines correctly or at all.

"Some of these patients returned to their doctors, their medicines having apparently failed, and were given other, often stronger drugs — further wasting the time and money of everyone involved."

The group said new research showed that plain English wordings could make about one in 20 prescription drugs more effective. That is 20 million of the 400 million prescriptions dispensed every year in England.

"More important, such wordings could even reduce unpleasant side effects and even deaths which have occurred through patients misunderstanding instructions."

The research, which involved 300 patients in London and Leeds, found that people made 15 percent fewer mistakes when trying to understand "plain English".

Of the patients asked, two-thirds preferred the plain English wordings, describing them as more "down to earth" and "human".

An example of traditional wording used with eye drops tells patients that drops should be "instilled" into the eyes, but then adds that the drops should "not be taken".

In plain English, the message is: "Drop one or two drops into both eyes four times a day. Don't swallow this."

The group will ask Tony Newton, the Health Minister, to review other wordings on medical labels which are difficult to understand when he opens the Clarity of Medical Information exhibition in London tomorrow.

Intellectual

'Problem one encountered that can be structuring is with messages of the.' Or, to put it another way, 'One problem that can be encountered is with the structuring of messages.' This example of a muddled-up sentence is perhaps a little far-fetched. But how often have we tried to make sense of a message whose content is badly organised? Once again, the crucial factor is our previous experience. We all have notions of logical sequencing, and when correct sequencing is observed, the problems are minimal. When it is not obvious — when it is illogical — the problems are much greater.

Another important factor is the 'pulse' of information. This refers to the speed at which facts are delivered. If we have experienced similar information before, we can consume it quite easily. When it is new to us, we need more time, and extra information will not be heard or understood if we are still trying to absorb an earlier idea or piece of information. If the information is cumulative (if it relies on earlier information to make sense), then we may give up altogether. Have you ever heard people say: 'I never really understood Maths at school'? This probably means that the pulse of information was wrong, causing them to feel progressively further and further left behind.

Presentational

Glance quickly at this poster (original size A4) and ask yourself a few questions.

- What is it about?
- Who needs to read it?
- What do they need to do having read it?
- Does the layout attract the intended audience?

West Midlands Computer **(C**

Education **(E**

TUESDAY 14TH OCTOBER   Group **(G**

'Why We Use What We Use'

A Guide to Software Selection

& Use in Schools by

JOHN WILSON, COLLEGE HOUSE JUNIOR SCHOOL, NOTTINGHAM

PLUS: Groups looking at:

Word Processing
LOGO
Simulations

7.30 to 9.00p.m.   **All welcome**

University of Birmingham

Faculty of Education — Room G33

Admission   Members FREE   Visitors 75p

You will probably have had quite a lot to say about this poster, but don't be too hard on the designer — he/she has made a commendable attempt! Posters are in competition with other messages to attract our attention, so they need to make an impact. Messages which fail to live up to our expectations may be rejected for that reason alone, so it is important to avoid conveying the wrong impression, for example by wrongly emphasising trivial information and by scruffy lettering.

┌─ **ACTIVITY** ───┐

Redesign the previous poster, in two or three colours, on A4, to create an irresistible design. You can modify, but not fundamentally change, the wording in any way you wish.

└───┘

It is also important to choose a suitable medium for a message. Although this sounds like a commonsense point of view, time and time again managers pin important memos to dreary notice-boards in remote corridors or draughty landings and wonder why they aren't read. (We dealt with this point earlier on page 48.)

It is not possible to avoid all these pitfalls all of the time. However, a few guidelines can be given which should help to ensure reasonably successful communication for most occasions.

7 POINT PLAN
for Improved Communication

1 **Identify your audience** — its age, social class, experience and cultural background.

2 **Choose a suitable code and medium** — every audience is different, so careful thought has to be given in choosing an appropriate code and medium.

3 **Use more than one medium** — a variety of signals will reinforce your message.

4 **Use redundancy** — make important points more than once and present information within a frame of reference with which the audience is familiar. But have a few surprises or people will become bored (see the section on redundancy and entropy for detailed guidance).

5 **Employ feedback** — look for clues about audience reaction, and don't ignore evidence of the fact that your audience doesn't enjoy or understand what you are saying.

6 **Empathise with others** — when people are telling you things, try to see how they perceive the information.

7 **Listen with a 'third ear'** — if there is emotional feeling involved, look for the hidden content, not just the apparent content, of the message. A speaker may not actually voice the real problem.

Solutions

Solution to the hazard warning signs on page 60. (1) Head protection must be worn. (2) Safe condition. (3) Foot protection must be worn. (4) Sound horn. (5) Use guard. (6) Use adjustable guard. (7) Emergency shower. (8) Wash hands. (9) Hearing protection must be worn. (10) Wear face shield. (11) Hand protection must be worn. (12) Keep locked.

Italian for THIS SIDE UP TO PREVENT DAMAGE (from page 60).

MEMORANDUM

From: Works Manager, Mr Alan Lewis

To: All employees

Date: 2nd April 19—

Subject: Concern at the number of thefts of personal belongings from employees

I refer to my earliest memo on this most important subject.

I am sorry to say that staff are still ignoring my advice to take the very greatest care of personal possessions while on the premises, despite the care that I went to in February, to circulate to all employees a copy of the new agreed guidelines from the joint employee–staff–management working party with regard to on-site security matters.

In the latest case it seems that an employee in the grinding shop noticed that a machine had developed a fault and switched it off. It seemed that probably one of the precision parts being produced had split and a splinter had dropped down into the rotary transverse oscillating spindle housing, and that this had caused the machine to 'run hot'. The employee called the supervisor's attention to it and the two men spent some time trying to remove the splinter. The employee who had been working the machine removed his overall in the process, and left it near to his machine on a crate of finished parts. As they were having no luck with the splinter, the man decided to borrow a pair of tongs from the forging shop. While he was gone, the supervisor was called away, and someone removed some money from the pocket of the man's overall. He had left his wallet in the pocket, containing £55.

The police have been informed and they are making enquiries. Nonetheless, I cannot stress too strongly this point about not leaving valuables about. Please re-read your agreed guidelines. I know some have been removed from the notice-boards by person(s) unknown and I am looking into this. I will arrange for some more photocopies to be made as soon as I can trace the photocopier fluid that has gone missing from my office over the weekend. In the meantime, I know I can count on you to be vigilant.

SCENARIO

Your boss, Mr. Lewis, has roughed out a memo for circulation to the workforce. He has asked you to revise it because his last memo had little impact on the staff.

TASK ONE / ANALYSIS

1 Using the terms 'redundant' and 'entropic', suggest whether this particular memo is likely to have the desired effect.

2 Which particular part of the message would you define as the most entropic?

3 What general advice would you offer to Mr Lewis to help him improve his communication skills?

TASK TWO / THE REVISION

Revise and rewrite the memo in a more satisfactory form. You may find it necessary to maximise the entropic content of the communication within a generally redundant format.

You need not adopt a memo format, nor are you obliged to communicate all the content of the original memo.

SCENARIO

This assignment is designed to encourage you to look at NEWS as it is reported in the press. You are to gather information from local and national newspapers on an important current issue and to analyse what this issue is all about.

You will receive group grades for skills shown in

- working with others
- written communication
- information gathering
- information processing

and you will receive an individual grade for oral communication.

PROCEDURE

- Get into groups of four.

- Between now and next week, each member of the group must obtain a different newspaper on four different days of the week, to achieve a group total of 16 newspapers. Agree amongst yourselves who will bring which papers — the important point is to ensure a wide range of 'qualities' and 'tabloids'. You will also need to bring with you a pair of scissors and glue.

Newsbeat

TASK ONE / PREPARATION

1 The following week, the members of each group are quickly to familiarise themselves with all the papers that have been brought in.

2 After conferring with the lecturer, each group is to choose a substantial news-story that has featured in the news during the previous week.

3 Cut out all references to this news-story and paste the cuttings onto the sheets of A4 that you have been given. The idea is to create a news-file, which records the progress of the story over several days, and the contrasting ways the different papers have reported it.

TASK TWO / THE ANALYSIS

1 Each group is to write a summary of the story. This must be in your own words and should, in addition, cover such points as

(a) When did the story first become newsworthy?

(b) What features make it newsworthy for the papers you have assembled? (Note positioning, illustrations and length of stories.)

(c) Which items appear to be factual and which convey the paper's opinions and attitudes?

(d) What are the implications of the story for the business and commercial world?

(e) What have you learned about the subject that is new to you?

2 What entropic techniques have the writer(s) used to draw and sustain the readers' attention? What form does the majority of the redundant material take?

TASK THREE / THE ORAL

When you have finished Task two, choose any other story that featured in your newspapers over the week. Then prepare an oral presentation in the form of a summary, based on an approach broadly similar to your written report. With each member of your group making a positive contribution, present your summary and analysis to the rest of the class.

CITY OF LOFTBOROUGH
The Personnel Department
Alliance House
Greyfriars Road
Loftborough L5 1BD

Summary of amended scheme
for the introduction of
FLEXIBLE WORKING HOURS
for administrative employees

1 Staff included

As many APT&C staff as possible, with the exception of those who clearly cannot be included because of the nature of their work and/or the extent of time that they are away from their administrative centre. Otherwise there is no intention to exclude senior staff or place any restriction on participation in the scheme because of status.

2 The working day

2.1 Under the Scheme the working day is divided into five periods.

Starting band	— 0800 to 1000 hours
Core time (am)	— 1000 to 1200 hours (all staff to be in attendance)
Lunch period	— 1200 to 1400 hours (minimum of $\frac{1}{2}$ hour to be taken)
Core time (pm)	— 1400 to 1600 hours (all staff to be in attendance)
Finishing band	— 1600 to 1900 hours

3 Flexible starting and finishing bands

3.1 During these defined periods, staff are generally free to start and finish work as they wish, provided that:

3.1.1 Their approximate times of arrival and departure are acceptable to their Supervisor and are consistent with the need to ensure that sections are manned during certain hours. This applies with particular force to the period from 0845 to 1715 hours (0845 to 1615 hours on Friday), but may vary according to sections or departments;

3.1.2 The Supervisor is satisfied that outside the period 0845 to 1715 hours (0845 to 1615 hours on Friday), work is available.

3.2 In any event, the Council reserves the right — which it will exercise reasonably — to require employees to be at work at any time during normal office hours 0845 to 1715 due to the exigencies of the service.

4 Lunch breaks

4.1 The minimum lunch break to be recorded, which must be between 1200 and 1400 hours, is half an hour on any one day. Up to two hours can be taken provided that this does not interrupt the work of the Section and that the period of absence is acceptable to the Supervisor. Whatever its duration, the lunch break must be recorded on the clock card on each day.

4.2 Failure to record the lunch break may lead to disciplinary action.

5 Time recording

5.1 Time clocks are installed and each employee is allocated to a particular machine by the direction of his/her Chief Officer. That machine only must be used and the clock card, having been clocked on the front of the card, placed in the rack adjacent to the clock and removed only when recording arrival or departure. Cards will be removed on Monday mornings for the purpose of totalling hours worked and calculating debit or credit.

5.2 Following totalling, the officer must sign the card in the space provided, acknowledging that the clockings and any other markings are a true and accurate record.

5.3 Under no circumstances is 'clocking' for other persons allowed. Any contravention of this may call for disciplinary action.

6 Time cards

6.1 Each day when an employee is present for the whole of the working day will require 'clocking' on a minimum of four occasions (arrival, departure for lunch, return from lunch, departure home). Every Friday afternoon, a new card will be placed in the appropriate card slot by the Chief Officer's designated representative, having previously been endorsed with the name of the employee and the week number. No blank cards will appear in the slots.

7 Totalling of hours

Unlike the times expressed at the head of this agreement, which are expressed in normal clock terms, the flexitime clocks record time in hours and hundredths of an hour. This makes for greater accuracy and simplifies the task of totalling hours.

8 Settlement period

The settlement period will be eight weeks.

9 Carry over

9.1 There can be carried over from one settlement period into the next up to 5 hours debit or up to 15 hours credit. Any credit over 15 hours at the end of the settlement period will be lost. If, in an individual case, more than 5 hours debit exists at the end of a settlement period, then disciplinary action may follow. This would initially consist of a warning, with a requirement to make up the deficit during the next settlement period, and, in respect of a second period of excess debit hours, the likelihood of a return to fixed hours working (0845 to 1715 hours — 1615 hours on Friday) for a period up to 12 months.

9.2 An officer who resigns and has a debit balance at termination of employment will be subject to an appropriate reduction in salary.

10 Staff absence

10.1 Other than in respect of official business, an officer shall not be absent during core time without specific authority from his/her Supervisor. Short absences for personal reasons (dental appointments, medical appointments, etc.) must, wherever possible, be arranged during flexible periods and intrude into coretime only with the prior approval of the Section Head. Individuals will be credited with such absence by reference to lost core time only.

10.2   Time off due to sickness, annual leave, day release or other approved special leave will be credited on the basis of $7\frac{1}{2}$ hours for a full day, pro rata for a lesser period of absence.

10.3   Where an employee goes home due to sickness after completing only a portion of the working day, he/she should be credited with $7\frac{1}{2}$ hours for that day regardless of time of arrival or the time of departure due to sickness.

10.4   On occasions where an employee takes half a day's annual leave/flexi-leave, the minimum of half an hour lunch break shall be taken, i.e. the earliest time to clock in is 1250 hours and the latest time to clock out is 1350 hours.

11   Inclement weather/industrial action by transport employees

11.1   Where, due to one or other of the above circumstances, an employee arrives at work after his/her normal starting time and he/she can show this to the satisfaction of the Chief Officer, then he/she shall be credited from that time. Such days will be designated by the City Personnel Officer and departments advised accordingly.

11.2   Such an employee cannot accumulate flexi-time on such a day other than by way of time actually worked as distinct from time allowed for late arrival.

11.3   An employee who, due to industrial action by transport employees or inclement weather, does not report for work at all on the date affected, will not receive pay for that day unless, exceptionally, the Chief Officer is satisfied in an individual case that the employee made every effort to attend.

11.4   Where employees are allowed to depart for home early — under the arrangements involving a decision by the Chief Executive and City Personnel Officer at times of inclement weather — then such employees will be credited in accordance with the time of 1600 hours, or actual time if this is later.

12   Flexible working hours leave

12.1   An officer may take up to a maximum of 2 half-days (or 1 day) in the first four weeks of the settlement period and, similarly, in the second four weeks of the period, subject to the exigencies of the service and prior authorisation in advance by the Supervisor. In order to qualify for such leave the officer, prior to the leave being taken, must have accumulated sufficient credit hours and, in the case of a half-day's leave, must complete the morning or afternoon session for the selected day (see Para. 10.4).

12.2   Any other credit hours can, of course, be taken during the flexible periods as laid down in this scheme.

13   Overtime

An officer authorised to work overtime during the bandwidth period, i.e. up to 1900 hours, must clock out before commencing such overtime working, which will be separately recorded. In general, overtime working will be authorised only where the hours cannot reasonably be retrieved through the flexitime system. Care must be taken so as to ensure that overtime authorised and worked is not included in normal hours for flexitime working hours calculation. In any event, it will not normally be paid unless 37 hours have been worked in that week.

14   General

The success of this Scheme, clearly depends on its thorough observance by staff. It follows that cases of abuse, will have to be dealt with — in the interests of staff generally and the Council — as disciplinary matters and in accordance with the agreed disciplinary procedure.

SCENARIO

As an expert on communication, you have joined a small action group that has been given the responsibility of communicating the council's flexible working hours scheme to its 750 eligible employees, and of 'marketing' the idea in the general community as part of the council's campaign to promote more flexible attitudes about employment. You appreciate that you must first read and thoroughly understand the scheme, even if this means that you have to check up on the precise meaning of a few terms used in the document.

PROCEDURE

It is the responsibility of the group itself to decide how it intends to inform council staff about the scheme and the techniques to be used for the publicity campaign. A useful method might be to 'brainstorm' both topics first to get some ideas. (Brainstorming is described in Chapter 7.)

TASK ONE / EMPLOYEE AWARENESS

Your team has come to the conclusion that:

- The information in the original document has to be made more 'accessible' and presented in a much more interesting format.

- A multi-media approach should be adopted to maximise the level of staff awareness.

- An opportunity should be given to staff to enable them to ask questions about the scheme.

Task one will be completed when your team has actually produced the materials to be used for the purposes of informing staff about the scheme.

You are also to explain how you intend to organise, publicise and conduct meetings (if these are required), again providing all the back-up material.

You might like to consider backing-up your employee awareness campaign with the use of video, if this facility is available. However, you will need to explain how you intend to use it, given the number of staff involved.

TASK TWO / PRESS AND MEDIA RELEASES

Loftborough's declared policy has always been to keep the local community fully informed of its actions and to 'lead the way' with its socially desirable employment strategies. The Council is convinced that the flexible working hours scheme offers advantages, not only to their own employees and themselves, but also to the community in general.

Your team has been charged by the Council with the responsibility of producing:

- A press release of about 500 words, plus one illustration if required, to be sent to the local paper and to the council's own paper *Council News* (see Chapter 6 for guidance).

- A 5-minute demo tape (perhaps a question and answer format?) to be sent to the local radio station *Brightsound*, who have already made enquiries about the scheme.

In preparation, your team might like first to consider:

- What are the advantages to the staff and their families of flexitime?

- What does the council get out of it?

- Are there any disadvantages?

- In what way does the community benefit?

- Do we need to write covering letters for the press releases and the demo tapes?

In this chapter we will be looking at the more important forms of written communication that are used in the running of a business. Although there has been a rapid and extensive introduction of computer-based systems of communication and word processors, this does not necessarily mean that the amount of correspondence written or generated by individuals has actually decreased. For example, think about the last letter, report, memo, minutes of meeting, or business document that you read. Although it may have been efficiently produced on a word processor or reproduced in several colours on an expensive photocopier, the chances are that the actual words and diagrams, beautifully presented though they were, had their origins in *human* creativity and imagination.

The business letter

In your morning post you receive a scruffy looking letter that has been addressed to a Mrs J. Smelley. Since you are a single woman and your name is Josephine Smalley, and the address on the envelope is roughly similar to your own, you open it to find a letter from a local firm. This is the text of the letter:

Dear Josephine,

<u>Re: employment inquiry</u>

With reference to your recent employment enquiry. Your quite right in assuming that the job for which you have applied requires a paper qualification. I am assured by our personel department that your BTEC certificate will be alright as far as we are concerned.

Regarding your inquiry about interview dates. We will not be able to let you know a definate time untill executive holidays are over. Your application will recieve attention eventually. We are expecting our selection proceedure to be finalised by the end of the week.

As far as your own forthcoming holiday is concerned, our firm will do it's best, should you be appointed, to meet your demands as best we can.

Yours faithfully,

DM

ACTIVITY

Make a list of the errors in this extract — then rewrite the letter incorporating your corrections. You may reorganise the letter in any way you wish to effect an improvement.

It is unlikely that any company would produce a letter quite as bad as this. One of the consequences of sending such a letter is not only the bad impression that it gives of the company, but the encouragement that it gives the job hunter to adopt attitudes and strategies that are to the company's disadvantage. For example:

- I wouldn't work in this company's office for all the tea in China. It must be a shambles. They can't even get my name right, never mind write a business letter. I think I'll stay where I am.
- This company is so bad that even someone as unskilled and inexperienced as I am could do well there. The interview is going to be a doddle.

From the employer's point of view both these attitudes are undesirable and unwelcome. However, they only have themselves to blame because they have failed to realise that readers make all kinds of favourable and unfavourable judgements, sometimes unconsciously, on the strength of first impressions. Since letters are often a first-contact mode of communication, it makes sense for us all to ensure that the letters we write are as attractive and as well written as possible.

ACTIVITY

Discuss the kinds of problems that have arisen as a result of faulty letter writing in your own line of work or in your personal experience.

Format and stationery

Most business letters are produced on either A4 or A5 paper and are sent in manilla C4, C5, C6 or DL envelopes.

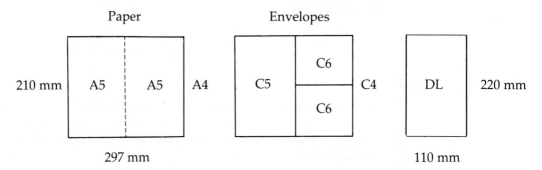

Put simply, C4 envelopes will take unfolded sheets of A4, and C5 envelopes unfolded sheets of A5. Since most letters are sent folded, C6 is the most common envelope size to accommodate an A4 sheet folded into quarters. Envelope size DL is also useful because it is designed to carry A4 paper folded into thirds.

ACTIVITY

What envelope size would you recommend for:

- a glossy 45-page holiday brochure (A4) and covering letter.
- a 6-sheet A4 report.
- a job application letter.
- a single A5 form and a DL stamped addressed envelope?

The vast majority of organisations know the marketing value of an attractive letterhead (sometimes in two or more colours and embossed) printed on both A4 and A5 stationery, and are prepared to spend a lot of money and time to get their designs just right. However, there are certain legal demands that have to be met first. In addition to the usual trading name and address, telephone and telex numbers, letterheads must carry by law:

- The company's trading name and its status as a limited company
- List of company directors and address of its registered office
- Registration number of company and location of registration

} *usually printed in small type at the bottom of the sheet*

As for the design of the letterhead, there are basically two types: the symmetrical design and the asymmetrical design. Here is an example of a symmetrical design, which simply means that all the design elements are centred on the sheet.

Tower Assurance Advisory Services Ltd

Tower House 5-11 Mortimer Street London W1N7RH Tel: 01-580 0617 Telex: 265495

In asymmetrical designs, the design elements are not centred on the sheet, so the left half of the design is different from that of the right.

Members of the West Midlands Chamber of Commerce.

136 Lawley Street, Birmingham B4 7XZ
Telephone: 021 359 0161 Facsimile: 021 359 0595

There are a few points worth noting about these examples. First the symmetrical designs tend to reflect an image of reliability and tradition (which explains why financial organisations favour them), whereas asymmetrical designs suggest an atmosphere of innovation and change (the modern technological office), although we must not take these ideas too literally. You will also notice the use of a logo in each example. Logos are visual symbols that help to project an image — it is important for businesses to project the most desirable image possible.

For the first two activities you are expected to invent appropriate trading names and other details. Dry transfer lettering is allowed.

1 Select one of the following logos and design a symmetrical letterhead.

2 Select a different logo and design an asymmetrical letterhead in two colours (one colour may be black).

3 Draw rough designs for logos to symbolise:
   (a) a company called Aquarium Products
   (b) a firm dealing in computer software
   (c) an insurance company.

Letter layout and style

We can now consider the way business letters are typed out on the page and the choice of punctuation styles available to us. Basically, there are three styles of letter layout and two forms of punctuation.

Letter styles	Punctuation styles
• Fully blocked	• Open punctuation
• Semi-blocked	• Closed punctuation
• Indented	

Which style of letter and punctuation that we choose to use for our particular business needs depends on what kind of image we want to project. There is no right and wrong style — although when we do decide on the most appropriate layout we must try to be consistent.

```
+--------------------------------------------------+
|               Company letterhead                 |
|  _____  |
|                                                  |
|  16 July 19—                                     |
|                                                  |
|  Mrs Edna Blake                                  |
|  35 Foremans Way                                 |
|  EPSOM                                           |
|  Surrey                                          |
|  KT19 7EN                                        |
|                                                  |
|  Dear Mrs Blake                                  |
|                                                  |
|  INSTALLATION OF GAS CENTRAL HEATING             |
|                                                  |
|  Thank you for your letter of the 13 July.       |
|                                                  |
|  We are now in a position to install gas         |
|  central heating in your home. Our engineers     |
|  have been instructed to begin the work          |
|  on Monday 24 July at 8.30am.                    |
|                                                  |
|  I hope that you or someone will be available    |
|  at that time to allow them access to your       |
|  property.                                       |
|                                                  |
|  Please contact me if you have any problems.     |
|                                                  |
|  Yours sincerely                                 |
|                                                  |
|  Roger Davis                                     |
|                                                  |
|  Roger Davis                                     |
+--------------------------------------------------+
```

Fully blocked and open punctuation

Fully blocked letters are typed to the left side of the sheet. There is no indentation of any kind. It projects a 'modern' image, but it does have the disadvantage of looking a bit lopsided, especially if the line lengths are short. Open punctuation means that there are no punctuation marks at the end of short free-standing lines, although this does not apply within the body of the letter. Generally speaking, open punctuation is becoming more popular.

```
+--------------------------------------------------+
|               Company letterhead                 |
|  _____  |
|                                                  |
|  Mrs Edna Blake,                                 |
|  35 Foremans Way,                                |
|  EPSOM,                        16th July 19—     |
|  Surrey,                                         |
|  KT19 7EN.                                       |
|                                                  |
|  Dear Mrs Blake,                                 |
|                                                  |
|      INSTALLATION OF GAS CENTRAL HEATING         |
|                                                  |
|  Thank you for your letter of the 13th July.     |
|                                                  |
|  We are now in a position to install gas         |
|  central heating in your home. Our engineers     |
|  have been instructed to begin the work          |
|  on Monday, 24th July at 8.30am.                 |
|                                                  |
|  I hope that you or someone will be available    |
|  at that time to allow them access to your       |
|  property.                                       |
|                                                  |
|  Please contact me if you have any problems.     |
|                                                  |
|                         Yours sincerely,         |
|                                                  |
|                         Roger Davis              |
|                                                  |
|                         Roger Davis              |
+--------------------------------------------------+
```

Semi-blocked and closed punctuation

Semi-blocked means that date and letter endings are ranged on the right side, with the heading in a centre position. Everything else is blocked to the left side. This style has the advantage of looking more balanced, but it may be a little more difficult to type. You can see that punctuation marks are used in a conventional way on line endings.

Indented

Indented letter styles are similar to semi-blocked letters except that paragraphs are indented, which means that there is extra space before the first word of every paragraph.

Of course it is possible to choose any combination of letter style and punctuation, although we must remember to address envelopes in a similar style if we are to be consistent.

Parts of a business letter

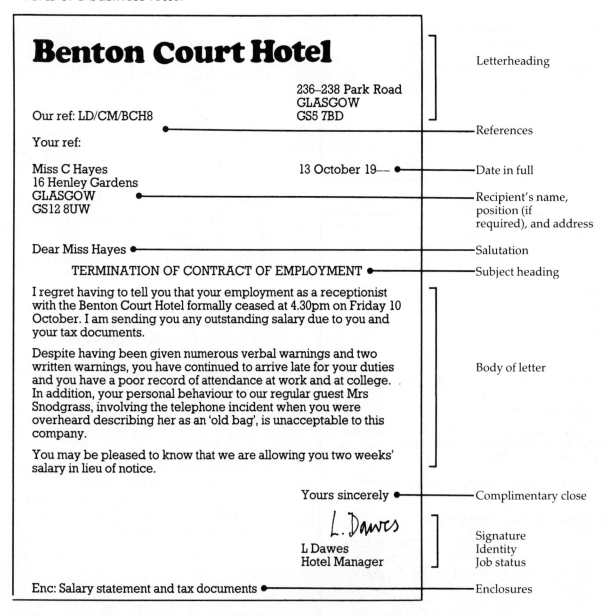

Benton Court Hotel

                236–238 Park Road
                GLASGOW
Our ref: LD/CM/BCH8   GS5 7BD   — References

Your ref:

Miss C Hayes   13 October 19—— — Date in full
16 Henley Gardens
GLASGOW   — Recipient's name, position (if required), and address
GS12 8UW

Dear Miss Hayes — Salutation

    TERMINATION OF CONTRACT OF EMPLOYMENT — Subject heading

I regret having to tell you that your employment as a receptionist with the Benton Court Hotel formally ceased at 4.30pm on Friday 10 October. I am sending you any outstanding salary due to you and your tax documents.

Despite having been given numerous verbal warnings and two written warnings, you have continued to arrive late for your duties and you have a poor record of attendance at work and at college. In addition, your personal behaviour to our regular guest Mrs Snodgrass, involving the telephone incident when you were overheard describing her as an 'old bag', is unacceptable to this company.

You may be pleased to know that we are allowing you two weeks' salary in lieu of notice.

              Yours sincerely — Complimentary close

           L. Dawes

           L Dawes   Signature / Identity / Job status
           Hotel Manager

Enc: Salary statement and tax documents — Enclosures

Letterheading

Body of letter

We can now examine in more detail the actual components of a business letter.

Letterheading

If we are writing to an organisation from a private address we would write our own address in the top right-hand corner, but we would *not* include our name. The format of a business letterheading has been described on page 85.

References

References help businesses to file and trace letters by providing an information key.

Our ref: = outgoing letter   Your ref: = incoming letter

The initials and numbers that follow both or either references indicate:

- Who has written the letter (first initials)
- Who has typed the letter (second initials, sometimes in lower case)
- Where the letter is to be found (third initials and numbers)

Example: Our ref: MT/jt/DS82 = Margaret Thatcher/Jane Taft/Downing Street file 82

Date

This is best displayed in order of day, month, year, without 'th', 'st', 'rd', 'nd' or commas.

Example: 17 January 19––.

Recipient's name, position and address

Letters are addressed either to private individuals, organisations, or to named individuals within a company or a department, followed by a postal address.

> Mr W J Morris, MA
> Director of Further Education
> Hatton County Council
> Market Street
> HATTON H30 2EA

Unlike addressing an envelope, we can afford to double up on lines to prevent having to start our letter too far down the page.

Knowing the correct way to address an individual, even when they have no official status, can be a problem. The usual forms of address are:

Men — Mr or Esq (Esq now rarely used and never together with Mr)
Women — Miss, Mrs or Ms (Ms is useful if you are unsure)
Male partnerships — Messrs (it literally means gentlemen who have formed a partnership)

We must always insert a person's qualifications or letters after his or her name unless we know that the person prefers them to be omitted. We must also address titled people correctly. Correct styles of address for dignatories can be found in the reference book *Whitaker's Almanack*.

Salutation and complimentary close

These describe ways of opening and closing the body of a letter and follow a strict convention that seems resistant to change. We are expected to use the affectionate 'Dear' as an opening in most cases, even though we may be writing to a total stranger.

Salutation (greeting)	Complimentary close
Dear Sir (Sirs, Madam, Mesdames)	Yours faithfully
Dear Mr Jay (Miss Jay, Mrs Jay, Dr Jay, Lady Jay, Lord Jay, Reverend Jay)	Yours sincerely
Dear Susan	Sincerely
Dear Mark	Kind regards

Subject heading

This helps the organisation to file the letter in the right place and tells the reader quickly what the letter is about. The subject heading should always lie between the salutation and the body of the letter, and is sometimes typed in capitals and/or underlined.

Signature, identity and status

Space is left under the complimentary close for signature, and the name is always typed (or handwritten in capitals) beneath, followed by an official job title. If the letter is to be signed by another person (e.g., a private secretary) the word 'for' or the letters 'pp' are written alongside the typed name.

Yours faithfully

Linda Smith

for F. Millward
Sales Manager

Enclosures

Any accompanying documents or materials are clearly indicated at the foot of the letter, along with a 'copies to' line if a third person is involved.

Envelopes

The address should be complete, legible and accurate, with each part of the address occupying a separate line. The envelope and its letter may be headed CONFIDENTIAL or PRIVATE AND CONFIDENTIAL only if this is strictly necessary.

CONFIDENTIAL

Mrs S. T. Sherman,
Forward Industries Ltd.,
135 Lofthouse Road,
WIDNES,
Cheshire,
WL5 2HJ

Planning the letter

Before we begin to write a letter we have to ask ourselves one important question: What is it that I want my letter to do? If we want to persuade someone to buy our products, or tender an estimate, or offer an apology for a delay in delivery, or thank a customer for her order, then simply thinking about the question will help us in our task. We must also respond to letters demanding a reply as promptly as we can, although we should allow ourselves time to think carefully about letters of a more serious nature. If we are foolish enough to rush into writing a letter, say, promising early delivery, we might find ourselves in an embarrassing position if we fail to deliver on time. We can get into even more serious legal and financial trouble if we make untrue and damaging statements in writing about other people's products, or if we carelessly send letters of dismissal that we later find to be based on false assumptions.

Unless our letter is to be short or very straightforward, we need to make a plan. Our first task is to get hold of all previous correspondence, financial statements, and documentation to familiarise ourselves with the background to the subject. We should read these carefully and make notes of any items to which we might refer later. We then begin to get a sense of how our own letter might be constructed. By making notes of the main points we wish to cover, and organising them into a logical order, we create a framework on which to construct our letter. In the following example addresses have been left out.

Example

You work in the Customer Relations Department of a national bus company that specialises in touring holidays. You receive this letter from a Mrs Bates, and your boss asks you to deal with it.

Dear Sir,

We have just returned from one of your coach touring holidays in Wales. I would just like to say how much me and my husband Harry enjoyed ourselves. We travel with you every year and we always get good value for our money. We enjoyed the friendship and the good humour of our driver 'Jimmy' Edwards.

But we do have a serious complaint to make about one of the hotels we stayed in. On the night of Thursday 7th July we slept at Duncannon Guest House in Llandudno. The next morning we discovered to our horror that we had both been bitten by bed bugs or fleas, and on our return home my husband had to go to the doctors for ointment for his legs. We complained to the hotel owner, but he said the sheets are changed regularly and there must be some mistake.

We do feel that we have a right to complain about this. It was a lovely holiday and it was such a shame that it had to be spoiled in this way.

Yours faithfully,
Ethel Bates

This seems such a nice letter that Mrs Bates has written. In fact you think she is being extremely reasonable considering the circumstances, and her letter deserves your fullest personal attention. However, before you put pen to paper you check your files to find that:

- There are several letters written by Mrs Bates, all of which describe previous holidays in the most glowing terms. You note that Mr and Mrs Bates have had eight consecutive annual holidays with the company.
- There have been previous complaints from guests about the Duncannon Guest House, but none very serious and none relating to insect infestation.
- There are copies of letters that have been sent to other clients on similar matters that might be helpful to you in the formulation of your reply.

This is your reply.

SPENCER TOURS

16 FENTON ROAD, WIGAN
LANCASHIRE, W5 6EB

Our ref: ML/PJ/FJ
Your ref:

Mr and Mrs Harry Bates
14 Preston Street   13 July 19—
WIGAN
Lancashire W12 1VD

Dear Mr and Mrs Bates

We are very sorry to hear about your unpleasant experience in the Duncannon Guest House Llandudno and we are most grateful that you have taken the trouble to write to us about it.

We are taking immediate steps to investigate the insect infestation in your bedding and we shall be writing to Mr Williams, the manager of the guest house without delay. We will also be instructing our senior investigator to visit the guest house and make a report on the incident. You can rest assured that we intend to get to the bottom of this problem.

We are most appreciative of your regular custom over the years and we will be delighted to continue to provide for your holiday needs. In the meantime, we would like you both to accept a box of chocolates as a token of our goodwill.

Yours sincerely

Marianne Lake

Customer Relations

Enc: voucher for box of chocolates

Notes on letter structure

- Acknowledge receipt of letter.
- Brief identification of problem.
- Establish friendly and supportive tone.

- Define precise nature of complaint.
- Acceptance of its seriousness.
- Detail actions for solving problem to re-establish confidence in company.

- The offer of a gift as a gesture of goodwill.
- Conclude on optimistic note.

This letter of adjustment will probably succeed in its purpose because it attempts to satisfy the needs of both the company and its customer. This leads us back to our original question: What is it that I want my letter to do? Once we know this and have done our research, we are in a position to set it out.

The way we set out or structure the body of a letter depends again on what we expect our letter to do. However, there are a few guidelines.

First paragraph

This is the most important paragraph because it tells the reader the purpose of the letter by giving it a recognisable context, often under a convenient heading. Generally speaking, we acknowledge previous correspondence and come quickly to the main point of our letter, without going into detail.

Here are three examples

1 MORTGAGE POLICY NO. 4869
   We would like to draw your attention to the fact that you have failed to meet your mortgage repayments for the …

2 I regret having to tell you that I am unable to supply …

3 I wish to rebuild and extend my garage and I would be grateful if you would let me know whether I require planning per …

Middle paragraphs

These are where the details or explanations are laid bare. Usually this can be done in just one or two paragraphs, each paragraph dealing with a separate issue. If our letter is to be long and complicated, we might consider a tabular approach to help the reader to assimilate the information.

1 I strongly advise you to contact your branch manager who will arrange to meet you and your wife to discuss …

2 Unfortunately, as this particular model is no longer in production all parts were withdrawn from stock on …

3 Here are some details of my existing garage:

   (a) Dimensions …
   (b) Location …
   (c) Materials used in construction …

   Details of proposal for the erection of new garage:

Closing paragraph

This is often used as a brief summing up of the main points of the letter or to re-establish the tone of goodwill (or otherwise) introduced in the opening paragraph. It is here that the reader is reminded of the action necessary to put right what is wrong.

1 I am bound to remind you that if interest on your mortgage is not repaid urgently, we will be forced to consider the repossession of …

2 Please feel free to contact us again. As you are well aware, we hold vast stocks of …

3 Will you please send me the relevant form and give me an idea of the procedures to get planning permission, if this is required.

As personal assistant to Ms Marianne Lake, you are asked to write to the manager of the guest house expressing your concern about the incident. You should make a few suggestions about what he might do to put things right and inform him of the steps you are taking to investigate the incident. You decide to be firm in reminding him of the consequences of a declining standard of customer service. The guest house is situated at 15 Manor Road, Llandudno, Gwynedd, LL2 2BL.

Letter content and tone

When we read a letter we are experiencing, as with all reading, a form of long-distance communication to which we are unable to respond immediately. Unlike having a conversation, say on a telephone, we can't stop our communicator to ask what he means if he uses a difficult word or an obscure phrase. Nor can we defend ourselves or argue a case if we are being accused unjustly — at least not immediately. This is why as letter writers we have a responsibility to do everything we can to help the reader to get the right message. Getting the right message across, as we have seen in the previous section, depends to some degree on why we are writing the letter in the first place. We can summarise the main reasons as:

- To give or seek information.
- To prompt some form of desirable action.
- To maintain or promote a satisfactory relationship or to end it.

In the letter sent by Spencer Tours, we can identify all three of these reasons, so we must accept that these separate categories are to some extent artificial. However, it is possible to classify most letters as being mainly in one or other of the three groups.

Make a copy of this table and leave plenty of space for your answers. Jot down a few notes, under one or more headings, to indicate the purpose of each letter. The first example has been done for you:

Classification of letter	Information exchange	Prompting action	Promoting relationships
Letter offering employment	The main purpose of the letter is to inform the applicant of their success. There may be a few details given about starting date and to whom they are to report.	The applicant is to confirm acceptance of post in writing.	There might be a brief and optimistic signing off sentence welcoming the new employee to the company.
Sales letter to customer			
Estimate of cost			
Complaint of faulty goods			
Query about cost			
Letter of credit			
Circular to staff			
Tender of final price			
Order for goods			
Letter of resignation			
Letter of adjustment offering to rectify a complaint			

Just how we tackle a particular letter depends on the precise nature of our intention. Since most letters we deal with are either asking for or giving information, then a neutral approach or tone is desirable. If, on the other hand, we are to give a favourable or unfavourable response to a request, or we are trying to persuade someone to buy our merchandise, then the tone and content of our letter needs to be shaped to suit our purposes. However, we should at all times try to follow these guidelines below.

Be aware of the reader

Being sensitive and informed about our correspondent's needs are important. We should adapt the tone and content of the letter not only to provide the quality and quantity of information we think is required, but also to be mindful of the reader's intelligence and status. Careless phrasing and over-familiarity are dangers we must avoid. For example:

1 One of our assistants told me that you bought a pair of shoes from the shop the other day and one of the heels fell off. I'm sorry about that. Why don't you call in and I'll get them changed for you? Ask for Mr Sharp — I'm the manager here. Thursday is a good day for me.

Be clear, simple and brief

We must try to say plainly what we mean in the fewest possible words so the reader is not misinformed or confused. Paragraphs should follow a logical sequence and we should avoid 'padding', over-long sentences, clichés and obscure wording. We should also resist the temptation to include convenient abbreviations and technical terms unless we know they will be understood by the reader.

2 Dear Miss Bissett

AC/NO. 3875/BH/LT/SECTION F

Looking through our extensive files on Thursday 8 June I observed with great regret that your account for the clothing supplied to you in May remains incomplete and outstanding, and we will be compelled in these circumstances to instruct our legal advisors to instigate legal proceedings against you on our behalf unless you are prepared to advance the appropriate moneys in prompt settlement.

Be accurate and complete

One of the most annoying things that can happen is when we get a letter that doesn't tell us what we want to know, and we are then forced into unnecessary correspondence. Before we seal up a letter we should check that we have dealt with all the points we intended to deal with and that we haven't omitted any crucial information such as names and addresses. It is also very easy to make mistakes with days, dates and times and we should check that these are accurate too.

3 Dear Mr Pringle

We would like to invite you for interview for the post of Clerical Assistant. Since we are anxious to fill this post urgently, we are holding interviews next Monday at 3.00 hrs. Please bring your documents.

Unfortunately, since these offices are in the process of being renovated, we may have to conduct the interviews in our Hendon Road branch office on Tuesday morning.

Perhaps you would like to ring Miss Burns before then at our Head Office in Hastings. She will let you know about the medical examination.

Yours sincerely

Be helpful and polite

Since the reason for writing a letter is often either to offer help in one form or another or to ask for help (usually it is both), then it is obviously in our interests to be considerate and polite. Unlike this correspondent:

 The lawnmower part you ordered (X23 — Model 7) is no longer stocked by this company. We consider this particular machine to be dangerous so we withdrew all models and parts from stock. We enclose brochures of our new models for your perusal.

Even when we are faced with having to write a 'strong' letter, this does not mean we ought to be either impolite or rude.

 Your offer of £750 to replace my stolen motor is ridiculous. I paid nearly £2000 for it six months ago and I expect at least £1500 now. That's why I insured fully comprehensively with you in the first place. I'm not standing for this. I'll go out of business if I don't get proper compensation — I rely on the van to run my business. Pay up or or I'll get my solicitor on to you.

Be tactful

Tact is sometimes most difficult to achieve because it is so easy, unintentionally, to slip in the odd word or phrase that can hurt someone's feelings. This is from the area manager of a 24-hour cleaning service:

 I am sorry about the damage to your dress that occurred at our Hettington Branch. I understand from the manageress that the problem may have been caused by a combination of inferior fabrics and an over-heated dryer. Please bring your dress back for examination.

ACTIVITY

1 Briefly explain what is wrong with the previous six examples of faulty writing.
2 Rewrite them in a more appropriate way, if necessary by introducing new material.

Circular letters

A circular letter is written with a mass audience in mind rather than an individual. Broadly speaking, circulars are used either for advertising or promoting goods and services, or for routine purposes within organisations. When circulars are sent to specific individuals by organisations they are sometimes referred to as 'standard letters'.

Advertising circulars

These are now so common that one pressure group is actively campaigning to limit their use because of the needless waste of materials and the damage done to woodlands. Although the vast majority of circulars are thrown away unread, there is no doubt of their selling power, especially since the widespread use of word processors has enabled personal details to be incorporated. Most circulars tend to follow a common format:

- An arresting first sentence.
- A glowing account of the advantages of the product in contrast with competitors' products.
- The offer of a 'bribe' in the form of a small gift, or advantageous terms to the customer who responds within '14 days'.

To help us to respond favourably, we are helped along with:

- An easy-to-fill tear-off address coupon to return in a free-post envelope.
- Free-phone telephone number.
- Call-back service, followed by a letter or a visit to the home by sales staff.
- More inducements, sometimes linked with a free competition or a '10% reduction in price if you bring this circular with you to the showroom'.

ACTIVITY

Study the extracts from a circular published by the Midland Bank before you answer the questions.

1 Summarise the techniques of persuasion used by the writer.
2 How effective do you think the circular is?
3 From which source do you think the bank derived its customer addresses? Which addresses might it have excluded from its list?
4 Can you suggest a few ways in which this circular can be improved?
5 There is one piece of information that the writer has chosen to play down. Do you know what this is? Why do you think it has been sidestepped?

Midland Bank plc
Customer Information Service

Dear Customer,

Wouldn't you like to be able to agree a loan <u>now</u>, then have
<u>6 months</u> to shop around for just what you want?

With a Midland Personal Loan that's exactly what you can do –
thanks to our Personal Loan Certificate.

This means that once your Loan Application is approved, you'll be
issued with your own Personal Loan Certificate, which agrees the
maximum amount you can borrow and the maximum repayment period
you can take.

Once you have your Personal Loan Certificate you can then take
as long as 6 months (the length of time for which your Certificate
is valid) to look around for exactly what you want.

You could have any amount from £250 right up to £10,000 (in
multiples of £10), you can spread your repayments over 6 months
up to a full 5 years, and you can use the money to buy whatever
you wish. For further details of loan amounts and monthly
repayments, please see the enclosed table.

Naturally, the Midland interest rate is as competitive as you'll
find elsewhere, but we also offer a combination of benefits you
definitely won't find anywhere else.

(continued)

As well as our Personal Loan Certificate, there's our CarOwner Plus package. Allow me to explain what this offers you.

If you obtain a Midland Personal Loan, and use it to pay for a car before the 6th October, we'll not only give you a voucher entitling you to a £30 discount off your next car insurance premium - valid for a full 12 months with one of Britain's leading insurance companies - but we'll also give you a form to enter our Free competition where you could win a new Porsche 911 Carrera!

Have a look at the enclosed leaflet for full details of our CarOwner Plus package.

There's the convenience too, of keeping your financial transactions all under one roof. And, with a Midland Personal Loan, your monthly Standing Order repayments can be made on the day of the month that most suits you.

Best of all, it couldn't be easier to apply for your Midland Bank Personal Loan: there's just one straightforward form which takes only a couple of minutes to complete.

Return the enclosed Personal Loan Application Form in the envelope provided (no stamp needed) or contact your branch and you could soon have your own Personal Loan Certificate to shop around with for up to 6 months!

Yours sincerely,

Routine or standard letters

Since many written transactions in organisations are similar, it makes sense not to waste money and time writing 'special' letters. It is even more sensible to have letters or cards pre-printed, so details relevant to a particular situation can be conveniently inserted. With word processors, it is now commonplace to store details of text on tape, and, by inserting personal details, create an impression that each letter is unique. However, since so much advantage is derived from one original letter, this means we can afford to spend time writing as perfect a letter as possible. It would be silly to abuse modern technology in the production of second-rate standard letters.

ACTIVITY

Draft a standard letter from your own organisation (or invent another if you wish), which could be sent to local colleges to inform them that an employee has ceased attending their course. You may design your own letterhead if you have time.

Applying for a job

The main purpose of a job application is to secure an interview with a prospective employer. Whether or not we get invited for interview depends on what we have to offer and how we convey this information. No matter how brilliant and capable we are, these are not enough in themselves unless we can convince the employing organisation to invite us for interview. We are usually asked to apply for a job by sending either:

- A letter giving full details
- A letter supported by a curriculum vitae
- A completed application form and covering letter.

Of course, if we are lucky, we might get interviewed on the strength of a personal telephone call made to an employer, or because our interview has been arranged by a careers officer or a job centre. Even so, the act of thinking through and planning a written application is in itself a valuable process, which may be useful to us later.

In an ideal world it should be possible to decide exactly what kind of job we want and then simply apply for it. With over 2 million unemployed in the UK, we might feel that almost any job will do. Unfortunately, landing a job that we know is unsuitable can eventually lead to misery and disappointment.

Having a rough idea of the kind of job we want, it is up to us to exploit every source of job opportunity available.

ACTIVITY

Here is a list of organisations and sources that provide job or promotion opportunities. Make a copy, and against each source jot down as much useful information as you can, based on your research. Data might include:

- Names and addresses, where appropriate.
- The range of services they provide (When? How? Where?).
- How to get the best out of them (specialist services provided/good and bad days to attend or buy).
- Some advantages and disadvantages.

Sources	Details of value to the job seeker
Job centres	
Careers service	
Local/regional/national newspapers/local radio	
Specialist publications and advertising circulars	
Private agencies	
Present employer Other local employers	
Other sources	

Once we spot a suitable job advertisement, say in a newspaper, we must take care to read it properly, because we may be about to put ourselves in a position to apply not for any job but for a *particular* job. We should be asking ourselves questions about what is actually on offer and what kind of employee the organisation is looking for.

1 Make a list of the qualities demanded of applicants in each advertisement.
2 Select one of the jobs advertised and suggest what other qualities and skills the employer might be looking for.
3 In your selected job, what vital information has been omitted? Draw up a list of questions that will help you to find out what you want to know.

SECRETARIAL ASSISTANT
(male/female)

required (due to retirement) to provide support services to secretary of small, long established Real Estate and Investment Company.

The work involves dealing with some pension and staff records, insurances and general office routine including preparation of reports and meeting minutes.

Some knowledge of commercial and company law and procedure would be a distinct advantage but good communication and administrative skills with friendly personality are more important.

Salary to be commensurate with experience. Please apply in writing enclosing full CV to: Mr J. Handley, Ogden Investment, 2 Fulham Road, Fulham, London LN31 6RA

HAVEN HOUSE

We are a charitable Association working in the Inner City area of Birmingham providing a wide range of accommodation and developing our work with groups and individuals to cater for those in the most urgent housing need. Applicants are invited for the post of:

HOUSING OFFICER

in one of our Housing Management teams. The person appointed will work under the direction of the Area Housing Manager and will be responsible for all Housing Management activities covering approximately 200 tenancies.

We are looking for someone with relevant qualifications and experience to take on this challenging post. The successful applicant will need to be adaptable and resourceful in order to deal with a variety of Housing duties and must be able to deal sympathetically yet positively with people and families in financial difficulties. Experience of working with Ethnic Minority groups will be a distinct advantage.

Salary within the range £6,309–£7,887, with a starting figure of £7,044 for a person with relevant qualifications.

Write to Mandy Lowe, Haven House, 14 New Street, Birmingham B2 8JL

▶ **CLASSICAL BUYER**
▶ **JAZZ BUYER**
▶ **PAPERWORK/CASH OFFICE ASSISTANT**
▶ **SALES ASSISTANT**

BIGSOUND Megastore, one of Britain's largest and busiest record stores, is looking for staff to fill the above positions. Applicants must have had previous work experience and be over eighteen years old.

We are offering a good salary, benefits package and opportunities within an expanding company to the successful applicants, who will be intelligent, enthusiastic, ambitious and have a good knowledge of music.

Convince us of your worth by writing to Ms Jane Chambers, Bigsound Megastore, 14 Adam Street, Cardiff CF5 2CE

Typist/Cashier

An exciting opportunity to join Britain's fastest growing national building society.

Britain's fastest growing national building society is also the country's most efficient.

We now have a vacancy for a Typist/Cashier to join this successful team in our Stratford-upon-Avon branch.

Applicants should be 18+ with at least 3 'O' levels (including English), have good typing skills and should also enjoy meeting and dealing with people of all ages. You will need to be presentable too, and although experience of work as a typist/cashier in a financial institution would be an advantage, it is not essential.

● In return you'll be working in attractive surroundings for a progressive but friendly organisation which offers a good starting salary and other benefits.

Please apply in writing with full details to Mr P. Glover, Area Manager, Swann Building Society, 17 High Street, Stratford-upon-Avon CV36 3BD

When we are fully aware of an employer's needs, we can tailor our application to meet those needs. This doesn't mean we should tell lies, because if we do, we will almost certainly be found out. But we should do our best to convince the employer that what we have to offer is what he wants and that we are worthy of an interview.

Curriculum vitae (pronounced cur-ric-u-lum-veet-i)

Anybody in the business of job hunting must produce for themselves the best possible curriculum vitae (referred to as the CV). It is simply an outline history of your life, which will be of interest to employers, and it is usually attached to your letter of application. Once you have made an up-to-date CV, it can be copied as often as you like.

ACTIVITY

Under the following headings, produce a CV of your own. Remember to place your most recent qualifications and work experiences at the top of your list to give them prominence. When you are satisfied with it, get a typed copy for future use.

Curriculum Vitae

Name   Status (Mr, Miss, Mrs, Ms)

Date of birth   Age

Address (including phone number)

Secondary schools attended (name of school, town, dates)

Colleges attended (name of college, town, dates)

Qualifications (name of exam, subject and grade)

Other qualifications, attainments or awards

Jobs held, including part-time and short training schemes (dates and titles)

Interests and hobbies

Referees (names and addresses of two people who will provide useful references for you, and telephone numbers if possible)

Application forms

Most applicants prefer to apply for a job by filling in a form rather than by letter. Unfortunately, it is very easy to make the most elementary mistakes unless we are prepared to take our time. The sensible thing to do first is to get a photocopy of the blank form. With our CV at hand to help us with the details, we are ready to:

- Read the whole form thoroughly.
- Understand exactly what we have to do.
- Draft a rough copy on our photocopied form.
- Check for errors, omissions and faulty presentation.
- When completely satisfied, complete the original form neatly in black ball point pen.
- Take a copy of the final form for future reference.

Letters of application

Most employers like to see a letter of application because it provides yet one more piece of documentation on which they can form a judgement about our suitability for the job.

Even when we are asked to fill in a form, we should always attach a covering letter to support our application.

For the great majority of job applications we can expect to write a fairly short letter because it will be supported either by a completed form or a curriculum vitae. In fact, if we are asked to apply in writing for a job, it is more business-like to write a short letter to which we can attach our CV. The purpose of the letter is therefore not to repeat the information on the form or the CV, but to interpret it in the most favourable light with regard to the advertised job. A letter also gives us an opportunity to explain why we want the job, the relevance of our qualifications and experiences, and acts as a vehicle for the presentation of the image we wish to project.

This letter was written by a 19-year-old applying for the post of 'Senior Sales Clerk, preferably with some knowledge of accounts'.

Your Ref: MEM/21

21 Faircliffe Road.
Lovington
Manchester
MC 29 2VX

Mr. M Anstey
Managing Director
National Retail Stores
14/18 The Parade
Manchester MV5 6PS

20 September 1988

Dear Mr Anstey

I wish to apply for the job of Senior Sales Clerk which was advertised in Thursday's 'Manchester Evening Mail'.

You will see from my attached curriculum vitae that I am at present working as a sales clerk in an office attached to a men's clothing store. In my two years there I have gained some useful skills and experiences, which I believe could give me a good start in your company. You will also note that I have continued with my studies at college and have gained a respectable qualification in accountancy. If possible, I would hope to continue with my accountancy studies in my new job.

Although I am reasonably happy in my present job, I do feel that I have more to offer and to gain in a larger, more enterprising retail company, where I hope there may be greater opportunities for promotion and more challenging work.

My present supervisor, Mr Carter, has agreed to give me a reference. I will be happy to come for an interview at a time suitable to you.

Yours sincerely

Helen Miles

Enc: curriculum vitae

The value of a short letter, whether it supports a curriculum vitae or an application form, is that it increases our chances of getting an interview because as this example shows, it:

- Conveniently introduces the applicant to the employer in a friendly business-like way and gives an immediate impression that she is competent and keen. The letter is also well written and presented.

- Draws the attention of the reader to the important features of her CV, again giving an impression that she is capable of sorting out the important from the unimportant.

- Suggests she is reliable and valued in her present post, but is capable of handling a more challenging workload in a larger company.

- Shows she has a particular skill to bring to the job (knowledge of accounts) and she is willing to pursue her studies at college.

What is more important is that a letter of this kind should ring true. It should be sincere, confident and convincing. If we boast, exaggerate or present a humble or cringing image we may fail to get shortlisted for interview. However, if we write a poor letter full of mistakes, we may not even be considered.

ACTIVITY

Choose one of the jobs shown on page 98 or select a similar job advertised in your local paper, and apply for it by letter, enclosing a full curriculum vitae.

The summary

A summary is a compressed version of a longer verbal or written account. All of us summarise verbally, almost without thinking. Here are two examples:

- When we tell a friend the plot of a film we have seen.

- When we explain what happened in last week's lesson to someone who missed it.

Written summaries are widely used by people in organisations whose jobs involve reading or writing a lot of reports. They are usually attached as a first page to long detailed documents and should help us to gain a complete picture of what follows. They also enable us to decide whether or not we want or need to read the full document by focusing our attention on the main points in it.

Unlike a précis, which is an accurate reproduction 'in miniature' of an original, a summary picks out only the significant points and need not display the same attitudes or points of view as the original. Thus, the type of summary required is determined by the person commissioning it, who usually states what part of the original he wants summarised. For example:

'Go through this file, please, and summarise the facts about the cancelled Ablex order. I'm seeing the Sales Director tomorrow and he's bound to bring it up.'

There are two common categories of summary.

Descriptive

Descriptive summaries describe the subject of the report in general terms without disclosing what was discovered or decided:

- The following report deals with the question of whether a snacks vending machine is needed in the office annexe. It considers the arguments for and against having the machine and examines the various types available under headings of cost, product range, installation and servicing. It makes recommendations based on these investigations.

Descriptive summaries are common in everyday social exchanges, but are not very helpful in most organisations. In the previous example, it would still be necessary to read the full report to find out what decision was made.

Informative

Informative summaries include details of findings, conclusions and recommendations:

- Vending machine — office annexe

The following report recommends the installation of the 'Chocovend' vending machine in the office annexe. The recommendation is based on a staff survey, an independent study and a cost/benefit analysis. An appendix lists comparative data on the four alternative machines that could be installed in the annexe.

In the same number of words, this gives more information on what was decided, what that decision was based on and what additional information is included. The original report probably ran to several closely typed pages and included a breakdown of staff attitudes to the proposed machine, the present catering facilities, and technical specifications of all the alternatives.

Writing a summary is not easy. It requires a steady concentration, judgement in the selection of relevant points, objectivity, and linguistic skills to enable us to express ourselves concisely without sounding jerky or confused. If we are asked to write a summary, the following points should help us to handle it effectively.

Establishing exactly what it is we are being asked to do

Are we being asked to:

- Summarise *all* or only *part* of the original?
- Summarise in not more than 200 words?
- Summarise on one side of a sheet of A5?

Reading, re-reading, then re-reading the original

At this stage it may be helpful to jot down or underline key words and phrases. We do not progress from this stage until we are sure that we understand both the general sense of the original and the development and structure of its facts and ideas.

Listing the essential points to be included and the sequence in which they should appear

At this stage we just use odd words to remind us what these points are and, as far as possible, make them *our own words*. This will help the finished summary to read smoothly and fluently. For example:

1 Title
2 First main point
   — subsidiary point or illustration
   — advantages and disadvantages
3 Second main point
   — etc., etc.

During this stage, we are analysing the structure of the original and our notes should reveal the order and development of our main points. By the time we are finished, our comprehension should be so thorough that we will be able to write the first full draft without any reference back to the original material.

Deciding on the most suitable format for our summary

This will depend on the instructions that we have been given or on the nature of the original material. The choice is between:

- Schematic presentation, under headed and numbered sections and indented subsections.
- Continuous prose, paragraphed if necessary.

In general, schematic presentations are preferable for business summaries.

Writing the first draft using our own words

We must try to keep near to any word or space limit we have been given, but not worry at this stage if the summary is slightly too long: it is easier to prune it down to the correct length than to add new points later.

Reading through and revising the first draft

We must ensure that:

- Waffle and 'lazy' words have been excluded.
- Items appear in a logical sequence.
- The whole summary reads well.
- Spelling and punctuation are correct.
- Full details of the original's source, its author and our 'brief' have been included.
- We have not altered or omitted points with which we disagree or which seem 'inconvenient'.

Giving our summary a title

The title is not a vague and meaningless phrase and not a tabloid-style headline, but a short, specific phrase which encapsulates the essence of the summary that follows. For example:

Useless title

Is the postman on his last legs?

Useful title

A summary of the advantages and disadvantages of electronic mailing systems.

Writing the final version

When writing the final version, we should add our own identity, our status and the date.

ACTIVITY

Summarise in about 250 words the article *Close encounters with stress* at the end of this chapter.

Telex

The long-established telex system is a combination of written and telephone communication, using telephone networks to transmit a written message, which will be received almost simultaneously. Communication can only take place between organisations that have the appropriate equipment and subscribe to the system. However, as it operates internationally, it is often used by multi-national organisations with offices all over the world.

The sender of the telex message dials the unique number of the recipient, just as if he was making a telephone call. He then types the message onto a keyboard, which transmits it down a special network of lines. Almost immediately, the message will be printed out on a teleprinter attached to the receiver's machine.

The advantages compared with a traditional letter are speed and confidentiality (and it can't get lost in the post), and it has the advantage over a telephone call in providing a permanent printed record of the message. Unfortunately, communication is limited to organisations in possession of the expensive equipment, and it is difficult to achieve the same person-to-person exchange of ideas possible during a telephone conversation. The modern version of telex is teletex, which forms part of an electronic mailing system that enables senders to transmit lengthy documents that are printed out on high-quality printers. You will be reading more about modern systems of data transmission in Chapter 5.

The most difficult task in sending a telex message, as with international telegrams, is having to reduce it to a minimum number of words. This is because cost rises steeply with time spent in transmission. It is therefore necessary to exclude all unnecessary minor words and to ignore normal rules of punctuation and sentence construction. However, it is vital that the meaning of the message is transmitted accurately and clearly. Let us suppose that you are faced with this problem:

Your boss is the reserve out of several delegates who were invited to attend a conference in Paris. You have just heard that one of the others has dropped out and advised the conference organisers of this fact, but not mentioned that someone else could attend as a substitute. Your boss is keen to go, but wants to make sure that accommodation will be available. There is no time to send a letter and the conference office is not answering the phone. Because she must leave soon, she asks you to telex that she is coming …

Your first attempt at the message might read:

Mrs Brown can attend the conference in place of Mr Drew, but will need a room and meals from Friday evening until after Sunday lunch. Can you provide this? She will arrive in Paris at 18.30 hrs.

ACTIVITY

Condense the previous message into a form suitable for transmission by telex, using the minimum number of words compatible with clear meaning and politeness (full marks for 6–8 words).

The memorandum

Becky: I've got a problem. I can't go on that computer course tomorrow afternoon. I'd forgotten about my son's dental appointment. Mrs Tracey isn't going to be very pleased with me.

Matthew: Why not phone her up now or go and see her?

Becky: I've tried that, but she's always at meetings. Anyway I don't fancy a long conversation with Mrs Tracey just now. I can't talk to her without getting myself all mixed up. It's hard to get a word in edgeways.

Matthew: I find that hard to believe. Why don't you send her a memo? Here's a memo pad. Why don't you write it out and I'll give you my opinion about it before you send it off?

This conversation illustrates how memoranda (memos) are used in organisations. They are nothing more than written messages sent by individuals to other individuals or groups, rather like internal letters or notes. Memos are most likely to be found in medium and large companies, and are just one of the many ways of communicating within organisations that have complex departmental structures, possibly spread through a multi-storey office block. Generally speaking, as organisations get bigger, so there is an increasing need for more formal written and spoken ways of communicating between staff. Memos are particularly valuable in this respect because of the organisation's demand for a permanent record on file of the more important messages that may have been distributed to all members of staff.

This is the memorandum Becky sent to Mrs Tracey. Becky of course would keep a copy for her own file. (The plural of memorandum is memoranda or memorandums — both are correct.)

COUNTY BUILDING SOCIETY

Memorandum

To   Mrs Emma Tracey, Manager   Reference

From   Ms Becky Hall, Clerk   Date   9/1/19--

Subject   Attendance on Computer Appreciation Course

Due to an unforeseen circumstance, I am unable to attend the Computer Appreciation Course on Friday afternoon (10/1/19--) at 3pm in Room 119.

My 5-year-old son, Ben, is developing a worrying abscess in his mouth and I have been forced to arrange a dental appointment for him at a time that clashes with your course. Naturally I have cleared the appointment with my supervisor, Mrs Peters.

I am sorry about this because I do find your course most enjoyable and worthwhile, and I hope to catch up on anything I've missed. I look forward to joining you all again next Friday.

The heading   Some organisations provide memo pads with standard printed headings, on which the writer fills in the details. The usual headed memo pad size is A5. It is important that names, titles, dates and subject descriptions are recorded correctly.

The message   Usually, but not always, the message is brief, accurate, polite, and completed on one side of a single sheet. Most memos carry only one paragraph dealing with a single item. Sometimes memos may extend to several sheets of A4 and deal with many topics under several headings. Most short memos are not signed, although longer memorandums may be signed and a note added to indicate where copies have been sent.

ACTIVITY

Write a memo on Mrs Tracey's behalf, which acknowledges receipt of Becky's memo and contains a suitable response. Include all the headings in your reply.

The style or tone we need to adopt in writing a memo is determined by a host of factors that relate to our own role and function within the organisation, as well as the specific nature or context of the message itself. For convenience, we can divide our approach to our memo writing style into four categories.

- Friendly personal
- Friendly formal
- Neutral
- Serious formal

Friendly personal

These are usually exchanged between staff who are on good terms with one another and are probably of equal status. Memos of this type form the backbone of the informal communication network within large organisations. Here are two examples

- What's this I hear about your engagement party next Sat night? How come you've invited Sandra from Sales but not me? By the way, my telephone extension is now 301. Give me a ring about the party.
- Don't forget I've moved the Director's meeting from Room 10 back to my office. I hope to see you and Margaret at 10am. Whose turn is it to buy the coffee and biscuits? I'm sure it's your turn!

Friendly formal

Probably the most common form of memo that is written both 'up' and 'down' the organisational ladder. The writer is usually conscious of the difference in status between himself and his reader and will modify the tone of the memo to take this into account. In the memo written by Becky Hall, you will notice the tone of formal respect that underpins its friendly style. This is the text of a memo written by an office manager to her secretary:

- Thank you so much for typing up that report for me during your lunch hour — it must have been inconvenient for you. I'm so grateful for your help during this rather difficult time and I promise to make it up to you when the flap is over. Thanks again.

Neutral

Memos of a rather neutral tone are often used by management to communicate fairly important but non-urgent messages to all staff. Because the recipients are likely to be drawn from all rungs of the organisational ladder, a too friendly or a too formal memo is bound to upset somebody. This memo was written by a Managing Director on the occasion of the company's centenary year:

- To all members of staff

  On behalf of the Directors, I am inviting you to join me for a celebratory glass of champagne in the Conference Room at 11am on Friday 3rd June. We will be joined by the Chairman, Sir Peter Hethington, who will invite us all to raise our glasses to 'the next 100 years'.

Serious formal

On occasions, management will see fit to distribute, usually to each member of staff, a memo that is meant to be taken very seriously indeed. The memo will be written in a language that is unmistakenly grave in tone and presentation and the reader will be left in no doubt about where he stands. In this extract, management has discovered an upsurge in pilfering of materials from a local government office:

• We take a very serious view of pilfering and will not hesitate to report any acts of theft, however minor, to the police. Nor will we hesitate to take the most urgent steps to deal with offenders, who will be summarily dismissed without notice and without a reference.

One important feature of memos is that they often finish up filed away as permanent written records of what was written or said at a particular time. For instance, a memo could be drawn up and signed by all parties to record decisions made as a result of an important telephone conversation or as a summary of a short informal meeting that took place in the staff canteen. Memos of this type should be written clearly, accurately, and be fair in their interpretation of what was said or agreed.

ACTIVITY

Draw up a suitable memorandum for each of the following situations. You may invent details where they are not given.

• Despite repeated requests to all staff for volunteers to form a first-aid class, you have failed to attract a sufficient number of people to justify running the course. You suspect the main reason for such a poor response is that although the course is to run mostly during working hours, staff would be expected to attend a 2-hour evening class each week without pay. You also suspect that some staff may feel nervous about the end-of-course test for their first-aid certificate.

• You are the manager of an office that is responsible for the administration of local bus services. Recently, there have been rumours of service reductions and massive redundancies among bus drivers and mechanics because of the threat of privatisation, and this is causing a lot of bad feeling and nervousness in your office. Although you know there will indeed be some redundancies among your own office staff, you feel you must make a statement quickly to counteract these exaggerated stories.

• You feel most upset because you have failed at an internal interview to get promoted to the post of assistant office manager. The job went instead to someone who had less service and fewer qualifications than you. You have repeatedly tried to approach the office manager, Mr Day, to discuss the matter, but he has fobbed you off to such an extent that you feel he could have hostile attitudes against you, which may have prejudiced the interviewing panel.
You make a decision to record your doubts and concerns on a memorandum, which you intend to send to Mrs Phelps, the Managing Director, whom you know happens to get on very badly with Mr Day.

• As a safety rep in a department store, you discover evidence of cigarette smoking in a room used for storing furniture. Management gives you permission to issue a memo to all staff to remind them of the non-smoking policy of the company and of the dangers involved.

Writing reports

To be asked to write a report for our boss or to deliver an oral report to a group of work colleagues is not something many of us would look forward to. How do you think you would cope with these situations?

• As a receptionist working in the office of a local public swimming baths, you witness a poolside accident in which a young girl seriously damages her spine after slipping on the stone steps leading into the shallow end. As the sole witness, you are asked by the baths manager to produce a written report within three days.

• Your office is burgled, ransacked, daubed with paint and other unmentionable fluids, and some equipment damaged. You are asked to call in at Head Office the next day to give a preliminary oral report to the area manager, who is trying to assess the degree to which your office can cope with its workload in the next few weeks.

- At an office party on Christmas Eve, your best friend and fellow clerk, who has had rather too much to drink, trips over a chair and spills a trayful of coffee over a pile of freshly-printed Directors Reports. Your employers are asking you to write a short report on the incident, which may be submitted in evidence at a disciplinary interview.

- As an office supervisor in charge of a staff of two, you are formally instructed to prepare, write and submit a formal written report recommending how your small office should be refurbished and re-equipped within an overall budget of £35 000.

If you think about what you are being asked to do here, you will grasp quickly that writing a report is not something that is practised only by faceless bureaucrats in massive organisations. Nor are the contents of reports of interest only to people who make decisions on our behalf. Reports that are written in our place of work, however long or short or difficult to write or prepare, usually affect us in one way or another, either in the short or the long term.

Here are just a few ways in which an employee at work can be affected by reports.

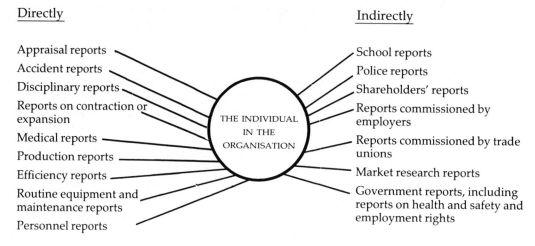

Directly

Appraisal reports
Accident reports
Disciplinary reports
Reports on contraction or expansion
Medical reports
Production reports
Efficiency reports
Routine equipment and maintenance reports
Personnel reports

THE INDIVIDUAL IN THE ORGANISATION

Indirectly

School reports
Police reports
Shareholders' reports
Reports commissioned by employers
Reports commissioned by trade unions
Market research reports
Government reports, including reports on health and safety and employment rights

ACTIVITY

Before you continue, discuss in groups in what ways the previous four reports are likely to affect the individuals or the organisation concerned.

Here is a rough breakdown of at least some of the points you may have touched upon.

Report one: The accident   As a public utility, a swimming baths has a legal responsibility to provide a safe environment in which members of the public can enjoy themselves. Any enquiry is extremely serious, especially one which may result from the disablement of a child. Your report may be used in evidence for claims for compensation and you will almost certainly be called as a witness in court.

Report two: The burglary   Since it is your office that has been burgled, you will share the same inconvenience and disruption as the rest of the staff. You will also have the added burden of having to present an accurate verbal report to the area manager at short notice. If you under-estimate the extent of the damage, this will undermine an accurate assessment of how much office work you can handle in the near future.

Report three: The Christmas party   Although this incident has an amusing angle, any report that is to be used at a disciplinary interview cannot be taken too lightly. You are, after all, contributing towards the decision-making process that will determine whether or not your friend will still have a job or get the sack.

Report four: The new office   It goes without saying that a report offering recommendations on the working conditions of employees is something to be taken seriously. It not only involves getting value for money, but also determines the type of equipment and furniture available to staff, which may in turn be related to increased efficiency and job satisfaction.

We hope that by now you appreciate the value of reports in commercial and industrial life. They are usually not something to be taken lightly or brushed aside as worthless pieces of paper. Important and far-reaching decisions are made on recommendations set out in written reports. This is the main reason why reports should be accurate, precise, true and well-written. There is a second reason why great care should be taken in the production of reports. This relates not to the report itself, but to the performance of the report-giver or the report-writer. For example, if you write a shoddy or misleading report, or speak badly or incoherently when delivering a verbal report to your boss because you haven't bothered to think the thing through properly, you may at best fail to get promoted and at worst make a fool of yourself.

ACTIVITY

Mention the subject or the title of any report that you have read, written or even heard about in the last year. Describe some of the content of this report and say whether it made any recommendations.

What is a report?

A report is a document which contains information, facts, statistics or advice that have been collected by a person or a group for the benefit of the organisation that has commissioned the report. Reports are written for many different reasons and may take any one of the following forms.

- A verbal exchange between two or more people or a talk given by an individual to a group (the Chairperson's annual report to shareholders).
- Letters or memoranda (an employee sends in a suggestion to improve productivity).
- Demonstrations, taking a practical form and supported with visual aids (a senior police officer reports on a new technique to contain violent demonstrations).
- Standard forms that are usually pre-printed for convenience (accident forms and social enquiry reports).
- Substantial documents that may have taken years to complete (government reports on education, housing or industry).

ACTIVITY

Can you suggest at least two more examples of reports for each of the previous five categories?

We are now in a position to look at the format of reports. For convenience we can divide reports into three types, although most report-writers prefer to use a mixed format.

- Informal reports
- Short formal reports
- Long formal reports

Informal reports

An informal report is a document, sometimes in the form of a letter or a memorandum, that deals with a specific point or issue. It is not usually set out under headings and subheadings like a formal report, and may have been written by someone who wishes to draw the reader's attention to a particular problem or idea. This is an example:

INTERNATIONAL COMPUTER SYSTEMS

MEMORANDUM

To: Mr Lewis, Managing Director   Ref: MH/DP/203

From: Margaret Hall, Personnel   Date: 3/10/19--

Subject: Crèche Facilities at International Computer Systems   Title

For some time now I have thought about the possibility of setting up a crèche on the ground floor, which would benefit both the company and our employees. Since the ground floor storerooms are now no longer in use, this would seem an ideal time to give the matter serious consideration.   Introduction

As you know, we employ an unusually high proportion of young women of child-bearing age and my rough calculations suggest that we would benefit considerably if we could encourage more women to continue to work for us by providing crèche facilities for their children. We would also benefit through the re-employment of trained women who have left in the last few years to bring up their young families at home. Although I haven't costed it properly, we will also make substantial savings by reducing training and induction costs associated with a high job turnover. We'll also save a lot of interviewing and advertising costs, too.   Main body of the report

Of course, there will be a price to pay for all this, especially in the short term. Clearing the storerooms,

---

furnishing, decorating, installation of kitchen and
bathroom facilities, safety barriers - and there
will be labour costs involved in running the crèche.

Main body of
the report

Nevertheless, setting up a crèche facility does seem to me
to be an idea worth pursuing. I do believe the ground floor
storerooms to be an ideal site for this, and I
therefore recommend that we instigate a more detailed
investigation as soon as possible.

Concluding
remarks

The most important point about reports that adopt an informal style is that they should be set out in a logical and orderly way. They should also be accurate, clear and as brief as possible. In the previous example, we can identify a title, an introduction which sets out the proposal, two paragraphs of information and argument, and a final paragraph which offers a recommendation. Therefore the word 'informal' does not mean or imply a sloppy or careless presentation. Here are a few examples of informal reports taking a more structured form.

Carcare Insurance

20 - 23 LOFTHOUSE ROAD, BARNSTABLE

D A M A G E   R E P O R T

Vehicle	1986 Honda Prelude D391DOL
Owner	Michael Fuller, 8 Howe Road, Barnstable
Insurance No.	2700399

Large dent and splitting on inside front wing and
shallow radiating scratches on passenger door.

	£
Estimated cost of replacement wing	85.00
Repair of door	20.00
Respray	35.00
Plus VAT @ 15%	21.00
Total	£161.00

I recommend approval   YES ✓   NO
should be given

Name of assessor J Smith

Date 31/1/87

In this example the investigator is asked to produce a short report on which a decision has to be made quickly

A report
that briefly
summarises past events
with a recommendation
about the future. Further
action is not usually
required

CITY OF BIRMINGHAM EDUCATION DEPARTMENT
MATTHEW BOULTON TECHNICAL COLLEGE
DEPARTMENT OF ARTS AND SOCIAL SCIENCES

SESSION 19 ....

EMPLOYER
Name ....
Address ....

Date ...... / ...... / ......

Signature of Authorised Officer:

STUDENT:
Name ....
Address ....

Stage .... Course Code ....

Course ....

SUMMARY OF DAY ATTENDANCES

	TOTAL ATTENDANCE IN HOURS DURING SESSION		Standard No. of Hrs. per Day
	POSSIBLE	ACTUAL	

FINAL REPORT ON STUDENT'S WORK

Subject Code	SUBJECT	Day or Eve.	ATTENDANCE IN HRS.			EXAM %	Class or Home Work %
			Poss.	Actual	%		

Recommendation: ....

YOU MUST PRESENT THIS FINAL REPORT WHEN YOU ENROL IN SEPTEMBER.

In this type of
report (page 1 shown)
the writer cannot
avoid providing the
fullest details

Form A1 (Revised 1984)

BIRMINGHAM CITY COUNCIL

Report of an Accident/Injury to An Employee/Non-Employee and/or Dangerous Occurrence.

DEPARTMENT:

REFERENCE NUMBER:

NOTE 1
This Form must be completed in respect of any Accident/Dangerous Occurrence/Injury (no matter how slight) to an Employee of the City Council whilst at work or on duty or to a Non-Employee on Council premises.

NOTE 2
The person responsible for filling in this Form is the injured person's Supervisor/Officer in Charge/Manager. Or, in the case of a Non-Employee, the person in charge of the place where the accident occurred.

1. SURNAME: FORENAMES	2. *Mr. Mrs. Miss Ms	3. Age:	4. Normal place of work Department/Division/Section/ Building, School/College Etc.,
5. PRIVATE ADDRESS:	6. *Employee/Home Resident/ Student/Pupil/Contractor/ Member of Public/Others		8. Activity At Time of Accident/Injury/ Dangerous Occurrence
Telephone No.	7. Employed As: Pay Roll No. or Check No.		11. Particulars of Injury/ Incapacity e.g. (Laceration left arm, scalded left foot
9. Precise place of Accident/ Injury/Dangerous Occurrence	10. Date and time of Accident		
12. Was the injured person treated at Hospital? *YES/NO. If Yes which one. Was he/she detained over 24 hours *YES/NO.		13. Was First Aid Given?	
14. Give a full account of the Accident/Dangerous Occurrence explaining how it happened and what the injured person was doing.			
15. To whom was the Accident/Injury/Dangerou. Occurrence Reported: NAME:		Continue on separate sheet	

*Delete as applicable.   POSITION: DATE:

ACTIVITY

There are complaints in your college about the range and quality of service provided by the canteen. Write a short informal report to the President of the Students Union, either in the form of a memorandum or a letter, pointing out some of the problems, and suggest a few ideas of your own that might improve the service.

Short formal reports

We can now look at the format of short formal reports. These are similar to informal reports, except that they are presented in a tabular form and set out under standard headings. They usually contain information and proposals based on research gathered by the report-writer, following an official request by the person who has commissioned the report.

Let us study a memo received by Margaret Hall from her boss Mr Lewis.

INTERNATIONAL COMPUTER SYSTEMS

MEMORANDUM

TO: *Maggie*
FROM: *Martin Lewis*
SUBJECT: *Crèche facilities*

REF:
DATE: *10/10/19—*

I like your idea of setting up a crèche. It's something I've had on my mind for some time. Could you put some sort of official report together for me with recommendations? Say in time for my next Board meeting on 10th November?

This is the sort of thing that might go down well with the Board. I know that the chairwoman, Councillor Day, is looking for something prestigious to impress them with at the Town Hall!

If you were Margaret Hall faced with the task of producing a formal report within a few weeks, how would you go about it? How would you find out what the employees think about the idea of a crèche? Would it be used enough to justify the expense? Do you require planning permission? What will the supervisory staff think about it? Will they resist its implementation? This is the report that landed on Mr Lewis' desk on 6th November:

REPORT ON THE PROVISION OF CRECHE FACILITIES AT

INTERNATIONAL COMPUTER SYSTEMS

I   TERMS OF REFERENCE

On the instructions of Mr Lewis, Managing Director (memo dated 10th October), to investigate the setting up of a creche for up to 15 children on the ground floor of International Computer Systems, and to make recommendations within one calendar month.

(continued)

II PROCEDURE

This report was compiled on the basis of:

A A visual investigation of the storerooms and of drawings and plans.

B Interviews with all supervisory staff (a total of 18).

C Interviews with a random selection of 10 women employees aged 18 - 45 years.

D Short anonymous questionnaires sent to all staff and to women who have left the company within the last 2 years (questionnaire attached).

E Discussions with the local planning officer, architect, and child care officer, and 3 estimates from local builders (summaries attached).

III FINDINGS

1 Staff attitudes and expectations

Non-supervisory staff

Based on interviews of 10 women staff and on the analysis of 52 completed questionnaires (a high 52% response), the following points emerged:

(a) The majority of staff (92%) were in favour of setting up a creche on the ground floor.

(b) Most staff (70%) thought that the facility should be made available to both mothers and fathers.

(c) The general view was that the creche should cater for children between 3 months and 5 years of age.

(d) Most respondents (68%) are prepared to pay between £2 and £3 per day for the care of each child.

(e) Some full-time staff (34%) thought that part-time staff should be excluded from the scheme.

(f) A majority of respondents (78%) said they would have made use of a creche had one been available.

(g) About 3% said the money should be used to improve canteen facilities.

(h) A substantial minority (28%) welcomed the idea, but did not wish to lose car-parking spaces.

Supervisory staff

There were no substantial differences of opinion between the supervisory and non-supervisory staff, except for:

(a) Most supervisors (75%) believed that the introduction of creche facilities would result in declining job turnover and recruitment costs.

(b) A minority (22%) believed there would be increased productivity because fewer trained staff would leave.

(continued)

(c) A minority (20%) argued that production levels might be threatened because a creche could encourage women to have children and take maternity leave.

(d) Up to 80% of supervisors preferred the care of children to be put into the hands of at least three fully trained staff (assuming a maximum of 15 children), and did not want a rota system of production workers to be introduced.

2 Existing site

The storerooms are presently unused and comprise one large room and two smaller rooms off. All rooms are heated and lit with fluorescent lighting, and there are fresh water supplies and sewerage connections. There are four windows and access is gained through an external door leading from the staff car part (see attached drawings).

3 Proposals for conversion

Following an on-site interview and tour of premises with a planning officer, architect, and child care officer, and on information derived from staff interviews and questionnaires, the following observations were made:

(a) The large storeroom could be converted into a creche area with only minor alterations.

(b) One small storeroom could be converted into a bathroom facility to provide:

1 Two lavatory cubicles (one adult and one child size)

2 Two wash basins with hot and cold press-down spray taps (one basin adult size, one child size), and one plastic baby bath.

3 Ancillary equipment: towel racks, wall mirrors, toilet paper holders, out-of-reach cabinets and first-aid box, nappy buckets, etc.

(c) The second small storeroom could be converted into a locked-door kitchen unit to provide:

1 A sink with hot and cold water and double draining board.

2 Washing machine and tumble dryer.

3 Electric cooker and small refrigerator.

4 Adequate storage: containers, cupboards, kitchen equipment, crockery and utensils.

5 Sterilizing unit for baby bottles.

(d) A substantial number of staff thought that an outside play area was needed. This requires:

1 The erection of a sturdy fence enclosing an area within the staff car park outside the creche entrance.

(continued)

The construction of suitable climbing frames and outside games furniture.

(e) Other useful ideas derived from staff include the provision of:

1 A telephone, with internal and external connections.

2 Metal safety meshes to cover radiators and windows.

3 Washable carpeting in play areas, bright and cheerful wall decorations, and pinboards for the children's drawings.

4 Toys, paints and crayons, paper, games, building bricks and cassette player.

5 Cots and bedding, sleeping mats, junior tables and chairs, play equipment, climbing frames, books and bookcases, coatracks, and large table.

IV CONCLUSIONS

The conclusions to be drawn are:

* The overwhelming majority of staff are in favour of a creche.

* The conversion of the ground floor storerooms and the staff car park for this purpose is feasible.

* There are no major planning or building obstacles.

* The initial cost of conversion is high.

* A minimum of three full-time or six part-time staff will be required to run the creche, assuming a maximum of 15 children.

* The running costs should be covered by a £2 per day child cover charge and a company subsidy.

* There are medium and long-term economic advantages to the company.

* It is certain that the demand for places will outstrip supply. A system of prioritisations will have to be drawn up.

V RECOMMENDATIONS

1 That this company authorises the conversion of the ground floor storerooms into a creche and gives approval for the work to start immediately.

2 That the company also authorises a small area of the staff car park to be used for a play area.

Date: 4th November 19--

Signed: *Margaret Hall*
Personnel Officer

Before we look at the individual sections of this report, we may have noticed the similarities with Margaret Hall's informal report:

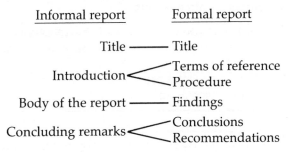

We can see also that the report is likely to succeed in its purpose of effectively drawing the reader's attention (and probable approval) to the need for a crèche because:

- It is written in a straightforward, concise and convincing style, which is unlikely to be misunderstood.
- It is well-researched, logically presented, neatly set out, and contains enough relevant information on which a decision can be made.
- It does not make any claims nor draw any conclusions that are not supported by evidence.

ACTIVITY

As a senior clerical officer at International Computer Systems, Margaret Hall asks you as a member of the newly-formed *Crèche Action Group* to discuss the problems of prioritisation mentioned in her report, and to make recommendations in an informal report. She asks you to consider the choices available as to which staff will be entitled to make use of the crèche, and which of these will have priority. The demand for places has been estimated to be over 50 from the full-time staff alone.

We are now in a position to study more objectively the main sections of a short formal report:

- *Title*   This usually begins 'Report on …' or 'Report into …' followed by a precise descriptive title. Avoid vague or incomplete titles such as 'Report on Smoking', when what is really intended is 'Report on the abolition of smoking in the staff canteen on the 4th floor'.

- *Terms of reference*   These define the scope and limitations of your investigation, usually within one short paragraph. They should include:

    — The name of the person or the organisation who asked for the report.
    — The date of request and the likely date of completion.
    — The exact subject of report, usually in greater detail than the title.
    — The recommendations, if required.

- *Procedure*   This section explains how the report was tackled and lists the methods of investigation used to find the information. These include:

interviews	questionnaires
meetings	memos to specific people
visits	direct observation
expert opinion	existing published sources
scientific measurements	unsolicited information

Go back to the tricky situations described on pages 107/8. Supposing you had to produce written reports:

● What do you suggest would be an appropriate title and terms of reference for each of the four situations? (You may use your imagination in the creation of names, dates and places, etc.).
● Suggest suitable procedures or methods of investigation that could be used in each case, giving reasons for your choice.

● *Findings* All information or opinions found out appear in this section. It is usually the longest part of the report and it is important to set it out in a logical way (e.g., advantages and disadvantages). Always state the sources of the opinion and present the facts in plain formal English.

ACTIVITY

Assume that TransEuro Haulage of Birmingham will shortly have to renew the lease on their headquarters office building in the centre of the city. As the lessees are raising the ground rent dramatically, TransEurope are looking for alternative accommodation, in keeping with their pan-European image. You have been asked to inspect an 18th century manor house, now at the centre of a Business Park near Redditch. You have gathered the following information so you are now ready to

● Arrange the points under suitable headings.
● Then put the headings in a sensible order.
● Then rewrite in appropriate English under the general heading: Findings.

Listed building, dating from the 18th century.
Alterations to form office accommodation have already been carried out.
Some floors will need reinforcing to accommodate TransEuro specialist equipment.
Internal design of building will mean sacrificing existing open-plan office layout.
Located within new Business Park — maintenance of grounds and estate security patrols are included in annual management charge.
All main services to site.
Current unemployment rates in Redditch are 14%.
Existing labour pool contains large proportion of unskilled workers/currently a shortage of experienced office and computer-trained staff.
Little rental accommodation available if existing employees decide to move.
Some low cost housing to buy, but prices above those of similar housing in Birmingham — and rising fast.
Site owners offer attractive leasing package with rent tapering from one-third in first year to full rental in third year of occupation.
Local council offers relocation grants to companies who agree to take on at least 25% of employees from local labour market.
Principal reception rooms in manor house will provide prestigious accommodation for meeting important clients.
Building is 400 metres from new leisure centre and restaurant/bars complex offering discounted membership to whole-company enrolments.
Industrial estate is within 2 miles of M42 intersection and access to new M40 will also be easy.
Local estate agents eager to assist senior managers to relocate have identified a number of select high specification residential developments suitable for executives.

Redditch station provides regular daytime rail services to Birmingham.
The A441 Birmingham–Redditch road is extremely congested – particularly at peak hours.
Local college has established computing centre on Industrial Estate providing consultancy and agency services.

- *Conclusions*   A shorter section in which conclusions are drawn from the evidence set out in the findings. It is where the writer uses judgement in stating the significant results of the research. It is not necessary to use the word 'I'. For example:

    As a result of the analysis of the findings, the following conclusions can be made:
    — The majority of staff wish to abolish smoking in the staff canteen.
    — A separate room for smokers should be provided for staff who wish to smoke and eat.

- *Recommendations*   These are included in the report only if they are asked for in the terms of reference. They point to specific actions that should be implemented, which may be to do something or nothing. For example:

    It is recommended that the company takes no action for the present on the question of smoking in the staff canteen, until a more searching investigation can be undertaken.

ACTIVITY

Draw up a report on the arrangements and equipment available for dealing with accidents, either at work or at college, and make at least one recommendation for their improvement.

Long formal reports

Long formal reports are similar to short formal reports except that they contain much more detail and usually carry a synopsis of findings following the contents page. By 'synopsis' is meant a summary which gives the reader a quick general view of the findings, which are later produced in greater detail. This is how the two types of formal reports compare:

Short formal reports		Long formal reports
Title or heading Terms of reference Procedure	Preliminary pages	Displayed title page or cover Table of contents Foreword or Preface Synopsis or summary of findings Terms of reference Procedure and research methods
Findings Conclusions Recommendations	Main report	Introduction Findings, presented in sections Conclusions Recommendations
	Supplements	Bibliography Appendices Index

You can see that long formal reports are substantial documents that are likely to run into a great number of pages. Mostly they are commissioned by large companies or government departments and may take months or even years to complete, following detailed research and analysis of findings. They are commonly presented to the reader via a title page or a printed cover, which give an indication of their importance. Here is an example:

THE IMPACT OF
OFFICE TECHNOLOGY
IN THE
MIDLANDS AREA

REPORT OF A SURVEY ON
OFFICE TECHNOLOGY
CARRIED OUT BY THE
MIDLANDS AREA
OF APEX

Head Office
22 Worple Road,
London
SW19 4DF
Tel:01-947 3131

Midland Area Office
27-28 Sherbourne Street,
Edgbaston, Birmingham
BI6 8NF
Tel:021-454 6848

APEX - Association of Professional, Executive, Clerical and Computer Staff.

It is helpful to keep in mind that there are often political reasons why reports are commissioned. This is to say that organisations ask for reports that tend to favour rather than oppose their aims. So trade unions are unlikely to commission reports that investigate low company profitability and employers might be unwilling to investigate the causes or extent of low pay in the service industries. However, report-writers are not always willing to toe the party line. The *Peacock Report* (1986) into the future of broadcasting produced evidence and recommendations that were unwelcomed by the government who commissioned the report. The report was described by a Minister as 'interesting' and promptly put on the shelf to gather dust. Integrity is never out of place in the art of writing reports.

┌─ **ACTIVITY** ─────────────────────────────────────

1 The following extracts have been taken from the *APEX Report on the Impact of Office Technology in the Midlands Area (1984)*. Rearrange them under these headings:

    A Terms of   B Procedure   D Conclusions
        reference   C Findings   E Recommendations

1 The lessons of the survey are clear. Trade unions need to be alert to new technology. New technology agreements should be negotiated with employers before its introduction and all aspects of training and job evaluation need to be considered.

2 We asked for the numbers of staff that had been lost as a result of these changes. This showed that the job losses were running at the ratio of 50–1 against those being created.

3 Only 3% of companies said that they had negotiated shorter hours as a result of the introduction of new technology and none had received longer holidays.

4 Replies to the questionnaire covered over 50% of APEX's membership in the area — a pleasing response indicating the interest of members in the new technology.

5 The survey provides firm evidence for the APEX case that unless new technology is introduced in a controlled and responsible fashion — and it is used to create wealth rather than to eliminate jobs — its benefits will be limited indeed.

6 Make your employer agree to a Training Programme for staff within our suggested guidelines, and ensure that it includes briefing seminars for staff reps.

7 59% of those surveyed said they had inadequate or no systems appreciation at all, and only 54% said they had received any training on computer principles.

8 62% of safety reps said that members had complained or suffered from some form of ailment, which they attributed directly to working on new technology systems. 56% complained of eyestrain, 25% complained of itching eyes, 19% of burning eyes, 29% of sore eyes, 52% of headaches, 22% of migraine, 19% of an arm ache, 27% of neck ache, 38% of back ache, 33% of fatigue and 36% of monotony.

9 The aims of the survey were to discover:
 — the extent of computerisation and office automation.
 — where unions had been able to reach agreement with management over the introduction of new technology.
 — whether new technology had caused an increase or decrease in employment levels.
 — the effect of new technology on health and safety.
 — what training companies were providing for staff operating the new systems.

10 30% of those replying said that it had resulted in the deskilling of jobs, and 40% said that it had increased skills in certain jobs.

11 Of the companies surveyed, only 8% had no new technology at all on their premises.

12 Ensure that an effective monitoring system is introduced at your workplace.

13 Questionnaires were sent to all APEX senior staff reps in the union's Midlands area. This covers 25 000 of the national membership of 110 000. The Midland area stretches from the Welsh border to the North Sea, with Stoke-on-Trent and Mansfield as its northern-most limits and Banbury and Northampton as its southern-most points.

14 The total number of employees employed in the companies surveyed amounts to some 77 000, of whom 11 700 are APEX members.

15 Only 12% said that improvements had been made in their salaries since the introduction of new technology.

16 Negotiate as soon as possible a New Technology Agreement.

(*continued*)

17 60% of the organisations surveyed were part of multi-national companies, for whom the introduction of new technology is going to have the greatest advantage.

18 In only 19% of those companies where new technology had been introduced had there been any attempt to amend their job evaluation scheme to cater for the new type of work being undertaken.

19 The survey reveals that the spread of new technology is undeniable — only 8% of respondents were unaffected by it. The survey identifies two particularly adverse effects of new technology: its tendency to destroy considerably more jobs than it creates and significant health hazards.

2 If an organisation representing the employers' interests were to investigate the impact of office technology in the Midlands area, in what ways do you think its report would differ?

Oral reports

Oral reports are commonly demanded when an answer or an explanation is required quickly, sometimes in the white heat of an emergency. We can accept, in the act of fighting a raging fire in an occupied high-rise office building, the importance of speed, precision and accuracy in the delivery of oral reports to the chief fire officer and the emergency services. On a more personal level, we can imagine being called to the boss's office at short notice to give an oral report on our work progress or to explain why we messed up a job, or to justify the nasty row we've had with an aggressive member of the public.

Although we will discuss in more detail the techniques involved in oral presentation in Chapter 4, we must not forget what we have already learnt in our exploration of written reports. Oral reports, like written reports, have to be thought through and preferably planned on paper, if there is time, *before* they are delivered. There is an even greater need to be logical and clear because we have to get it right the first time, unlike a written report that can be rewritten as often as we choose. Suppose your newly appointed boss has arranged to give you the opportunity to report on what your duties are at work and to talk about how you see your future at the company. The least you can do is to jot down a few headings and notes in preparation for your interview.

Personal details
Name, age, qualifications, how I got the job here.
How long I have been working here.
How happy I am with my job and the nice people I work with.

Job description
My job title and how long I've been doing it.
My main areas of responsibilities and other responsibilities.
The kind of team I work with and the name of my section boss.
Other departments and outside bodies that I liase with.

College attendance
Day release attendance at technical college and type of course.
Degree of success so far and what I hope to achieve.
Other courses that I attend in my own time and other relevant interests.
Courses I plan to join in the future.

Plans for the future
Try to continue with the successful progress in my present job.
Would like to further myself with promotion if given the chance.
Am prepared to consider changing jobs or departments if asked to do so.
Willing and eager to learn new technology on short courses.
Would like to go in for first-aid certificate.
Would like to go as far as I can on my college courses.

Although these notes are far from perfect, you can appreciate that delivering an oral report is not something that you would choose to do without preparation. Making plans about what you are going to say gives you an edge; it also allows you freedom to deviate or to add anything relevant that comes to mind at the time of delivery. The actual process of making notes in itself will prepare you for your oral chore. In fact you may find that it is not even necessary to consult your notes at all, since you will be so well prepared.

ACTIVITY

You are asked to give an oral report of between 5 and 10 minutes to a small group on one of the following subjects. Your report may apply to either a college or a workplace setting.

- First-aid facilities
- Heating systems
- Accident and emergency procedures
- Disciplinary and grievance procedures
- Fringe benefits
- Canteen facilities and organisation
- Retraining opportunities
- Trade union or student union membership and responsibilities
- Personnel recruitment methods.

Remember that you are expected to deliver an oral report based on your research notes. This is *not* the same as reading aloud the contents of a written report. You may be asked questions about the contents of your report in the discussion that follows.

Forms and questionnaires

Business forms

In virtually every sphere of life we are obliged to 'fill in a form' before we can make any progress. We can't start a college course without being asked to fill in a form, we can't get a job, we can't get dole, or save money, or get a mortgage, or drive a car, and we can't flee the country to escape from forms unless we are prepared to complete a passport application form. For those who work in offices and banks or for the council, the sheer number of forms seems to grow by the minute. Why is this? Why are forms so important that some of us would be out of work without them?

The simple answer is that forms enable organisations to run more efficiently than they would if they had to rely on more conventional modes of communication. Imagine how difficult it would be if we had to process personal details from letters or telephone conversations before we could issue a passport or a driving licence. We can summarise the value of a form in this way:

- It tells the form filler exactly what to do and how to do it, and controls the quality and quantity of information with the use of precisely worded questions and the allocation of space available for answers.

- It helps the organisation by providing identical and specific pieces of information that can be processed economically, so fair judgements and comparisons can be made. For example, which applicants are the most deserving in the allocation of council housing.

Designing forms is a difficult and time-consuming business. Ideally, a form should be a brief, attractive document that is easy to fill in because the questions are simple to understand and to answer. Although the introduction of computerised data processing has made form design an expertise in itself, it is possible that you might be asked to design a new internal form or re-design a poorly-designed existing one. These are the kinds of questions you ought to ask before you begin:

- What questions do I need to ask? Do I really want to know the applicant's address, age, or whether they are married or not? Are there any important questions that I've left out? Have I asked for signature and date?

- Are questions clearly written? Are they capable of misinterpretation? Why do so many people find it difficult to answer questions like: How old is your eldest child? Do you require a repayment mortgage or an endowment mortgage? Are you suffering or have you suffered from any serious diseases?

- Is there enough room to answer the questions? Is there too much room for some answers but not enough for others? Do I need 'lines' to write on? Should I leave space for answers or provide tick boxes instead? Can I get everything on one complete side of the sheet? Do I want to use the space I'm left with?

- Have I given the correct instructions? Do I want the applicant to use capital letters and a ball point? Is he/she to attach anything to the completed form? What's he/she supposed to do with the completed form? (Don't answer that.)

ACTIVITY

1 Make a list of the faults to be found in the form opposite.
2 Re-design the form in a more satisfactory way. You may alter, delete or add anything you wish.

```
INTERNAL


                      HOLBECK SALES AND SERVICES


APLICATION FOR STAFF CAR PARK STICKER AND KEY

(Please tick Yes or No were required)
Name                                    Christian names


Adress                                    Mr    ┌─────┐
                                                ├─────┤
                                          Mrs   ├─────┤
Departmental phone number                       │     │
and home number                           Age   └─────┘

                         Yes            State make, regestration
Do you own a car                        number, colour, and year
                         No             of purchase

                         Yes
Do you drive
                         No



Is the car parking facility for your own use or does it
include your spouse                              Yes/NO

Do you wish to apply for key and sticker or for either?   Yes/No

If there is to be a deposit to be payed for the key, are
you willing to pay?                              Yes/No

Do you accept that all parking facilities are at the owner's
risk and the company do not accept liability?    Yes/No


Please give this form to my secretary, Mrs Burns.

You can pick up your key and sticker from Mrs Burns in your own time



                                        Name

                                        Date
```

The questionnaire

Questionnaires are often used in organisations to gain first hand information about people's behaviour and attitudes. This is achieved by asking a representative group a series of questions and then analysing the responses, often with the aid of a computer. If we wanted to find out what 10 000 employees in a nationalised industry thought about their jobs, we might select 250 of them at random for our sample. Sometimes because of time pressures and the difficulty of getting in contact with people, we may be forced to use our judgement in the selection of a representative group.

Great care has to be taken with the wording of questions. They should be short, straightforward and written in such a way that they cannot be open to several interpretations. For instance: Do you go to the pub a lot? Questionnaire writers cut out vagueness by supplying a series of coded answers:

Do you go to a public house for a drink:
(a) rarely, (b) once a month, (c) once a week, (d) 2–4 times a week, (e) 5–8 times a week, (f) more than 8 times a week?

You can appreciate that coded answers help when you are ready to analyse your results. Other pitfalls we should try to avoid when compiling questionnaires are:

- Obscure wording (Do you prefer malt or blended whisky?)
- Unreliable questions (Do you tell lies?)
- Leading questions (Most people are in favour of hanging, are you?)
- Double questions (Is your name John Smith and did you murder your wife?)
- Assumption questions (When did you last smoke a cigarette?)
- Irrelevant or offensive questions (Do you like being fat?)

Before you attempt the next exercise, you might like to explain what is wrong with the questions in brackets.

ACTIVITY

The following questionnaire has been badly written. Examine each question carefully and say why you think it is unsatisfactory.

ATTITUDES TOWARDS WORK

We are conducting a survey into the unwholesome attitudes of young people at work and we think you can help us with our research. Please answer the questions as honestly as you can by drawing a circle around the correct answer.

1 How old are you? −12 12–13 13–14 14–15 15–16 16–17 17–19 19–20 20–21 21+
2 How often are you late for work? Occasionally Sometimes Frequently
3 How would you characterise your attitudes towards authority?
Hostile Cooperative Indifferent
4 What is your marital status? Married Single
5 Do you travel to work by public transport? Yes No
6 Do you prefer to work alone or in a team? Yes No
7 What sex are you? Male Female Other
8 Do you approve of the conduct of trade unions? Approve Disapprove
9 Which fringe benefit do you desire most?
Sick pay Luncheon vouchers Company pension scheme
10 Do you think you are paid enough? Yes No

One of the things you may have noticed about this questionnaire is the careless order of the questions. Questions should follow a sensible sequence. Questions dealing with similar aspects of a topic should be grouped together so that the sense of the questions is obvious to the respondent. Several types of questions can be asked:

- *Classification questions* These cover details such as the age, sex and group of occupation of the respondent. It may be possible later to draw different conclusions about different age groups or sex types using this information.

- *Factual questions* These seek direct information: At what age did you learn to drive?

- *Knowledge questions* It is important to find out how much the respondent knows about a subject before asking questions: Do you know whether you can join the students' union?

- *Opinion questions* These seek opinion on the topic in hand: Do you think the students' union is well publicised? A list of coded choices can greatly help with this type of question.

- *Motivational questions* These often follow a factual question and try to discover the motives behind a person's actions: Why did you enrol on this particular course?

ACTIVITY

Re-design the previous questionnaire 'Attitudes towards work' in a more satisfactory way. You may decide on a new set of questions. The introduction requires re-wording.

The usual way to present findings is in a report. The method of presentation varies, but report-writers attempt to draw our attention to the more significant findings by presenting their percentages diagrammatically. Here are a few examples taken from a national survey recently published in the *Observer* magazine:

The easiest way is to present simple percentages

QUESTION I am going to read you some statements which have been made about modern society. For each, please tell me whether you agree or disagree? (Don't know figures not shown.)

		ALL	MEN	WOMEN
It is important for both partners in a marriage to remain faithful	AGREE	92%	91%	94%
	DISAGREE	4%	5%	4%
Adultery is more tolerated by society nowadays than it used to be	AGREE	86%	89%	84%
	DISAGREE	11%	8%	13%
Young people nowadays mature sexually much earlier than they used to	AGREE	85%	83%	87%
	DISAGREE	13%	14%	11%

Visually more interesting because of the use of a bar chart. A pie diagram would be just as effective.

QUESTION If more men were to look after the home and children and more women worked as the main breadwinner, do you think this would be a good thing or a bad thing?

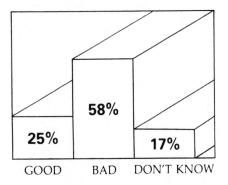

GOOD 25% BAD 58% DON'T KNOW 17%

127

Using the simple shape of a hand, it is possible to give extra meaning to cold statistics.

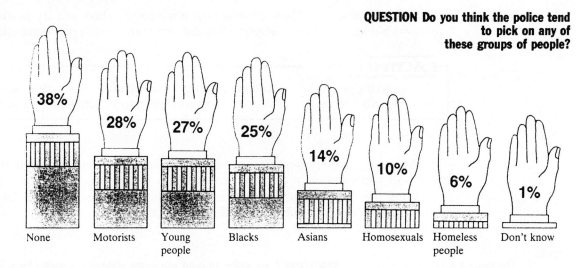

None	Motorists	Young people	Blacks	Asians	Homosexuals	Homeless people	Don't know
38%	28%	27%	25%	14%	10%	6%	1%

By contrasting the responses of old and young, a striking difference in attitude is brilliantly demonstrated.

ANALYSIS							
NONE							
18–24							
25%	26%	44%	31%	17%	13%	9%	1%
Pensioners							
55%	27%	12%	13%	7%	5%	2%	2%

ACTIVITY

Using your re-designed questionnaire, conduct a survey on a sample group of young workers on their attitudes to work. Present your findings in an interesting way.

SCENARIO

You are to attend the first meeting of the Crèche Action Group at International Computer Systems. You receive this memo in the internal post.

INTERNATIONAL COMPUTER SYSTEMS

MEMORANDUM

TO: All members of the Crèche Action group   Ref: MH/119
FROM: Margaret Hall, Personnel Officer   Date: 21/11/19__
SUBJECT: Running the creche

At your first meeting I would like you to discuss the day-to-day organisation and running costs of the proposed crèche facility as outlined in my report. It would be helpful if you produced a short formal report for me setting out your proposals and recommendations. I am enclosing a copy of my original report, which might be useful (See pages 113/116.)

The company is willing to contribute up to 50% of running costs and you can assume that the crèche is fully equipped with the items outlined in my report. You will have to make decisions about:

- Hours of opening, to provide a service for employees who work from 8.30 am to 4.30 pm, Mon to Sat.

- Staffing the crèche, part-time or full-time staff, hours, pay, organisation of working day, etc.

- Arrangements for children's and babies meals.

- Organisation of the children's day.

- Parents' contributions in terms of cash, clothing and food.

- Consumables, main items and costs.

Might I also suggest that you seek as much advise as you can from any available source, including the mums themselves. I would also like you to attach to the report a simple balance showing a weekly income and expenditure estimate - ignoring such costs as lighting, heating, rents, rates and telephone.

TASK ONE / THE AGENDA

Produce an agenda for the meeting based on Margaret Hall's memo.

TASK TWO / DISCUSSION AND QUESTIONNAIRE

At the meeting, take notes of the discussions, and the decisions arrived at, in preparation for your report. Produce a short questionnaire that will help you to find out from mums what kind of consumable items will be required in the day-to-day running of the crèche.

TASK THREE / THE REPORT

Write a short formal report that deals with the points mentioned in the memo. Don't forget to attach a simple balance sheet.

TASK FOUR / PUBLICITY

Produce a poster on A3 to advertise the crèche and a publicity handout on A4, that gives more details of the facilities on offer.

TO ALL EMPLOYEES

FROM PERSONNEL DEPARTMENT

SUGGESTION SCHEME

We operate a suggestion scheme to encourage all employees to make suggestions that will benefit the company. The major features of the scheme are:

— A maximum award of £2000
— Open to all employees up to but not including Department Heads

The procedure is to:

1 Submit a suggestion which must save money, increase income, or benefit the organisation in some way. The only restriction is that the idea must *not* fall within the normal duties and responsibilities of your job (if in doubt, submit your suggestion).
2 Your suggestion should be presented in the form of a confidential memo, which should be sent to the Personnel Department in a sealed envelope.
3 Await the decision of the Assessment Panel — you may attend the meeting of the Panel to explain your idea if you wish.

SCENARIO

You find this memo on your desk.

TASK ONE/THE CONFIDENTIAL MEMO

First jot down a few ideas or suggestions about improving your own place of work or college and then develop your most promising idea for submission to the Personnel Department.

TASK TWO / THE FORM

Design a suggestion form that in future could be used instead of the confidential memo.

MEGASTORE/memorandum

To: C. Andrews, Manager/Sportswear Ref: AD/L20

From: D. Davis, Sales Director Date: 21/10/19––

Subject: Sale of De Angelo tracksuits

It has been brought to my notice that the sale of ladies' and men's tracksuits has decreased considerably. I should like you to consult your staff about ways of promoting better sales. I am quite prepared to receive suggestions from individual members of staff in short reports, and I hope in due time to be able to offer a substantial cash award to the member of staff whose ideas effect improved sales.

SCENARIO

Under the chairmanship of Chris Andrews you and all the shop assistants in the Sportswear Department have been invited to a meeting to discuss your ideas about ways to increase tracksuit sales.

INFORMATION

- Price — Men's tracksuits £30/£40, depending on size.
  Ladies' tracksuits £20/£30, depending on size.

- Colour — Men's in grey/blue/navy.
  Ladies' in grey/pink/blue.

- Sizes — Men's in small, medium, large and extra large.
  Ladies' in sizes 10–18.

- Material — Polyester and viscose, towelling texture.

- Situation — On adjacent rails at the back of the Sportswear Department.

TASK ONE / PREPARING NOTES

As you are to be asked to report your ideas orally to the meeting, you had better plan what you are going to say on paper. Chris Andrews has given you this information.

TASK TWO / THE REPORT

At the meeting you will be expected to explain your ideas to the rest of the group. After discussion, each group member will produce an informal report for the Sales Director based on the best ideas from the discussion. You may need to use your imagination and invent certain details.

SCENARIO

You are a member of your company's Health and Safety Committee. Read all the tasks before you begin.

TASK ONE / THE RESEARCH

Read carefully *Close encounters with stress* and make notes of the more important points in preparation for a short article and a company research file. Extend your knowledge of occupational stress by investigating the subject more thoroughly in the library, and gather as much information and documentation as you can from other sources, including

— your own and other companies
— trade union sources
— health promotion organisations
— local office of Health Education Council.

TASK TWO / THE ARTICLE

Write an interesting and informative article of about 750 words on the recognition and dangers of occupational stress for your company's magazine *Forthright*. You are allowed to use one illustration, which you must try to draw yourself.

TASK THREE / THE QUESTIONNAIRE

Draw up a questionnaire of at least ten questions of a similar type to those shown in the panel *Test your tension*. You will need to devise your own system of answer coding. Conduct your survey on one of the following pairs of sample groups of workers.

— Men and women in similar jobs
— Young and old (define terms)
— Supervisors and subordinates
— Manual and non-manual workers
— Any other contrasting groups of workers (e.g., in different departments).

TASK FOUR / THE REPORT

Produce a short formal report based on your survey. Present your findings in a visually interesting way. Draw conclusions from them, but do not make any recommendations.

TASK FIVE / THE RESEARCH FILE AND MEMO

Your final task is to compile and submit a research file containing all your written work, plus materials and documents relating to one aspect of occupational stress. The idea is that each member of the committee will contribute a personal file on a different aspect of stress, which will be deposited in the company reference library. File titles might include:

— Smoking
— Alcoholism
— Absence from work
— Industrial accidents
— Stress, injuries or diseases
— Specific industrial diseases
— Mental problems

Attach to your file a short memo addressed to the manager, Mr Riley. The memo will point to the specific financial benefits of reducing stress in the workplace and will make a few suggestions about how to minimise stress without having to spend a great deal of money.

Close encounters with stress

Stress is the disease of modern times and it is a serious, growing complaint which British industry tends to ignore, believing that the work environment is not the place to display personal problems.

Not so, says Professor Cooper, who is Professor of Industrial Psychology at the University of Manchester Institute of Science and Technology and an expert on occupational stress who has carried out considerable research into the problem.

Stress, whatever its cause, *is* a work problem because it manifests itself at work in a number of disruptive ways – accident proneness, absenteeism (either through sickness or lethargy), and alcoholism which can lead to impaired judgement, all of which mounts up to a heavy financial loss to the company in manpower and productivity.

Industry may be reluctant to take on the problems caused by stress because it seems to be an abstract term. Not so, says Professor Cooper again. The stress problem can be directly linked with the incidence of coronary heart disease – and Britain has the second highest number of fatalities from CHD in the world – which means that British industry has a huge stress problem that it is not even attempting to cope with. "You can't wreck a person's life by giving him work problems and then absolve yourself of all responsibility when he suffers from stress," said Professor Cooper.

"Why?"

Medical men will look at the alarmingly high incidence of CHD and attempt to prevent its physical causes by advising on high blood pressure, diet, advocating exercise and giving up smoking, says Professor Cooper. A psychologist on the other hand will ask the question "Why?" Why does that person have high blood pressure? Why does s/he smoke so much? Why does s/he feel unwell? Why is s/he so unhappy?

According to Professor Cooper, there are three main causes of stress which often interlink but, either way, they must be treated as a whole. These are: the problems we have within ourselves as personalities; the problems we have in our private lives; and the problems our employment gives us. Whatever the cause, it is taken into the workplace and manifests itself in either mental ill-health; upset behavioural patterns; in social consequences such as divorce, separation etc; or with direct consequences in the workplace – accidents, absenteeism, alcoholism etc.

Different occupations have different stress levels and each person's stress tolerance level is different: One man's adrenalin booster is another man's coronary, but we all come close to the edge of our tolerance level at certain times in our lives. How long we attempt to stay poised on the brink of our tolerance level can decide whether or not we suffer a serious, life threatening illness (either physical or mental) which we may, or may not, survive.

In the United States, Canada and Australia companies have recognised the need to deal with stress among employees and in many companies it is quite common to find counsellors employed for the workforce working on Employee Assistance Programmes.

Most companies in Britain, according to Professor Cooper, react to employee stress problems by saying: "It's *your* problem; don't bring it to work." In the States, apart from the Employee Assistance Programmes, they have gone one step further and many middle to large companies hire consultancy firms where the employee can go to receive help and advice.

Stress factor

JOB	RATING	JOB	RATING
Miner	8.3	Farmer	4.8
Police	7.7	Armed forces	4.7
Building work	7.5	Vet	4.5
Journalist	7.5	Civil servant	4.4
Pilot (civil)	7.5	Accountant	4.3
Prison officer	7.5	Engineer	4.3
Advertising	7.3	Estate agent	4.3
Dentist	7.3	Hairdresser	4.3
Actor	7.2	Local govt.	4.3
Politician	7.0	Secretary	4.3
Doctor	6.8	Solicitor	4.3
Taxman	6.8	Art/designer	4.2
Film producer	6.5	Architect	4.0
Nurse/midwife	6.5	Chiropodist	4.0
Fireman	6.3	Optician	4.0
Musician	6.3	Planner	4.0
Teacher	6.2	Postman	4.0
Personnel	6.0	Statistician	4.0
Social worker	6.0	Lab technician	3.8
Manager	5.8	Linguist	3.8
Marketing	5.8	Banker	3.7
Press officer	5.8	Computing	3.7
Pro footballer	5.8	Occup.therapy	3.7
Shop salesman	5.7	Beauty therapist	3.5
Stockbroker	5.5	Vicar	3.5
Bus driver	5.4	Astronomer	3.4
Diplomat	4.8	Librarian	2.0

Alcoholism

JOB	RATING	JOB	RATING
Doctor	8.6	Photographer	6.0
Journalist	8.5	Businessman	6.0
Advertiser	8.4	Psychiatrist	5.8
Policeman	8.4	Diplomat	5.2
Prison officer	8.4	Civil servant	5.2
Social worker	8.3	MP	5.1
Dentist	8.2	Milkman	4.9
Actor	8.1	Market worker	4.9
Psychologist	8.1	Nanny	4.8
Vet	8.0	Secretary	4.3
Lawyer	8.0	Architect	4.2
Estate agent	8.0	Optician	4.1
Nurse	7.8	Bank clerk	4.1
Professor	7.8	Vicar	3.9
Surgeon	7.7	Landscaper	3.7
Chiropodist	7.6	Auctioneer	3.7
Engineer	7.5	Serviceman	3.5
Computer op	7.5	Plumber	3.5
Artist	7.4	Farmer	3.2
Sales rep	7.1	Hairdresser	3.0
Press officer	7.0	Planner	3.0
Publican	7.0	Manicurist	2.9
Solicitor	6.9	Statistician	2.9
Probation offr	6.8	Astronomer	2.8
Bank manager	6.8	Museum worker	2.7
Stockbroker	6.6	Taxi driver	2.5
Chemist	6.4	Librarian	2.2

▲ *Extracts taken from* Occupational Safety & Health, *June 1985*

Lost opportunity

Lest it be thought that CHD is an "executive" problem, the statistics show that this is higher amongst blue collar workers, white collar workers tending to suffer more from mental breakdowns. Professor Cooper believes that blue collar stress is largely to do with a feeling that the employee has no control over his job. S/he is not involved in decision-making by supervisors or management and the jobs are boring and repetitive. He cited Scandinavia and Japan as examples of how you can control these adverse elements. CHD is not a problem in Scandinavia and it is almost non-existent in Japan. He attributes this to the way in which these companies organise their work: they vary it, allow the employees to have an influence in decision making and, generally, involve them much more. At the Saab-Scandia car plant the work is varied and people work in small groups, taking and making their own decisions. Although this system means a slower output, they do not have the wastage problems due to incorrectly made goods and the product is better. They also have a financial benefit in that they do not experience high labour turnover figures.

In Japan they noticed that as they began adopting western management techniques and ideals, they began to experience stress problems. Now in Japan they have reverted back to the paternalistic ideal: job security is guaranteed through permanent employment with the company for life and there is no competition for promotion – the one with seniority gets it as a matter of course. This may seem to have many flaws to Western eyes but, according to Professor Cooper, the most important relationship we have is the relationship with our parents and people are looking for this same protective relationship with their employers. In Japan they prefer it; In the UK we should think about it.

Respect

The non-participative role of the blue collar worker creates pressure. Professor Cooper believes that the "don't speak unless you're spoken to" attitude is completely wrong. The more autocratically one is managed, the more damaging it is to one's health. Employees want (and should be) treated with respect and praised for what they do. People at the top level of a company should be made aware of what stress is and how it filters down through the hierarchy of a company. They should ask themselves: is work structured to provide as much control as possible to the employee? Are employees rewarded for their work? Do we need to have to control so much of the job? Can we investigate the possibilities of delegation?

There is no doubt that stress creates unhappiness at home and disruption at work. If only for financial reasons, companies should start to consider introducing stress-reducing programmes at work but also they should perhaps remind themselves that the HSW Act requires companies to ensure, so far as is reasonably practicable, the health, safety and *welfare* of employees at work and a stressed employee is someone whose health, and possibly his life, is at risk.

Job satisfaction and the Occupational Health Nurse

In the day to day running of an Occupational Health Centre, the OHN will meet employees with stress-related problems. A high percentage of these problems are quite likely to be related to inadequate job satisfaction. An employee can become dissatisfied with his job for many reasons:

The nature of the work is boring.

The work is too demanding.

Insufficient remuneration.

Difficult inter-relationships with colleagues.

Working away from home.

Overbearing superiors.

Inadequate management supervision.

Inadequate amenities.

Inadequate facilities.

Regulation

This final section deals with life in general and how the stress of life, taking both its advantages and disadvantages into consideration, has much to teach us in the way we must regulate our lives. Regulation of our lives might at first seem a rather dominant oppressive term, but as human beings we need to be able to regulate ourselves both for and against close encounters with stress. When we fail in this regulation process, the encounter can, as we have seen, become unbearable, and therefore we need to take notice of those people who offer us the chance and the real possibility to increase the quality of our lives here on earth, and in a very special way we refer once again to the role of the OHN.

Equipped with the necessary knowledge, the OHN can advise many employees in the correct way to both prevent and increase the amount of stress in every-day life. People will require different levels of stress in their lives. We have seen that we all act differently, and the OHN will take this into consideration. A modicum of stress is part of life, and is not necessarily always bad. Joyful events such as marriage, a birth, a new job, can be stressful because of the changes they entail in the person's life. The key issue is not how stress can be avoided, but how it can be coped with to advantage.

In a MORI poll conducted for the Daily Express in 1983, 2000 adults were asked which of 20 things they did most at weekends. The most popular activity was watching TV, regardless of sex or age groups.

Further results from the poll showed that 16 per cent of those surveyed donned their walking or running shoes in preference to anything else and that the pursuit of fitness was keenest in the towns. The MORI poll suggests that the work of Health Education Council is having a very marked effect on the public at large

However, before we can become complacent in our attitudes regarding stress at work and its total annihilation, a recent study performed by Sheila McKechnie, Health and Safety Officer for ASTMS (the Association of Scientific, Technical and Managerial Staff) soon puts our feet squarely on the ground. In their policy document on the subject – *Occupational stress*, ASTMS point out that although some work has been done on remedying the effects of stress, nothing positive has been done about eradicating the causes. And, says the union, this is possible with some thought and care on the part of management without too much in the way of cost. They suggest measures such as:

Ensuring the workforce has some control over the flow of work.

Ensuring there are regular breaks in between particularly stressful jobs.

Making the work varied and more interesting.

ASTMS say that although top management might indeed be under pressure, at least they have the authority to delegate work out; that is not so easy the further down the hierarchy you are. In publishing this latest in a series of policy documents, the union say they want discussions about eradicating causes of stress brought into negotiations about pay and conditions of work, and they also call for stress to be made a compensatable disease.

SHORT TERM EFFECTS OF STRESS

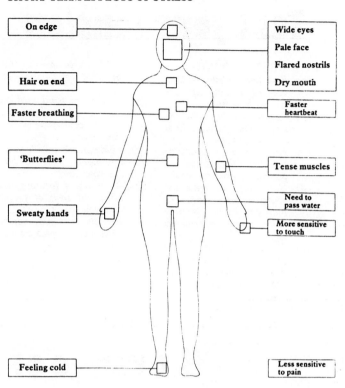

LONG TERM EFFECTS OF STRESS

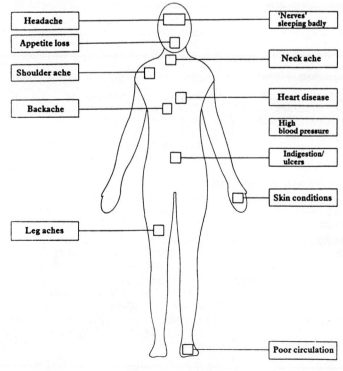

Test your tension

HOW OFTEN DO YOU:

(a) *Feel that you have too little authority to carry out your responsibilities?*

(b) *Feel unclear just what the scope and responsibilities of your job are?*

(c) *Not know what opportunities for advancement or promotion exist for you?*

(d) *Feel that you have too heavy a work load, one that you cannot possibly finish during an ordinary day?*

(e) *Think that you will not be able to satisfy the conflicting demands of various people about you?*

(f) *Feel that you are not fully qualified to handle your job?*

(g) *Not know what your supervisor thinks of you, how well he evaluates your performances?*

(h) *Find yourself unable to get information needed to carry out your job?*

(i) *Worry about decisions that affect the lives of people that you know?*

(j) *Feel that you may not be liked and accepted by people at work?*

(k) *Feel unable to influence your immediate supervisor's decisions and actions that affect you?*

(l) *Not know just what the people you work with expect of you?*

(m) *Think that the amount of work you have to do may interfere with how well it is done?*

(n) *Feel that you have to do things on the job that are against your better judgement?*

(o) *Feel that your job interferes with your family life?*

The range of symptoms

Heart and circulatory system	Explanation
Rapid pulse Palpitations Pounding in chest Raised blood pressure	Increased rate and force of heart contractions.
Cold hands and/or feet Pale face	Diversion of blood flow away from non-important organs to muscles for fast powerful action.

Respiratory system

Tightness of chest Rapid breathing Shortness of breath Asthma	Breathing rate increases to allow increased oxygen supply to muscles. Increased muscle tension in chest muscles. Not a direct cause of asthma, but can aggravate if already present.

Digestive and urinary system

Nausea/sickness Stomach-ache "Butterflies"	Speeding up of transit through digestive system.
Diarrhoea/frequent bowel action Frequent urination	Disposal of waste such that subsequent strenuous activity will not need to be interrupted.
Indigestion/acid stomach	Rapid transit of stomach contents leaves digestive juices acting on stomach.
Dry mouth	Digestion a non-important activity; therefore salivation inhibited.

Psychological

Worried Nervous On edge Irritable Jumpy	Self-explanatory
Loss of interest/enthusiasm No energy Tired all the time Sleeping all day Impotence/loss of sexual drive Can't concentrate Poor memory Absent-mindedness	As far as the mind is concerned, recreation/socialising is taboo until problems are resolved – it has its own priorities. Sleep may be a technique (subconscious) of legitimising withdrawal from social/recreational activity.
Tearful Sad/low in spirits/down	Stress is a depressing experience
Increased use of drugs Alcohol Cigarettes Prescribed Illegal Food	Usually in an attempt to circumvent stress or to alleviate symptoms. Alcohol and illegal drugs often compound rather than relieve stress.

Skin

Sweating	In preparation for dissipation of heat generated by strenuous activity.
Itching Acne Dry skin	Consequences of sweating.

So far in this book we have considered the ways in which many organisations are structured, examined the methods and purposes of their internal communication systems, and studied some of the more important documents that are used in this communication process. Our purpose in introducing these topics has been a desire to relate each of them to the people who work for organisations.

This chapter is about the way in which organisations deal with their workpeople and how companies and the people they employ come into closer contact with each other to achieve their aims, which of course are not always identical. We will look at four broad areas.

- The personnel function — why it exists and what it does
- Person-to-person contacts — how to deal with other people
- Dealing with supervision and the management of people
- Interviewing — for a new job, for appraisal purposes, and for counselling.

The Personnel Department

If you work for a large organisation, then it is likely that it will have a Personnel Officer, perhaps even a separate personnel section. Indeed, if you are reading this book as part of your BTEC National Certificate course, then your training course may well have been arranged by somebody from personnel. If, in addition, you have only recently joined the company that is organising your training programme, it is likely that staff from the Personnel Department were involved in your selection, in helping you to settle into your new job, and in dealing with queries about pay, holiday entitlement, National Insurance contributions, and so forth.

Nonetheless, as we saw in Chapter 1, personnel departments are usually created relatively late in the growth of organisations, and they are an easy target for contraction or amalgamation when a company is going through a 'bad patch', which is ironic because it is often at just such a time that employees, worried by problems of closure and redundancy, feel the need to turn to personnel for advice and guidance.

ACTIVITY

In your own company, which staff members or departments usually handle the following duties? Take a copy of the chart and include as much detail as you can.

Duties	Who usually carries them out, and under what circumstances
1 Selection of new staff	
2 Taking disciplinary action	
3 Organising and monitoring training	
4 Handling staff grievances	
5 Welfare (pensions, canteen, protective clothing, etc.)	
6 Health and safety matters	
7 Writing job descriptions	
8 Arranging induction programmes for new staff	
9 Promotions	
10 Drawing up rules and regulations	

We can summarise the main duties of the Personnel Department in terms of:

- *Manpower planning*: anticipating the demand for labour in the organisation and matching it to existing staff expectations.

- *Advising other departments on all matters concerning recruitment*: including job design, drawing up job descriptions and advertisements, shortlisting applicants for interviewing, conducting interviews and making arrangements to help new staff settle in.

- *Encouraging staff to achieve full potential*: organising appraisal processes, implementing appraisal or advising specialist departments, designing training programmes, providing off-the-job training, handling promotions and instigating suggestion schemes.

- *Trouble-shooting*: both for individual problems and when an industrial dispute with part or all the workforce seems likely.

- *Liaison*: with trade unions recognised by the employer, and outside bodies such as safety inspectors and MSC training officials.

- *Staff welfare*: organising canteen facilities, pension and sick schemes, fringe benefits and social and medical facilities.

- *Handling discipline*: disciplinary and grievance interviewing, especially of a more serious nature involving written warnings and dismissals.

- *Legal expertise*: giving advice and determining policy on current and pending laws affecting employment, such as the employment rights of women and ethnic minorities.

- *Organisation and method studies*: ways of performing clerical and other duties that lead towards more efficient information-gathering functions.

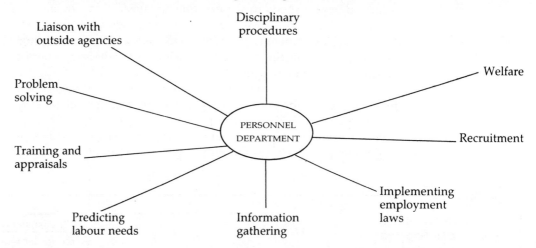

▲ *The main functions of the Personnel Department*

As you can see, the functions performed by the Personnel Department are quite formidable. However, there is a mistaken view held by many people that the Personnel Manager is some sort of in-between person who protects the vulnerable employee from the worst ravages of an uncaring management. This is not the case, nor is it the role of the personnel team. The Personnel Manager is a *manager* in his (often her) own right, who is an integral part of the management team, and whose primary aim is to maximise the *human resources* of the organisation. Most people agree, of course, that the best way to do this is by creating the most pleasant working conditions and treatment for the staff. In fact, all managers, to varying degrees, are involved in some form of personnel management in their day-to-day activities.

Sometimes personnel departments emerge as a result of a crisis, when the absence
of a specialist department to deal with a 'people problem' suddenly makes itself felt. For
example, a company may be plagued with disputes with its workforce, with low morale,
or with a high staff turnover. The result is the birth of a department to deal with the
problems, and the Personnel Officers who are called in to handle these problems usually
hold a professional qualification from the Institute of Personnel Management, as well as
other academic qualifications.

It is now widely recognised that both the specialist knowledge and the skills
appropriate to the personnel function are such that it is unreasonable to expect line
managers to have a grasp of them as well as their own specialist skills. This point is
borne out in these extracts by a leading industrialist Sir Harvey-Jones, ex-Chairman of
ICI. He first describes what people in management were thinking when he joined the ICI
as a young man.

How I see the personnel function

There appeared to be a belief
in industry that the primary job of the manager
was to do the technical task for which he had been
appointed. In my early days that was duty as a
work-study officer, and subsequently in the purchasing and supply function. There was a feeling
that the good manager should always be available
on his telephone, and time spent actually with the
people for whom the manager was responsible
while they were working was almost considered to
be dereliction of duty. There was no systematic
training, except the old-fashioned policy of sitting
with daddy and little attempt to inculcate values of
the organisation.

My early experience convinced me that personnel should not primarily be a specialised isolated
function but should be the responsibility of every
line manager, and that that responsibility should
be made clear from the earliest days. However, the
opposite side of the same coin is that there is undoubtedly a very large amount of personnel expertise which must be kept up to date and, indeed,
where the background of knowledge must be
sufficient to enable the development and
adaptation of the best current ideas and theories
to the particular circumstances of one's own
organisation. I therefore start with the view that
'personnel' ideally should not be a totally separate
career on its own. I see great merit in putting line
managers through a period of personnel work
and, indeed, in an ideal world would like to feel
that every chief executive had had some experience
of it. Simultaneously I believe, albeit somewhat
regretfully, that the levels of expertise are such
that it is inevitable that there are some specialists
who remain in the function for a large part of their
working lives.

Many of the industrial problems with which we
are trying to deal in this country have to do with
change: changes of values, changes of methods of
working, the introduction of new technology,
changes in the perceived career patterns and adaptation to changes in external social values and
expectations in our country. I have believed for a
great many years that there is a considerable
amount of expertise and experience available in
how to manage change, and since change is almost
impossible without some degree of conflict, that
there is a great deal to be learned from the constructive use of conflict. While I believe that the
knowledge, study and thinking of these areas must
be, at the end, the responsibility of line management, I also believe the personnel function has a
particular responsibility for stimulating and
making line management aware of both the theory
and practical experience that can be adapted and
applied to the circumstances of the organisation in
which one works.

The great change in our society, and a long
overdue one, is that it is totally impossible to
achieve anything in industry without the freely
given collaboration of all people in the organisation. The job of the manager is to enlist that
collaboration, and a primary role of the personnel
department is to equip the manager with the skills,
the systems and the stimuli to manage this process. I have always been fascinated about the integration of all the various factors which go to lead
and motivate people, and for a long time it has
seemed important to me to make sure that they are
all congruent and mutually reinforcing. The whole
business of the reward system, which must be
motivating, be able to tolerate difference, be non-
bureacratic, stimulative and in addition must
contain an element of punishment as well as
normal disciplinary activities, must be co-
ordinated with the whole business of recruitment,
assessment, selection and the development and
training of people at all levels. We badly need a
clearer concept of a motivating career for people
on the shopfloor. Both these areas of activity have
to be linked with administrative and other systems
which encourage open information and effective
and real joint consultation — including very open
disclosure of the business situation and of the
factors which affect the individual at his or her
place of work and are likely to cause change.

▲ *Personnel Management, Sept 1982*

┌─ **ACTIVITY** ───┐

1 What does Harvey-Jones mean by the phrase that there was 'little attempt to inculcate values of the organisation'?

2 Why do you think the Chairman of ICI believes that it is 'totally impossible to achieve anything in industry without the freely given collaboration of all the people in the organisation'? Why should this be more true now than say 20 years ago?

3 The writer believes that the introduction of change in working practices usually involves a degree of conflict.

(a) What form would this conflict be likely to take if change involving the redeployment and retraining of staff were proposed in your company?

(b) In what way could personnel help to ease the shock of this proposal?

The role of the Personnel Department cannot extend to monitoring the thousands of everyday exchanges between individuals. Nonetheless, such conversations are the bread and butter activities of many employees, certainly of those who work in administrative, sales, management and supervisory roles. Most of us accept that these spoken exchanges are important, but perhaps few people realise just how important they really are. Certainly, such evidence that researchers have begun to amass suggests that we should regard our behaviour in dealing with other people as every bit as valuable a skill as mastering accounting or programming computers.

Person-to-person communicating

Communicating orally is popular and fun. It's also quite easy to do, although there are a few pitfalls, as we discussed in the previous chapter. However, this does not mean that all forms of oral communication are universally popular. People who are quite happy gossiping with their workmates in familiar surroundings may become shy and reticent when confronted with a group of relative strangers in another office or section.

┌─ **ACTIVITY** ───

Here's an opportunity for you to assess your own degree of confidence in tackling a range of activities involving speaking. Look at the following list of situations, and score them in the column depending on how confident you would feel in each of them. If you think you would be very confident, score 5 points, and if you think you would be very worried about the prospect described, score only 1. Lesser and greater degrees of confidence or difficulty can be scored between 5 and 1. So, for example, if you think giving a talk to the rest of your class at college is something you would rather not do, but are nonetheless quite prepared to do if necessary, then you should put a tick in column 3 on your copy of the table.

Confidence →

ORAL ACTIVITIES	1	2	3	4	5
First day in a new job					
Attending a party where you don't know any of the other guests					
Going out with a member of the opposite sex for the first time					
Complaining about poor food or service in a crowded restaurant					
Attending a social function at which most of the other people present come from different cultural backgrounds					
Speaking at committee meetings or working parties					
Giving a talk to your class at college					
Dealing with a customer who is complaining over the telephone					
Asking a noisy neighbour not to use a typewriter on a Sunday afternoon					
Staffing a reception desk/enquiry counter at work, and dealing with queries from visiting members of the public					
Asking colleagues of the same status at work to do tasks which they should have done, but haven't					
Correcting the antisocial behaviour of young people (not known to you) in a public place					
Giving a group of important visitors a tour of your place of work					
Telling your present boy/girlfriend that you don't want to see them any more					
Answering questions during class at college					
Returning defective goods to the shop where you bought them					
Having to complain to your boss about some aspect of his/her behaviour which is upsetting you or your friends					
Meeting the family and parents of your boy/girlfriend for the first time					
Asking the bank manager for a loan or an overdraft					
Dealing with a high-pressure door salesperson					
Being interviewed for a new job					

Make a list of those responses which indicate your confidence level, by picking out the 3 situations in which you felt the most and the least confident (total of 6). Does any pattern emerge? Now compare your answers with those of friends in your class. Did their answers surprise you? Discuss each other's responses as honestly as you can.

Two common elements that will probably be found in your own and your friends' responses will be those of *success* and *familiarity*. The situations in which you felt most confident will be those where you have previously experienced success, which are usually activities with which you are familiar. On the other hand, where you anticipated the most difficulty, or have actually experienced failure, it may be simply that you have had little experience, in which case the activities are relatively unfamiliar.

The extent to which you felt comfortable in a particular situation will in turn be related to the likelihood of being humiliated. This explains why we are more nervous about talking to large groups of people than we are of addressing individuals or small groups, where the possibilities of embarrassment in the event of a mistake are very much reduced. 'Loss of face' is a real fear for many people, perhaps all of us, and is frequently responsible for making us pass up opportunities to communicate, or for choosing inappropriate methods of communicating. For example, a supervisor who wants to tackle a problem of persistent lateness on the part of a subordinate, would be well advised to interview the person directly. However, doubt on the part of the supervisor about his ability to handle the interview may lead him to take the easy way out, by choosing a time when he knows the subordinate will be out of the office, and leaving a note on the wrong-doer's desk instead, which will probably be thrown in the bin and ignored when he returns.

Before you blast our fictitious supervisor for cowardice, just check back to your own list and see how you scored in comparable situations! It is also important to realise that the problem of tackling deviant behaviour is more of a problem for supervisors if the person being reprimanded has the support of his peer group. It is precisely just such a consideration that has influenced government campaigns against drug abuse, and to warn people about the spread of AIDS. In neither case was a moral stance adopted. Instead, an attempt was made to win support for the government's case amongst a wide range of those thought to be at risk.

The Affair

Trudy Austin, who is in charge of a small section in the office of a large manufacturing company, is responsible for the work and output of five girls, none of whom is married. Until recently the section's work has been excellent, but some weeks ago it became common gossip that Amanda Hall, the junior of the girls, was 'having an affair with a married man'. The work of the whole section had become affected for the worst, and the other girls were jealous and hostile towards Amanda. They continually bickered and their work deteriorated, particularly Amanda's who, apart from allowing her work to suffer, now had frequent late attendances, and often asked for time off. When Trudy finally refused to grant time off, she was overruled by Mr Reed, the manager responsible not only for promotions but also for serious breaches of discipline.

Today Trudy discovered that without doubt the man with whom Amanda was having an affair was Mr Reed.

ACTIVITY

1 If you were Trudy Austin, how would you handle this situation? Explain in detail what you would do about
   — Amanda
   — Mr Reed
   — the morale and behaviour of the rest of your workteam.
2 In the previous question, which problem do you think would be the most embarrassing for you to deal with? Explain why.

Non-verbal communication

If you think the situation in the previous activity would present you with few problems, then that might be because you have the 'gift of the gab', or a special talent for handling tricky face-to-face problems. Perhaps you have the type of personality that lends itself to this sort of thing. Whatever is the case, there is a generally accepted view that successful speakers have 'a way with words', although we can't be sure that this is an ability we are born with or whether it is something we pick up as we go along.

In fact, skill with the mechanics of speech is not even half the story. Psychologists who study the way we behave in a social setting have begun to demonstrate that it's not what we say that counts, so much as what we do or don't do while we say it! In particular, the gestures and facial expressions that accompany speech, together with the voice characteristics of speakers, are now thought to be of particular importance in communicating information about the speaker and in bringing about changes in the behaviour of the listeners.

This is a very significant and illuminating discovery, but if you think about it for a moment, it is very straightforward and commonsensical. In some recent research published by the Open University, it has been shown that the success of teachers is directly related to what have previously been regarded as secondary communication skills, such as posture, facial expression, eye contact, gesture, tone of voice and so forth. What the research has shown is that where teachers fully exploit these skills, they are more successful in influencing their pupils than those who transmit inappropriate messages that suggest defeat, lack of confidence and disinterestedness.

This field of research is not new, and writers like Desmond Morris, with his *Manwatching* and later books, have done much to draw our attention to this area of human behaviour which is known as **non-verbal communication** (NVC for short). It is a topic that must not be underestimated because so many important and far-reaching decisions are made about us, whether we like it or not, on the basis of non-verbal messages that we transmit to others. Here is a Personnel Manager and a foreman having a discussion about a prospective job applicant:

'Did you see that bloke outside waiting for the interview?', the manager asked.
'You mean the fella pacing up and down the room?'
'That's it. The nervous bloke. I wonder what's the matter with him?'
'Probably got the elbow from his last place. Whatever happened I reckon he's a bit dodgy. Notice his ear-ring? God knows what'll turn up next.'
'We've got to interview him', the foreman said.
'I suppose so but I've almost made my mind up already.'

Just in case some of you are sceptical about the importance of NVC in the process of communication, then try the following activity. For this you need to work in pairs and you should put the book aside while you find someone to work with. You should find it both fun to do and informative.

ACTIVITY

Arrange your chair so that you sit back-to-back to your chosen partner. One of you will then select and describe an illustration to the other, who will draw the shape that you describe. You may describe it in any way you wish, but it is important that your partner cannot see either the book or you while she is attempting the drawing. Try one of the drawings first without allowing any opportunities for feedback (and if you've forgotten what that is, turn to page 65). *It is important not to allow your partner to see you or the open book.* Each pair should attempt to describe and draw about three examples from the set of twelve.
→

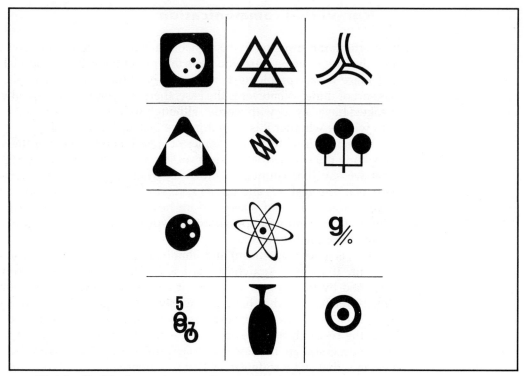

Finished? We hope it wasn't too argumentative an experience for you both. However, we also hope that it showed you some of the difficulties of communicating without being able to use the supporting techniques of NVC. Here are the various forms of non-verbal communication whose absence you probably regretted.

Gesture

There was no point in drawing any of the shapes in the air with your hands, which is what we mean by gesturing, because your partner couldn't see them. Even so, it would be surprising if no gestures were used because they so frequently accompany speech. In giving directions we often reproduce shapes or movement with our hands, partly for the benefit of the listener and partly for our own benefit. Try asking a friend to describe a spiral staircase, and watch what they do with their hands. It is likely that they will support their verbal description of the staircase with a gesture, perhaps with a finger pointing at the ceiling, slowly rotating and moving it upwards to suggest the direction and shape of the stairs.

Spatial gesturing or 'space drawing' of this sort is only one type of gesturing employed during speech. Usually a gesture is used to reinforce or to convey an attitude. The following illustrations show how we employ gesticulation to emphasise not only the content of the message but how we feel about it.

a

b

c

d

e

f

g

h

ACTIVITY

Describe the circumstances in which a person might employ these gestures.

Of course, we don't always employ gestures deliberately, they are sometimes an unthinking ingredient of our normal behaviour, but if the gestures are observed by others then they are open to interpretation by them. Some gestures are an outlet for nervous tension and they can be seen even among people who otherwise seem to be quite confident. Such gestures are known as 'leakage' and you can spot them easily. They often take the form of self-touching, particularly around the head and face. Alternatively, pointless alteration or fussy correction to appearance are other examples of leakage. One well-known TV comedian has actually built a form of leakage into his act by making it a feature of his performance (in his case, the obsessive brushing of non-existent fluff from his trouser leg while seated — no prizes for guessing who).

Some types of gesture have specific meanings, and these have to be learnt. In professional sport it is easy to see how universally-played games need signals from umpires and referees that are understandable, whatever the language of the players. Deaf people have their own coded international sign language, and motorists employ an amazing range of gestures to deliver silent abuse to each other.

Other gestures are specific to particular cultures, and signs representing abuse and derision vary from country to country. Whatever their purpose, our tendency to use gestures can be best illustrated by watching people when they speak. If you can't hear what they are saying, so much the better. Almost certainly you will not be disappointed, because they will accompany their speech with a form of almost continuous semaphore, not perhaps of a specific kind but of less precise movements which they have picked up by observing how other people behave when they too are speaking. Gesticulation becomes so habit-forming that we perform it even when no-one is watching. This illustration shows a person using a telephone, gesticulating and smiling to an unseeing listener. If you are honest, is this something that you do too?

Eye contact

This is also very important to speakers. The eyes of a listener tell us where the listener's attention is directed. In addition, the muscles around the eyes are responsible for giving us clues about the listener's reaction to our comments, either before or during their spoken reply. It is also popularly supposed that looking people 'in the eye' is a measure of integrity. Regrettably, some people become practised liars by learning to master the technique of 'eyeballing' others while telling blatant untruths, an unpleasant characteristic to which popular love song lyrics (e.g., The Eagles' *Lyin' Eyes*) bear testimony. Nonetheless, avoidance of gaze between speakers can signal nervous tension, for example when the speaker is saying something that is irrelevant, hostile or regarded as untrue by the listener. One conclusion to be drawn from this is that there is no straightforward way of reading NVC. It is often a matter of cultivating skills based on our own experience, but helped along by a study of human communication behaviour.

ACTIVITY

Select one of the following human moods and try to convey its meaning mainly by the use of your eyes. Your partner has to judge which mood you are trying to communicate.

- Suspicion
- Hostility
- Boredom
- Terror

- Surprise
- Love
- Interest
- Shame

Another useful eye function is the way in which they help us to 'take turns' in conversation. This is a complex process involving a number of skills which combine to secure an ideal pattern of communicating behaviour in which there are frequent exchanges of speaking and listening roles, but without the fear that one speaker will dominate (or pressurise another into yielding the right of reply) while at the same time avoiding any embarrassing silences in the pattern of talk. As we discovered in Chapter 2, our society values highly those who can easily sustain conversation whilst in the company of others. This is not easy, and it is for this reason that much social chatter is accompanied by props to fill in any awkward pauses. Obvious examples are sipping drinks, nibbling crisps and peanuts, even smoking — all providing something to do while new conversational topics are sought. Even the process of buying and exchanging these refreshments is of value, often breaking the ice and even providing topics of conversation in themselves.

This does not mean that people who talk endlessly are therefore popular. Your own experience will suggest the reverse is true. That is why it was suggested that the ideal conversation is one where all those present feel able to contribute, in which there are frequent exchanges of the speaking role. Handling this exchange of roles requires care, however, and a number of clues are used to bring it about. For example, when a listener wishes to say something their posture and facial expression will indicate this, perhaps in the way they lean forward and raise their head or eyebrows several times. If this does not have the desired effect, they may add sound by saying 'mm' or even a 'yes' in accompaniment with their head-nods. On the other hand, disagreement or doubt about a speaker's point may be conveyed by frowning, averting the gaze, shaking the head, and if the speaker has still not yielded, vocalising either a quizzical 'er?' or repeating the word 'no' in conjunction with head shaking.

Other spoken signals also coordinate conversation. Sometimes these are explicit and take the form of invitations to speak (What do you think?), or they may be implicit. Tone of voice, for example, indicates whether a speaker has finished or whether they propose to continue. A speaker's pitch normally falls at the end of an utterance, but if they intend to continue, the voice pitch rises just before they take a breath to indicate there is more to come. We learn that it is impolite to interrupt a speaker, so listen for a falling pitch before beginning our own utterance. If you feel inclined to interrupt a speaker you may be excused if you begin with a conciliatory phrase such as 'Look, I'm sorry, but …'.

ACTIVITY

About six students will be formed into a discussion group. They will be asked to discuss the proposition *Convicted drunken drivers should have their vehicles confiscated.* The rest of the class will be asked to observe the group's NVC and make a few notes on a copy of the following table. In the discussion that follows, opinions will be sought as to who exercised the most interesting, effective, or unusual skills in NVC. You should make observations during the discussion like this:

Names of participants	Types of NVC observed
1. Carl	Pointed a lot — for emphasis and to pin down the opinions of others. Taps his teeth when he is thinking.
2. Amreeta	Watched other speakers carefully — leaned forward when trying to join discussion. Stared hard at opponents.
3.	
4.	
5.	
6.	

Head-nods and facial expressions

Although we discussed these in the last section, it is important to restate their importance. Head-nods (or head shaking) are powerful tools that are used mostly to express approval or disapproval. They enable us not only to reinforce a verbal message, but make it possible for us to get a clear message across to everybody present without having to interrupt a speaker. Nodding, of course, is an encouraging sign for a speaker to observe, as it means that their point is at least being understood and perhaps even approved of. This is even more clearly transmitted if the nods are accompanied by a smile.

The importance of the smile as a facial expression is clear from the faces which beam at us out of holiday snapshots. Put us in front of a camera and a manic grin creeps across our faces as we attempt to convey our keen sense of enjoyment to the pages of the family album. Similarly, it is the mask to be worn when meeting people. In our culture, the smile is the sign of pleasure and a token of goodwill. However, the smile of the adult is not necessarily the same thing as a baby's chuckle of contentment. Sometimes smiling can be overdone to give the observer an opposite impression of phoney charm, and you may have noticed in films that are meant to frighten us, how evil characters use the smile at chilling moments.

With simple contractions of facial muscles, the whole range of human emotion can be visually transmitted to others. By twisting our lips we can sneer, by opening our mouth and raising our eyebrows we can convey surprise, and by frowning and pouting our mouth we can express doubt.

ACTIVITY

How well do you read faces? Study these stylised expressions and guess at the emotion each attempts to convey.

When you have finished, discuss your results with others in your group. How do your interpretations compare with theirs? Are there any glaring differences? What could be the consequences of misreading facial expressions in real-life situations?

Orientation and proximity

A highly contrived feature of the activity where you sat back-to-back to your partner and described shapes was your unnatural position. Usually a shared activity will have you seated next to your partner, perhaps even facing them. Our physical position in relation to our partner's position is what we mean by 'orientation'. Certainly you wouldn't choose to sit facing in opposite directions. Indeed such an orientation in ordinary circumstances would amount to 'giving someone the cold shoulder', which simply means ignoring them in a social setting.

Sitting or standing directly opposite someone gives maximum opportunity for eye contact. As such, it is the ideal orientation for lovers, or for those about to engage in either physical or verbal combat. As few of our social contacts achieve either of these extremes, we are normally quite happy with orientations that place us more or less at right angles with those whom we need to address. This arrangement facilitates eye contact, enables us to see facial expression, head-nodding and posture, but gives us the opportunity to look away from time to time without appearing disinterested or devious. It also improves hearing reception and the chance to lip or face read if we are confronted with an unfamiliar accent. You may yourself have experienced difficulty in understanding someone because this visual channel was not available to you.

Proximity is also important in cementing relationships. Have a good look around you at work, or in your classroom, library or canteen, and see what distances people choose to place between each other when they have a choice. These distances, or proximities, are what social anthropologists call 'personal space', which refers to the territory surrounding us into which we usually allow only those with whom we are prepared to be intimate. People who wish to become intimate with us sometimes 'invade' our personal space to see what our reaction will be. If we repel them, or retreat, the sensitive intruder will interpret this as a rejection, although a more persistent intruder may take longer to get the message — as you no doubt have experienced for yourself.

Although our personal space gives us enough territory to allow a certain mobility, we may choose to fix that space in a form of permanent ownership. For example, at work we often like to have at least a locker, perhaps even a whole desk, which is 'our corner' of an otherwise anonymous workplace. Even in a library, seated users will mark their territory by a spread of books and personal objects, and according to an experiment carried out by Desmond Morris, leaving clothing on a library chair 'reserved' the seat from use by others for a period of 70 minutes on average.

▲ *In this photograph, the people queuing for a bus have as much personal space as they need, and you can see clearly who are together and who are strangers to each other.*

There are circumstances in which we are unable to sustain the usual social distance. Can you think of any examples from your own experience? What about using the lifts at work or in a large store, or travelling in the rush hour? In lifts, we go to great lengths to avoid having to look at each other by staring mindlessly at the illuminated buttons or the roof. On public transport reading is a popular activity. It not only passes the time but provides a temporary barrier to shield us from fellow passengers and to indicate to others that the people sitting next to us are strangers.

ACTIVITY

1 Think about the working and social relationships that exist between colleagues at work. Is there a link between those relationships and the layout of the workplace, especially the orientation of supervisors and their subordinates?

2 Jot down any examples of territorial behaviour you have observed on the part of your workmates or your classmates at college.

3 What useful tips about orientation and proximity can you give to someone who is about to
   — deal with an awkward and aggressive member of the public
   — inform a member of staff of the death of their closest relative
   — conduct a disciplinary interview at work?

Touch

It is unlikely that much touching will occur at work. Some ritualistic handshaking will be permitted with visitors, perhaps, even though the origins of this custom are now quite forgotten by the participants and are probably irrelevant for 20th century men and women. (If you don't know when this custom began, then find out.) Touch is more common in our society between women than between men, but because organisations are often designed and managed by men, male behaviour patterns tend to dominate. Touching that can be observed is likely to be confined to the back, shoulders and arms and is used to guide, control or gain attention from others. In recent years, the doubtful practices of men who exploit their positions by touching low-status female employees have been the subject of corrective campaigns, supported by trade unions and women's groups.

Posture

Although we are no longer asked to walk about with books on our heads in order to cultivate an erect gait, our posture, or the way we present our bodies, continues to be used as a barometer of our attitudes. For example, when we are being interviewed for a job, sitting stiffly on the edge of the chair with arms folded can give an impression of aggression, though this is probably better than being slumped in the chair like an old sack. Whether it is reasonable to draw conclusions about a person's character from the way they arrange their bodies is very dubious, but people still do so, and public schools frequently discipline young boys who walk about with their hands in their pockets.

Appearance

Although we can't do much about the face we are born with, or for that matter the ravages of time on our bodies, it is still possible to alter our appearance considerably. Hair, face, hands and figure are the principal areas of interest and we spend a great deal of time and money to achieve appearances that will either shock or stimulate approval from others.

Some organisations are so concerned about the appearance of their employees that they insist on staff uniforms. If you are employed by an organisation that is semi-militaristic, such as the police force or the prison or fire service, you will have been told that your uniform allows you to be easily identified by members of the public and by colleagues, as well as promoting a sense of loyalty to the organisation. It also reduces the sense of individualism, which can be counter-productive in a job that demands instant obedience in response to orders, some of which could expose you to great personal danger.

ACTIVITY

These extracts are taken from a staff induction guide of a large British company.

APPEARANCE AND BEHAVIOUR AT WORK

Workwear

If you have been issued with workwear it must be worn during business hours.

You must ensure that you always keep it clean, in good repair and neatly presented. Spare buttons are available from the Branch Manager or Staff Officer.

Any alterations to the garments which may be considered necessary should be carried out only after management approval has been given.

Footwear

All members of staff are required to wear sensible, comfortable footwear in the interests of health and safety.

Shoes should be well-fitting and provide adequate protection. Special footwear is available for male porterage staff.

Heels must be of a safe and comfortable height, and shoes must have flexible soles.

Shoes must be smart, suitable in style and colour for business wear and be kept clean and in good repair. Extremes of fashion style must be avoided.

Trousers

Trousers are not considered appropriate wear for female staff who during their normal working day are required to appear on the sales floor.

Female staff who are required to wear trousers for religious reasons may do so; but the colour and style must complement the workwear — jeans are unacceptable.

Accessories

Accessories such as brooches, bracelets, scarves, etc. must not be worn at work. If staff wear earrings they must be discreet, as must rings worn on the hands.

THE PERSONAL TOUCH

YOUR HAIR … must be well-cared for and dressed in a style to suit your work and our business image. Long hair must be kept neatly under control.

YOUR HANDS … and nails are an important element of general appearance. They must be kept clean and neatly manicured. If nail polish is used it must be of a discreet or natural shade and be perfectly applied.

PERSONAL FRESHNESS … day-long freshness is important to customers and colleagues who meet you in your daily job. The warm atmosphere of the branch and the nature of your work requires that you give this matter careful attention.

1 What kind of organisation do you think is being represented here?
2 Do you think these rules are reasonable? Explain which rules or advice you take exception to.
3 What rules governing appearances are laid down by your employer?
4 What justification, if any, is given for them?
5 What is your own attitude to these regulations? Do others share your attitudes?

Uniforms also bestow a mark of authority on the wearers. We tend to associate them with the armed forces, with individuals who have more power than we have, and who can inculcate a sense of respect in others. For employees who take risks in potentially stressful situations, this can be a positive advantage. Railway guards, air stewardesses, bus drivers, even doormen and 'bouncers' are examples. Otherwise the uniform is a means of ensuring that a favourable image of an organisation is created for customers, either by repeating a 'house-style', which may exist in advertising and promotional material, or by laying down a common standard of smartness and appearance. Even if there is no prescribed uniform at the place where you work, there may, in practice, be a fairly narrow range of acceptable outfits. This is not because one way of dressing is superior to another, but because certain forms of dress convey their own meaning at particular times and in particular places.

Paralinguistics

The last type of non-verbal communication we will consider involves the way in which the sounds of speech are actually made. Strictly speaking, paralinguistics is a form of verbal communication, but it is useful to think of it as a type of NVC because we are not concerned here with the explicit content of the verbal message, rather with its added meanings. In the same way that gesture, eye contact or appearance can give us important clues as to the identity and emotion of the speaker, and can be highly influential in determining our response, so the *way* we portray our message is probably at least as important as the literal meaning of our words.

Paralinguistics can be best understood as being the intonation of the message and the accent with which it is spoken. Intonation is the pattern of stress which we give to our spoken words — and stress can be very important in making clear the precise intention of the message. Sarcasm, for example, is often delivered by tone of voice. Write down a sarcastic message and it will look like a compliment!

ACTIVITY

Speak out loud the following sentences, and by changing the emphasis, see how many different meanings it is possible to arrive at.

— We can always rely on you to do a first class job.
— This is the only suitable job left for you.
— What a lovely dress that is.
— Your intelligence appears to have no bounds.
— You are nice you are, really nice.
— Great.

We have already discussed how the pitch of the voice can indicate whether an utterance is completed, or whether it is to be continued. Intonation also helps us to differentiate questions from statements. Even when sentence and word order remain the same, the tone of voice can indicate that a question is being asked. Try saying 'This is your house' as a statement, then as a question. Easy, isn't it. Or should it be: Easy, isn't it?

Intonation also provides emphasis, although it is important that we shouldn't overdo it. Purists would suggest that we say '*This* is the car', rather than 'This is *the* car', unless the car really is unique. Yet monotone speech can be very dull to listen to, so the important thing to remember about speech is that it is not only important to keep the content interesting, but also its mode of delivery. This demands variation in pitch, pace, and in the length of pauses, although we must remind ourselves that however interesting we sound in projecting our voices, there is bound to be a limit to our listener's patience.

In commenting on the intonation in speakers' voices, you may have said something about **accents**. It is sometimes supposed that it is possible to speak without an accent, but if you think about it, you will see that this is not so. An accent is simply a habitual way of pronouncing the language, so no-one can speak without one. Those people who fancy that they do speak 'without an accent' are merely using an accent with which they are familiar and consider to be a natural form of speaking. In Britain, the accent most popular with the middle classes, and therefore held in high regard by the business community, is that which might be termed 'BBC English'. It is the accent of the newsreader and TV presenter — and one which is widely thought not to be an accent at all. Probably its status now exceeds that of what used to be called 'received pronounciation', which was an accent used by the upper classes and 'received' at court.

Also under threat from the spread of BBC English are the regional accents which have long been a feature of speech in Britain. As the social importance of radio and TV, accompanied by state education, have grown, so local accents and dialect words have waned. It remains to be seen whether the speech of West Indians and the languages of Asian families will endure. Some signs of revival of regional and national language forms are seen in the attempt to encourage more Welsh speaking and the reintroduction of the ancient language of Cornwall. The importance of regional accents may have declined, but judgements and attitudes towards speakers, based on their accents, are still being made. These judgements include guesses about a speaker's position or status, personality and intelligence. The interrelationship of factors can be represented as:

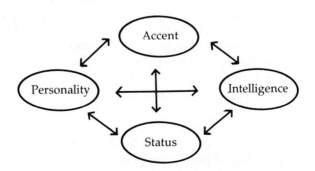

┌─ **ACTIVITY** ───

1 What accent do you speak with?
2 Do you have attitudes towards other accents? Check with other people to see
  whether they share any of these attitudes.
3 Do you believe that accents are likely to be of benefit or a hindrance to people at
  work? What accents might be thought to be disadvantageous in your part of the
  world?

Influencing other people

If you are hoping to find here a magical formula for bringing the rest of the world to heel, you will be disappointed. However, it is possible to influence other people, quite considerably, because we are all susceptible to some very simple stratagems.

Reinforcement

Here is a tactic that every dog owner will be familiar with. When your subordinates behave as you wish — reward them — *always!* It is easy to take other people's hard work for granted after a while, but this can lead to resentment. Unfortunately, rewards in the form of cash or promotion are seldom available, but employees are often content to know that somebody is noticing and appreciating their efforts. A simple response such as a smile, a nod, or a thumbs-up gesture is sometimes enough, coupled if possible with a friendly compliment. On the other hand, undesirable behaviour should be met not only by withholding rewards, but with frowns, looks of disapproval, and if necessary spoken criticism. Some of these techniques can even be applied to those in high status positions, although it would be inadvisable for subordinates to voice criticisms unless invited.

Other non-verbal signals

We have already drawn your attention to research that shows how teachers depend heavily on non-verbal signals for keeping control. We can all learn from this, for teaching usually involves persuading others to do what they would otherwise not wish to do. Let us examine some 'tricks of the trade' from the teacher's repertoire. First, most teachers stand while their students sit. This is not done to ensure the comfort of pupils, but to make it easier for the teacher to dominate a large group. A similar but slightly different tactic is used by teachers handling deviant behaviour. Here, the culprit is sent to the study of a senior teacher and made to stand in an empty space before the teacher's desk, which is a symbol of their authority. Supervisors can borrow these ploys. Just as the policeman prefers to look down at a sitting motorist, so, like teachers, a standing supervisor can reinforce his authority if necessary by talking down to a seated subordinate. If there is a more serious problem to deal with, the supervisor can interview the employee in the manager's office. Not only does this separate the wrong-doer from any support he/she might get from his/her peer group, but it allows the supervisor to be surrounded with the trappings of authority on his/her own ground. A few subtle ploys can be introduced to heighten the effect. If the subordinate is kept waiting outside for a while, that will remind them of their weak position. Making them knock before allowing them to enter will shore up your authority, and inviting them to sit down not only sounds polite but actually reinforces your control over the action.

Of course, only the more serious disciplinary problems demand this form of action and you will deal with most challenges without recourse to this pantomime. The best way to avoid problems is to stop them from happening in the first place. Like cats, teachers often puff themselves up to seem more dominant than they really are. They do this by drawing themselves up to their full height and pulling their shoulders back. If necessary, they will tilt their head back so that they appear to be looking down their noses. Finally, they try to make themselves more commanding by making positive gestures with their hands, suggesting a bold resolve and strength of purpose. In certain circumstances, these tactics may prove useful in the office.

The simplest way to command attention is by raising your voice. Talking loudly can give you an air of confidence and authority. Try using a confident and cheerful tone, and smiling occasionally, but watch for leakage, which your subordinates could identify as inner tension. If they want to argue with you or attempt to question instructions unreasonably, consider interrupting them. People of equal status can do this only at the risk of being thought ill-mannered, but higher status individuals are able to avoid criticism if such conduct is appropriate to their position.

A word of warning. As was pointed out earlier, there is no simple formula for ensuring the willing compliance of others and any of these techniques can produce confrontation rather than cooperation, particularly if it is not employed within a climate of trust, collaboration and a reasonable respect for authority. However, they do provide a useful guide to help you to deal with those tricky personal situations which can otherwise get out of hand.

The coffee machine

Your company has introduced vending machines and has withdrawn the off the trolley service which used to dispense refreshments to all the office staff. The machines have been giving trouble lately and suppliers say a lot of it is caused through ill-treatment by staff, who have been seen banging the machines in order to get their drinks.

One coffee break, Philomena Dobbs, a youngish clerk with a reputation for a short temper, but regarded by most as a good worker, is seen by you throwing a half-full cup of coffee at the machine and kicking it violently with her right foot. As Philomena's supervisor, you ask her to stop and to get a cloth to clean up the mess. She then turns to you and says: 'I'm fed up, and if that's all the service I can get for my money you can sod off and clean the machine yourself.' With that she gathers up her things and storms out of the office.

Next day, she returns to work and carries on working as though nothing has happened.

ACTIVITY

Although you have reported Philomena's behaviour to higher management, you are expected in the first instance to handle problems yourself. Serious written warnings and dismissals are of course a matter for management.

1 Suggest several different possible approaches that are available to you as a supervisor.

2 Describe in detail how you think you ought to conduct yourself in the interview if you are either Philomena or the supervisor.

3 Interviews will now be arranged in which you will play the role of either Philomena or the supervisor. The rest of the group will make comments on your tactics in the discussion that follows.

Make them like you

We will always do more for people we like, or to whom we owe our allegiance, than we will for people whom we dislike or distrust. But how *do* we persuade people to like us or trust us?

This is a complex question, and if you are again expecting a three-point plan to quick popularity, it simply doesn't exist. However, there are a few points that are worth thinking about. For one thing, liking and disliking is often a two-way process — which means that if someone seems to like us, we will probably like them. So taking a friendly interest in someone else will probably bring dividends. Second, the most popular employees are often those who help, encourage or cheer up others, while those often least liked are the attention-seeking, the aggressive and the boastful. Finally, none of us likes the feeling that we are being exploited, that others are taking advantage of our friendship. So it is a smart idea to do a few good turns for your colleagues, and when you have need to cash in on them, they will not feel that you are being selfish.

ACTIVITY

For some people, the finding and making of friends is a difficult process. In the previous section, three conditions influencing friendship formation are described. Can you think of any others? Use your own experiences at home, in your social life or at work to illustrate your answers.

Persuasion

We cannot hope to influence others only by our non-verbal signals or just by being nice to them. From time to time, we may have to persuade them to change their minds or behaviour even when they don't want to. Once again there are no easy answers, but a scrutiny of the tactics used in teaching may be helpful. First, there will be a need to change the pupils' views of what looks like unpopular activities by drawing attention to their more attractive features. The snag with this tactic is that people will not fall for it twice. The shopper who buys a product that he/she previously did not find acceptable simply because it has been packaged more attractively is no more likely than before to become a regular customer. Even so, it is often highly desirable to change people's perceptions, and schools are trying to do this at the moment with the introduction of new exams, new subjects and new methods of assessment.

Another ploy is to appeal to group loyalty on the part of the individual. 'You don't want this class to get a reputation for being lazy?', a teacher might ask, hoping that the lazy few will be motivated to try harder for fear of damaging the standing of the group. Under certain circumstances, this is a potent force which may lead individuals to make enormous personal sacrifices. In war time people will even lay down their lives for their country or for an important principle, or to save their comrades from danger.

A third and rather desperate tactic is to deny that any harm will befall those who follow our suggested course of action. 'It can't do any harm to try it, can it?', is a frequent conversational device used on those who are looking for an excuse not to do something. A much more detailed section on persuading others appears in Chapter 6.

Power

Although it might be argued that respect for authority in our society has waned, there is still general acceptance that people with legitimate authority and responsibility should not be ignored. If ever you achieve promotion, this is an important point to remember. We all tend to expect direction and control from those occupying positions where power is located — so long as we feel that power is being used legitimately. An interesting experiment carried out in the 1970s demonstrated this, albeit in a rather bizarre fashion.

Ordinary members of the public were asked to pass what they thought to be 450 V electric shocks through people, who appeared to show every sign of intense suffering and even collapse. In fact, the sufferers were professional actors playing the greatest roles of their careers, but the subjects did not know this. Incredibly 65 per cent of them had accepted the authoritative instructions of the experimenters because they believed the experimenters must know what they were doing!

Finally, it is important to restate a point already made. None of these techniques is foolproof and they cannot be regarded as a substitute for a regime in which employees believe their efforts are valued and their opinions sought and considered. In addition, they are of course the characteristics of assertive but not aggressive behaviour.

Summary and checklist for giving instructions

- Is the employee suitable for the task?
- Are the instructions for the task clear and unambiguous?
- Will you check that the employee has understood what is required of him or her?
- Is the employee aware of the need for the task?
- What manner of issuing instructions is most suitable for this employee?
- What opportunity will the employee have to influence the manner in which the task is carried out?
- How will you check to ensure that the instruction is being carried out?

I heard it on the grapevine

Here are two typical examples of extreme views held by managers.

Personally, I deplore the existence of a grapevine. It's nothing more than idle tittle-tattle—people wasting their time destroying reputations and depressing morale. I wish we could stamp it out here at Universal Communications

HOWARD GRIPE-HALL
Accounts Manager

The grapevine? It's very valuable—a super safety valve, and by keeping my ear to the ground, I can often spot problems early and nip them in the bud before they get out of hand.

MOLLY BRIGHT
Personnel

In truth, grapevines are something of a mixed blessing, but as there is virtually no chance of getting rid of them, organisations just have to learn to live with them as best they can, and try to harness what benefits there are for the organisation and its employees.

What is a grapevine? It would be wrong to regard them simply as random flows of gossip around the workplace. In fact, grapevines are complex informal communication networks that are usually highly efficient. Although the pattern of information exchange is not easily identifiable, grapevines have some important characteristics which give us clues as to their likely channels of information.

- Grapevine communication often follows the official channels of communication through an organisation. This is not as strange as you might think if you remember that official channels bring people into contact with each other and provide ideal opportunities for exchanging gossip.

- As a result, information is often slow in reaching departments which are at the end of official organisational processes or which are remote from the hub of the workplace, e.g., annexes.

- Grapevines are selective. In general, information is passed to those for whom it is relevant, and gossips often avoid passing information to those who would be offended or feel slighted by it.

- Speculation thrives in the absence of official information. When organisations withhold information or make statements that contradict what key but low-status personnel regard as suspect, staff will simply fill the gaps with their own details, which may or may not correspond with the official version.

Are grapevines something that management should worry about? The answer is probably yes because they can do great harm. Try to imagine how you would feel if you thought that everybody at work was talking about you behind your back, making references to your supposed incompetence, laziness, double standards, ruthless ambition, poor dress sense and bad breath. Not the sort of thing to make you eager and confident, is it? So the Accounts Manager in the illustration is right: it can depress morale, particularly if the grapevine is buzzing with news of falling sales, declining investment and proposed redundancies. This may lead to a lack of commitment on the part of employees and even to the loss of key personnel who start looking for alternative employment before the crisis hits the local job market.

Fortunately, these disadvantages are compensated by two important benefits. Managers who are alert can pick up rumblings about possible problems and act to prevent their development. The grapevine can also be used to help break bad news to a workforce. The tactic here is to start a rumour about some horrendous eventuality which is far worse than the reality. The rumour is allowed to spread through the organisation before an official statement is made to 'counteract the misleading rumours that are circulating'. The statement, while still bad, is much better than the grapevine suggests, so the staff feel relieved and grateful — at least, that's the theory.

The important conclusion to be drawn is that if managements cannot control the grapevine, they can control the environment in which it operates. As has already been suggested, grapevines will be most active in a climate of uncertainty. The answer is to ensure that employees receive adequate information from official sources to stop misplaced speculation damaging morale.

Job interviews

You will already have spent a lot of time at school or college preparing and thinking about job interviews, and have no doubt been pumped with advice about the importance of arriving on time, suitably dressed to make a good impression. Although there is a lot of commonsense advice available, there has been little research into exactly what job interviewers are looking for or the value of the techniques that they use in the selection process. For example, as a candidate you might be rejected because of a badly written letter of application or because you fluffed the interview with a couple of stupid answers. Yet no-one is certain whether these actions are fair or even sensible ways in which to assess your potential, say as an engineer or a shop assistant. Nonetheless, you will in future be involved in interviews, either as a candidate yourself or eventually as a member of a selection panel, so it is worth looking at a brief summary of the existing knowledge of interviewing practices.

Why interview at all?

Interviews cost money. Besides the administration and advertising costs, there is the work sacrificed by the employees on the interviewing panel and the travelling expenses paid to candidates. However, as a means of exchanging information, especially between people who may not have met before, the face-to-face interview probably has no equal. It is particularly helpful for these reasons:

- It is important to see whether the candidate will 'fit in' with the organisation and its employees. As most people work in groups, choosing a person who might upset group cohesion can be a serious mistake.

- Since we know that appearance, facial expression, eye contact and voice qualities are often more important than the content of messages in assessing a speaker's personal qualities, it is sensible for an organisation to want to take a look at potential employees.

- An interview gives candidates a chance to assess the suitability of the employer. A candidate who discovers undesirable features about a job can withdraw before damaging both parties.

- The interviewing process provides an opportunity to confirm or modify opinions about a candidate, to ask further questions, correct false impressions and clarify information on both sides.

How are interviews carried out?

Unless a potential employee has been 'headhunted' (invited to work for an organisation directly), employers normally sift through the pile of applications, quite ruthlessly and quickly rejecting those that are thought to be wholly unsuitable for whatever reason. Taking greater care and interest in perhaps the best ten remaining, these are whittled down to a short list of about six candidates who are then invited for interview.

The favoured format for interviews is the *panel*. This is where a candidate is interrogated by a group of senior employees for about half an hour. This has the advantage that all the panelists see and hear the same evidence on which to form judgements, but it is an intimidating and stressful experience for the applicants who are asked to sit in an exposed position while questions are fired at them. A good panel chairperson will try to reduce the stress by putting the candidate at ease by gently explaining what is about to happen and by giving them the opportunity to put questions to the panel at the end.

An alternative format is to interview each candidate on a one-to-one basis, but using the same number of panelists in rotation. In effect, each candidate would be interviewed alone, say four times, by a different person. The advantage of this method is that it is less stressful for the applicants, who may do themselves more justice as a result. As it is possible for the candidates to be interviewed simultaneously, there is no reason why this method should be any more wasteful of staff time. At present, this method is still little used in organisations. It also has some disadvantages too. Can you think of any?

ACTIVITY

You have been asked to plan a series of job interviews for the post of clerical assistant. The candidates have all been invited to your firm for 11 am. Produce two alternative timetable programmes, one based on a traditional interviewing panel and another on single candidate interviewing.

The interviewers

Jane Hollis, Office Manager
Samantha Smith, Section Head
Jonathan Harvey, Finance Officer

The interviewees

Mandy Robinson   Judy Lofthouse
Louise Gubbins   Stephen Morse
James Malpas

What are interviewers looking for?

This seems a rather pointless question because each job is different from all other jobs, not only in the skills, knowledge or experience demanded, but because work is a social activity in which we are expected to get on reasonably well with our fellow workers. So organisations vary enormously in their approaches to filling vacancies. However some common denominators do emerge.

Panelists are usually looking for people who are like themselves

As was said earlier, a main concern will be to choose somebody who will 'fit in' and perhaps this explains why panels are drawn towards candidates with whom they feel the most comfortable. It would account for the difficulties women have traditionally experienced in gaining promotion (panelists being almost all male) and why non-whites have similar problems (panelists being almost all white). However, there are other factors by which an applicant can appeal. These include similar social backgrounds to the panelists, going to a particular school or university, even being in a particular age group or holding certain political or social opinions all play an important part in the selection process.

Initial impressions count strongly in the assessment of candidates

This is because we have an irresistible urge to jump to conclusions about people when we meet them for the first time. Just think of the people who believe in 'love at first sight' or how easy it is to like or dislike someone within minutes of meeting them. We can always change our minds when we get to know people better, but this isn't of much use to the candidate being interviewed. A considerable amount of convincing has to take place before we will accept that our first impression was wrong.

Presentation of self

Research suggests that the more successful candidates are those who smile, nod their heads, talk in an interesting way, and generally give an impression of confidence and keenness. It is significant that many of these are non-verbal characteristics.

What problems are there for candidates?

Candidates usually have to contend with three major difficulties.

- The first of these is simply nervousness. The problem with interview by panel is that the risk of humiliation is much greater than when being interviewed by an individual. In addition, it is more difficult for us to assess what a group of people is looking for, therefore we have difficulty in modifying our behaviour to our advantage. Suffering from nerves can cause us to perform badly, and knowing that we have performed badly, to become more nervous with a further deterioration in our performance.

- The second problem is the risk of over-selling ourselves. It is the custom in Britain to applaud modesty and deplore vanity, so many of us have learned to understate our achievements. However, in an interview, self-criticism can be a serious handicap. On the other hand, conspicuously drawing attention to personal qualities can sound boastful. There are no easy answers.

- Some jobs require a person to be assertive, even dominant. However, there is a problem about displaying these qualities in an interview, where we are expected to take our cues from the panel members. Under the circumstances it may be wiser to assume that the panel will infer the presence of these qualities, rather than turning them on the panel itself by raising our voices or by being argumentative.

Checklist for interviewers

- Decide in advance how the candidates are to be assessed.

- Plan how the interview is to be conducted by compiling a few common questions and deciding who will ask them.

- Carefully read all the documents that relate to each candidate, such as the application form and references.

- Make candidates feel as much at ease as possible.

- Explain exactly what is going to happen.

- Try to avoid being influenced only by first impressions.

- Make the candidates feel the interview has been worthwhile. They may be either a potential customer or suitable for another post in the future.

- Ask open-ended questions, not ones which are self-answering. (We expect our staff to work overtime. Are you prepared to work overtime?)

- Give candidates a chance to ask questions at the end.

Checklist for interviewees

- Find out something about the organisation, and if possible the actual job, before the interview.

- Read and understand any documents that have been sent to you.

- Remember the importance of first impressions, so allow yourself plenty of time for the journey. Take care over your appearance, but don't overdo this by being too glamorous.

- Use non-verbal signals. Look at all the panelists, not just the questioner — and don't be afraid to meet their eyes. Smile and nod occasionally to give an impression of confidence and optimism.

- Don't answer questions tersely. The panel will want to hear not only what you have to say, but how you say it, because they are forming judgements about your attitudes.

- Don't ask questions just for the sake of it, but do have an interesting question up your sleeve just in case.

- At the end of the interview ask how and when you can expect to hear the outcome.

Personnel selection is further explored in Chapter 8.

Appraisal interviews

Interviews are not used solely for the purpose of selecting new employees. In many organisations existing employees may be invited to attend 'appraisal interviews' at intervals of at least once or twice a year to discuss their individual progress and performance with their immediate superior. Though most companies have their own reasons for holding appraisal interviews, there are common advantages for all organisations.

● They help management to decide what increases of pay or any other reward should be given on merit grounds.

● They provide data on which to confirm the existing status of employees, or whether to promote, transfer, demote or even to consider dismissal in certain circumstances.

● They identify training needs and point to where improvements might occur if extra training were provided.

● They are a valuable person-to-person communication channel, which management can use to get across the culture of the organisation.

● They motivate the employees to do better in their present jobs by providing them with knowledge and recognition of their achievements and the opportunity to discuss problems and prospects with their superior.

As you can appreciate, the interview itself has to be handled with great skill by the interviewer, whose main job is to spur the interviewee to greater success in the future. In order to do this effectively, the interviewer has to have information at hand relating to the employee's previous work performance. Sometimes this information is passed on through word of mouth or the supervisor may be required to provide a written report. The following appraisal form, which is filled in by a supervisor, is used by a major retailing company. You will notice that the interviewee is expected to sign the form at the end of the appraisal interview.

STAFF APPRAISAL

√ as appropriate

JOB SKILLS	Above standard	Acceptable	Below standard	Unacceptable
Documentation	Very neat and 100% accurate ☐	Usually neat and accurate ☐	Untidy and not always accurate ☐	Very untidy and inaccurate ☐
Cash register operation (if applicable)	Very quick and 100% accurate ☐	Quick and accurate ☐	Rather slow and not always accurate ☐	Most unreliable ☐
Cash handling	Always balances immediately ☐	Usually balances ☐	Frequently makes mistakes ☐	Never able to balance ☐
Sales ability	Self-motivated and extremely effective ☐	Generally capable and effective ☐	Quite capable — could be more effective ☐	Incapable and ineffective ☐
Overall job knowledge	Highly proficient ☐	Good — with further potential ☐	Still much to learn ☐	Severely lacking ☐

PERSONAL QUALITIES:

Appearance	Invariably clean, tidy, well dressed ☐	Generally very well turned out ☐	Often untidy, inappropriately dressed ☐	Persistently unkempt ☐
Speech	Extremely clear, concise, correct ☐	Clear and easily understood ☐	Has some difficulty expressing him/herself ☐	Difficult to hear, understand ☐
Manner	Courteous, confident and cheerful ☐	Lacking in one of these qualities ☐	Lacking in two of these qualities ☐	Lacking in all three qualities ☐
Timekeeping/attendance	Beyond reproach ☐	Seldom subject to criticism ☐	Frequently subject to criticism ☐	Persistently subject to criticism ☐
Relationships with: Customers Staff Superiors	Friendly, cooperative and even-tempered ☐ at all times ☐ ☐	Usually friendly, cooperative and ☐ even tempered ☐ ☐	Occasionally adopts hostile uncooperative ☐ attitude ☐ ☐	Indifferent, truculent aggressive ☐ ☐ ☐
Initiative	Takes correct action without supervision ☐	Usually acts on own initiative ☐	Requires frequent direction ☐	Requires constant detailed direction ☐
Adaptability	Adapts willingly, easily to change ☐	Generally adapts easily, quickly ☐	Has some difficulty with new situations ☐	Very slow and unwilling to adapt ☐
Hardworking	Never stops ☐	Seldom flags ☐	Requires some prompting ☐	Requires too much prompting ☐

Any training thought necessary and now to be provided by the Manager	
Promotional potential	

Interviewed by:.........................   Signature of employee: ....

Position: ....   Name of employee: ....

Interview date: ....

ACTIVITY

1 Using this form as a guide, design a new appraisal form that would be suitable for either junior staff in your own firm, office workers in general, or for students attending your college.

2 Team up with a person you know reasonably well, either as a working colleague or a friend at college, and fill in your form to record their abilities. Do try to be fair, but don't over-estimate their abilities.

3 In the appraisal interview that follows, talk through the assessment with your partner as constructively as possible, by pointing out their successes and where there is room for improvement. You should both sign the form at the end of the interview to indicate your agreement before you both change roles.

Counselling interviews

When you get promoted to a supervisory position you can expect to be approached from time-to-time by staff who wish to discuss personal problems. These interviews can be difficult to handle, for whatever training you may have had in the management of people, it is unlikely that you will have received coaching in counselling techniques. Faced with unfamiliar demands in stressful situations, it is not surprising if our first reactions might be ham-fisted and of little benefit to the person asking for our help.

ACTIVITY

What follows are examples of mistakes that we can all make in our relationships with other people. Identify the mistakes Mr Barnstable makes in each example and suggest what he should have done or said instead.

Dorris — *Oh, Mr Barnstable, my boyfriend's run off and left me and I can't afford the rent we owe and I'm worried about going back to my parents and what will all the people here say when they find out? I'm so unhappy ...*
Manager — *Don't worry. I'll speak to Payroll and see if we can't fix you up with a loan. That should sort your problem out, Dorris.*

Fred — *Er ... Mr Barnstable ... I wanted a word. I'm going to have to ask you for some time off. You see, I think I've got a touch of Herpes.*
Mr Barnstable — *Herpes? When I was your age I'd got VD in the army. 1952 ... in Cairo. I was in agony. Doctor said he'd never seen so virulent a case, almost a medical landmark I was. Makes your spot of Herpes look a bit insignificant, eh?*

Mandy — *Mr Barnstable, what is my entitlement to maternity leave?*
Manager — *But ... but ... you're not even married.*
Mandy — *I know. I've been seeing this fella, and I think it's his.*
Manager — *You* think *it's his? Then you'd better get married at once.*
Mandy — *I don't think I love him enough to marry him.*
Manager — *Perhaps you should have thought whether you loved him enough to let him father your child!*

Steve — *Mr Barnstable ... I think I'm gonna fail my college course.*
Manager — *Don't worry. I'll ring your tutor at college — he's a friend of mine. You'll be all right.*
S — *One of my problems is that I haven't got a copy of the text book.*
M — *No problem. I'll get one of the lads in the office who's done the course before to lend you his copy.*
S — *That's good of you, but I need it now really. I've got to do an assignment to hand in tomorrow.*
M — *Oh very well then. Bring me the questions and I'll tell you what to write.*

Barry — *Mr Barnstable, can I have a word. It's about ...*
M — *Don't tell me. I think I can guess. Your drink problem, right?*
B — *Yes, that's right. You see ...*
M — *I know, Alcohol Dependency Syndrome. Seen it many times before.*
B — *The thing is ...*
M — *No need to explain. I know all about your broken home background — picked it up from your personnel file actually.*
B — *Well, it didn't really start, until ...*
M — *Yes, that bust up with your wife. Marriage Severance Syndrome the experts call it.*
B — *Well, I ...*
M — *Now take a tip from someone who knows. You pop down to Dr Gubby's clinic for chronic alcoholics. He'll dry you out.*

Amanda — *I hope you don't mind my telling you all this, but you're such a good listener, Mr Barnstable. None of the women in the office seem to understand me the way you do.*
M — *Oh, that's perfectly all right. After all, what sort of manager would I be if I wasn't interested in my staff.*
A — *Sometimes when I've had a row with mother at home I wish I could do what I do here at work ... you know ... just have a word with you about it. You're so capable. I wonder ... is it possible to ring you at home?*
M — *Well ... I suppose so. Of course, you must do so whenever you want to.*
A — *Oh, that would be really nice.*

Robert — *Waaa! Waaa! Waaaa! ... I can't stand it any more ... sob ... sob ... That new VDU is the last straw ... sob ... sob ... but coming on top of everything else ...*
Manager — *OK Parsons. Here, have a tissue, man. For God's sake, stop blubbing and pull yourself together. Dry your eyes — that'll make you feel better to begin with.*

We can briefly summarise the chief mistakes as:

A   *Clockwatching*   The manager isn't really prepared to listen to what she has to say. *Dealing with the 'easy' problem.* The woman has a number of difficulties, but he chooses to deal only with the easy and possibly less important one.

B   *Going one better*   Instead of dealing with the employee's problem, he merely 'caps' the employee's story with a more dramatic experience of his own.

C   *Imposing own standards*   The manager doesn't answer the girl's question, but attempts to impose his own moral attitudes.

D   *The expert*   Rather than listen to what the employee says, he instead 'shows off' his own supposed knowledge of amateur psychology.

E   *Mr Fixit*   This is where he takes all the employee's problems and solves them himself, making it unlikely that the individual will face up to the responsibility for his own actions.

F   *Getting emotionally involved*   The relationship between manager and
    subordinate is getting out of hand. The normal boundaries between staff are
    being ignored and the manager is in danger of becoming too personally involved
    — perhaps in something he is going to regret.

G   *Suppressing emotional display*   All he succeeds in doing is making the employee
    keep his despair bottled up, something which Robert may have been doing for
    some time already. Occasionally we all need to work off our emotions before we
    are ready to investigate rational solutions to our problems.

A checklist for counsellors

- *Give people time* — Listen to them carefully, and don't interrupt. Make sure people know what time the interview is due to end so that no-one feels hurt when it does end.
- *Don't try to deal only with the first problem mentioned* — Refresh your memory by referring to the 7-point plan for improved communication on page 74. The first complaint may only be a symptom of the underlying concern.
- *Keep your distance* — Avoid identifying with other people or forcing yourself to be popular by offering to do everything.
- *Don't judge others* — People come for help — not a sermon.
- *Treat people with respect* — The best help anyone can have is a sympathetic and constructive listener who is genuinely concerned for their welfare.

Above all, it is important to remember that counselling is a two-way communication process in which an individual is seeking help or information often about extremely private and personal matters. Obviously counselling can be successful only in an atmosphere of mutual trust and confidence.

ACTIVITY

Re-enact the seven illustrated situations as role play. Start off exactly as described, but with the manager putting into practice what he has learnt about counselling. You will need to think about your role carefully before you begin.

GEORGE AND LINDA

George Seagull, the middle-aged office manager of *Carlton Insurance*, stretched his rather fat arms above his balding head, spread them out slightly as though he had all the time in the world, and indulged himself in a huge yawn. Life is very satisfying at the moment, George thought, sitting alone with his feet across the corner of his polished desk, office junior to Office Manager in 18 years. There's no reason why he shouldn't enjoy himself a little more, take it easy like, let everyone see how comfortable he was controlling 20-odd staff. Maybe he should buy himself a couple of new suits, those lightweight ones he's seen the youngish executives wearing in *Dallas*.

George thought he heard a knock on his door, a timid knock, a knock that sounded as though the caller wished they were somewhere else. George whipped his feet off the desk, sat himself upright, selected a fairly healthy looking ball point from a bristling container, and poised himself, pen in hand, over some freshly typed letters. 'Come in … come in' he managed to croak, surprised at the sound of his own voice.

A disembodied face peered around the half-open door, a worried, white face. 'Have you got a minute, Mr Seagull? I'd like a word with you, if you don't mind.'

'Come in … er … luv … er … Linda, isn't it?'

Linda slipped quietly into the room and stood by the door, fumbling at some yellow beads at her throat. 'Yes', Linda said, 'I won't keep you a minute.'

'Take a seat, luv', George said, pointing with open hands to the carefully placed visitor's chair on the other side of his desk, 'I don't think you've been in this office before, have you?'

The way Linda sat down gave George an impression that he was in for a bad time. Not another staff demand, he moaned silently to himself, bracing his body for the onslaught. This time he intended to take a firm hand with any silliness.

'Can I take Friday off to go to the hospital?' Linda gasped rapidly, staring for no apparent reason at a jug of water on his desk.

'Ah … not feeling too well … eh … I suppose you don't want to tell me about it … eh … woman's trouble I suppose. Actually I went to the General only last week … on my day off, mind … I'm having trouble with my big toe-nail. Ingrowing … my God, the pain …' George's eyes were swivelling around madly in his screwed up face as he relished an exquisite agony. He was enjoying himself.

'No, not that,' Linda interrupted abruptly, 'I'm not sick. I want to visit my gran.'

'Visit your gran? Visit your gran? What do you mean, visit your gran? We're not a charity you know. We're running a business here, Miss Short, not a charity. You know Friday's our busiest day. That's our balancing day. What would happen if we all took Friday off? Tell me that?' George was by now building up a head of steam. He clutched, white knuckled, the edge of his desk, pulled himself up to a standing position, and boomed on 'Who's going to type up the financial report, if you don't? Do you think I'm going to do it? This isn't on Miss Short, this isn't on. No way. No … What's the matter?'

Linda had buried her head in her hands and was sobbing and shaking uncontrollably. 'But my gran, Mr Seagull, she's dying … she's dying … she's got breast cancer … oh … I'm sorry … I'm so sorry.' With a final great sob Linda looked up to see Mr Seagull pouring a glass of water. He was sitting now, looking a bit sheepish. Then Linda's necklace snapped and the bright yellow beads began bouncing all over George's desk.

'Oh, never mind the beads. I didn't realise ... never mind the beads ... here, have a sip of this ... my mother died last year you know, but it's different with close relatives, isn't it? Come to think of it, I hardly ever met my grandparents when they were alive. If we all had time off to visit all our relatives in hospital we'd never do any work, would we?' George was an old hand, you see, he'd heard all the old sob stories before.

'But I live with my gran. My parents are divorced. My gran is like a mum to me. The hospital has asked me to bring her clothes and things on Friday. Then I have to see to the house and everything. While my gran's in hospital, I'm going to stay with my friend, Tracey. So, on Friday, I'll need to pack my clothes as well and lock the house up.' Linda had never said so much to Mr Seagull in all her two years at Carlton Insurance. Her confidence and her colour were returning. She managed a little smile.

'But why didn't you tell me all this when you came in', George responded, 'it could have saved us a lot of unpleasantness. Anyway leave it with me to think about. Perhaps we can help you out on this one.'

ACTIVITY

1 Identify in this story examples of the following types of non-verbal communication:

facial expressions	paralinguistics
gestures	orientation and proximity
posture	eye movements

2 Suggest a few more examples of NVC that have not been identified but are likely to have been exhibited by George and Linda.

3 What is your overall opinion of the way George handled this interview? Identify the exact moments where you think he made his more serious misjudgements.

4 What advice would you give Mr Seagull about interviewing staff with personal problems?

5 If you were Linda, how would you have handled the interview?

6 Playing the part of either Linda or George, re-enact the interview.

THE SAUSAGE ROLL

Scenario

This case study concerns an incident in the company canteen. You will be asked to play one of the following roles:

Mike Johnston — *Personnel Officer*
Jennifer Hall — *Personnel Officer*
Helen Miles — *Personnel Officer*
Joanne Carr — *Office worker and wife of Robert Carr*
Robert Carr — *Insurance salesman and husband of Joanne*
Melvin Harrison — *Company van driver*

Summary of incident

Joanne Carr and Melvin Harrison are sitting in the canteen enjoying a cup of tea and a chat. Robert Carr, who is sitting unsighted at another table, throws a sausage roll at Melvin, which hits him in the face. Melvin shouts back 'If you're looking for trouble, your're going to get it.' Robert walks towards Melvin and immediately attacks him. Melvin retaliates, and a vicious fight develops between the two men, with shouting and bad language. Chairs are scattered, tables upturned, food and cutlery thrown about and plates smashed. Joanne joins in the fight, at first trying to pull the men apart, and later hitting them over the heads with a dinner plate. All three are immediately sent home and asked to report to the Personnel Office at 9 am the next day.

Personnel Officer's brief

You are a Personnel Officer and it is your team's responsibility to sort out this mess. One thing you are all certain about is that you are not prepared to tolerate this animal behaviour by anyone, no matter what the excuse. You have in front of you a short report from the canteen manager. He points out that at least £20s worth of damage has been caused and that does not include two broken chairs and three hours of overtime worked in order to clean up the mess. The real cost probably amounts to about £60. You are aware that bad feeling has existed between the two men for some time, but you are not sure why this is so. You intend to find out. You also intend to find out who is going to pay for the damage. All three workers have satisfactory records at the company and there have never been any problems before.

You dig out a copy of the company's disciplinary procedures to give yourself a bit of background information.

The procedure in operation

When a disciplinary matter arises, the supervisor or manager should first establish the facts promptly before recollections fade, taking into account the statements of any available witnesses. In serious cases consideration should be given to a brief period of suspension while the case is investigated and this suspension should be with pay. Before a decision is made or penalty imposed the individual should be interviewed and given the opportunity to state his or her case and should be advised of any rights under the procedure, including the right to be accompanied.

Often supervisors will give informal oral warnings for the purpose of improving conduct when employees commit minor infringements of the established standards of conduct. However, where the facts of a case appear to call for disciplinary action, other than summary dismissal, the following procedure should normally be observed:

(a) In the case of minor offences the individual should be given a formal oral warning or if the issue is more serious, there should be a written warning setting out the nature of the offence and the likely consequences of further offences. In either case the individual should be advised that the warning constitutes the first formal stage of the procedure.

(b) Further misconduct might warrant a final written warning which should contain a statement that any recurrence would lead to suspension or dismissal or some other penalty, as the case may be

(c) The final step might be disciplinary transfer, or disciplinary suspension without pay (but only if these are allowed for by an express or implied condition of the contract of employment), or dismissal, according to the nature of the misconduct. Special consideration should be given before imposing disciplinary suspension without pay and it should not normally be for a prolonged period.

Robert Carr's brief

You have been working at the company for three years. You are 23 and have been married to Joanne for two years, although you haven't been living together or seeing each other for six months. Since your break-up you have been living at home with your parents. Everything seems to have gone wrong for you lately. You still love Joanne but she has gone off with that nerd Melvin. Seeing them in the canteen together holding hands under the table was too much for any man to bear. The grapevine has been buzzing about them for the last three months. Melvin deserved what he got for taking away another man's wife and bragging about it around the offices.

Melvin Harrison's brief

You are 20 years old and have worked as a van driver at the company since you started there two years ago. The fight in the canteen came as a bit of a shock. You had no idea that Robert felt that way about things. You had always assumed that their marriage had finished. After all, it's a bit much getting punched up like that. You feel that you are the innocent party — a victim of violence. As a single man you were minding your own business and having a good time. In fact Joanne had encouraged you to take her out, and you had both talked about sharing your lives together — after the divorce. Now you have a black eye and have had a sausage roll thrown at you — maybe you ought to report the assault to the cops?

Joanne Carr's brief

You feel deeply ashamed of what happened in the canteen. Having a broken marriage is one thing, but having a fight and a row in front of all your workfriends is another. And you might get the sack! With unemployment being what it is, there's no chance of getting another job. You find it difficult to understand why Robert started the fight. He was such a quiet person, too quiet even. You have been separated for about six months and as far as you are concerned the marriage is finished. In fact, the divorce papers have already been sent to him. There's your own future to think about, and you hope that future includes Melvin.

PROCEDURE

Joanne, Robert and Melvin are sitting outside the Personnel Office at 8.55 am the next day. The personnel team of three are sitting at a desk deciding how to deal with the problem. You are playing one of the six roles.

TASK ONE / PREPARING FOR THE INTERVIEW

As either Joanne, Robert or Melvin, you are to think carefully about how you are going to play your role and what you are going to say in the interview — your future will depend on it. As one of a team of personnel officers you have to plan what questions you intend to ask and how to conduct the interviews (e.g., whom to call in first), or you may decide to interview them together (or both).

TASK TWO / CONDUCTING THE INTERVIEW

Conduct the interviews in a properly organised way. There should be no preconceived notions about the exact outcome of events. Decisions will be based on what actually happens, although individuals may have a general idea about what they would like to happen.

TASK THREE / IMPLEMENTATION

At the end of all the interviews the personnel team will, after full discussion, come to a decision about each of the three employees. The task will be completed when these decisions, accompanied by a short explanation, have been conveyed to the three employees, who should remain silent.

TASK FOUR / THE APPRAISAL

On a copy of this chart, make an appraisal of the interviewing performance of the other five participants (or all six if you are an observer) based on: 1 = excellent, 2 = above average, 3 = average, 4 = below average, 5 = poor.

	Evidence of preparation	Verbal skills	Non-verbal techniques	Leadership qualities	Persuasive skills	Overall performance
Helen Miles						
Jennifer Hall						
Mike Johnston						
Joanne Carr						
Robert Carr						
Melvin Harrison						

1 Which participants, other than yourself, were the most convincing in presenting themselves? What was so special about them?

2 Which features of your own performance were you most pleased with?

3 If you had to repeat the experience, which elements of your approach would change? In what way would you change them?

Wiring up the office

Within days of the introduction of computerised share dealings in the Stock Exchange in 1986, the sight of hundreds of well-dressed men shouting and rushing around buying and selling shares in a large open floor area was never to be witnessed again. What then began to occupy people's thoughts were the opportunities a huge empty floor space could offer. Some suggested its reversion to a coffee house, others to a skating rink. There was one suggestion that it might be transformed into an open prison for insider traders. Whatever the fate of the building, the significant point is the speed with which working practices in the City of London have changed to make the old Stock Exchange obsolete. The brokers and jobbers who once crowded the floor of the exchange to perform their own quite separate functions, now do their own and each other's jobs in front of a VDU on their own desks, and are able to deal not just on the UK market but on international share markets. All this without setting foot outside the office.

That this has happened just four months after the introduction of a microelectronic system is an indication of the urgent pace of change in business practices that the wiring up of offices dictates. This chapter will examine the nature and applications of the technology that is creating these major changes and make some predictions for the path along which the new technology is leading. As we will be using some jargon in this chapter you might like to take note of the glossary on page 209, entitled 'What everybody should know about computers'.

New technology?

Although the advances in microelectronics and the equipment that they have spawned are often referred to as *new technology*, it would be wrong to see their arrival as a sudden and exceptional phenomenon. In fact, a glance around your own office, particularly if it has yet to tool itself up for the 'new age', should convince you that a quite dramatic process of change has been underway for a long time.

ACTIVITY

Jot down a list of 'modern' materials and equipment that are used in offices. From your nearest library find out when each of these items was introduced or invented. A few examples can be found at the end of this chapter.

Some familiar items in today's office have been with us for a long time, and the application of microelectronic circuitry to both the equipment and the processes of office work is merely a development in a long history of the transmission of recorded information, which began with the early forms of writing in the ancient world. The invention of writing was a vital ingredient of civilisation. It became possible to produce records, and societies that introduced writing were liberated from their dependence upon human memory. It made possible greater precision in measurement and the storage of information across generations. Just how important an advance this was can be appreciated if you try to recall the contents of the documents that you worked on say on Monday of last week. No doubt you would say 'I couldn't tell you without looking in the file', or something of the sort.

Along the way, humankind has refined the methods of recording information, the means of storing it, and of sending it to other people who might need it. Nobody today is surprised by the ball-point pen, the filing cabinet or a Telex machine chattering away in an outer office. Yet there are youngsters now in school who will take for granted in the near future the efficiency of the laser pen, the capacity of electron beam computer memories and the versatility of electronic document transmission by means of fax machines.

Systems

There is a temptation to talk about new technology in much the same way as someone might brag about a car or a new stereo system: about what it can do and how they might be envied for owning one. It is true that many exciting developments have arrived or are about to arrive, but simply to wallow in the wizardry of new equipment can be dull for those who can't see the point of it, and frightening for those who see the future in terms of a struggle for supremacy between themselves and the computer, which might eventually lead to their own job loss.

It would be more useful if we examine the way in which the new technology is being applied to existing office procedures. In this way, computerisation can be seen for what it is: a new and possibly better way of doing what is being done already, and as natural a development as the replacement of manual typewriters by electronic ones. So in looking at the current and likely applications of computers, it is necessary to examine the typical procedures for handling work. These procedures are known as *systems*, and a system can be defined as a process by which a company organises the production of a service or product which it seeks to provide. In manufacturing, a system is the process by which the products are made, so that when *Austin Rover* introduced the *Metro* at the beginning of the 1980s, they had to design not only the car, but the system by which it would be made. This meant organising the processes by which the materials, skills of the workforce, and the ready-made components were deployed in order to produce the new car. In systems jargon they are known respectively as the *inputs*, the *process* and the *outputs* of the system. Clearly, each element needs careful thought. How much steel is needed to arrive by what date? When will it need to be reordered? In what order are the parts of the car to be assembled? Will each assembling process progress at the same speed or will there be a log-jam in the system? These are examples of questions that need to be asked when a manufacturing process is being undertaken.

In offices, the same concept of system applies, although usually it is the provision of a service (frequently the transmission of information). Indeed, the inputs and outputs of an office system may be similar, consisting of pieces of paper, albeit with different formats or information recorded on them. Another important feature of office work, as anyone who has ever worked in one will know, is the *storage* of information not currently needed, but which may be wanted in the future. Similarly, office procedures could become lax if no-one was checking to ensure that tasks were being done efficiently, so any office system needs an element of *control*. Finally, if the various parts of the system are to function in harmony, they must have available at least one channel of *communication*.

These elements of systems, whether in offices or factories, can be illustrated in a diagram.

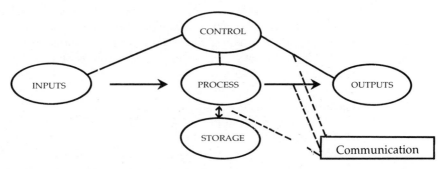

▲ *Model of a business system*

The elements in the system can be further defined as:

- *Input(s)*: the elements that are fed into the system.
- *Output(s)*: the end-product of the system.
- *Process*: the means by which inputs are converted into output.
- *Storage*: the means by which information is kept and made available for retrieval.
- *Control*: the means by which the system is supervised and decisions in exceptional cases made.
- *Communication*: the channels through which information flows within the system.

This does not make the application of the idea of a system very clear, so let us consider how it applies to the treatment of an insurance claim.

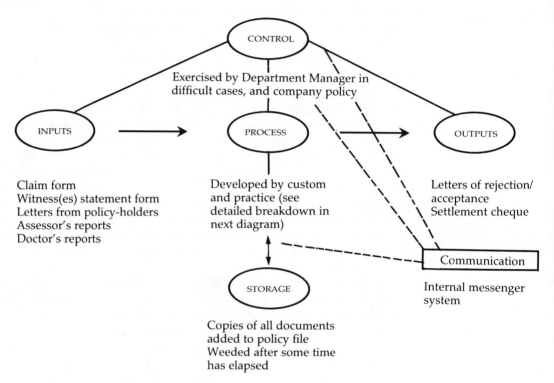

▲ *Model of an insurance claim system*

A process such as the checking of an insurance claim and making a decision about any payout is often quite complex, perhaps involving professional judgements acquired after many years of experience. In addition, there is enormous variety in the nature of claims and of the circumstances in which they arise, and systems used in such circumstances may have developed on a trial-and-error basis over many years. On the other hand, perhaps because of the need for computerisation or because of existing inefficiencies, a new system may have to be designed. This will mean the use of a method known as **systems analysis**. This involves a careful appraisal or analysis of all the stages in the existing process and of the possible outcomes of each of these stages. When these are set down on paper, potential problems can be identified and a new or revised process drawn up. This will have the advantage of standardising procedures, removing inconsistencies, and will enable newly recruited staff to function effectively because they will be working to a 'blueprint'.

The resulting system can be issued to staff, either in whole or in part, in the form of a **flow diagram**. Such diagrams represent, step-by-step, the typical questions or dilemmas posed for employees in handling routine enquiries or problems. They also set out standard responses to these dilemmas which have been adopted as organisational policy. Here is an example of a flow diagram. It is used by staff in supplementary benefit offices and deals with the current entitlements of 16- to 18-year-olds in part-time education who are applying for benefit.

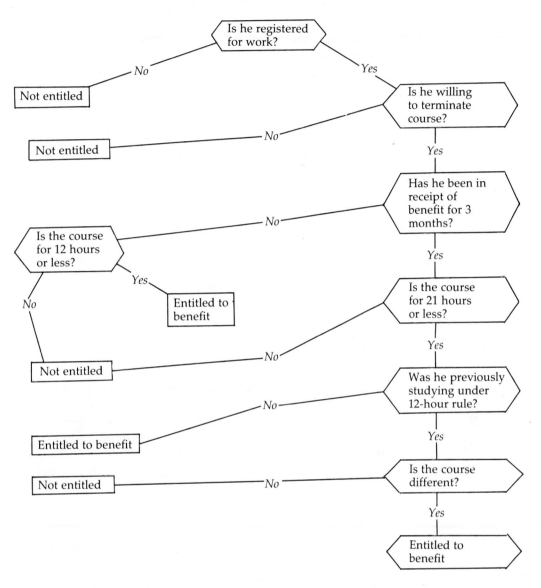

▲ *Supplementary benefit, part-time education 16- to 18-year-olds 1987*

ACTIVITY

1 Why do you think it is important to ensure standardisation in the payment of supplementary benefit?

2 What is the difference between the stages represented by lozenge-shapes and those represented by rectangles?

Perhaps you noticed that there are never more than two alternative responses to the questions posed in this example of a flow diagram. You will also have spotted that questions are identified by the lozenge shapes and outcomes by the rectangles. This process of providing only two choices is known as **binary opposition**, which happens to be the process by which information is handled by a computer.

All data is processed in computers by means of switches, which can only be either on or off, a process that is carried out thousands of times a second in the machine. It is no coincidence that network or flow diagrams have this basic binary structure because their development stems from the programming of early computers for which information had to be presented in a similar format. Experienced employees, of course, do not need to consult a flow diagram to know how to deal with the majority of the transactions that form part of their work. However, if we can simplify these human decision-making processes by means of systems analysis and flow diagrams using binary alternatives, it also means that a computer can be programmed to do it too, only a great deal more efficiently.

ACTIVITY

1 Using the symbols and binary structure given in the example, design your own flow diagram to show how to make a call from a public telephone box. Compare your diagram with that of a friend's.

2 Identify one transaction that you perform at work and, using the same technique, produce a flow diagram that could be used to simplify the process for new employees. If you don't have a job, design a flow diagram for one of the transactions you know of at college, perhaps the marking of an integrative assignment by a lecturer.

3 Discuss in class how easily you think this task could be done by a computer.

Office systems and computers

Computers are already widely in use. Sometimes they permit something quite new to be done, when for example we draw cash from our bank account at round-the-clock cash or service points. On other occasions they provide an improved way of doing what was done already, as with the introduction of computerised check-outs in supermarkets. Many of the functions of computer technology in offices fall into the latter category, and so in the rest of the chapter we will explore how the traditional elements of office systems are changing in response to the availability of new technology. Later we will consider the impact this has had on the nature of organisations and on the people who work in them.

Inputs

Most inputs into office systems are still paper-based. If you think about your own office, you will realise that the majority of inputs arrive by post: letters from customers or suppliers, forms of one sort or another, invoices, delivery notes, and so on. Some will be generated within the organisation and arrive in the form of memos, internal forms, even telephone messages, while others may originate in your own section. If they are paper-based, some may be hand-written. Writing is a valuable skill and it is not likely to disappear for a long while. Pens and pencils are cheap, portable, easy to use, and they will not fail during a power cut. Most inputs will be typed, possibly on electric or electronic, rather than on manual machines, and some will have been prepared on word-processors.

In offices where systems are partly or wholly computerised, it is necessary to convert manual inputs into a form which the computer can deal with, and in most cases this means feeding information into the electronic system using a **keyboard**. This is the entry point for data into the machine's memory, and in form it is like a conventional typewriter keyboard, with the addition of 'function' keys arranged above and/or at the side of the letter-keys.

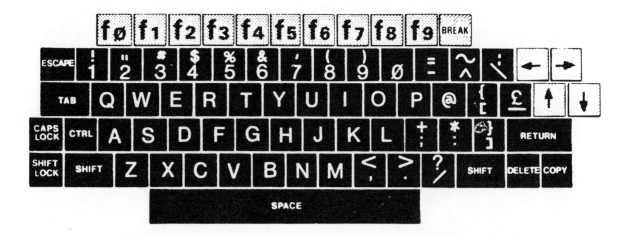

▲ *A typical microcomputer keyboard*

Most keyboards have a QWERTY layout of keys, even though the mechanical factor which dictated this layout on typewriters is not needed on computers, where circuits, not levers, convey instructions from the keyboard to the machine. The function keys, however, do not have counterparts on the typewriter keyboard, as they are the means by which an operator gives instructions to the computer about what to do with the information which has been or is about to be entered.

Not all inputs are paper-based. You may have people who call in person to speak to you or who ring up with information. These also form part of the input to an office system. At present, you may write down what your visitor or telephone caller says, or you may feed it straight into a computer via a keyboard. Holiday booking agencies, motor vehicle insurers and regional gas boards are among those organisations who have equipped their telephone answering staff with their own computer terminals at which they can enter bookings, application details or queries from callers, without having to write anything on paper to pass onto another section at a convenient moment. This has the advantage that the operators can call up on their screen a file giving relevant details of earlier transactions with the customer, or in the case of holiday bookings, whether the holiday is already fully booked.

In the future, writing notes on scrap pads and tapping out data on a keyboard may be unnecessary. Although such systems are by no means perfect, computer manufacturers are hurrying forward with **voice-systems** to give to all operators to use to give instructions directly to a computer. Such systems would work on exactly the same principle as every other computer programme, because instructions or data would be converted to binary digital electrical impulses upon which the computer would then act. Already Japanese businesses are using such devices, and though Japanese is phonetically simpler than English, their introduction into this country is just a matter of time. Alternatively, computers fitted with **optical scanning fonts** will be able to 'read' documents that are fed into them, thus avoiding the need to transfer data from a sheet of paper by keying it into the system. Already in the UK computers are in use that can scan typed or printed documents, and not too far behind are computers that can read written inputs, either in hand-written forms (providing the lettering is tidy and confined to pre-printed boxes), or hand-written messages composed on a special electronic message pad, which is either sensitive to the pressure made by the operator's pen or responds to a **laser pen** (see overleaf) of a kind that has been in use for some time as part of library and supermarket check-out systems.

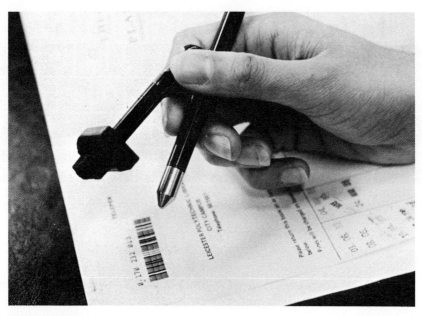

▲ *The library laser pen*

Communication

This is the means of transmitting data within the system, particularly of conveying inputs, whether written, printed, spoken or electronic. A great deal is probably communicated between staff by word of mouth, and some material may be conveyed using an internal post or messenger system. Some organisations use mechanical devices to transport documents, but this is largely confined to the retail sector, where cash handling in some stores requires cash and customer bills to be conveyed in cylinders under pressure along tubes to a cash room, where receipts are issued and any change returned to the point-of-sale along the same tubes.

However, computers are also communication devices and this rather dated form of transaction handling in stores can serve to illustrate the enormous advances that computers offer. A reference has been made already to the use of laser pens at supermarket check-outs, but now more sophisticated 'intelligent' check-outs are being installed by multiple retailers like *Sainsbury's*. These have optical scanners fitted to the counter and check-out operators pass each item from the shopping trolley (which is probably a more important invention) over an optical scanner so the computer can read the individual product code printed on each item. Stored in the computer's memory is a list of all the prices of goods currently on sale, so that it can record the value of each item purchased and produce a total price for the customer's bill. It also registers the sale on a stock-handling programme so that goods can be called up from the storerooms as the shelves are emptied, and reordering from warehouses takes place as soon as the computer recognises that stocks have fallen to the programmed reorder point.

► *Product bar code from a tin of Sainsbury's soup*

A further development will be the use of these check-outs for computerised cashless sales. Customers will be able to pay with a form of credit card, for example Barclays Connect card, which will authorise the computer to debit the holder's bank account and credit the store's account with the value of the grocery bill. Exciting though these developments are, they should not blind us to the fact that all these functions are already being performed with manual or mechanical systems. For example, there is nothing new about cashless sales and it is probable that your or your family buy groceries either by cheque or credit cards. What the computer does is to provide a more rapid and efficient means of communicating by sending data to the store manager about takings and sales; keeping the store and warehouse staff much better informed about the need to restock or reorder; and debiting or crediting bank accounts at the moment of sale, rather than two or three days later. At this moment, these techniques have not been introduced on any significant scale in the UK, but they will soon be common enough in the High Street. However, there is no reason to suppose that the same techniques will not be introduced by most commercial organisations.

ACTIVITY

1 (a) By what methods does your organisation collect money from its clients or customers?

(b) What would be (or are) the advantages and disadvantages of computerised debit/credit systems?

2 In Japan, most people plan their video recordings with the use of a laser pen. In the Japanese equivalent of the *Radio Times*, each programme carries a bar code printed alongside. By pressing the pen across the codes you can set up your video to record your favourite programmes within seconds.

(a) What further possible use could laser pens have in commerce or industry of the future?

(b) Suggest a range of clerical chores that could be carried out more efficiently using this type of technology.

Electronic communication

How do computers communicate with each other? There are a number of possibilities. First, it is possible for several **microcomputers**, which are small free-standing computers with limited memories, to be linked with other machines in the same building in a **network**. A network is a cable running round an office into which communicating equipment can be connected. By keying a destination code into a machine, it is possible to send a message to any or all other terminals, which will read the destination code(s) and extract the signal from the system.

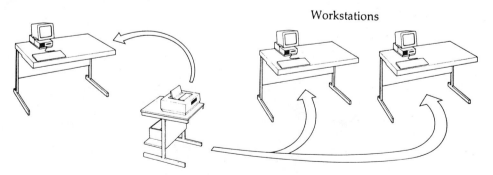

Workstations

Remote printer

▲ *Networking: free-standing microcomputers are linked to other machines 'locally' (i.e., within the same office or building)*

Alternatively, a company might install a mainframe or mini computer with 'peripherals' or 'on-line terminals', as they are also known. This means that the system's memory and the link-ups between machines are restricted to those determined by the computer's central processing unit (CPU).

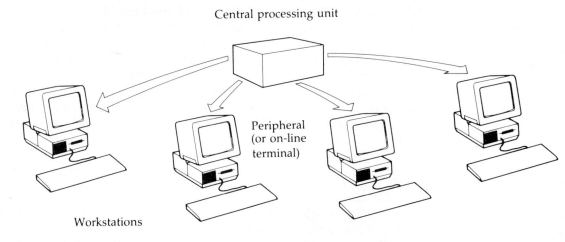

▲ Mainframe: terminals communicate with the computer memory and with each other via the central processing unit. Heavy use of the CPU can lead to delays in calling up data

However, it is increasingly likely that an organisation's computers will not only be linked to each other, but also to external systems. A great deal of this will occur over cable, rather than via broadcast signals, because off-air signals are not compatible with computer systems without the use of a converter unit and they are susceptible to interference. As it is, much computer communication travels over telephone cables, and in order to handle the expected boom *British Telecom* have been laying thousands of miles of a new type of cable as part of their System X digitalised telecommunication network. This glass-like material is an optic fibre, which uses light rather than electrical impulses to convey signals. This means that there is less degradation of the signal during its journey (very important if the signal is going to make sense when it arrives at its destination), and that thousands of messages can be carried simultaneously along the same cable in both directions.

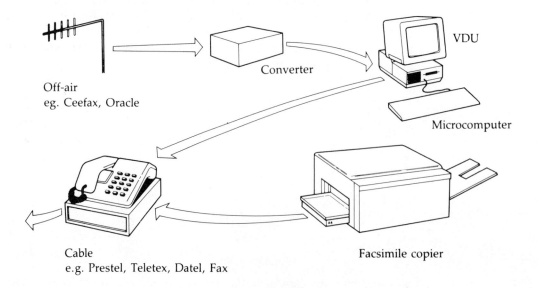

▲ Landline and off-air communication and interactive services

The services that computers can receive in this way include a number of viewdata services, the most useful of which is British Telecom's *Prestel* system. Viewdata is an electrical filing system which can be displayed on television sets or visual display units. The information is stored by 'page' and each system has a menu of contents from which the appropriate page(s) is(are) selected·by users. Some of these systems — Ceefax and Oracle — are carried by television signals, which make them less suitable for computer users because they are not transmitted as a digital signal. Prestel on the other hand utilises digital transmission and is therefore compatible with computers, enabling remote computers to store the information in their own memories and to make responses to the service. In the case of Prestel, it is possible to send, via a computer, an order for goods or services, which can then be relayed to the company that is advertising on Prestel. This makes viewdata services genuinely interactive, whereas consumers who wish to order from Ceefax or Oracle have to make a separate phone call to an advertised number.

Prestel is also an example of a **value-added network**. This means that, in addition to transmitting data, the system provides a number of other services which add to the value of the technology once it has been installed. If a business wishes to transmit and receive information between itself, its suppliers and customers, then it will probably use British Telecom's *Datel* system, which involves the leasing of linetime on the telephone network to switch messages between terminals. Even so, the number of value-added services offered by Prestel is limited, and British Telecom is now developing a new service known as *Teletex*. This will provide transmission facilities and it will be topped up with an attractive range of value-added services, including:

- Data processing
- Text editing
- Data storage and retrieval
- Access to 'external' information (as with Prestel at present)
- Multi-addressing mail facilities
- Facsimile transmission
- Store and forward capabilities
- Route switching
- Internal destinations

Organisations with Teletex are able to send postal material electronically. For example, a circular can be sent to all customers by feeding one copy into Teletex, along with a list of customers' names and addresses. Each customer will then receive their own copy of the message.

This means that owners of microcomputers will be able to obtain services that previously have only been available to bigger organisations that could justify the cost of installing a mainframe computer with a large memory. However, it is important not to get over-excited with the possibilities that technology will open up. While it may be possible to send an 'electronic letter' to a commercial customer in Hong Kong, which will arrive almost as soon as it is sent (computerised cable systems can search out routes and move messages from congested paths to those with low-message loadings), it is much less likely that your organisation will use electronic mailing to reach its thousands of small domestic customers in Wigan or Handsworth, because they do not possess a domestic microcomputer on which to receive these messages.

Another interesting development is that of sending documents electronically, such as legally binding contracts, using **facsimile transmission**. This is a process that involves breaking down illustrations that might be printed on official documents into binary digital signals to deter forgery. These are then transmitted to a remote receiver where they are converted either into a pattern of dots on a visual display unit, or printed out using a **dot-matrix printer** or a more sophisticated laser ink-jet printer, laser printer or electrostatic plotter. At present, there are growing numbers of facsimile transmission and copying machines popularly known as **fax** machines.

Unauthorised communication

Organisations have always been vulnerable to sensitive information finding its way into the hands of competitors. Confidential information is leaked for various reasons. Sometimes it is a question of principle, as when a chemist notified the EEC about the illegal activities of a multinational drug company for whom he worked; and sometimes for financial gain or political advantage, an activity known as industrial espionage. Although a serious problem in the days of paper technology, it has intensified with the introduction of wired offices because disloyal or greedy staff might take easily concealed tapes or discs home, copy them, and sell the copy to a rival organisation. The interactive nature of computer systems also increases the possibility of a database being raided by a computer buff with a domestic microcomputer, or by a rival organisation using a commercial Datel or Teletex service.

One preventive measure that is adopted to protect sensitive information is the use of **passwords**. A password is a computer code giving access only to parts of the computer's memory. Without the correct password the computer will not allow access. However, passwords can be learned or broken, even if changed frequently, and this is one reason why computer manufacturers are urgently pressing ahead with voice recognition and optical scanning devices, which should restrict the opportunity for unauthorised access to confidential information. Other security measures include **encryption** (scrambling information during transmission) and physical removal (taking the programme out of the computer and locking it away).

Storage

Every system needs to store information. This might be short-term information, in which case there may be an **in-tray**, or long-term information which will require a **file**, a document wallet or index card either hung in the drawers of a filing cabinet or arranged laterally on shelving or in a rotary cylinder. However, such storage systems are expensive in terms of floor-space and this explains the interest in alternative methods of long-term storage such as **microfilm** or **microfiche**. This is a process in which original documents are photographed and stored on 16 mm film, either in continuous rolls, or in the case of microfiche, on sheets of film. The impact that such systems can have is underlined by the fact that microfilm requires only 2 per cent of the storage space taken up by the original documents. There are disadvantages, of course, in the initial cost of the microfilm equipment, but these can be offset by the reduced demand for floor-space. Retrieval need not be a problem if the individual frames representing the original documents are clearly identified, but in general microfilming is applied only to *archive* material — by which is meant any filing that is no longer 'live' and that is unlikely to be needed in the ordinary course of business.

▲ *Rotary filing system. Rotary systems enable an employee to obtain cards without having to leave her seat.*

Material in paper storage systems is usually stored alphabetically. However, geographical and numerical indexes, based on account numbers, are also common. One problem with all filing systems is that files may need to be accessed by several staff. This means that if a file has been removed from its storage point, it has effectively 'disappeared'. In some offices, staff will leave a receipt slip in the empty sleeve to show who has taken the file, but in practice people are unwilling to do this on the basis that: 'I'll only keep it for a minute or two'. It is very annoying to open a filing cabinet to find neither the file nor any clue as to its whereabouts. Indeed, the filing and retrieving of documents is a major irritation and it is for this reason that the job is often given to new young staff, while experienced employees busy themselves with less boring work. The same attitude seems to be taken towards the weeding of files. **Weeding** is the process of removing unimportant paperwork, such as outdated memos and progress sheets. It is necessary to do this occasionally to prevent space being wasted and to make the retrieval of 'live' documents easier.

Electronic storage

As soon as scientists discovered a method of storing information electronically, the role of computers as databases began to open up. Computers offer the following important advantages over traditional filing systems.

Space

There are big savings in terms of space. As with microfilm storage, the mass storage of information on computer disc or tape is much less space-consuming than paper systems.

Time

There are savings in time. One entry on the computer can cause all related files to be simultaneously updated and nobody has to convey files to or from a cabinet or shelf before or after use.

Flexibility

The equipment is flexible. Computers are multifunctional, unlike the typewriter, filing cabinet and telephone, which all have single functions. A computerised work station can create text, store it, and send it elsewhere.

These advantages have to be set against a few minus points.

Down-time

This term describes the period when a computer is out of action because of a technical fault.

Erasure

The memory on a computer can be lost, perhaps by being wiped accidentally by an inexperienced operator, or by the physical deterioration of the storage medium, or even by a programme fault.

Error

Mistakes fed into the memory of a computer can have damaging consequences. Although the loss of a computer during a breakdown can be serious, the most catastrophic is the loss of a file. Machinery can always be replaced, but the Open University once lost the equivalent of fifteen years of research work when a fire destroyed computer tapes. Holding back-up copies of tapes and discs on- and off-site reduces this risk, but updating needs to be done at the end of each day. Indeed, many organisations have a dual system with a parallel paper file to use in the event of computer failure.

Computer memory is either internal or external. **Internal memory** is built into the computer either in the form of a chip or a bubble, but any data in an internal memory is lost every time the power is switched off. **External memory** is not integral with the computer, but comes in the form of discs or tapes that are inserted into the computer to give it access to the memory. Such memory is therefore not lost simply because the current is disconnected. Internal memories are those that enable data or text to be created, while those that store data are the external media. These media currently include the following.

Magnetic tape

This medium can be used for both mainframe and microcomputers. The disadvantage is that material is stored in linear sequence, like recorded music on cassette. You will know if you have a cassette player that finding a particular track can be time-consuming. The same is true with computer memory. For this reason magnetic tape, although widely used for home micros, is not very suitable for office use as too much time is spent searching through the memory.

Magnetic disc

This medium — whether floppy or rigid — despite storing information in linear sequence, gives faster access to data. It is for this reason that it is preferred for office uses.

Videodisc

At present, storage requirements are either for data or text, but in the future image-storing (e.g., for use with fax machine) will also be necessary. This requires high capacity storage, and videodisc or digital tape is the format ideal for data, text and image-storing.

The possibility also exists that internal computer memories will be capable of expansion and of retaining information even when the power is disconnected. This is an attractive proposition as they are 'solid state' functions, which, having no moving parts, are unlikely to go wrong. They also allow random access, which means they do not have to be scanned in linear sequence to locate data. Developments are moving fast in this field and this information may be out of date by the time you read it. Nonetheless, it is important to keep our feet firmly on the ground. Many organisations still have to maintain paper files for those customers who continue to communicate on paper, quite apart from providing cautious organisations with a fail-safe in the event of computer failure.

ACTIVITY

1 What forms of information storage are currently in use at your place of work? How effective are they? Take a copy of the chart and compare your answers with others in your class. Can you suggest any improvements to the methods used? We've made some suggestions to start you off, but leave plenty of space for your own.

Storage period	Medium used	Storage purpose	Effectiveness
Temporary	Filing basket	Work pending and completed	Good, on the whole. Can see what's left to do, but 'problems' can get forgotten at the bottom of the in-tray.
Medium term			
Archive	Microfilm.	All file material more than 5 years old.	It's a real bore finding things and not easy to read through the viewfinder – it strains my eyes! System collapses if there is a power cut, or if the equipment breaks down.

2 How much space is allocated at work for the storage of data? Calculate the ratio of storage space to other floor space in an office that you know. You may get permission to research your college office facilities if necessary.

3 If you believe that floor space and costs used in document storage could be reduced, draft a memo for submission to your section head outlining the possible ways in which this could be achieved. You may first wish to discuss this issue with your *Finance* and *Organisations in their environment* lecturers.

Information storage — the age of Big Brother?

Earlier we discussed the capability of computerised workstations to monitor employees' output and the possibility that a database might be raided by unauthorised computer operators seeking confidential information. The alarming prospect that organisations might be transmitting and receiving secret and possibly inaccurate information about us has increased demands that we should be able to see this information and that the people holding it should have a duty not to divulge it to others, at least not without our consent.

This led to the 1984 *Data Protection Act* which sought to safeguard individual citizens from malpractice. However, the Act only covered computerised records and many critics attacked it for not dealing with paper records as well. Since then the right to examine all records has been introduced, and school, housing and social service records are now available for inspection by those to whom they refer. The main provisions of the Data Protection Act are:

- All organisations and individuals who hold personal records on computers must register with the Data Protection Registrar (the government's watchdog).

- They must tell the registrar
  - what type of information they hold
  - what use is made of it
  - to whom the information may be disclosed
  - how they collected it.

- The Registrar has a duty to see that the data conforms to certain principles:
  - it must have been obtained openly and fairly.
  - it shall be held only for lawful purposes.
  - its uses and possible disclosure must be declared to the Registrar.
  - it must be relevant to its purpose.
  - it must be accurate and up-to-date.
  - it must be destroyed when it is no longer needed.
  - we are entitled to know what information is held and to challenge inaccuracies.
  - it must be protected against access by unauthorised persons.

- Organisations that do not comply may be liable to compensate us if we suffer as a consequence.

- There are, however, exceptions to the right to receive compensation. These include:
  - data that has been supplied by ourselves.
  - data that has been acquired with 'reasonable care'.
  - data held for payroll or pension purposes.
  - data held for statistical purposes, from which it is impossible to identify individuals.

Process

At the heart of any office system is the process by which the system inputs are converted into outputs. This will almost certainly be part of your role if you work in an office. But what tasks or stages are covered by the general heading of 'process'? This is a question that you can answer yourself by thinking about the jobs you see going on around you every day. They will almost certainly include:

- Sorting
- Checking and correcting
- Calculating
- Synthesising (or bringing parts together)
- Deciding

For example, when an accident insurance claim arrives at an office, it will be one of a large number of communications that needs to be **sorted** according to a predetermined procedure, say by letter of the alphabet. Documents received may first be entered in a post-book (a record of postal deliveries) and then despatched to the appropriate person for attention. Here the claim will be **checked** for completeness and accuracy. If unsatisfactory, additional details will be demanded. Meanwhile the business of **synthesising** various, perhaps conflicting versions of the accident on which the claim is based will be undertaken. This means amalgamating all the information until an acceptable version of events is agreed, on which the merits of the claim can be judged. Some **calculations** may then be made which reflect the options open to the company and a **decision** can be made about the offer (if any) in response to the claim.

Electronic processing

These sorts of tasks are those with which the microprocessor is designed to deal. Sorting, calculating data, editing and merging text are basic functions of computers. There may at the moment be a reluctance to allow computers to make 'decisions', but since the method by which we make decisions is probably no more than a process of elimination, it seems likely that computers could cope more rapidly and more fairly than we could ourselves. The calculation of statutory sick pay entitlement, for example, could easily be undertaken by computer, freeing payroll staff to concentrate on more complex, individual problems, where detailed investigation is demanded.

Computers process either data or text. Data processing involves all the activities we have been discussing, the most obvious being calculating. However, if only a simple calculation is required, a pocket calculator will be much quicker. Where a computer scores over a calculator is in its ability to integrate calculation with its other functions. The best example of this is known as the **spreadsheet**. This is a computerised data organisation programme, rather like the old-fashioned office ledgers. But instead of having to manually enter corrections or alterations to columns of figures every time one figure is changed, the spreadsheet will do this automatically, whenever the corrected figure appears in the account. There is still an initial need to enter the data manually, but once done the computer will rapidly and accurately perform functions that will save time and reduce boredom, and even produce additional information as a bonus. The ability to produce constantly updated financial projections or up-to-date cash flows, for example, is of enormous benefit to business managers.

Business accounting is probably the commonest use of computing in offices. Much of it began in the early days of computing, long before the present generation of mainframe and micros were even dreamt of. One common early application was to **payroll**, with the computer calculating total weekly or monthly pay and deduction rates. Since all employees who work for at least 16 hours a week are entitled by law to receive a detailed written pay statement, it is easy to see why this particular administrative chore was computerised. Even today, in large organisations, payroll programmes are more likely to be handled by a mainframe computer because the memory in a micro is unlikely to be capable of storing all the data. Here is how a computer might produce a pay slip.

HOW YOUR PAY SLIP IS PRODUCED BY COMPUTER

Your pay slip probably contains the following items:

— Your name, payroll number and work location
— Your grade and rate of pay
— Number of hours worked
— Gross pay (before deductions)
— Deductions, including tax, insurance, superannuation and voluntary stoppages
— Your net pay

Even though all of these items are not printed on your pay slip, the computer will need to have the details so your pay can be calculated. Some information is fairly static and does not require many changes, such as your payroll number, grade, rate of pay, Income Tax and National Insurance contribution. These are therefore held in the computer's memory. The only item which might vary from one pay period to another is the number of hours worked, so this is usually entered manually at the end of each pay period. These statistics are entered when they become available, but they may well be 'batched' and fed into the computer department by department. When this work is done, pre-printed blanks are loaded into a printer and pay advice slips printed out, either in payroll number order, by department, or even alphabetically. If a cashless pay system is in operation, the company will instruct its bank to credit the accounts of individuals with the net pay shown on their pay slips. This information is then transmitted to the bank using manual methods or electronically via cable data transmission.

Name	Hours 1	Pay 1	Hours 2	Pay 2	Hours 3	Pay 3	Hours 4	Pay 4	Basic Rate	
	A	80.00 B	2 C	6.00 D	1 E	4.00 F			2.00 G	

Date	Salary	Other Pay 1	Other Pay 2	Other Pay 3	Other Pay 4	Other Pay 5	Other Pay 6	Gross Pay
30.8.85.	80.00 H	10.00 I	I	I	I	I	I	90.00 J

Dept	Pers. No.	Tax	N.I.	Co. Pension	STD. DED. 1	STD. DED. 2	STD. DED. 3	Other DEDs.	Total DEDs
2 K	123 L	14.10 M	8.11 N	0.00 O	0.00 P	0.00 P	0.00 P	0.00 Q	22.21 R

Tax Code	Period No.	Gross to Date	Tax to Date	N.I. to Date	Co. Pen to Date			N/Tax Allce.
220L S	21 T	1906.20 U	303.90 V	171.74 W	0.00 X			Y

NET Pay
67.79 Z

EXAMPLE PAY SLIP

A Hours worked at the basic rate of pay.
B Pay due at the basic rate.
C Hours worked at time and a half (overtime).
D Overtime pay due at time and a half.
E Hours worked at double rate overtime.
F Pay due for double rate overtime.
G Basic hourly rate of pay.
H Total basic pay due.
I Total overtime pay due — any other extras, e.g. seasonal bonus, commission or any sick pay due will appear in the 'other pay' boxes.
J Total pay for that week.
K Department reference, e.g. accounts dept.
L Person reference. This is used for the company's personnel department's filing purposes.
M Income tax payable on the gross pay for that week.

N National Insurance contribution payable.
O Company pension contributions (if applicable).
P Standard (fixed) deductions for union subscriptions, voluntary savings schemes etc.
Q Other deductions, again either by arrangement or with a written explanation from the employer.
R Total deductions, fixed and variable.
S Tax code. The current normal code for a childless single person is 220L. This indicates the total amount you may earn in a year before your wages are taxable, in this case £2,200. This is then calculated as a weekly figure, in this case £42.30, which is deducted from your gross pay and the remainder is taxed. The person in the example therefore pays income tax on £47.70 of his/her gross pay. The actual amounts are calculated by the Inland Revenue and issued to employers as tax tables.

T Period number. This refers to the relevant tax week, counting the full week commencing around April 6th as week 1.
U Gross pay to date — the person in the example has earned £1,906.20 to date over the previous 21 weeks.
V Tax paid to date.
W Total National Insurance contributions paid to date.
X Total company pension to date. You may not be in a pension scheme, in which case this will not affect you. If you are and you leave your job, you may be eligible to receive a refund of part of your contributions.
Y Non-taxable allowance. For certain specialised jobs, you will receive a non-taxable allowance which usually covers out of pocket expenses necessary for you to do that job, e.g. special clothing allowance.
Z Net pay. This is the amount you finally receive.

▲ *Example of a pay slip, courtesy of the Midland Bank*

The processing of text is handled by word processors. It is a mistake to think of a word processor as a glorified typewriter, although there are similarities, especially when it is used to produce letters for customers and suppliers. However, a word processor has a number of additional features, which increase its range of functions. For example, it is now possible to buy dictionary programmes so that any document can be checked for spelling mistakes before it goes out. Another valuable function is its ability to improve the image on the page. Because a letter can be held in a word processor's short-term memory, it is possible to make alterations to the layout before it is printed on paper. For instance, it will **justify** text or rearrange it so that each full line of text is exactly the same length as every other line by minutely varying the spaces between words. This used to be a time-consuming job for printers and impossible to do on most typewriters, but computers perform the task in the twinkling of an eye.

Text as entered into word processor

Text 'justified' to ensure lines of equal length

Text 'centred' — useful for notices

Text arranged in columns — useful for newsletters

▲ *Text arrangements on word processors*

Alternatively, the text may be arranged in columns, say when producing a newsletter for clients or for a house newspaper. Centring of text, instead of working to a left-hand margin, is also possible, as is the arrangement of text into numbered pages ready for printing, which is very useful if the document being prepared is a lengthy formal report.

A word processor will also **merge** text. This means that a letter, for example, can be personalised by merging unique details with a standard text. So if an organisation wishes to chase up a bad debt, the standard letter can be accessed from the word processor's memory and the machine instructed to insert the specific details — account name, number, amount outstanding — into the text, without the chore of writing or typing details on a pre-printed letter.

Another advantage is in the production of circular letters which look exactly like individually typed and addressed correspondence. The text of the circular is keyed into the word processor with blank spaces. It is then 'merged' with the existing list of customer names and addresses held in the machine's memory. When instructed to print the merged circulars, the machine can be safely left to print the letters by itself while the employee collects the printed letters, puts them through the folding machine and supervises their insertion into envelopes, which are also addressed by the word processor.

ACTIVITY

Collect a few examples of circulars produced by word processor. Do the functions described — editing, justifying and merging — appear to enhance the impact of the circular? Circulars, as a vehicle of communication, are discussed in Chapter 3.

Outputs

In our discussions about the various elements of office systems, particularly 'inputs' and 'communication', we have covered much of the media used in the process of outputting.

ACTIVITY

Think about your own office systems and suggest a few examples of outputs that utilise each of these media.

- Spoken (face-to-face)
- Telephone call
- Hand-written
- Typed or printed on word processor
- Printed
- Electronic transmission, other than phone calls

It is likely that each medium is regularly in use and that you were able to identify many examples. The verdict to a successful candidate at an interview may be delivered *face-to-face*; a *telephone call* may be used to authorise a purchase; a *hand-written* letter of congratulation to an employee may seem more sincere than its type-written equivalent. On the other hand, *typed* letters to customers give a business more status than hand-written ones, and a catalogue or sales pamphlet will certainly be *printed*. Even an office that is not wired up for new technology may still possess its faithful old Telex machine for the *transmission* of text.

Voice systems

The telephone has been used for input and output in office systems for generations. However, the telephone on your desk today is different from that which existed only ten years ago. Most businesses now have a PABX (private automatic branch exchange) that allows internal calls to be made between extension telephones without going through an operator. External calls can be made 'direct', although most organisations restrict this facility to designated phones or to a defined geographical area (usually by charge band), so that expensive trunk calls have to be logged individually. The difficulty is to strike a balance between overwhelming the switchboard and running up expensive bills as talkative employees ring colleagues in remote branch offices.

ACTIVITY

As manager of the Claims Department of *Imperial Insurance* you learn that telephone charges for your department were 25 per cent above target for the last quarter. You are told to 'toughen up' by your board and bring costs down within budget. Prepare a memo for all staff in your department, outlining the action you intend to take.

Some recent innovations in telephone technology include the following:

Answering machines

These are cassette recorders that have a short loop message which is played to callers when no-one is available to take a call — perhaps at night when the office is shut. Incoming calls are recorded on the answering machine and the matter attended to when the office reopens. Two variants on this are possible. First, people travelling can telephone their own answering machine and instruct it to play back messages that have been left, or second, the machine can be used as a 'filter' if somebody wishes not to be disturbed or is being bothered by nuisance calls at home. (Genuine calls can then be taken by switching off the machine and talking directly to the caller.)

Rerouting devices

If an extension does not answer within a specified time, or if already instructed to do so by the user of the extension, a phone will transfer a call automatically to another line where someone else can answer it.

Loudspeaker telephones

These devices permit the caller or the receiver to be heard in or to speak from any part of the room. They also permit both hands to be free for taking notes or dealing with paperwork. The argument for their introduction is that they avoid time wasted in getting back to the original caller, and retrieval or calculations are possible while continuing the dialogue.

Internal memory

Handsets can now be programmed to memorise frequently called numbers, avoiding the need to press a sequence of digits.

Automatic redial

A handset with memory can be instructed to redial a number if it was engaged or the person sought after was unavailable at the previous attempt.

Queuing

Calls can be 'stored' so that as soon as a line is free the next call in the queue will be switched through. This explains why a phone will often ring again as soon as the receiver goes down and why we can never get an outside line!

Store-and-forward

If we wish to make a call but can't get through, the telephone will keep trying until successful, while the employee gets on with some useful work.

ACTIVITY

1 Think about the amount of time you spend on the phone each day.

— How much time is spent on incoming calls?
— How much time do you spend making calls?
— How effective is the time you spend on the phone?
— Do your callers always get the answers and help that they want?
— How much of your time making calls is wasted because the number you want is engaged or the person isn't available?

Discuss these and other points that come up in discussion within your group.

2 Draft a policy statement for new staff, giving them advice on effective telephone technique, both as receivers and senders of calls. It should describe the technical capabilities of the system as well as reminding them of their role as embassadors for the organisation.

Typed and printed systems

The most basic item of equipment in the office of the 20th century has been the typewriter. These machines still produce the bulk of the documentation that represents the output of most office systems. Despite recent advances, *manual typewriters* continue to be bought, both for business and domestic use. They require no electrical power source and they are portable because of their lightweight construction. Furthermore, businesses which have few office functions (e.g., small painter/decorator like Ken in Chapter 1) continue to use manuals because more expensive typewriters are simply unnecessary.

A manual typewriter has a movable carriage through which the paper is fed. However *electrical typewriters* have dispensed with this cumbersome device in favour of a 'golf ball' or 'daisy wheel' head, which moves across the page instead. The advantage of electrical machines over manual ones is their greater speed and the more even quality of the printed image.

▲ *Manual typewriter showing direction of carriage movement*

▲ *Daisy wheel disc*

▲ *Golf ball head*

The new generation of *electronic typewriters*, which retain the fixed carriage of their electrical predecessors, represent a further advance by incorporating a memory for storing text and a small built-in display — although this shows only a limited number of characters at any one time. It is therefore similar to a word processor, although it has two advantages.

- It is an integral unit and therefore occupies less space.
- It is cheaper than a word processor and it offers comparable print quality.

Word processing, nonetheless, represents a major advance in the preparation of documents, as we have discussed earlier. You will remember that a word processor is a computer designed to produce text rather than data, but it can also be one of the functions of an integrated workstation in a wired office — a point which we take up later. The production of documents by word processor is a function of the *printer* in the system. The two basic types of printer are:

- *Impact printers* in which images are printed by means of impacting (e.g., typewriters print by striking the letter shape through a ribbon onto the receiving page).

- *Ink-jet systems* in which ink is sprayed onto the receiving page.

Impact printing using either a daisy wheel or a *dot-matrix* printer is most common. Daisy wheel printers are cheaper but slower than other methods, but access to a wide range of print faces and sizes is possible simply by changing the daisy wheel. Dot-matrix printers produce dot-like configurations on paper that represent the desired image, whether text, heading or illustration. This allows a keyboard operator to produce both text and *graphics* and an example of output from a dot-matrix printer follows. You can form your own judgement of the system on the basis of this example.

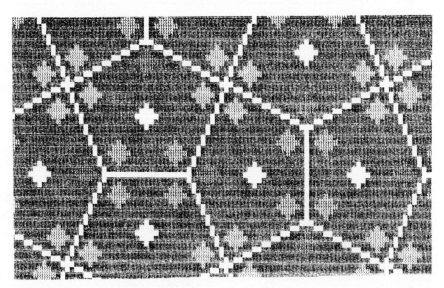

```
ABCDEFGHIJKLMNOPQRSTUVWXYZ[\]^_`abcdefghijklmno
BCDEFGHIJKLMNOPQRSTUVWXYZ[\]^_`abcdefghijklmnop
CDEFGHIJKLMNOPQRSTUVWXYZ[\]^_`abcdefghijklmnopq
DEFGHIJKLMNOPQRSTUVWXYZ[\]^_`abcdefghijklmnopqr
```

▲ *Text and illustration produced with a dot-matrix printer*

Ink-jet printers produce good quality images — with the difference in quality between dot-matrix and ink-jet systems particularly marked. Not only do ink-jet printers give good results, they are also very fast. Some machines can now print whole pages at once by first transferring the image to a special paper electronically, before being sprayed with ink. As the ink only adheres to the electronic image, the surplus ink is washed away. The system is so fast that this whole textbook could be printed in less than a minute. However, such systems are clearly designed for publishing output and do not belong in the everyday office.

ACTIVITY

1 How are letters produced at your place of work? Estimate the proportions by putting a percentage in the box:

	%	
Hand-written	☐	Your total
Electrical typewriters	☐	should
Electronic typewriters	☐	add up to
Word processors	☐	100

2 Does your organisation have a typing pool? How are instructions about letter content sent to typists?

	%
Handwritten drafts	☐
Dictated tape-recorded messages (e.g., dictaphone)	☐
Dictated to short-hand/speed	☐
Composed by senders directly onto word processors	☐

3 Is it likely that in future all staff will need to possess keyboard skills? What effect will this have on existing typists and on the specialist functions of the typing pool?

Other image systems

The remaining image producers used in offices are the *copiers* and *duplicators*. Copiers generate new images from original documents by one of three processes: electrostatically (Xerox is the best known machine), by heat transfer, or photographically. The latter is the most common method in use in offices. Although not expensive, the ease with which documents can now be copied can lead to a proliferation of paperwork, some of which is unnecessary. Messages can be produced at a tremendous rate because the means to do so cheaply now exist, and not because the recipients need the information. Yet, as we have already discussed in Chapter 2, this means that because information is distributed indiscriminately, staff are unable or unwilling to sort out the important from the unimportant.

Traditional duplicating in offices has utilised the following processes.

● Spirit duplicators (e.g., Banda)
● Ink duplicators (e.g., Gestetner)
● Offset duplicators (e.g., Rotaprint)

Spirit duplicating

This requires a master written or typed on a carbon sheet to transfer the carbon image to the receiving paper, which is then washed with spirit during the duplicating process. Though cheap to use, it is unsuitable for long runs (i.e., more than 100 copies) and the quality of the reproduced image is poor.

Ink duplicating

For this, masters are produced on wax stencils. These are either cut mechanically by a typewriter or electrically using a scanner to burn minute dots into the surface of the stencil. The stencil is then secured to the drum of the duplicator and ink is forced under pressure through the stencil onto the paper. Highly absorbent paper is needed otherwise the image smudges before the ink dries during the printing process. Because the paper is coarse, this process is also unsuitable for the production of good quality documentation.

Offset duplicating

This process also uses ink and produces an image, not directly from a master, but indirectly from a 'blanket', to which the image is transferred. It is this indirectness which gives 'offset' duplicating its name. A paper, plastic or flexible foil plate is first made from a photographic copy of the original artwork and attached to rollers in the machine.

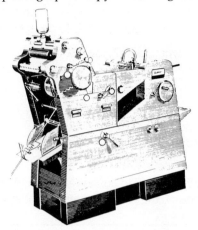

► *An offset duplicator*

Paper plates are less expensive than foil but they are less durable. About 5000 copies can be expected from a paper plate, although a foil plate with a good image can produce up to 50 000 copies. This is a versatile and efficient printing process, and an organisation with a sizeable output of paperwork is likely to have reprographic facilities. Although initially expensive, the long print runs and superior results make offset duplicating cost-effective.

New generation copiers

Recent developments in photocopying techniques are leading many organisations to utilise new 'big' or 'super-copiers' as an alternative to traditional imaging services. The new generation of copiers are highly versatile machines. In addition to copying, many are capable of reducing, enlarging, distorting, lightening or darkening the original image. Nor is it necessary to feed originals individually into the machine. Artwork originals for an entire booklet can be loaded into a 'big' copier and the machine will then make copies on both sides of the receiving paper, collate into page order, and staple the finished product ready for use. 'Super-copiers' go one stage further. They incorporate a type-setting capability and can therefore be used to originate materials as well as copy them.

Desk-top publishing

These new copiers can be useful in complementing the new concept of desk-top publishing. This represents the fusion of three important computing capabilities.

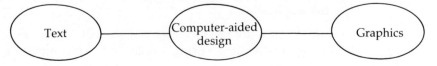

This has revolutionised the publicity and promotional output of many organisations. Publicity leaflets and newsletters for customers can be prepared in-house without the need to turn to a specialist agency. It is now possible for an employee with a word processor to compose the titles and text for a leaflet at his/her own workstation. Typefaces and illustrations can be accessed from a library in the computer's memory, and combined to produce a layout. The layout, too, is composed on the operator's VDU, before being printed on the desk-top laser printer to produce an original for use either with the offset printer, or for direct photocopying. If a super-copier is available, there is the possibility of sending the composed layout electronically to the copier, where an image is produced and then copied by just one piece of machinery. An example of what a desk-top publishing programme can do is illustrated. It is taken from a promotional leaflet showing the *Aldus Page Maker* from Apple Computer (UK) Ltd.

 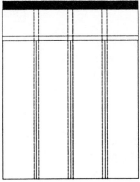 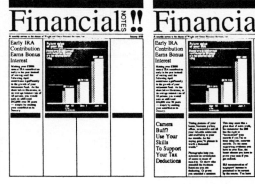 

I

Begin page production as usual: by preparing text, illustrations and graphics. With PageMaker, you key text into your word processor, defining type specifications as you go.

Later, you can revise and copy specifications at will with the built-in text editor. By creating illustrations or graphics with MacPaint or MacDraw and bringing them directly into PageMaker, you avoid the delay and cost of camera work.

II

Next, you develop a page format to use throughout the publication. (PageMaker automatically accommodates left-right page orientation.) Begin with the blank page on the screen and define the margins, the number of columns, their width and the space between them.

Your screen shows these as dotted lines to guide you in placing text and graphics on the page. On-screen rulers also assist placement. You can scale your screen ruler to work in inches, millimetres or picas and points.

III

Now, you bring the text or illustration into PageMaker, move the pointer to where you want it placed and click the button. Page-Maker "fills" a column with text, then allows you to flow remaining copy to another column or page. It lets you crop or proportionally scale the illustration to fit a given space.

As you add copy and illustrations to the page, you can change columns, type styles and other elements as you wish. A built-in library of borders and fill patterns lets you add designer touches such as grids and diagonal lines.

Background tints and reversed type allow you to produce high quality layouts - quickly and easily.

IV

Once the page looks the way you want, print it on the Laser-Writer. Use your page as camera-ready artwork and send it to a commercial printer. PageMaker will have saved you time and money.

Electronic output

In order that human operators can read computer data, the data is converted into a visual display: a monitor containing a cathode ray tube. These monitors are known as **VDUs** (visual display units). The remaining electronic outputs — electronic mailing, Teletex facsimile transmission — have already been dealt with earlier in this chapter.

Control

So far in this chapter we have looked at office systems and examined the ways in which electronics have further enhanced processes that have been evolving over many years. What has come through clearly is the remarkable versatility of computers, especially their application as a means of communicating, storage, processing, inputting and outputting to and from the system. The one element we have not so far considered is that of control.

Control is normally in the hands of managers and supervisors. However, computers not only can handle tasks, they can also supply management with information about the progress of such tasks. This information can be helpful in identifying:

- Peaks and troughs in demand
- Congestion points in the system
- Delays in dealing with tasks
- Elements in the system that need to be replanned
- Resource needs

Access to this information is not just rapid — before computerisation it may not have seemed worthwhile even to collect it. Management now has a great deal more data, a much more responsive feedback loop. You will remember reading about feedback loops in Chapter 2, and some of the uses to which such information are put are dealt with in the section on Method Study in Chapter 9. You might find it helpful to read these before you continue.

The office of tomorrow

What are we likely to find in the office workstations of the future? Although at present paper storage and handling are the determining factors in desk-top management (hence the 'clean desk' mentality), and paper transactions in some business activities will continue for the foreseeable future, there is no doubt that the key trends in tomorrow's office will be based on electronic equipment. The items illustrated in the following diagram are likely to be found on your desk before very long — perhaps they are there already!

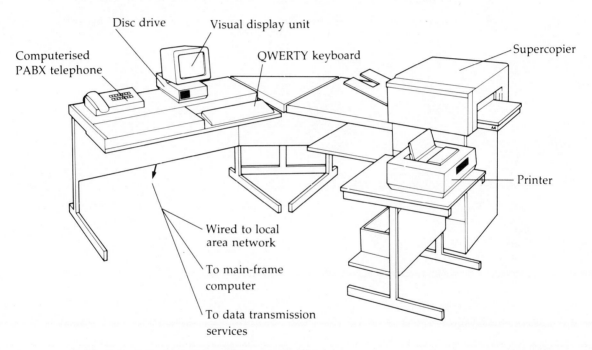

▲ *The layout of a typical late 20th century office*

All this assumes that offices of the future are likely to exist, but since the introduction of the microprocessor has made the Stock Exchange building redundant, and almost overnight rendered some economic textbooks out of date, could not the actual habit of working for an organisation be similarly undermined? If ours is to become a genuinely wired society, with the benefits of computerised communication widely available to us for domestic purposes, why then should the same equipment and transmission services not be used for work as well? It is this realisation that has made many people face the possibility that the salaried office worker of the 20th century may become the freelance home-based worker of the 21st century, communicating with other workers through a small centralised HQ by means of computer.

Such employment already exists and is known as **networking**. To date, the best known example of this work-from-home system is *F International*, a company started by Steve Shirley for freelance computer programmers. However, the important difference between this approach and the radical decentralisation envisaged here, is that *F International* began as a way of giving mainly working women an opportunity to continue their work from home, something which many women have to forego during child rearing. *F International* and its related companies do have headquarters premises and something akin to the traditional bureaucratic organisational structure that was outlined in Chapter 1. However, the company is evidence of the success that can be achieved with a predominantly networked workforce working from home.

A final thought. Some employees can be forgiven for taking a 'Luddite' view of the wired society. Luddites were early 19th century workers, who, fearing that mechanisation and the introduction of factory methods in the textile industry would ruin their livelihoods, broke into the new mills and smashed machinery. Indeed, there is a bit of the Luddite in all of us. When the office manager unwraps the new micro that 'is going to do the work of you lot in half the time', and then spends two days failing to get it to work, there is great satisfaction expressed in the canteen! Nonetheless, there is another side to this coin and we must keep in the forefront of our minds that computerisation:

- Frees employees from less rewarding duties and allows them to concentrate on more stimulating work.
- Erodes divisive status differences between managerial, clerical and secretarial staff.
- Enables organisations to take on a greater volume of work.

More information on office development can be found in Chapter 9.

WHAT IS A COMPUTER?

A computer is an electronic data storage system. The structure of a computer is therefore very similar to that of the office system described in this chapter. It can be represented in a simple diagram:

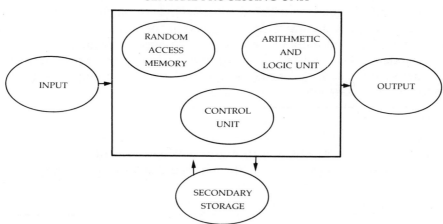

Input devices include keyboards, optical scanners and, in older computers, punched tape or card-readers. When information is fed into the computer it is first held in the random access memory (RAM), which is volatile. In other words, when the computer is switched off, that information will be lost unless it has previously been transferred to a non-volatile form of secondary storage. This will be either a disc or a tape. The scope of the volatile RAM is measued in the number of bits of information it will hold, usually a letter or number that can be displayed on the visual display unit. These are frequently called 'bytes' but because these are small units, computer jargon refers to RAM capacity in terms of kilobytes (i.e., 1024 bytes). A typical office computer has a 64 K memory; that is an approximate capacity of 64 000 possible letters or numbers. The two other elements of the central processing unit are the logic unit, which determines the operational limits of the computer, and the control unit, which integrates the hardware elements with the software elements.

The software in a computer is the programme that determines the applications to which the hardware will be put. As explained earlier, programmes and memory are formatted either on tape or disc. This makes it easy for a variety of programmes with differing applications to be loaded into the computer, making it a general-purpose device capable of tackling a range of problems.

As we have seen already, computers are communicating devices. As such, they need to communicate internally between application programmes and central processing unit. They may also need to communicate with each other and with their human operators. The languages used by the computers themselves are usually specific to a particular manufacturer's equipment. There is a sound commercial reason for this. Incompatibility between suppliers means that having bought the hardware, a user is compelled to buy software from the same source!

The basis of all computer language is the binary code. You will be familiar with binary number systems from your maths classes at school. However, all symbols in computer language — not just numbers — are represented in binary form. Because of the need to read digits quickly, modern computer designers have replaced digits with mnemonics (symbolic codes). This provides the computer with a language, which is then 'read' by a programme known as an assembler.

Although this may explain what goes on within the machine, a further set of operator languages also exist, usually to permit programming. The two best known are BASIC (beginners all purpose symbolic instruction code) and COBOL (common business orientated language). Fortunately, the need to master such language is starting to diminish, as is the need to employ specialist computer staff. The availability of an increasing number of off-the-shelf packages for standard office applications makes the need to master programming and the associated specialist languages unnecessary for the employee who wishes to sit at a workstation and 'get on with the job'.

Read the accompanying article *What is a computer?* You have been asked by your departmental head to give a short presentation to a group of newly recruited staff, outlining the role of computerisation in your office. She tells you that 'as you are doing this course at college, you can put it to some good use'.

TASK ONE / MAKING NOTES

Draft notes for your talk, drawing on:
— the article
— other information about computerisation in this chapter
— your own experience.

TASK TWO / YOUR TALK

In small groups, use your notes to deliver your talk. (See Chapter 6 for hints on talking to groups.)

Afterwards jot down any new material that you learned from other people's presentations.

Your manager is so impressed by your talk that she invites you to take the matter a stage further by asking you to review existing clerical duties and to recommend any computerisation that could provide benefits.

TASK THREE / THE REPORT

Prepare a short formal report examining existing clerical procedures, and making recommendations, where appropriate, for additional computer applications in your own office.

Note: Use the checklist to organise your thinking. You may wish to contact some manufacturers to ask about the software and hardware that is currently available. Here are some useful addresses:

Apricot Computers Ltd, Fulbourn Rd, Cherry Hinton, Cambridge, CB1 4JN

ICL Ltd, ICL House, Putney High St, London, SW15 1SW

Apple Computer (UK) Ltd, Eastman Way, Hemel Hemstead, Herts, HP2 7HQ

IBM (UK) Ltd, 389 Chiswick High Rd, London, W4 4AL

Office technology checklist

There are four stages in the process of identifying areas to which new technology can be applied.

Stage 1 — *Analyse* the existing system.

Stage 2 — *Identify problems*. Are there delays in the existing system? Are there activities you want to tackle more quickly? Are your competitors quicker than you?

Stage 3 — *Solution*. Could any or all problems be solved with improved manual systems or with computerisation?

Stage 4 — *Equipment*. What hardware (machinery) and software (programmes) are needed to enable the computerised solutions to be implemented?

In stages 1 and 2 of your deliberations you may find it helpful to remember the model of office systems discussed earlier.

Input

- Do any of your customers/clients have data/facsimile transmission capabilities?
- Would you be more attractive to potential customers if you had these facilities?
- Do you need to use any of the large information databases (e.g., Prestel)?

Communication

- Would you benefit from being able to keep in touch with remote staff through telecommunications (e.g., 'paging' devices or car phones)?
- Does your existing telephone system let you down? Could it be modernised?

Storage

- Is your filing system a lengthy business?
- Does it take up a lot of floor space?

Process

- Is book-keeping a labour-intensive operation?
- Does it involve the duplication of effort in many departments?
- How easy is it to update or retrieve 'short-term' information (e.g., to check on progress or to reschedule appointments and meetings)?

Outputs

- Does your organisation issue many routine letters or documents with substantially similar phraseology?
- Do you need to send data rapidly to clients or other parts of your organisation in remote locations?

Control

- Does your organisation have all the management information it needs to maintain or improve efficiency?
- Could computers be used to improve forward planning?

SCENARIO

Your organisation runs a *Suggestion Scheme*, which provides generous cash payments for the best ideas put forward by staff that are subsequently adopted.

Portable computers on the road

DO YOU really want to compute on your lap? How many times have you urgently needed to transmit data to headquarters while negotiating Spaghetti Junction?

Not very often. But most computer-makers have, rather rashly, expected high-flying executives to scoop up as many portable computers as they can fit on their laps. There are at least 15 different battery-driven computers small and light enough to sit on a knee. All are powerful machines capable of doing a number of office jobs. a system which has helped it cut, by up to a third, the time it takes for orders to be executed.

Portable computing is only successful when the machines are part of a larger system made up of bigger computers and the telephone network. Cake-mix manufacturer Pillsbury has such a system which has helped it cut, by up to a third, the time it takes for orders to be executed.

Pillsbury makes a range of cake-mixes and pre-baked dough products which it sells to shops and super-markets throughout the UK. Twentyfive representatives, based at home, visit shops and take orders.

' Retailers want a turnaround within a week. To meet this, we had to computerise,' says Stuart Johnson, Pillsbury's technical data processing manager.

Pillsbury had to streamline the process of entering the orders into the main computer which runs the firm's order-processing system. Johnson and his colleagues had two options: they could either set up their own system, which would have cost around £200,000, or they could use an outside computer bureau to channel the orders into the company. The bureau was a far cheaper option, so Pillsbury chose Telecom Gold, a British Telecom company that runs an electronic mailbox service.

Telecom Gold, and similar companies, are computerised versions of telephone message services. Instead of leaving a message with a person, it is placed in a large computer which has parts of its storage area divided into personalised ' mailboxes.' To use the service, you need a computer, a modem and the telephone.

Once the rep has typed the order, the information is not altered or retyped. This ' single-keying ' saves consider-able time and effort.

The system was introduced slowly, starting in Scotland. ' The reps were very keen to use the portables because it saves them rushing home to get orders into the post by 6 pm. It only took them about half a day to learn how to use the machines,'

' The next stage in our plans is to send the reps information, like journey plans, special offers and new accounts, in the same way,' The combination of portable computers, which cost around £400 each, including the soft-ware, and the mailbox service has helped Pillsbury cut its delivery times by up to one third. The customers, the most important factor in computeris-ing, receive their goods faster.

TASK ONE / THE MEMO

Read the accompanying article on portable computers, which was published in the *Observer* (March 23 1986) and write a memo containing a suggestion for applying this technology to your own organisation. You should consider how it could be used by:

— field officers
— delivery staff
— agents
— sales representatives

or any other staff whose work takes them away from their office base.

Now read the article about working from home as a 'networker', which was published in the *Independent* (2 March 1987).

Your organisation is about to launch a pilot scheme for networked staff. It is likely that the first batch of networkers will be current 'on site' employees, who, for a variety of reasons, prefer to work from home. However, they first need to become self-employed by losing their status as full-time employees.

How it pays to hang around the house

Clare Raffael reports on the trend towards working from home

A potential "cold fish across the face". This was the description of Roger Walker, the first Rank Xerox networker, of an increasingly common working practice.

Mr Walker was involved in an experiment pioneered by Rank Xerox in October 1981, under which employees who could no longer be employed full-time were sponsored to set up their own businesses and continue working for Xerox from computer terminals at home.

Mr Walker, whose company now has 63 employees and a turnover of £750,000, would not change his way of working now "for the world". But although he says the benefits are unlimited and indisputable, he also believes that before networking is undertaken, questions must be asked of all involved to avoid mistakes.

Neither he nor his family, for example, had any idea of how their lives would change. They found it difficult to adjust, though in the long term he believes their life will be better. Working longer hours, Roger Walker spends far more time with his children than he ever did when he was working "on-site". They in turn have developed a healthy understanding of business and the pressures of self-employment.

Other networkers feel that the increased flexibility in their working lives adds to their satisfaction in other ways. ICL "off-site" workers have moved from London to Manchester with scarcely a hiccup. The possibility of living in rural areas without the need to commute, and the chance to pursue a hobby more easily, make it attractive. For many disabled people, networking is the only way they can pursue a career.

In physical terms adjustments are needed. Although computer equipment is becoming progressively smaller and neater, working at home takes up space: about 100 sq ft seems to be the consensus. Some newly built housing in Oxfordshire incorporates specially designed computer workspace.

Financially, the networker is unlikely to lose money. Both Rank Xerox and ICL said that those working off-site would not be paid less, task for task, than on-site employees. For the self-employed working at home there can be tax advantages. The Inland Revenue is loath to be explicit, but a 20 per cent allowance on total housing costs (including mortgage) seems to be normal.

Any employer considering implementing a computerised network scheme for homeworker will become aware of the man constraints. It is rare that an exist ing job can be translated exactly into a home-based one; most new networkers will find themselves filling different functions. Only certain jobs are suitable, particularly those involving processing information.

Social contact in an office, as well as giving a feeling of belonging, provides a forum for ideas. "Neighbourhood" offices, where networkers can meet periodically, help to fill these gaps, though the office atmosphere can never really be replaced. Most networkers emphasise that they rely to a large extent on the emotional and professional support of the mother company.

The three main companies to have implemented networking systems, Rank Xerox, F-International and ICL, all agree that success lies in the psychological make-up and motivation of the individual.

It is a common myth that as technology develops, so will the use of employees working at home. In fact, the technology is almost incidental. Much more important is the attraction of home working to the employees. Many people, for example, feel isolated. The classic introvert could develop into a "Bunker Bill", losing all sense of purpose or of the world around him.

Diana Hill, who manages 160 of ICL's off-site employees, stresses that candidates are put through a rigorous selection process. The company looks for self-starters — people who can demonstrate independence and initiative, and who find a particular satisfaction in working alone. They are generally highly qualified people who are expert in their field.

A high level of motivation is vital. Rank Xerox believes that networkers should form limited companies, gaining a sense of ownership that encourages them to go beyond their initial assignments. Financial responsibility helps to dampen the natural tendency, as one networker points out, to mow the lawn if the sun is shining, rather than sit indoors in front of a computer terminal.

ICL's approach is very different. All off-site workers are employees, with the same job security and fringe benefits (pro-rata if they are part-time) normally applied throughout the company. The majority are women with young children who were unwilling to give up work and forfeit ICL's investment in training them. With the new system, both parties win.

There is a general feeling that networkers have less opportunity for promotion, and the preponderance of women supports this. But for those who are self-employed that is not the case. Roger Walker's success story is somewhat overshadowed by the ebullient Mrs Steve Shirley, whose company, F-International, has just celebrated its silver jubilee. From an initial capital of £6 and first year revenue of £700, the company has grown to a group that is well up in the league table of UK-based computing services firms, providing work for more than 1,000 people.

Where productivity is concerned the experience of all concerned is unanimous — Diana Hill estimates that about 25 hours of home-working is equivalent to a traditional working week. The experience at Rank Xerox is more startling — networkers are hour for hour consistently twice as productive; and the effect on earnings is obvious. These estimates take no account of the savings that are made on substantially reduced overheads.

Figures published by the IMS in the spring *Labour Force Survey* show a slow but steady decline in the relative size of the "permanent" workforce, from 70 per cent of the total workforce in 1981 to 66 per cent in 1985. The decline is consistent enough confidently to predict a figure of 64 per cent for this year. The requirement for increasingly flexible work patterns is not disputed, and the potential application of networking is wide.

So why have so few employers exploited the obvious benefits of networking? Roger Walker has been asked for advice by many companies. His only explanation is that, while they are right to be cautious, "they just aren't seeing outside the square".

TASK TWO / THE ARTICLE

Prepare a 250-word article for your organisation's in-house newsletter, announcing the introduction of a networker scheme, and outlining its possible attractions for members of staff. You should point out any factors that you feel might make it unsuitable for some categories of personnel.

TASK THREE / THE QUESTIONS

Draft a list of at least 10 questions on behalf of your Personnel Department to be used by panelists interviewing staff members who are interested in becoming networkers. You should draw on the reported experiences of organisations using networkers in the article. Ensure that the questions are probing and do not merely require 'Yes' or 'No' answers.

Love them or hate them, computers are an important part of our lives. You may know how to use one, but do you understand how they work? Test your knowledge with this quiz compiled by Chris Bigos and published in *Office Secretary* in September 1986. You can find the answers at the end of the chapter.

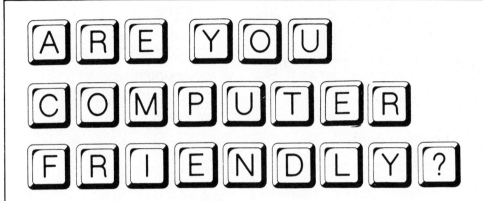

1 BACK-UP refers to:

a The pile of draft letters in the in-tray to be word-processed, which builds to a peak around 5 p.m.

b The regular copying of your computer files in case anything corrupts the originals.

c The physiological condition induced when your boss demands a change to the report you've just typed (only applies if you don't use a word processor).

2 FLOPPY DISK refers to:

a A moist, anti-static pad used to clean computer equipment to prevent the build-up of dust.

b The medical condition suffered by computer operators using badly designed workstations.

c A thin, flexible disk a computer uses to store information on.

3 MICRO-CHIPS are:

a Small, black, "chip-shaped" mites with 16 legs that can breed inside dusty microcomputers.

b Tiny pieces that could be chipped off the corners of a microcomputer if a protective sheet is not spread over it when not in use.

c Small, black, "chip-shaped" objects, usually with 16 legs, that can be found inside modern computers.

4 DISK OPERATING SYSTEM refers to:

a A program loaded from disk into your microcomputer which controls the operation of your system.

b A rota drawn-up to ensure that the computer equipment is regularly cleaned with floppy disks.

c A surgical technique used in the treatment of computer operators suffering from floppy disks.

5 SPREADSHEET refers to:

a The protective sheet that is spread over a computer when not in use to prevent damage.

b A sheet of paper spread with a matrix of printed "cells", into which data are entered.

c An anti-static sheet spread under a computer, which also protects the carpet from computer bugs, and prevents micro-chips from being trodden-in.

6 MATRIX PRINTER refers to:

a An output device with a wheel-shaped printhead, consisting of a matrix of "petals" in the form of a daisy.

b A specialist printer who produces forms with a matrix of empty "cells", which are used to create a spread-sheet.

c An output device that creates characters by striking a ribbon with a group of pins.

(continued)

7   COMPUTER BUGS are:

a   16-legged mites that inhabit the inside of dusty microcomputers. Also known as "micro-chips" due to their shape.

b   Unseen problems in a programme that can cause computer malfunctions. Said to be named after the small insects that jammed early mechanical computers.

c   Moth-like insects that breed in dirty spreadsheets and feed on the soft clothing worn by computer operators, hence their nickname of "soft-wear bugs".

8   HARD DISK refers to:

a   The temporary back complaint that afflicts computer operators after treatment for floppy disks.

b   A rigid magnetic disc that can contain computer programmes, such as the Disk Operating System.

c   A cleaning pad (floppy disk) that has dried out. Must not be used in this condition as it can damage the computer housing, creating micro-chips.

9   TAPE STREAMER refers to:

a   The apparatus used to load a new computer tape onto it's plastic reel.

b   A small explosive novelty that ejects streams of coloured tape, traditionally used when celebrating the installation of a new computer.

c   A device that copies all your computer's files onto tape in a continuous stream, for safe storage.

10   MICRO-PERFORATIONS are:

a   Used on continuous computer stationary to fool people into thinking their letter was typed manually.

b   Damaged areas in spreadsheets and in soft-wear caused when computer bugs are allowed to breed freely.

c   Used in special tea-bags made so computer operators can brew very weak tea, otherwise their tannin intake can exceed the daily dosage.

11   COMPUTER MONITORS are:

a   An output device that can be used to monitor the progress of a computer programme.

b   Programmes that run permanently in the background of a computer to monitor printers and other devices.

c   People designated to ensure sufficient stocks of computer supplies, switch off the computer at night etc.

12   MICRO MOUSE is:

a   A cartoon character used by a famous computer manufacturer to advertise its personal computers.

b   A rodent that inhabits untidy computer installations and feeds on softwear bugs.

c   A device used to input data to a microcomputer, and which looks similar to a mouse.

13   WIMP is:

a   A very simple user interface running on a computer. Can be used by almost anyone with no training.

b   A very simple user. Cannot use a simple interface running on a computer with training.

c   Someone in the office who can't manage to lift a full box of listing paper.

14   LOCAL AREA NETWORKS are:

a   Groups of computer users in one locality, who get together occasionally to share information, etc.

b   Groups of computers in one locality, which communicate together occasionally to share information, etc.

c   Groups of computer dealers in one locality, who get together to provide better service and maintenance, etc.

15   8–BIT MICROS are:

a   An older generation of microcomputers that physically consist of 8 "bits".

b   An older generation of microcomputers where a "byte" of data consists of 8 "bits".

c   An older generation of microcomputer that can only transfer data 8 "bits" at a time.

WHAT EVERYBODY SHOULD KNOW ABOUT COMPUTERS

Computers have a language of their own. But by knowing just a few key words you should be able to hold a conversation with anybody.

Acoustic coupler Enables you to connect your computer to others through a telephone handset.

Bit A *binary digit*, the ultimate unit of computer information.

Buffer A temporary memory store, holding information while the computer is busy.

Bug An error in a program.

Byte A group of eight *bits*, sufficient to define a character, and the unit handled by most computers.

Chip A tiny square of silicon 5 to 6mm square that is etched to provide the equivalent of tens of thousands of transistors. The entire growth of microcomputing depends on its development.

CPU Central processing unit. The "brain" of the computer. The microelectronic revolution has made it possible to put the functions of a CPU on a *chip* – a microprocessor. This in turn has made it possible to make powerful computers that will fit on a desk top or even be portable.

Crash A computer has crashed if it stops working and will not respond to any instruction. Often the only cure is to switch off and start again.

Cursor A symbol on the screen of a computer showing where the next character will be printed. When you are editing text it shows you where the changes will occur.

Database A store of information in a central computer that can be made available for other computer users. Big companies have their own databases and there are also public databases.

Disk, *floppy disk*. A permanent magnetic memory store. It looks like a small gramophone record, and is used with a disk drive and a magnetic head that "reads" the information. It is much quicker to use and holds much more information than a tape cassette.

Hardware The parts of a computer that you can see and touch – keyboards, circuits, chips etc. Contrasted with *software*.

Language Instructions are given to a computer in a stylised form called a computer language. A "high-level language" closely resembles normal speech. Examples are Basic, Cobol, Logo, Pascal.

LCD Liquid crystal display, the kind of display used on pocket calculators and watches. Some small computers and word processors use an LCD and not a TV screen.

Listing A computer program, shown on the screen or in print. One way of seeing a listing of the program that is in a computer is to use the command "LIST".

Mainframe A large computer, the kind that fills several offices. It is essential for processing large amounts of information. At one time there was no other kind of computer.

Matrix An array in rows and columns. The word may be used to describe one type of printer in which the letters and numbers are formed by patterns of dots. An alternative is an "impact printer" where the letters and numbers are printed by some variation on a typewriter mechanism.

Micro or microcomputer. The small computer that fits easily on an office desk. Home computers are micros, as are the computers used for small businesses.

Mini A mid-sized computer, smaller than a normal desk. It is smaller than a *mainframe* computer and, in size, comes between it and the familiar microcomputer.

Modem A device for connecting a computer to the telephone system for passing information around the country and to other countries. It achieves the same result as an *acoustic coupler*.

Monitor A specialised display for the computer that looks like a TV but does not have the circuits to receive TV programmes. A computer connects more directly to a monitor than to a television and therefore gives a clearer picture.

Network A group of computers that are joined by the telephone system and by special cables so that they can communicate with each other. Inside a company there may be a local area network (LAN). There are also public networks available to anyone who cares to subscribe. These can be used to send electronic mail.

PCB Printed circuit board. A way of making the wiring that connects the components of a computer. The *chips* in a computer are plugged into the PCB.

Peripherals Devices that can be added to a computer – printers, *acoustic couplers*, etc.

Port, *IO port* (input/output port). A socket for connecting the computer to other devices.

RAM Random access memory. The built-in memory that a computer uses to store programs and the information it is working on. RAM is transient and disappears when the computer is switched off.

ROM Read only memory. Unalterable memory, usually used as a permanent store of programs. Often it takes the form of a *chip* that is plugged in to the computer.

Scroll To move the text or picture shown on a computer screen up or down. In horizontal scrolling, the text or picture moves sideways.

Software The instructions given to a computer and the information it works on. It usually comes in the form of cassettes or floppy *disks*.

Spreadsheet A method of bookkeeping on computer. A formula connecting different columns can be written into the program, which then shows the overall effect of the change you have made.

Time sharing A technique that lets a number of people use a central computer. Each person has a terminal, and the computer is programmed so as to give each person the impression that nobody else is using the computer.

Word processing Writing and editing text on a computer. The text is first written into the memory of the computer and read on the screen. It can then be refined and corrected: words and paragraphs can be added or deleted or moved around. Substitutions can be made for words or phrases. The text is printed only after editing.

SOLUTIONS

Activity on page 174

A few examples of 'modern' equipment and materials and the year of their introduction.

Paper	100 AD
Printing text in books	1450
Mechanical typewriters	1874
Telephones	1876
Electric typewriters	1920
Teleprinter and Telex	1930
Computer with memory	1949
Photocopiers	1950s
Laser beams	1960
Floppy disc	1971
Post Office 'System X'	1980
Fibre optics transmission and voice inputting	1980s

Answers to computer quiz

1b 2c 3c 4a 5b 6c 7b 8b 9c 10a 11a 12c 13a 14b 15c

If you have *guessed* any answers, knock one point off your final score.

How did you rate?

12–15. Well done. You have an excellent grasp of today's computer jargon and good knowledge of the technology. Even if you are not sure of exactly how everything works, it is an advantage to be able to converse with dealers, etc., in their own terms.

8–11. Not quite the office expert, but you obviously have some knowledge or interest in computers. You could easily learn more through reading magazines, etc. if you are so inclined.

4–7. You can consider yourself 'normal', definitely not a computer-type. However, you should consider finding out a bit more about computers, as they will play an increasingly important part in office life.

0–3. It is statistically impossible to score so low, so you must have worked at it! You hate computers and will have no truck with them. Consequently, you will probably live happily to a ripe old age.

6

Winning the argument

Why did you buy this book? Were you persuaded by the cover, or did you scan the contents pages in a bookshop and liked what you saw? Was the book recommended by your college tutor, or is it one that a friend of yours has told you about? What we can say is that you will not have seen it advertised on TV or in a magazine. There are of course endless TV and magazine advertisements, some of which undoubtedly succeed in their purpose of persuading us either to part with our money or to change our brand loyalties. One of the most striking features of late 20th century life is the sheer numbers of people and range of techniques employed in marketing and selling goods and services to us. However, in most of our purchasing decisions, there are few impartial advisors. We are usually at the mercy of slick advertising presentation or the salesperson's appealing patter.

It is not just advertisers and salespeople who try to persuade us. Politicians, pressure groups, religious organisations, teachers, even our own families and friends, regularly attempt to get us to change our behaviour. It is likely that even you try to influence others. But how successful are you? Do you wish you could be more influential with your family, workmates and friends? Some simple strategies have already been outlined about influencing others using non-verbal communication and paralinguistic skills in Chapter 4. However, not all the circumstances in which we wish to persuade others involve face-to-face encounters between employees and supervisors. A great deal of persuasion may be undertaken by means of information presented on paper or within a formal business meeting; so it is important to know what we are trying to do and how we can best achieve our objectives.

In this chapter we outline a straightforward approach to the business of persuading others under the heading *Putting your case*. Then we go on to examine ways in which it is possible to spot weaknesses in a counter-case which an opponent might be presenting in the section *Tricks and flaws of argument*. Thirdly, we set out ways in which an argument can be made more compelling by using visual presentations of statistics in *Bringing your information alive*. In the fourth section we apply these points to the business of making a case to a meeting under the title *Giving presentations*, and finally we examine the ways in which organisations can improve turnover by changing the image that their customers and potential customers have of them in *Projecting your image*.

Putting your case

There is now a whole industry of people engaged in the business of persuading us to change our minds and our social behaviour. Not only are there advertisers and salespeople, but also public relations consultants and media advisers who make a living out of selling expertise to businesses that are anxious to make a hit with the public. Not that there is anything new in the art of persuasion. The ancient Greeks had a name for it: they called it 'Rhetoric', which is the art of writing or speaking effectively. At times, rhetoric was so much admired that it was included in the school curriculum. However, it is doubtful that rhetoric is an exact science, with a series of mechanical rules, which once absorbed will guarantee success. Rather, it is best to have a clear objective in mind, and then make decisions about how that objective is to be achieved. Indeed, by their very nature, rules tend to make things dull and predictable, and that is the opposite of what advertisers and persuaders have in mind. Here is a six-step-plan for putting your case:

```
Step one    — Know your objective
Step two    — Know your subject matter
Step three  — Know your audience
Step four   — Interest your audience
Step five   — Inform your audience
Step six    — Give them something to do at the end
```

A glance at these will show you that the first three steps are part of the process of preparing, while the last three are steps to take during the delivery of a presentation, which may be written or spoken. We can now look at them in more detail.

Know your objective

Make up your mind about what you want to happen. Do you want them to appoint you to the post, or to take up your suggestion about a new method of filing? Are you trying to persuade them to buy your firm's products or services, or to refund money or replace defective goods? Or do you want someone to marry you, or to be set free from them? Whether your objective is work-based or personal, the more firmly you hold it, the more likely it is that you will achieve it. Having formed a clear-cut objective, you are in a position to plan more positively the route by which it can be accomplished.

Some objectives will be easily achieved. You will need no powers of persuasion to tempt an alcoholic to join you in a 'wee dram', but if the only holidays you have spent to date have been with your family, granny and dog in a caravan at Mablethorpe, you can expect to have problems persuading your parents that you are ready for a hitch-hiking and camping holiday across Europe with a group of drinking friends from 'down the pub'. This is an important point. Not everyone is going to be persuaded just on your say-so. Their attitudes and opinions may be long-standing and may take a great deal of time and evidence to modify. After all, an opposing negative objective can be as strongly held as a positive one. Even when attitudes do change, they do not necessarily lead to an immediate change of behaviour.

Anticipated difficulties, however, are not a reason for not trying. If getting people to stop smoking or to consume less alcohol and foods high in cholesterol were easy, then there would be virtually no sales of such products now. Yet despite the ingrained habits and tastes of people in Britain, organisations such as the *Health Education Council* continue to battle against these health hazards with growing evidence that their campaigns are having some effect.

ACTIVITY

Rank these persuasion tasks in order of anticipated ease or difficulty:

- Persuading staff in your office to allow you to buy them a meal.
- Getting your parents to lend you their car for a touring holiday in Yugoslavia.
- Persuading your supervisor to let you leave an hour earlier for 'personal' reasons.
- Convincing your manager that you are the person most deserving of the next promotion in your office.
- Persuading an attractive member of your class to visit your home to see your collection of compact discs.
- Persuading the staff at work to take more exercise.

Identify the elements of each of these tasks which make them easy or difficult. Compare your answers with those of others in your group.

Know your subject matter

Knowing the objective will help to clarify your thinking about the facts that you need to gather in support of your case. Facts are very persuasive. They have an objectivity, an indisputability, to which everyone is susceptible. But even though some facts may not appear to support your case (indeed they could be useful to an opponent) that is no reason to close your mind to them. Anyone who seeks to argue a case convincingly must have a thorough grasp of the subject and be prepared to concede or respond to counter-arguments. Looking only for 'helpful' facts will create the impression that your knowledge is only partial, and therefore flawed. Such an impression is not persuasive.

ACTIVITY

Summarise the arguments that might be made for and against the introduction of flexitime in an office similar to your own. (See Assignment at the end of Chapter 3 if you are not familiar with flexitime.) How would you respond to counter-arguments or alleged weaknesses in the flexitime system?

Know your audience

Next time you are watching a programme on commercial TV, think about the advertisements that are scheduled during the breaks or immediately before or after the programme. Try and see whether there is any connection between the programme itself and the products or services being advertised. This is especially the case during tea-time transmissions, when there are lots of adverts for toys, confectionery and fast-foods. Advertisers know that when children are viewing in large numbers, they form a ready-made audience at which child-targeted products can be aimed. You will also detect a similar link between programmes for young adults and the nature of the advertising that surrounds them, which often reflects the more outrageous or distinctive features in youth culture.

ACTIVITY

1 Suggest the type of TV programme and/or preferred times of transmission that advertisers might recommend for marketing and advertising the following

- Electronic colour copiers.
- The dangers of drinking and driving after office and work parties.
- Executive limousines for hire.
- Heavy duty hand-cleansing jelly.
- Digital tapes for recording.
- Government grants for industry in the regions.

2 Recommend at least two publications or mass media channels for each product in which an advertisement could be used to advantage.

Any attempt to persuade requires an evaluation of what is likely to be most persuasive, and no such judgement can be made without first knowing more about our potential audience.

In our day-to-day encounters with work colleagues, family or friends, this poses few problems. Our acquaintances are well enough known for us to guess their likely reaction to any proposal we are about to make. With some, we can expect agreement; but what are we to do with those who are hostile or indifferent? The way forward is to begin with whatever common ground exists between us and them. Emphasise those things which you can agree about and which you have in common. Try to strike a sympathetic chord with your audience. Later you may move on to more contentious matters, but try always to present them from a perspective that appeals to a potential opponent. This tactic was used by the reformers of capital punishment in the 19th century. They persuaded land owners, who formed the bulk of the members of parliament, that hanging criminals for sheep stealing was ineffective because juries were unwilling to condemn people to death for such offences, and so brought in verdicts of 'not guilty'. The reformers did not use a moral argument because it would not have worked. Exactly the same tactics are used today by advertisers. They don't say 'Buy this product to keep us in jobs' but instead play on the worries and ambitions of their audience: 'Buy this product and look better, smell better, and *be* better!' If you seek to persuade, you must start to see things from the other person's point of view.

Knowing what our customers think is easy when we know them personally, but for an organisation that seeks to persuade potential customers to use its services, the audience is no longer knowable on personal terms. It is now a great mass called 'the general public', or at best a subgroup made up entirely, say, of young people or mortgage holders, perhaps 'all those people who have bought something from us during the last twelve months'. Predicting audience response is now less certain, and we are forced to make guesses about them and their reactions. Fortunately, as we are all members of the same society, we have many things in common which bind us together. For example, most of us believe that keeping clean and going on holiday are good things: thus we can predict the need for soap and cheap package holidays.

In addition, there is information available to us from commercial and government sources that can be used to sharpen our judgements about the audience we are trying to reach. If a company knows that a customer has bought a product or service from it in the past, there is a fair chance that the same customer will be willing to buy in the future. Many firms retain the names of customers on a mailing list so they can be sent circular sales letters, catalogues, invitations to product launches and other promotional material. Alternatively, a company seeking new markets and customers can acquire someone else's mailing list, usually for a small fee, and use that. Members of trade or professional associations are often swamped in a deluge of such mail, all carefully targeted at specific groups, such as medical workers, farmers, teachers and motorists. The names and addresses on the electoral register can also be bought for this purpose.

ACTIVITY

1 Identify the likely audiences for promotional or publicity material for the following services, activities or products.

  - Your existing colleges' courses.
  - A pub singer and entertainer.
  - Office furniture.
  - Save-on-your-tax-bills computer program.
  - Greyhound racing.
  - Council rest homes for the retired.

2 Suggest a few organisations or addresses to which promotional material could be sent for each of the products. (Check the *Yellow Pages*.)

Interest your audience

Knowing our audience is half the battle, but we will never persuade anyone if what we have to offer is boring. It is first important to draw their attention, and then to keep them interested. One way to do this is to ensure that our presentation, written or spoken, is kept as short as possible. Think about your own concentration span. How long are you able to concentrate on the text of this book, for example, before your mind wanders off onto other things? Remember, a brief message is best.

Brevity is not enough on its own. It must be linked to stimulating material. Some topics are potentially more interesting than others, and we cannot consider interest-value independently of the audience we propose to address. We may be a keen collector of butterflies, but we know that our enthusiasm is unlikely to be shared by work colleagues. Nonetheless, there are organisations that manage to create products of daily interest to their customers, which provide a useful insight into subjects that seem to be of interest and concern to society as a whole. These products are, of course, mainly newspapers, television and radio. A glance at a day's output in the *Sun*, *Mirror* and *Star* is enough to give us an idea of the level of interest in crime (particularly if violent), sex (particularly if scandalous), royalty, sport, TV personalities and money. Whether these subjects reflect a genuine interest or whether they are manufactured for readers by the papers themselves is an interesting question you might like to discuss.

Yet even an interesting topic can be ruined by a dull presentation or style. An old newspaper maxim is always to make the first word or phrase of any report a 'hook' for the story. Every first word should be 'active' in the sense that it encourages the reader to go further, especially after being 'caught' by a snappy heading. Here is an example of what to avoid, and what to do instead.

LOUSY

West Midland Regional Manager of Inter-Europe Holidays (1987) Ltd, Mrs Amanda Cleary, 31, said in a statement today: 'Our company's new package holidays available to senior citizens to destinations in the Iberian peninsula have exceeded the targets set for the package when it was launched last year'. She confirmed that a recent strike by dockers had resulted in a few shortages in Spanish shops and hotels.

LIVELY

Grannies jet to the sun

Jet-setting pensioners are flying off to holiday destinations in sun-soaked Spain and Portugal by the plane load, according to a leading West Midland's travel firm.

Raven-haired Amanda Cleary, 31, regional manager of Inter-Europe Holidays, told reporters that sales of their Spanish 'Riviera' holidays to gad-about pensioners had gone through the ceiling and exceeded the company's wildest expectations.

Eighty-year-olds Mr and Mrs Maurice Phew from Cleethorpes said that their holiday had been wonderful, but wished they had taken a bottle of brown sauce with them because of shortages in strike-bound Spain.

Writing in a lively and interesting way is important. Later in the chapter we will be saying something about the techniques involved in preparing Press Releases.

Many subjects you have to write or talk about will score few points in terms of audience interest. This should not be a cause of despair. Professionals in advertising agencies have to solve these problems day after day. Some of their solutions have come in for criticism, as in the case of motor vehicle repairers or parts suppliers who traditionally use photos of scantily-clad women in newspapers and calendars to attract what is thought to be a male audience. On the other hand, not all their strategies are questionable. A striking example is the recent campaign for advertising a type of instant porridge. Now there are few foods as unappetising as porridge: its appearance is against it and its texture is unappealing. Yet the agency promoting a brand called *Ready Brek* has come up with an interesting solution. Instead of selling porridge to mums as nutritious and warming, they have decided to encourage children themselves to think of this product as friendly fun. They have devised a cartoon character called 'Ready Eddie' who is amusing, capable of taking on several varied but similar identities, and of glowing health and vitality. The product is therefore linked to an image of fun and amusement. This is an important point to which we shall return in the last section of this chapter.

▲ *Ready Brek's 'Ready Eddie'*

Holidays

The annual leave year runs from 1 April to 31 March.

Annual Leave entitlement in addition to public holidays is:

Basic annual salary	Basic entitlement (in days)	After 5 Years	After 10 Years	After 15 Years	After 20 Years
Up to and including £7329	20	25	26	26	27
Above £7330 but at or below £9114	22	25	27	27	28
Above £9114	24	27	28	29	30

New entrants to the Service are entitled to annual leave proportionate to the completed months of service during the leave year of entry, e.g. an Officer who commences duty on 16 August will complete seven full months by the following 31 March. The entitlement for that year will therefore be 7/12ths of the appropriate annual leave entitlement during the leave year.

New entrants to the Local Government Service are not entitled to paid annual leave until they have completed six months' service. However, in certain circumstances, which will be explained by your Finance and Administrative Officer, it is possible to arrange that annual leave may be taken before six months' service is completed.

On leaving the service of the Authority during a leave year other than on transfer to another Authority, an Officer's salary shall be adjusted to take into account any leave taken in excess of his entitlement. An Officer transferring to another Authority takes with him his leave entitlement.

Inform your audience

Having carefully researched our case we are now ready to present our material in the most effective way possible, keeping in mind the exact purpose of our delivery. Here are a few questions we should ask ourselves in preparing our case, which will help us to get our message across.

Which facts and statistics are really helpful to my case?

We have already commented on the general admiration for 'facts'. No less convincing is information and statistics collected from reputable published sources, such as government reports, quality newspapers and social surveys. These have an objectivity which members of the audience and opponents — who probably lack this information — will find difficult to challenge.

Can I think of any examples to support my case?

Are there any instances of my proposal proving successful elsewhere? Could they be used to show that my ideas are not crazy or risky? If you have actual personal experience, your own testimony may be very persuasive, once you have established credibility with your audience, perhaps by having shown them how like them you are in attitude and outlook.

Are there any pictures or models I can use?

One of the tricks of successful communication that we discussed in Chapter 2 was the use of more than one channel of communication. If words alone are not persuading your audience, give them some evidence that they can *see*.

Can I involve my audience in any way?

Nothing is as convincing as personal experience. Motor dealers always offer a 'test drive' in selling cars and you wouldn't dream of buying a TV set without first seeing it working. However, if this sort of involvement is too difficult to arrange, an alternative strategy is to direct questions at your audience, which will lead them to the answers that you want. Politicians do this all the time in speeches by asking rhetorical questions which cause their listeners (they hope) to think in exactly the way the politicians want them to think. They might ask: 'Do we really want this government returned to power?' or 'If the other lot are elected, we know what that means for unemployment and inflation, don't we?', hoping that the audience will agree silently that the result will be awful. People are always prepared to be convinced by those arguments that are closest to what they already believe; which takes us back to the need to know an audience before we start.

What objections will be raised?

This is a vital point. We must anticipate that some people may have reservations about our ideas, or even demonstrate a marked hostility. What arguments can they use against us? Often it is possible to refute their arguments. But if they point to genuine disadvantages, it is often wiser to give way gracefully and argue that they do not outweigh the desirability of our scheme as a whole.

ACTIVITY

Assume you are trying to encourage people from other parts of the UK to come and spend a day, or longer, as tourists in a major British city. From these photographs select two that you would use to illustrate a publicity leaflet. For each photograph that you select or reject, write a few lines explaining your decision. Compare your results with others in your group.

Give them something to do at the end

If we are trying to persuade somebody, it follows that we wish them to do something that they are not doing or thinking at the moment (to buy a different product or support an alternative idea). It is important, therefore, not just to take them to the point where we have made our case, we should go on to indicate what we hope they will now do. In a circular sales letter this might mean enclosing an order form or reply-paid card to prompt a favourable response. Frequently, this will be coupled to an inducement to reply quickly, say within fourteen days, so that the inclination to buy or act is not lost through delay or forgetfulness. In a sales interview it may be possible to urge that the deal is closed quickly: 'This offer closes at the end of the month', but in other interviews good manners will deter us from pushing people towards a decision too quickly. However, it may still be possible to indicate that we are hopeful of a favourable outcome, and that we would like to know that outcome as soon as possible.

Spotting the flaws

When we are listening to an argument that is being put to us, or if we wish to challenge a contrary point of view to our own, it is important for us to be aware of any flaws in the case being presented. This does not simply mean being on the lookout for mistakes or even lies, because our own knowledge may be too limited for us to be able to identify such errors and deceptions. Instead, we should concern ourselves with the structures and devices being used in the presentation of the case.

ACTIVITY

Examine the following statements and see whether you can spot any unsatisfactory elements in them. When you have finished, you can check your answers against the information given later in this chapter.

Statement	What's wrong
Youngsters these days have no sense of responsibility. The number of kids on the dole proves that.	
Welshmen are so unromantic. I'm telling you it won't last between him and our Brenda.	
There's now an extra 33 per cent more flavour in new improved *Wilson* cigars.	
Everyone knows the BTEC National Certificate is a walkover. Only a cretin could fail the course.	
Another crazy suggestion — just what we've come to expect from Mr Smallman. It's typical of the fairy-tale nonsense he always comes up with.	

Structuring the argument

In a criminal court, the procedures for dealing with the accused are well known. First, there is the *charge* against the defendant. Then comes the *evidence*, which is followed by the *interpretation* of that evidence. The trial is concluded with the *verdict*, and on that basis a *sentence* is given. A similar approach may be used for presenting an argument in less formal surroundings, say in a report or a business meeting. First, we state our *assertion* — that is, the point we are seeking to prove. Next, we present our *evidence*, usually the facts and figures that we believe support our assertion. The evidence is then subjected to *interpretation* to demonstrate its relevance and reliability. This is followed by a *conclusion*, which is a judgement based on the evidence, and this in turn is followed by the *decision* to which the audience has been led.

We can summarise the steps in the presentation of a case in the following way.

```
ASSERTION

EVIDENCE

INTERPRETATION

CONCLUSION

DECISION
```

In meetings, the presentation of an argument is likely to be dynamic. In other words, there will be several people taking an active part, with subgroups developing, some of whom will favour or oppose the argument in varying degrees. If we have to speak at a meeting ourselves, we will be putting our own case and responding to the criticisms of our opponents. In a letter or a report, however, we are wholly in control of the argument (though this does not mean that our readers will not later respond critically) and it is up to us to present both sides of the argument, even though we might present the opposing view in order to knock it down again.

In order to be able to assess other people's arguments, and to test our own to ensure that it will stand up to cross-examination, here is a simple procedure to follow:

Testing an argument

Step one — Identify the assertion
Step two — Identify the evidence
Step three — Determine what evidence could prove the assertion
Step four — Decide whether the evidence offered does prove it

ACTIVITY

Apply this test to the following arguments. Do you think the assertions have been satisfactorily proved in each case? Explain in detail.

1 Our present levels of unemployment are almost entirely attributable to the numbers of married women who now exist in the job market. Figures show that unemployment has risen at the same rate that the numbers of married women registering as available for work have risen.
2 Public schools have a far higher proportion of their pupils gaining places at university than their counterparts in the state sector. This illustrates the enormous gulf which exists between the quality of education in the public and the state schools.
3 In 1983 the Conservative party won a 160-seat majority over all their opponents in the General Election. This proves that an overwhelming majority of British people wanted that party to form the government.
4 The most popular record at any time in Britain can be heard on the BBC Radio Top Forty programme every Sunday afternoon. It will have sold more copies than any other during the previous seven-day accounting period.

CRIMES OF VIOLENCE SOAR

Rape, assault, gang warfare, hooliganism and muggings have reached epidemic proportions in British cities.

A government report published yesterday, called *Urban Violence*, points to a rapid rise in all reported violent crimes against the person in the last five years.

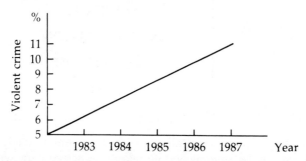

Police Superintendent Mike Dare of the Metropolitan Police said that it is now unwise for women to walk the streets unescorted and that old people should not even open their doors to strangers.

He said that the victims and perpetrators of most crimes of violence are young men aged between 14 and 23 years.

Spotting the tricks and flaws

If you wish to polish up your own argument to make it harder for your opponent to defeat, or to develop skills in identifying errors your opponent is making, you should find the following guide to flaws in argument helpful.

1 The imprecisely stated assertion

e.g. 'Insurance clerks are pretty boring people.'

The problem with this assertion is that it is vague and lacks definition. This is often a sign of poor argument. Does the writer mean *all* insurance clerks, or most of them, or only some? If it means all clerks, it will be easy to disprove. It is necessary to find only one fascinating and interesting insurance clerk for the argument to collapse. On the other hand, if the writer is saying that some clerks are boring, then it is questionable whether this is worth saying in the first place. Here are some other examples which fail the 'all' or 'some' test.

- Socialists are compassionate and caring people.
- Young people have little respect for their elders and betters.
- Accountants are people who have a way with figures.

Until the writer or speaker makes clear his statement in each case (i.e., all, most or some), no satisfactory discussion can take place on any of these assertions.

2 Starting from a false premise

Many arguments seem reasonable, even though this conceals the fact that the conclusion is based on an invalid premise or proposition. For example

Welshmen are unromantic.
Dai is a Welshman.
Therefore Dai is unromantic.

This argument is based on a form of reasoning known as a syllogism. Syllogisms have three components:

1 Premise
2 Development
3 Conclusion

These are represented in simple terms as:

All A is B
C is A
Therefore C is B

Let's look at an example of a valid syllogism. Just to show yourself that you understand, identify the three elements A, B and C:

All women are mortal.
Edwina is a woman.
Therefore Edwina is mortal.

Pretty obvious stuff you might think (and, yes, women = A, mortality = B and Edwina = C). However, exactly the same argument was used to conclude that Dai was unromantic, although this cannot now be accepted, because the premise — that all Welshmen are unromantic — is clearly false. Indeed it leads us towards another common flaw found in argument.

3 Appeal to prejudice

e.g. 'We don't employ gay people here. We'd have an epidemic of AIDS before we knew where we were.'

Statements like this appeal to fear and ignorance. They attempt to get round the need to make out a real case by feeding the listener or reader with stereotyped images. Stereotypes are simplified views of particular groups of people that seek to justify attitudes that are held towards them. As such, they are very powerful and help to explain how many ordinary Germans came to support the Nazi persecution of Jews, who were the target of pernicious stereotyping during the 1930s and 1940s.

4 Using selected instances to prove a case

e.g. 'People in Finance have a really snooty attitude to everyone else who works here. Only yesterday Mrs Boothby ignored me in the canteen.'

This is an example of an argument that is supported by only one piece of evidence to back up a much wider contention. Mrs Boothby may indeed think herself superior, but an example of one person's behaviour on a single occasion (when her mind may well have been on other things) is not proof of her whole department's attitude.

5 Abusing statistics to support an argument

Here is an example of an abuse of statistics presented in the form of a bar chart. It appears to show that Sefton College is significantly more effective than its neighbours in preparing students for BTEC National Certificate. Now look closely at the vertical axis and you will see that it is not calibrated. It is not clear therefore whether it starts at zero or at a mid-way point, say at 50 per cent. The designer probably hopes that we will see it as a zero and the top of the chart as 100 per cent, because it gives a distorted but flattering view of that college's success.

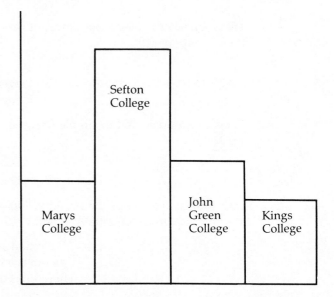

Percentage of BTEC National students gaining certificates

Sefton College

Marys College

John Green College

Kings College

It is worth remembering the old saying: 'There are lies, damned lies and statistics', because it reminds us to be sceptical about figures until we are reassured about a few basic points. Do they give us enough information, for example? In the previous article, *Crimes of violence soar*, we cannot be sure whether violent crimes have actually increased or whether it is because we either now report more violent crime to the police (rape and muggings), or the police themselves have improved their detection rates in a particular type of crime (football hooliganism). Have the statistics been presented with integrity? Even governments (especially before an election) have been known to cook the books. It is possible, for example, to conceive of a company wishing to select the most favourable statistics to give shareholders an exaggerated picture of the present management's trading position. Do the figures actually mean anything? At the beginning of this section we gave an illustration of a cigar which offered '33 per cent more flavour'. It is worth asking whether qualities like flavour can be quantified in this way. Finally, it is worth probing to find out what might be concealed by statistics giving averages. The average attendance for a class of students might be acceptable, but it may hide wide variations in patterns of attendance, including that of a few students whose records are atrocious.

┌─ **ACTIVITY** ───┐

Without changing the relative positions of the colleges in the previous chart, present the information to give a *different* impression to the reader.

└──┘

6 Name-dropping

e.g. 'Experts have shown conclusively that ...'

This sounds impressive, doesn't it, but exactly which experts are being referred to? How valid is their expertise and is there an alternative point of view? Is a well-known personality being used just to look impressive? Many TV commercials use stars or media figures to promote products on the basis that their popularity will encourage us to copy their behaviour as consumers. In order to judge the value of any quoted expert, it is worth asking two questions. First, what is the commercial motive of the expert, and second, does he really have a thorough knowledge of the subject matter?

7 Brow-beating

e.g. 'You surely don't still believe in that outdated notion, do you? Gosh, have you just fallen off a tree?'

Brow-beating is a form of intimidation in which people are persuaded or bullied into believing that their arguments are naïve, eccentric or socially undesirable. The trick is to associate an opponent's point of view with outmoded thinking and to embarrass those who hold such views by suggesting how old-fashioned and stilted they are. It is similar to character assassination.

8 Character assassination

e.g. 'We might be able to believe what Mr Thomas is telling us now if only he could make up his mind what he actually thinks. Only last week he was trying to get us to believe exactly the opposite of what he is saying now.'

Here an opponent is responding not to the actual content of an argument but to some characteristic of the person advancing it, in this case somebody whose views are supposedly unreliable and inconsistent. People who can't think of any immediate reason to oppose an argument may use this technique as a way of defeating an opponent, or it may be used to supplement an attack on a proposition that is put forward.

9 Using anaesthetic language

e.g. 'As a result of our reorganisation a number of non-essential personnel can be released into the job market.'

This is an example of using language for the purpose of desensitising people to unpleasant realities, in this case the reality that some employees will be made jobless. It is a way of using language to make the unacceptable acceptable, by closing off some possible meanings and leading people to other preferred meanings. Here are a couple of real-life examples:

- In South Africa, a carefully devised policy of separate development has been fostered. This ensures that different ethnic groups are encouraged to develop at different congenial rates. (*Official comment on apartheid*)

- Military personnel have been involved in the rectification of borders in Afghanistan. (*Russian comment on the invasion*)

The author of the novel *1984*, George Orwell, called this use of language 'political language' and said of it that it was 'devised to make lies sound truthful and murder respectable'.

ACTIVITY

1 Using these nine categories, identify the tricks or flaws of argument contained in each of the following statements.

(a) Tax offices are notoriously slow in dealing with queries — everybody knows that.

(b) Well, now we've heard the two suggestions, you can either accept mine or the Marxist gibberish that Ms McLehan has put forward.

(c) In a recent research paper, Dr Ferdinand Izel has shown conclusively that staff who wear traditional office suits and clothing stand a better chance of promotion compared with staff who wear casual clothing.

(d) People who are experiencing a prolonged spell of unemployment will be offered an opportunity to take part in a stimulating regime of counselling, retraining and reappraisal of their financial needs and the best way in which these may be met, given the many demands on a limited resource.

(e) It is indeed remarkable that despite the advantages that a modern non-sexist education is supposed to bring, there are still people who appear to believe in the outmoded concept of romantic love.

2 From a copy of today's newspaper, extract an example of each of the nine tricks and flaws used in argument. Please take headlines into account.

Bringing our information alive

Earlier in this chapter we stressed the importance of keeping our audience interested in the message we have for them. Whether our presentation is printed, spoken or electronic, no opportunity should be lost to support our presentation with visual or graphical illustrations. Not only does this provide a second channel for our message, which should improve its chances of being received in the way we would wish, but a visual or graphical message is also likely to be more redundant. You will recall from Chapter 2 that redundancy has a specific meaning in communication theory. A redundant message is one with a high degree of predictability, and high predictability makes decoding messages easier than it would otherwise be. Put simply, pictures and graphs are likely to make our message more effective than masses of words. A glance at newspaper advertisements from a century ago is enough to convince us of this. In those days, there were no pictures at all, but today advertisements without pictures are a rarity outside the classified columns.

Fortunately you don't have to be a crack commercial artist to beef up a leaflet, report or presentation with drawings or illustrations of your own. Quite apart from computer packages, which are making the production of graphs, cartoons and line drawings a relatively easy task, there are dry-transfer illustrations and books of camera-ready artwork which can be dipped into to provide even the hamfisted with usable illustrative material. The following illustrations have been taken from an artwork catalogue, which allows the purchaser to reproduce any of its drawings. You will find an example of the capabilities of a desk-top computer on page 197.

▲ *The Graphic Communications Centre Ltd*

In this section we will emphasise and explore the importance of presenting information in ways other than in close-knit text. In particular, we will deal with the treatment of statistical information. Later we will make a few suggestions for ways in which ideas and facts can be presented in alternative formats.

Tables of statistics

The problem with tables of statistics is that they are intimidating to many people. This is because they are unfamiliar except to those accustomed to dealing with them. They are what we might call 'entropic', which means that they have such a low level of predictability that we have to be well-motivated to make sense of them. If the purpose of the table is to communicate information, the first question to ask is whether a table is the best way of doing it. In general, a form that is visually more interesting is to be preferred, but there are occasions when so much detailed information is to be conveyed that a statistical table is desirable.

Graphs

You will certainly be familiar with graphs from subjects you studied at school. A graph has two axes — a horizontal axis and a vertical axis — each representing a different value. The points of intersection of these values are plotted on the graph and then joined up in a line to show changes. Here is an example from *Tesco*'s annual report.

▼ *Stores analysed by sales area sizes* (Tesco's annual report)

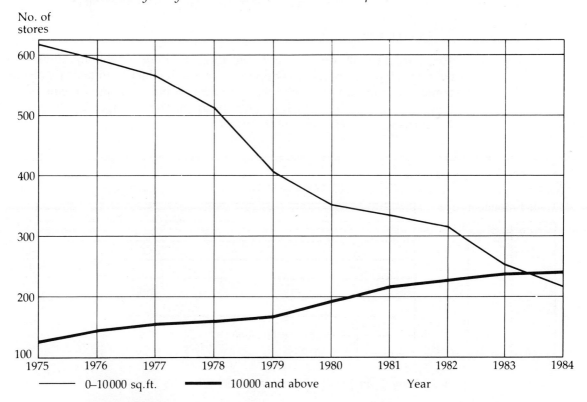

┌ **ACTIVITY** ┐
1 What do the vertical and the horizontal axes on this graph represent?
2 What do the thick and thin lines represent?
3 What general trends about the development of Tesco supermarkets is obvious from this graph?

Graphs are suitable for the presentation of rapidly changing figures, and they have the advantage that a number of related factors can be plotted at the same time, so long as the values of the axes are relevant to all the trends that we wish to represent. On this example, a number of related but rapidly changing factors are illustrated.

▼ *Pegasus Transport Ltd*

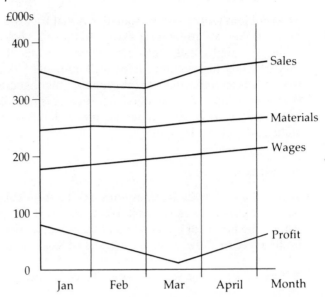

Bar charts

These are a variant on the graph, but they are more suitable for summaries of figures over a fixed period of time, as opposed to a graph which is suitable for changing figures. Sometimes they are presented with the bars (or blocks) rising (or sinking) vertically, or they can show the bars in a horizontal position. This example from the annual report of Cadbury-Schweppes shows both formats.

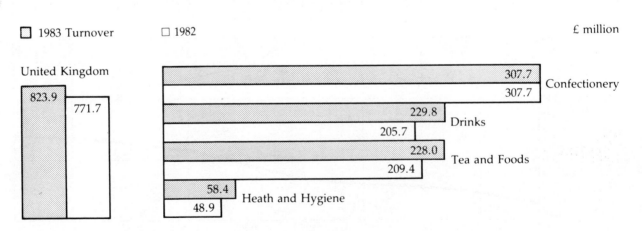

▲ *Cadbury–Schweppes turnover 1982–1983*

The same bar can show a number of values simultaneously. In this chart, each bar represents a given year and a percentage level of employment. Because the bars are placed side-by-side, it is also possible to see trends in employment over a 7-year period.

▼ *People in employment: by sex and occupation*

Great Britain

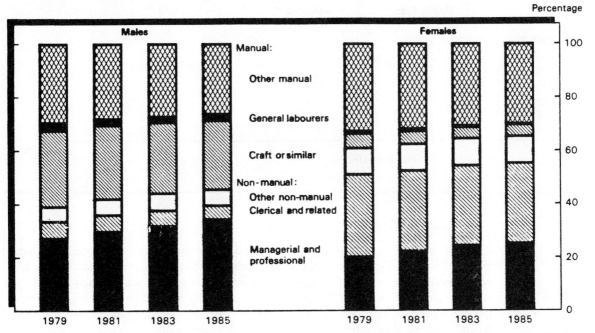

Source: Labour Force Surveys, Department of Employment

ACTIVITY

1 Approximately what percentage of males and females in 1985 were employed in
— managerial and professional occupations
— clerical and related jobs?

2 What is the general employment trend in manual and non-manual jobs over the 7-year period?

3 There is a growing percentage of people that are employed in the 'managerial and professional' category. Suggest six jobs that could be described as 'professional'.

4 On the evidence of this chart, what is the overall difference between the types of jobs women do and the types of jobs men do? Is there any evidence to show that this difference is diminishing?

Histograms

Histograms are similar to bar charts. However, while the calibrations on the axes of a bar chart are uniform (e.g., month, year, etc.), those on a histogram may not be, and represent variations in time periods or in the scope of the groups sampled. For example, the age groups given on a histogram may differ in their range. One bar may cover 18- to 21-year-olds (3 years) and another bar 60 years and over (potentially 30+ years).

Construct a chart to represent the statistical data for *Pegasus Transport Ltd.*

Year	Commercial Division Profit/loss	Courier Services Profit/loss	Private Hire Profit/loss	Profit/loss Total pre-tax
1980/1	150	−70	17	97
1981/2	135	−65	15	85
1982/3	145	−35	15	125
1983/4	95	−15	17	97
1984/5	125	−12	19	132
1985/6	145	0	20	165
1986/7	150	5	23	178

(all figures in £000s)

Pictograms

This is a method of presenting statistics in a user-friendly way. Although it is similar to the bar chart, the bar is replaced with a column of symbols, which should ideally bear some resemblance to the subject of the pictogram. A table of road deaths could be set out as a row of coffins, each coffin representing 1000 road deaths in a given year, and injuries could be similarly presented with crutches! Trading surpluses, on the other hand, could be shown by whole or partial cash bags, as in this example.

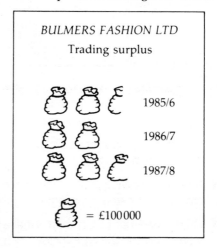

It is possible for pictograms to depart radically from the bar chart layout and employ a much more visual presentation, even though the purpose and the end result are similar. In this example, expenditure for a local authority is depicted.

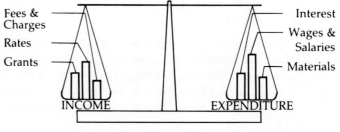

▲ *Brightshire County Council*

Pie diagrams

This is a familiar form of pictogram which takes its name from its likeness to a pie, with proportions or 'slices' of the pie being allocated for particular purposes. The diagram shows how a typical city council allocated its funds to client groups. You will know that in order to convert a percentage into the degrees of a circle you have to multiply by 3.6.

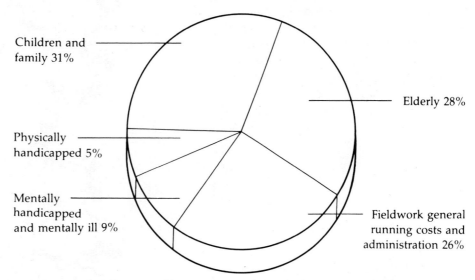

▲ *Allocation of financial resources to client groups, 1986/87*

ACTIVITY

Study the figures for income and expenditure for the Woodland Trust for 1986, and produce pie diagrams to illustrate them. Remember to caption your diagrams properly.

	1986 £	£
Income		
Membership	426,551	
Legacies	120,108	
Appeals	649,326	
Grants for woodland purchase	457,843	
Woodlands	106,292	
Trading	43,600	
VAT repayment	64,656	
Sundry	60,865	
TOTAL INCOME		1,929,241
Expenditure		
Fund-raising and membership information	294,107	
Administration	257,931	
Financial	24,152	
TOTAL EXPENSES (excluding cost of Woodland Management)		576,190
		1,353,051

Maps

A map is a useful alternative to the pictogram or bar chart. Technically, these maps are called cartograms, an example of which is produced for you. It is based on information contained in the report of the Woodland Trust and shows clearly the general scatter of Woodland Trust properties in Britain. The importance of maps in helping us to orientate ourselves is considerable. They are also invaluable as a guide to getting us to where we want to go.

THE WOODLAND TRUST SAVES A WOOD EVERY WEEK

Key

● Woodland Trust properties

▲ *The Woodland Trust*

Many organisations produce their own sketch maps to help customers to find their premises. This example provides a lot of information to help clients find their Employment Training Advisory Service (ETAS) office.

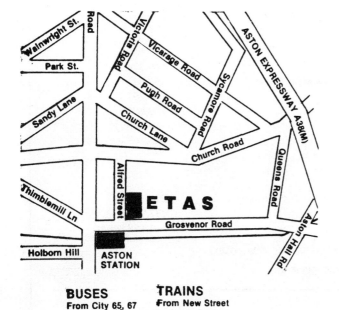

BUSES
From City 65, 67

TRAINS
From New Street to Aston Station

▲ *How to get there*

ACTIVITY

Draw a sketch map to show the route to your present place of employment or college, from either the nearest motorway junction or railway station. (If there is no such facility in your area, choose an important geographical feature.) After adding other helpful information, exchange your map with somebody else in the group, and make comments about the usefulness of their map.

Matrix

A matrix is a convenient way of setting out information that is repetitive in nature. It has a great deal in common with a graph in that a matrix possesses two axes, and information is read off at the point at which values on each axis join. An example of a well-known matrix is the table of distances by road between major towns in the UK that can be found in most road atlases.

▶ *Check your weight*

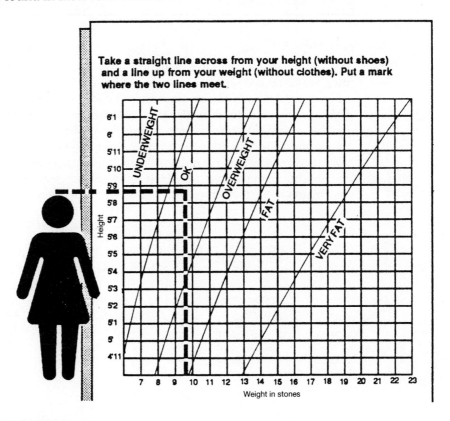

Take a straight line across from your height (without shoes) and a line up from your weight (without clothes). Put a mark where the two lines meet.

> ### ACTIVITY
>
> Using the above matrix, conduct a survey on a group of staff or students in your college and produce a chart to illustrate your findings.

	Good looks	Youngish	Lots of cash	Unmarried	Fun to be with	Considerate	Sexy
Bob	✓	✓	✗	✓	✓	✓	✗
Cedric	✗	✗	✓✓	✓	✗	✓	✗
Walter	✗	✓	✗	✗	✓✓	✓	✗
Mike	✓	✗	✓	✗	✓	✗	✓✓
Wayne	✗	✓	✓	✓	✓	✓	✗
Mitchell	✓	✓	✓	✓	✓	✓	✓

▲ *Amanda's suitors*

Matrices can also be used to make comparisons between competing services or products. In this fanciful example, you should assume that Amanda is beset by male admirers from whom she has decided to choose a potential husband. The qualities she is interested in are listed along the horizontal axis and the men currently seeking her favours are listed down the vertical axis. Where a suitor possesses the desired quality, Amanda ticks the column, and if he possesses it abundantly, she ticks twice, but if it is completely absent an X is recorded. This matrix helps Amanda to clarify her thinking. Although this is a frivolous and probably sexist example, there is an obvious application in, say, choosing a holiday destination or making a selection from comparable makes of consumer goods. It could also provide members of interview panels with a useful reminder of the merits of the candidates being interviewed.

Time-line

If you have to give people instructions, it is worth asking whether the manner in which they are given is as effective as it might be. We have already seen how useful a map can be in supporting written or spoken instructions on how to reach a destination. However, if you have ever assembled flat-pack furniture or model kits, you will have been grateful for the *exploded diagram* accompanying the printed instructions. Although it is unlikely that you give instructions for product assembly in your own job, you may have to give guidance on how to carry out a process. If the instructions are to be printed and left with the machine or process to which they relate, one variation of the 'list' method of instruction is the time-line, which sets out the sequence of tasks in diagrammatic form.

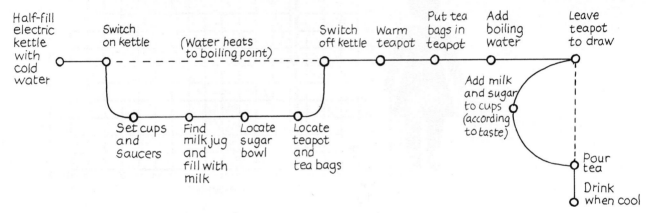

▲ *Making a cup of tea*

The tasks being undertaken by the operator are represented by the solid line (which incidentally represents the way to make a *real* cup of tea — none of this brew-in-the-cup-nonsense) – while those tasks that are performed automatically, or remote from the operator's control, are represented by the broken line. Circles represent stages in the process.

Flow diagram

A flow diagram is yet another way of representing instructions, but it differs from the time-line in allowing for the possibility of more than one outcome. Normally a diagram has limitations in representing all organisational processes, but so useful are such diagrams in standardising behaviour that a company might actually redesign its processes around it to eliminate anomalies and inconsistencies. An example of a flow diagram can be found on page 177.

Venn diagram

This form of representation is common in what used to be called 'new maths' syllabuses and you probably encountered examples when you did 'sets' at junior school. This example shows how group loyalties can be represented diagrammatically.

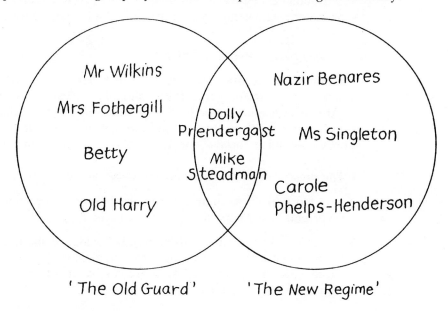

▲ *Divided loyalties in the office*

All nine people work in the same office. Unfortunately, they are divided broadly into two camps. Those wholly in the left circle have been in the office for a long time, and they are used to the old ways. Those wholly in the right circle are new employees, including Ms Singleton, brought in by management to bring the office into the 1990s. In the middle, where the circles overlap, are two staff members who are neither wholly modernist nor reactionary. That they have a foot in each camp is illustrated by the overlap of the two circles. If you are sceptical of the value of this form of representation, think about the amount of explanation that would be needed to express the situation with words alone. Then ask yourself which represents the conflict most dramatically.

Models

One way of explaining theoretical relationships is by the use of models. Although these can be three-dimensional, as in the case of some scientific models, they are more likely to be presented as a diagram. This example of a model of the communication process dates from 1949, and though it has been refined many times since (including the one on page 57), it is still regarded as the mother and father of much work in the area of communication theory. It owes its charm to its deceptive simplicity.

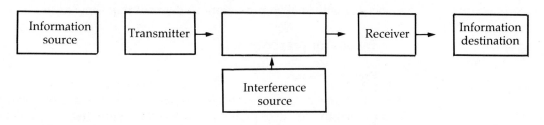

▲ *Shannon and Weaver, 1949*

Giving presentations

When we discussed the points to consider before communicating with an audience, we suggested that these points are equally applicable whether we intend to write or speak to our audience. However, there are some special factors that need to be explored if a spoken address is being contemplated, and it is to these we now turn.

Why give presentations at all?

The attraction of presentations — which are widely used for training purposes, interviews, selling and general promotional activities — may not be obvious immediately. After all, the information to be imparted is usually available in some other form, such as video tape, brochure, leaflet, application form and training manual. The answer is that a presentation is a social event which provides three main advantages.

1 The presence of a presenter and audience allows for feedback on *both* sides.

2 It is more likely to motivate listeners because they may have a sense of personal involvement and experience some excitement.

3 It provides an audience with non-verbal evidence about the presenter, which allows them to check the integrity of verbal signals with non-verbal ones (e.g., looking an audience in the eye and speaking in a confident and level voice may be registered as a sign of honesty and reliability).

Why do presenters get nervous?

The advantages of a presentation do not necessarily mean that presenters view the forthcoming event with enthusiasm. Indeed, many otherwise confident and effective individuals become frozen with terror at the prospect of having to address even a small group. There are usually three reasons for this.

1 An unfamiliar role. In assuming the role of presenter, speakers feel there is an obligation to live up to the expectations of an audience that has been conditioned by the high standards of delivery and content shown by presenters in the media.

2 Lack of confidence in public speaking. Despite the fact that we all spend a great deal of time in conversation, this seldom includes addressing groups.

3 Dealing with problems. With many eyes turned on us, we are aware of being observed, yet we are unable to employ any of the conversational devices for monitoring audience reaction that are available in one-to-one encounters. It is simply more difficult to keep control over what is happening. In addition, the size of the audience is also related to the extent of the humiliation if things do go wrong.

Fortunately, many difficulties, if anticipated, can be overcome. In devising your plan for a presentation, thinking about what we discussed earlier, such as the likely attitudes, needs or interests of the audience, should be very helpful. However, the problems associated with spoken presentations demand that some tactics be planned in advance.

Tactics for presenters

Preparing notes

You must first prepare yourself some notes. It is important to plan your presentation, and the self-discipline of preparing notes will ensure that you do not get over-confident and assume that inspiration will come as you walk in to address the board of directors. Remember that in Chapter 4 we concluded not only that non-verbal signals were important in determining other people's perceptions of us, but that first impressions are difficult to alter once formed. A careless and badly planned presentation will create entirely the wrong impression. On the other hand, it is equally important not to lose our listeners' attention by reading from copious notes. Reading aloud to a group is almost always less arresting than speaking with spontaneity, and it is a sure way of losing their attention. Each member of the audience has to feel that we are talking to them personally.

A suitable format for notes is illustrated. The notes should be large enough to be read at arms' length, or with a quick glance at the desk, but we should include only such details as are needed to jog our memory. After all, if we have researched our topic (as recommended in step two of *Putting your case*), we should not need to refer to detailed notes. The points we wish to make should be part of our memory by now, and the purpose of notes is to prevent us from departing from the logical order of our talk.

> Notes for talk to
> Holiday Tour Operators
>
> 1. Welcome to Wigan
> 2. Explain purposes of 'Wigan for Holidays' event
> 3. List attractions
>   - location
>   - cost
>   - not touristy
> 4. List events
>   - Wakes Week
>   - Arboretum illuminations
>   - visit to Wigan Pier
> 5. Conclusion
>   - summarise
>   - repeat welcome

An exception to this advice is the set-piece speech to a large gathering. This is frequently read aloud, often through a microphone, but it tends to suffer from a lack of vitality and creates a feeling of distance between speaker and audience. A way of getting round this has been the development of the so-called *sincerity machine*. With this device the text of a speech is reflected from TV screens onto two glass screens at eye-level on either side of the speaker. The screens are visible to the audience, but the text display is not, so a speaker appears to be speaking without notes while at the same time looking through the glass screens at the audience. As far as the audience is concerned, the speaker appears to be talking to them naturally without having to refer to notes. In the same way TV presenters face a device known as an Auto-cue.

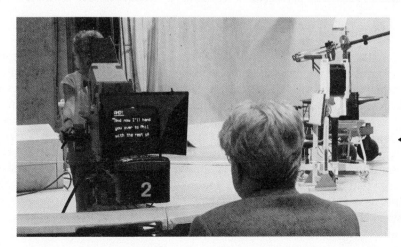

◀ *An auto-cue*

Beginnings and endings

The next thing to think about is the beginning and ending of our presentation. One tactic is to outline at the start what we intend to cover during the talk, and at the end, to summarise our main points. This is what happens in TV and radio news bulletins. The reason for this is that people find it easier to absorb information if they are alerted to the likely content in advance, and will remember it better if they are reminded of it again at the end. However, it is also necessary to give some thought to ways of attracting attention at the start of our talk, and of ending with a telling phrase or an interesting conclusion. One way to start is to tell a joke. This communicates to our audience that we are relaxed enough to invite them to laugh with us. Another way is to ask a rhetorical question, which we will later answer. This alerts them to some deficiency in their knowledge or understanding and hopefully provides them with a motive — other than mere politeness — for listening to us. A third opening is a statement that will shock our audience into taking notice. Whichever way we begin we must be sure that our opening remark is authoritative enough to demonstrate that we are now in charge. We can do this by waiting for quiet before speaking in a confident and loud voice that can be heard by everyone. If people are chatting, we must look them in the eye and say 'Can we make a start, please' or 'I think we're about ready'.

Ending on a positive note is important. There are two dangers here. One is to go on and on because everything seems to have gone well and we are enjoying being at the centre of attention. If this continues long enough, it may wreck an earlier good impression. The second error is to arrive abruptly at an unsatisfactory and hesitant conclusion. Avoid blurting out 'Er … well, that's about it … er … thanks …'. Instead aim for balance by returning to your opening theme. If you began with a joke, return to the punch line; if you began with a question, remind your audience that they have had their answer; if you began with a surprise, remind them that what was surprising before has now been made plain. For example, 'I began by suggesting that one out of three people in this room will die of cancer. I hope that now you can see a way of reducing this figure by adopting some of the more healthy practices that I have outlined this afternoon'.

ACTIVITY

Following some basic research, prepare in writing suitable opening and closing remarks for one of the following presentations.

- A service or product offered by your employer.
- Starting a BTEC course at college.
- Dangers in the office.
- Computers in the office.
- Equal opportunities at work.

Visual aids

A matter for careful thought is the use that can be made of illustrations and displays. Remember that a message is more likely to be received if it is transmitted through several rather than through one channel. Fortunately, a number of devices that permit this to happen are available in most commercial organisations. You may find that you are able to use a *whiteboard*. These are similar to the *chalkboards* of your schooldays, except that they are written on with felt-tip pens and wiped clean with a damp cloth. They are excellent as visual support for your talk because they allow you to jot down briefly your main points as you give them. A similar device is a *flipchart*, which is an easel to which a large pad of paper is attached. Again key points are jotted down for the audience before the next clean sheet is exposed by 'flipping' it over. A portable flipchart enables a speaker to stand closer to the audience, as opposed to a fixed whiteboard which often puts 'distance' between them.

Whiteboards and flipcharts have drawbacks. First, the act of writing on an upright board forces a speaker to turn away from the audience. Writing long items on either boards or flipcharts therefore risks breaking up a fluent talk with irritating pauses. Second, writing on such surfaces requires practice because it is not as easy as it looks. Words and drawings may be too small to be seen at a distance and the inexperienced user tends to allow his writing to drift at alarming angles. Such media should be used with restraint and only if the speaker is reasonably proficient.

ACTIVITY

To get in a bit of practice, reproduce the previous paragraph on either a whiteboard or a flipchart. Ask somebody at the back of the room to make critical comments.

An alternative form of display is the *overhead projector* (OHP). This device transmits images on a transparency onto a screen located behind the speaker. Overhead projectors are used to convey a range of written and illustrative material. This material should be prepared in advance of your talk and assembled in the order in which it is to be used. However, if it is intended to use audience reaction as part of the presentation, it is possible to write on transparencies during your talk. The advantage here is that you are able to face the audience while writing on the transparency and thus avoid having to turn your back on them. But be prepared for technical problems by familiarising yourself with the equipment beforehand. Finally, don't pin all your hopes on the projector. If things go wrong, you should still be in a position to put a good case.

If you intend to use photographs, make arrangements to borrow a *slide projector* for 35 mm transparencies. Once again, beware of gremlins, and make sure you can continue even if it breaks down. Some projectors require you to stand at the back of a darkened room. Nervous souls may find this attractive, but a better idea is to have a projector that is operated by a remote-control unit. This allows you to go either forwards or backwards through the sequence of slides and to adjust the focusing without losing the advantage of being in full view of the audience. Even in the half-light of a slide show, this is preferable to being at the back hidden from view.

Many forms of photographic and illustrative displays are possible, providing the material is of *poster* size, but it should be prepared and pinned up before you begin. Illustrations that are so small that only eagle-eyed members of the audience can see are a waste of time, and the same applies to any *plans* which you want them to look at. Under no circumstances should material be passed around while you are still speaking, and this also applies to any *samples* or *models* which are not big enough to be seen properly by the whole audience. When material is in circulation, there is far too much shuffling and whispering for you to continue effectively. Make sure that such items can be inspected afterwards. However, it is important not to be put off by these kinds of difficulties. Visual aids are an essential part of the process of 'bringing your information alive', which we dealt with earlier, and it is worth quoting again that 'one picture is worth a thousand words'.

You may have an opportunity to use *video tapes* or *close-circuit television* facilities to illustrate your talk. Although a professionally made video can be impressive, it is not a substitute for a presentation. There is still a need to use such material *within* a properly organised and interesting talk. Even so, if you do intend to take advantage of video or TV, you must ensure that you are technically competent to handle the equipment.

Finally, it is necessary to say something about *duplicated notes*. If the content of your talk is important and new, perhaps for a training or induction session, you will want your audience to have a more permanent record of important points. At college, such a record probably takes the form of hand-written notes, but you may prefer your audience just to listen while you speak. If you do decide to work in this way, make sure you don't hand out your duplicated notes until the end, otherwise they will provide a potential source of distraction.

The presentation

You first need to think about whether you intend to stand or sit when you deliver your presentation. As we saw in Chapter 4, it is probably better to stand to address a formal audience as this conveys an aura of authority. However, in less formal presentations, perhaps to a small group (as in an interview), standing would seem odd. Whether standing or sitting, one point to remember is not to attract attention away from what you are saying by nervous and distracting movements. You will recall that this is known as 'leakage', and as we are all guilty of it, there are a number of ways of handling it. For example, if you are projecting illustrations on a screen, what could be more natural than to make gestures which draw your audience's attention to the points you are making? This not only provides an outlet for releasing tension, but it also helps nervous speakers by allowing them to direct attention away from themselves to the illustrations they are showing.

If there is no obvious target to point at, you may find an outlet for leakage in a range of acceptable gesticulations. Counting off points on the palm of your hand, raising a finger to give emphasis, opening arms in a gesture of honesty or appeal, clasping and unclasping hands to suggest intensity of feeling — whatever the gesture — as long as it seems appropriate, your audience will scarcely be aware that you are doing it. But if your gesture is obsessive and repetitive (head shaking, tongue poking, face rubbing and scratching), your audience will begin to pay less attention to your utterances and more attention to this unusual form of communication. At best, it will become a source of embarrassment to both you and them; at worst, a flash point of ridicule and disruption. A similar point might be made about walking around during a presentation. Occasional movements may be helpful, if only to keep your audience alert and interested in what is happening, and especially in what is about to happen. However, ceaseless and meaningless pacing is very irritating.

One way of assessing audience reaction is to look them in the eye. Don't stare obsessively at anyone in particular, but let your gaze wander round the whole group. If someone is not paying attention, it is permissible to fix them with your gaze, just to let them know that you know that they are not playing the game. If this sounds a bit heavy handed, don't worry. Most social encounters are made up of interlocking roles. For every speaker there must be listeners: their roles interlock. The polite listener listens with his ears *and* eyes, and he knows it! Another trick is to tease your audience with pauses. When you are about to say something remarkable, pause beforehand, just for a second, and then deliver your bombshell. It adds a moment of drama to the occasion. A last tip is to vary the pitch and pace of your delivery. No doubt you will give some thought to your appearance before giving a presentation, so why not give thought to the intonation of your voice? Remember you do have an obligation to be interesting and entertaining, so there should be variety not only in content, but also in the way you deliver the content to your audience.

To be really effective, these techniques need to be brought to the point of **absorbed actions**; that is, they should be done unconsciously, in the way that we automatically check our rear-view mirror before performing driving manoeuvres. Yet we cannot reach this level of skill without practice, so try them out in front of your bedroom mirror before presentation day, and why not incorporate some of them in your everyday conversations. They may seem a bit theatrical, but you might be surprised by the results.

ACTIVITY

Prepare to give a 3-minute talk on a subject that you feel strongly about. Try to absorb at least some of the advice we have given you in the section *Tactics for presenters*. Then arrange for your talk (make it really dramatic) to be recorded on video tape. Play it back so that you can see yourself as others see you. Play it back a second time without the volume on. What do you notice about your gestures, facial expressions and body movements during your delivery?

Promoting an image

If potential customers are unaware of your organisation, then business opportunities are being wasted. The more people that know about your existence obviously increases your chances of being successful. However, knowledge may not in itself be enough to encourage custom. What customers believe they know about your organisation may not be conducive to making a sale, especially if the image they have is one of an unreliable, costly and unattractive business with uncompetitive products. So most organisations seek to create a favourable image for existing and potential customers. Raising or sustaining the awareness of people about a business is known as *promotion*. It differs to some extent from *advertising* in its purpose, for advertising is concerned with selling products or services. Nevertheless, there is clearly some overlap between the two, and most organisations will use one activity to complement the other.

One way of differentiating the two functions is to examine the cost headings allocated to each in company accounts. The cost of advertising will almost certainly be large, involving as it does the use of perhaps specialist agencies and the buying of space or time in newspapers, magazines and commercial broadcasting. Promotion is more or less a constant activity largely carried on in-house. What is being promoted is the *corporate image* of the organisation, and by this is meant the impression of the company that its management wish people to have of them. The idea of a corporate image is that it should be present wherever the organisation or its products are available for consumption, and sometimes beyond even this. The corporate image is there to create a favourable impression of the company and to that extent it may be in part created by advertising. However, advertising alone is not enough, and money and thought have to be expended on the design of stationery, labels, uniforms, etc., to reinforce the advertised image. Means of promoting a corporate image is shown in this diagram.

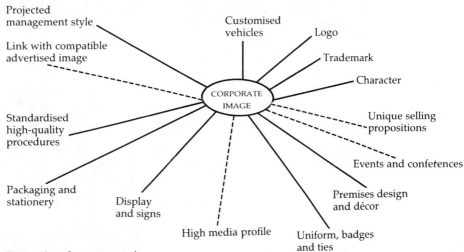

▲ *Promoting the corporate image*

239

Organisations that have the best-known corporate images are those that promote them hard to the wider community. Some images become so powerful that they are absorbed into our culture and language. We might *hoover* a carpet, or ask for a *kleenex* to blow our noses, or buy our toiletries from *Boots*, not thinking that these are actually brand images and not real words at all. If we are invited to reflect on such company names as Rolls-Royce, McDonalds and Woolworths, we tend to conjure up similar images in our minds. It is simply not possible to think of Rolls-Royce other than in terms of luxury and quality, and McDonalds in terms of fast food and hamburgers. McDonalds has in fact, almost single-handed, changed public eating habits in Britain in the last ten years — it has been a dazzling success story for the corporate image. Woolworths provides an interesting contrast. Here we have a company whose traditional image is one of a cheap-multi-item-store, whose management has lately put colossal efforts into changing our thinking. We are now being invited to think of Woolworths as an up-market store specialising in a more limited range of goods. We wait to see whether this happens.

ACTIVITY

It is proposed to create a wall display headed 'The Corporate Image'. Your task is to assemble a set of visual images used by your own or any company that projects a corporate identity. Look at the previous diagram for ideas and consider using photographs if necessary.

The total effect of all the elements involved in promoting a corporate image is to create a high profile. In the case of McDonalds, each restaurant has a distinctive but instantly recognisable appearance. A potential customer can identify the premises, not only by the shop-sign facing the High Street, but from the logo which usually appears on a hanging sign in the street and on doorpanels. Once inside, we experience customised design, décor and display, with the company name prominent on uniforms, packaging and in-store displays. There is never a question in our minds as to where we are or whose food we are eating. Children are attracted by the clown character of 'Ronald MacDonald' which appears on hats and displays. Once a year 'Ronald' visits each store and photographs are taken of young consumers with the celebrity. Adults, on the other hand, are more likely to be impressed by the high standards of cleanliness for which the company strive and for the speed of service and courteous manner of staff.

McDonalds are not alone in seeking a successful corporate image. Most organisations strive for similar goals, although methods and style differ. Does your employing organisation have its own logo? A **logo** is a graphical symbol used to project the company image, and you can find some examples on page 84. As a graphical symbol it is more redundant than the full name; it is therefore recognised more quickly. At one time, coats of arms were fashionable as symbols, but today most organisations prefer something less formal. An example is the red and blue 'heart' adopted by Birmingham City Council as part of its new corporate image policy. This symbol has largely supplanted the old city coat of arms.

▶ *The old Brum coat of arms*

► *The new corporate logo* **City of Birmingham**

Sometimes a logo accompanies a **trademark**. The trademark is often the name of the company incorporated as part of the logo design, as with the Birmingham logo. However, where a company makes several products, the trademark may be supplemented by the **tradenames** of the various products or services.

ACTIVITY

Logos are now widely used and you will surprise yourself by how many of them you know. In your notebook, make drawings from memory of the logos representing these organisations:

- McDonalds
- Lloyds Bank
- British Rail
- Volkswagen
- Olympic Games
- Bradford & Bingley Building Society

However effective these devices are in putting a company name before the public, it may be that this image is not right for the entire market. So the corporate image may be supported with a **character**, which attempts to give an attractive slant to what might be perceived as a rather impersonal organisation. We have seen how Ready Eddie (Ready Brek) and Ronald MacDonald (McDonalds) do this for their own companies. However, adults can be equally susceptible to this approach, and one of the most successful inventions was the cartoon character 'Buzby', a talkative cartoon bird who settled on telephone wires and made friends happy with his calls. Although abandoned by British Telecom during the early 1980s, this cartoon figure did much to dispel public hostility to what was regarded by many as an expensive and unreliable telephone service, and encouraged greater use of off-peak calls. An alternative to cartoon characters is the use of celebrities who have established themselves as entertainers or sports stars. The risk here is that exposure is often more beneficial to the superstar than it is to the organisation which has hired them!

Although more a feature of advertising, employing a **slogan** or catch phrase is yet another way of promoting a company image. Slogans have become potent image makers that are especially valuable in TV commercials. But organisations need to be very careful in choosing the right form of words — they have to be both exciting and sympathetic to the image that the organisation is trying to promote. Slogans are known to advertising people as **USPs (unique selling propositions)**. The idea is that they expose those features of the product that none of its rivals possess; in other words, characteristics which make it unique. If the slogan is effectively promoted, it alone can trigger mental images with which no other form of corporate image can compete. We only have to catch a glimpse of 'All because the lady loves ...' and 'We're getting there' for us to form a mental picture of the product or organisation involved.

When these elements — logo, trademark, character and unique selling proposition — are combined with advertising, stationery, premises and delivery vehicles, and reinforced by uniforms, interior decoration, and high-quality standardised procedures, they have a powerful effect, not only on customers, but also on employees. The corporate image, if it is a positive one, plays an important role in improving the morale of staff, who come to believe that they are working for a successful company. Here are some questions to think about:

- How aware are customers of the standardised high-quality procedures of your organisation?
- How aware are staff of the need to maintain these standards?
- How does management ensure that these standards are kept up to scratch?

```
┌─ ACTIVITY ─────────────────────────────────────────────────────┐
```

1 With which products do you associate these slogans:

Join the professionals
Cookability
More cats than ever before now prefer
Simply years ahead
We'll take more care of you
Flexible friend

2 Suggest or design suitable characters and slogans to promote these organisations:

Green Shield Garden Centre
Daltons Word Processors
The college you currently attend

Meeting the media

So far we have examined the elements of an organisation's corporate image and how this is developed through promotion and direct personal experience. However, a corporate image can also be helped along by using the publishing and broadcasting media. The advantages of this to an organisation are:

- Press publicity is free publicity.
- Customers' attitudes to press reporting are very different from their attitudes to advertising.
- It can reinforce and complement other attempts to build a corporate image.

How to interest the media

If you think that you have something to say that the media would find interesting, there are several methods of making contact.

Issuing a press or media release

A press or media release is a neatly typed statement issued by an organisation to the news media. It is the single most reliable way to get a story published accurately. From the reporters' point of view, a press release is the easiest, least time-consuming way of getting a story. We will take a longer look at how to write press releases later.

Calling a Press Conference

This is a meeting between representatives of an organisation and invited reporters, at which a prepared statement is made, followed usually by questions from reporters. It is a technique suitable when the story is a big one and in circumstances where reporters are likely to ask many questions. Typically they are used during police investigations, for major political developments, for new product launches and during major crises. Unless there is already a high level of media interest, editors will not release reporters for local or low-input stories, so it is important not to be over-ambitious.

Holding a Press Reception

This is a variation on the Press Conference at which extra facilities are made available to reporters. There may be food and drink, the opportunity to interview and photograph a guest celebrity, or a chance to preview a new product. This is more expensive to organise, but may make a reporter more favourably disposed towards your organisation. However, we must be wary of anything that smacks of bribery! And there is nothing that can be done about the sort of hack who sent a review of a new play to his editor before he discovered that the theatre had burnt down minutes before the first act.

Phoning a paper or radio station

Don't do this unless the story has blown up at the last minute. If you just ramble on to the reporter, don't be surprised if the printed version is a hashed version of what you said originally. Better to prepare what you want to say in note form, and then dictate it slowly.

Responding to a phone call from a reporter

If your organisation receives such a call, don't be bullied into saying something you'll regret afterwards. Here are some tips.

- Refer them to someone who knows more about the topic than you do, and then phone them and warn them of what's coming.
- Say you will phone them back in ten minutes, then find out fast what's happening.
- Only say 'No comment' when it's something you really don't want to get involved in.

If you are expecting the press or media to contact you, check to find out whether your organisation has appointed a particular employee to deal with enquiries.

Sending a 'letter to the editor'

Remember that letter pages are the least read sections of papers. Try to get your story onto the news pages first. If a correspondent attacks your organisation, don't enter into a long-running private war in the letters column. Big organisations who try to squash the voice of the outraged individual seldom emerge with any credit, even when they have a strong case.

What do you tell the press?

First, think about the sort of things that papers like to publish. Second, make sure that you always give them good news, and never display your weaknesses. Here are a few ideas about things you can feed the press and media.

Biography

Are you appointing a new Managing Director, a Branch Manager, or just taking a few hard-pressed youngsters off the dole? Give the papers a good quality black and white photograph and some biographical details of the people concerned.

Routine

There's often a story in the nuts-and-bolts of day-to-day operations, although beware of facts you would probably rather nobody knew about. Annual statistics, sales trends, new orders, export drives and company reorganisation: these all provide extra inches for a local editor eager to fill his columns.

Human interest

Births, marriages, golden weddings, star apprentices, retirements and acts of bravery can all provide column-fodder for a local paper. Of course, the pay-off for your organisation is not immediate, but it can create a favourable impression of your company among potential employees as well as in the community as a whole. Look particularly for 'COUNCIL STAFF RAISE £500 FOR CHARITY' stories, which encourage a caring and responsible image for your organisation.

Comment

This is one area where your organisation may have less to say because getting involved in local or national controversies can be counter-productive. However, here are some suggestions: banks could comment on a change in interest rates; CBI chiefs on proposed rate rises; police on crime or accident statistics; and local authorities on changing legislation and the effect it will have on their policies.

Campaigns

The launch of a new product or service should always be backed by coverage in the press. Make sure they know what your organisation is doing. Often, the press can be persuaded to do an unashamed 'puff' for your product if you've given them helpful and reliable information in the past, or if the success of your new product will generate or secure employment prospects in their circulation area. Placing advertisements in a paper/magazine may also persuade the publication to take a favourable attitude towards you. Nor should you forget to give your campaign a 'pulse' half-way through, by staging a stunt or releasing successful statistics to keep the story 'on the boil'.

ACTIVITY

Suggest one topic for each of the previous five categories that could form the basis of a media news-story to promote a favourable image of your own organisation.

When to contact the media

Having decided to release a story, when is the best time to do so? There is no single correct answer. Instead, it is necessary to build a relationship with and knowledge of your local media to know which days are generally short of news and when their deadlines are for accepting stories. Often the content of evening papers and news bulletins is decided quite early in the day.

Writing a press or media release

A press release is not a letter. Nor is it the item which will eventually appear in the paper or on the air. Instead it is your organisation's statement that provides an unknown reporter with sufficient information *on its own* to enable him to write an article. A helpful structure, therefore, should include:

- An attention-grabbing headline.
- A strong first paragraph that summarises the main point of the story.
- A range of points that you wish to make, in descending order of importance. (This is because news items are often cut down in length by deleting final paragraphs.)

Here is an example of a professionally written release produced during the evangelist Billy Graham's visit to Britain in 1984.

press release

BILLY GRAHAM
mission:england

FOR INFORMATION CONTACT: ATTENTION: NEWS/PHOTO EDITOR
Maurice Rowlandson   )
Larry Ross   ) 021 358 3730
Derek Williams   )

2nd July 1984

PRESS CALL
Young Evangelists Conference

There will be a Press Call at 1.30 p.m. at The Supporters Club at Villa Park
Stadium on Tuesday 3rd July. This will provide an opportunity to meet
participants in a unique event during the whole of this summer's Mission England
activities. Evangelists Leighton Ford (Billy Graham's brother-in-law) and Doug
Barnett (British evangelist with the Saltmine Trust) are leading a Young
Evangelists Conference to coincide with the Billy Graham meetings at Villa Park.

This is a strategic conference for a rising generation of British preachers. The
participants will also be available for interview or questions.

The 29 students who come from all over Britain will be taught how to prepare
sermons, organise missions, train counsellors, give an appeal to people to make a
public commitment to Christ, and how to develop their own personal and family
life. They will also act as counsellors during the Billy Graham meetings.

They will be on a practical open-air witness exercise at St. Martins in the
Bullring on Wednesday from 2.00 p.m. to 3.30 p.m. and photographers are welcome to
attend that exercise.

Annotations (right margin):
- Identifies nature of document
- Authentic printed heading
- Contact point
- Recipients
- Date and subject heading
- Opening paragraph containing essential information
- Important details underlined

Writing press releases needs practice, particularly as writing in journalistic clichés is seldom the best way to do the job. This checklist offers some useful advice.

PRESS RELEASES — a checklist

1 Type on one side of the paper only.

2 Use DOUBLE spacing and leave reasonable margins at either side.

3 Always put a heading on the release. Keep it to the point.

4 At the end of the release type the word 'ENDS' in capitals after the final line. If the release covers more than one page type the word 'MORE' in capitals at the bottom right hand corner of each page which has a follow-on. Number the pages if there are more than one.

5 Date the release in full at the end. For example, 20 November, 198–. When mentioning a day in the text, for example, 'today', 'tomorrow', 'last night', include the date and day in brackets afterwards. For example — 'at a meeting last night' (Thursday 19 November) …'.

6 The date and time your release can be published should appear at the start of the release, preferably at the top right hand corner of the page. If there is no embargo, type 'FOR IMMEDIATE RELEASE'. If the release is embargoed, state the time and date of the embargo. For example — EMBARGOED: NOT FOR PUBLICATION BEFORE 00.30 HRS, FRIDAY 20 NOVEMBER, 198–. Use the international 24-hour clock.

7 When referring to people by name use both forename and surname in the first instance.

8 Do not use jargon, clichés or short-forms. Only use abbreviations, e.g. CFE, MSC, YTS, after stating the organisation, etc. in full and giving the abbreviation in brackets the first time it is mentioned. You may need to give a brief, popular explanation of some terms.

9 Always try at least one usable direct quotation. Quotations should be checked with the person being quoted, and that person should receive a copy of what he/she has been quoted as saying.

Press Releases … continued

10 Use the 'pyramid' style, i.e. the first paragraph should contain the main points of the story — who, what, when, where and why (the five Ws). Each succeeding paragraph should be of less importance than the one preceding it.

11 Use vigorous language. Keep sentences short and simple. Express yourself positively.

12 Ensure that it is clear from whom and where the release has come. Give at least one contact name with day and evening telephone numbers. Ensure that your contact/s will be available when the release reaches the media.

13 Always keep a copy of the release that you send out.

ACTIVITY

Find out from the Students' Union or a lecturer about an event or initiative that is about to take place at your college. Draft a press release to publicise this, for circulation to the local paper and radio station.

The case for a change in our habits

SCENARIO

Your company (or college) has suddenly become health conscious, and has agreed with the local health authority to do what it can to increase staff (student) awareness of the dangers of poor nutrition and faulty diet.

THE UK has one of the highest rates of coronary heart disease in the world. The main risk factors are known to be cigarette smoking, high blood cholesterol, high blood pressure and lack of exercise.

In the USA and Finland, heart attack rates have fallen after community campaigns to alter risk factors including diet.

In recent years, the National Advisory Committee on Nutrition Education (NACNE) and many other expert committees have looked at all the evidence about diet and health and made recommendations for a healthier diet that will reduce the risk of heart attacks and other conditions.

The recommendations are:
● *REDUCE FAT INTAKE*

Aim to reduce percentage of calories supplied by fat from 40% to 30% by a reduction, mainly in saturated fats (meat, dairy produce).
Expected benefits:

Reduce heart attacks and other cardiovascular problems.
● *INCREASE FIBRE INTAKE*

Aim to increase fibre intake from 20 to 30 grams per day, especially by eating more wholegrain cereals.
Expected benefits:

Reduce incidence of constipation

Reduce incidence of haemorrhoids (piles)

Reduce diverticular disease and perhaps a reduced risk of colonic (bowel) cancer.

● *DECREASE SUGAR INTAKE*

Sugar provides only calories and no other nutritional benefit and can safely be avoided.
Expected benefit:

Less obesity (fatness)

Less dental caries (fillings)
● *DECREASE SALT INTAKE*

In this country we consume several times the minimum necessary amount of salt. Some people may therefore develop a high blood pressure from taking excess salt.
Expected benefit:

Less hypertension (high blood pressure)
● *DECREASE ALCOHOL INTAKE*

Alcohol is increasingly recognised as a major contributor to physical and mental illness. The risk of alcoholism is related to the average alcohol consumption of any society.

Safe levels of drinking are now thought to be 21 units per week for men and 14 units per week for women (1 unit = half a pint of beer/lager, or 1 single of spirits, or 1 glass of wine).
Expected benefits:

Decrease alcoholism.

Decrease cirrhosis of the liver and numerous other health benefits. (Alcohol at present contributes to about 10 per cent of all hospital admissions).
Other points to note:

Healthy eating habits are likely to bring greatest benefit if followed from childhood or early adult life.

TASK ONE / THE RESEARCH

After reading the article, which was published by the local health authority, decide which one *or* two of the five recommendations for a change in diet your team wishes to research in greater detail in preparation for a publicity campaign. The task will be completed when you have gathered sufficient information and background material with which to launch a campaign. Your primary aims are to:

— inform people of the facts
— offer them guidance on how to change habits of a lifetime
— persuade them of the advantages of doing so
— make recommendations to management about the canteen services.

(If you prefer, you may direct your campaign at reducing cigarette smoking or encouraging staff to take more exercise.)

TASK TWO / THE CAMPAIGN

Your team is now in a position to put together a package which contains all the materials, visual aids, and tactics that it intends to use in its campaign. It is entirely in the hands of each team to decide on its strategy, but materials and plans must be produced in time for a presentation to management.

TASK THREE / THE PRESENTATION

You are now to make a presentation of your materials and ideas to a management panel (made up from other teams) for advice and comment. You should be in a position to know roughly the total financial cost of your package.

SCENARIO

You are employed in the Publicity Department of Langdon Borough Council. As a member of a small team, your main job is to publicise and explain the work of the council to the public in the most effective and attractive way possible. Your biggest challenge so far is the Council's plans for the 'Brambles'.

▶ *Plan of the BRAMBLES*

Existing site

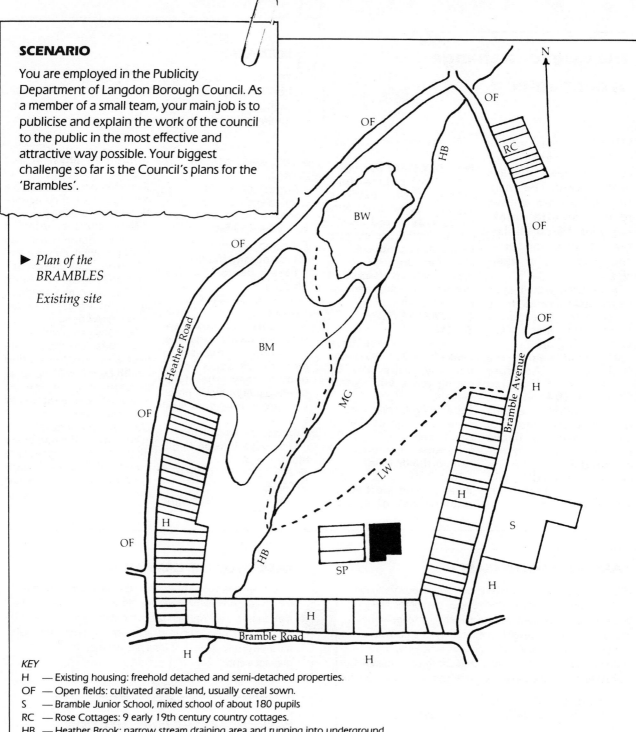

KEY

H — Existing housing: freehold detached and semi-detached properties.
OF — Open fields: cultivated arable land, usually cereal sown.
S — Bramble Junior School, mixed school of about 180 pupils
RC — Rose Cottages: 9 early 19th century country cottages.
HB — Heather Brook: narrow stream draining area and running into underground culverts beneath roads and housing.
MG — Marshy ground.
SP — Derelict sports pavilion and tennis courts.
BM — Bluebell Meadow: grassed area used for recreational purposes.
BW — Bluebell Wood: woodland containing many species of trees and plants.
LW — Lovers' Walk: a pathway famous for prickly brambles and courting couples.

Langdon Borough Council, 49–52 High Street, Langdon, L5 1EA

The proposals

The Council has put forward a scheme, as part of a new development policy, under which they are to acquire the entire 60 acres of common land known as the 'Brambles'. This is a triangular parcel of flat land lying north of Bramble Road, bounded on the east and west by Bramble Avenue and Heather Road respectively.

This 60 acres is roughly divided in half by Heather Brook, which itself splits in two for part of its course. At its widest, this waterway is never more than 2 m. The piece of land enclosed on all sides by Heather Brook is marshy, water-logged ground.

The land north of Heather Brook is largely taken up by Bluebell Meadow and a small wooded area. South of Heather Brook is rough open ground on which is situated a small derelict sports pavilion and three overgrown and abandoned tennis courts.

Outline proposals

The Council proposes to build a three-storey open hostel for long-stay, elderly men (maximum accommodation for 150 staff and inmates) on a site south of the wooded area in Bluebell Meadow. Some of the inmates will be ex-offenders. The hostel will have gardens, grounds and car parks of about 8 acres, including minor roads.

South of Heather Brook, on a site cleared of the derelict sports pavilion, will be built a substantial sports stadium containing a large multi-purpose sports hall, squash courts, swimming pool, games room, sauna and changing rooms. An adjoining site of 16 acres will be levelled and grassed over, and marked out for outdoor sports (football, cricket, tennis, etc.). Although the hostel residents will have preferential rights, these facilities are available to local residents at a reasonable cost. The marshy ground will be drained and grassed over and the brook redirected along a single channel. All the remaining rough open land will be landscaped and trees planted. The Council insists that these proposals should be accepted in total and there is very little room for manoeuvre. For example, they are not prepared to build the sports complex without the hostel. However, they are prepared to listen to proposals that involve only minor changes.

Look at the proposals on the next page.

▼ *Plan of the BRAMBLES*

The proposals

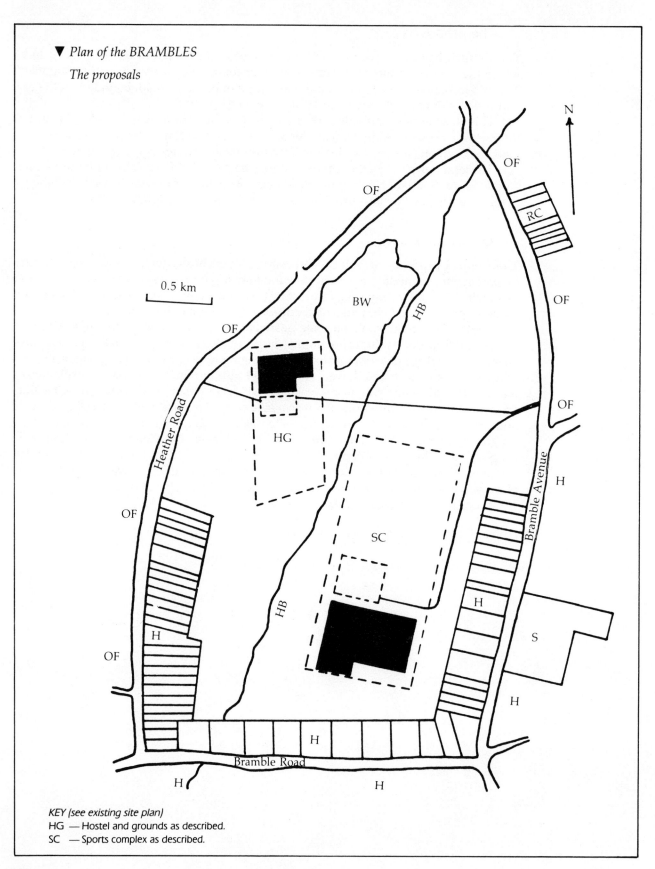

KEY (see existing site plan)
HG — Hostel and grounds as described.
SC — Sports complex as described.

TASK ONE / PUBLICITY

Your team is aware of the delicate nature of these proposals and accepts that only a well-planned campaign is likely to succeed. After much discussion, you decide to prepare:

- A 200/300 word press release for the local paper and radio station.
- An A3 poster announcing a Public Meeting to be held in the Town Hall.
- A circular letter to be distributed to residents living in and near the Brambles area, explaining the reasons for the new developments and inviting them to write or phone in with their comments. (Circulars are covered in Chapter 3.)

TASK TWO / THE PUBLIC MEETING

Your team is to prepare and deliver a 20-minute presentation to an audience made up of other teams. Making effective use of visual aids, the basic purpose of your talk is not only to remind people of your proposals, but also to relieve their anxieties. Fortunately, you do have a few clues as to what might be worrying local residents as a result of their phone calls to the Council offices. Here is a summary.

Extracts from telephone calls received at the office

1 Have you considered the effect of all the extra cars in the neighbourhood? How much extra traffic will result from the sports centre and visitors to the hostel? Will there be a later demand for road widening schemes?
2 Will there be more young people hanging about the sports centre during the summer months? Will this mean an increase in vandalism to nearby houses?
3 The Brambles is now a neat and pretty area. What is it going to be like in the future? How much litter is there going to be?
4 Will the increase in traffic endanger our children? Will we need a Pelican Crossing?
5 What about the Pony Club? Does it mean that we can no longer use the Brambles for our learner riders?
6 This area has a good reputation. How long will that last when people hear about the 'old lags'? Maybe even their friends will start visiting the area. Will this mean more police cars?
7 Will people have to keep their doors bolted at night? What about increases in theft?
8 What's it going to be like living here when they start the construction? How much noise and inconvenience are they going to cause? Will we have lorries charging up and down country lanes? How long is all this misery going to last?
9 Old lags today — what do we get tomorrow? Maybe the Council has plans for a 'Super Centre' for criminals, perverts and junkies?

TASK THREE / THE CORRESPONDENCE

Meanwhile letters have been arriving at your office in response to your circular letter and press release. After careful reading, you select three letters which seem to merit an individual reply. Draw up suitable replies, taking into account that the final plan has yet to be approved by the Council.

The letters

THE BRAMBLES SPORTS AND LEISURE ASSOCIATION
Geoff Fawkes, Secretary
16 Bramble Avenue

Dear Sir

In the light of the public discussion about the proposed development of the 'Brambles', I would like to take the opportunity on behalf of my members to express this Association's point of view.

Much of the public discussion so far has centred on young families, and while their wishes and needs have to be considered, I would like to make it clear that there are other needs in the area.

There is very little in the way of sports amenities for local teenagers and the proposals put forward offer a golden opportunity for changing this situation. There is a demand for tennis facilities, squash and football and many other recreational activities and the proposed development of the 'Brambles' can only add to the area and improve the social life of the local population.

Please take these requirements into account.

Yours faithfully

THE BRAMBLES RATEPAYERS ASSOCIATION
Mrs Clara Hyde, Acting Chairperson
'Lilliput'
87 Bramble Road

Sir

Concerning the proposed development of the area of natural parkland known as the 'Brambles', I would like to take this opportunity of informing you of the points raised at the last meeting of the Ratepayers Association.

1 The Brambles is a rich area of natural beauty, adding much to the quality of life of local residents. It allows parents the opportunity of instructing their children in the pleasures of the English landscape.
2 While appreciating that hostels have to be located somewhere, concern was expressed on the adverse affect this siting will have on the price and value of property.
3 The area has a high proportion of children under twelve and concern was expressed that 'social undesirables' in the area could bring needless worry to parents.

The Association would like to make it clear that it has no objection to ratepayers' money being spent on such proposals. What is at issue is the location of the site. Given the nature of the hostel, it seems to the ratepayers that it would be more appropriate if the hostel was sited in an area that would be more familiar to the hostel residents.

This is a highly desirable area and its amenities are far more appropriate for young families than for men who are undergoing some form of social rehabilitation.

Yours sincerely

Certain words have been deleted from this correspondence.

From Sammy Johnson
6 Rose Cottages

Dear Sir

I bet by now you have got dozens of letters and telephone calls from so-called 'concerned' citizens telling you how sorry they are for these old men who have nowhere else to live. I bet they say that they should go somewhere else and not spoil such a beautiful place as this with new developments.

It's just because round here they are a load of toffee-nosed ★★★★ snobs. They don't really care about the countryside anyway. They like the countryside because they think that they can get more money for their ★★★★ little houses when they come to sell them.

I've been living round this district for over 60 years. There was nothing when I first came here. We didn't object then to having houses built round here, did we? If we did, then these ★★★★★ people wouldn't be living here now, would they?

What do these ★★★★★ town people know anyway. Somebody told me that some people were moaning about the council draining that sinking marshy ground near the brook because it was part of nature. What a load of ★★★★ rubbish! That ★★★★ bog killed my best dog. One minute it was barking, then the poor ★★★★★ was gone, sucked down and drowned. How can anyone want such a ★★★★★ place as that.

And as for Bluebell Meadow, well that's a joke. What it is really is for rich people to ride their horses all over the place, which is dangerous, and there's so much dog ★★★★★ around, it's like an obstacle course. I think it's all right really, but to call it a meadow is ★★★★★ ridiculous.

I say live and let live. I'm glad these old folk are coming — it will give me some company. I'm glad they are making something decent out of that waste-land. I'm glad about the sports place as well. I like to see young people enjoying themselves. I hear they are having a games room built for the old folks where we can play dominoes and bingo.

When they build these places the folks round here will be able to walk in peace across the Brambles without funny-looking people pestering them.

Thanks

THE BRAMBLES NATURE SOCIETY
Thomas Beech, Secretary
'Nightingale'
29 Heather Road

Dear Sir

I would like to outline the views of the membership of the Brambles Nature Society regarding the proposals for the development of the 'Brambles'.

It goes without saying that this is a very scenic area which captures the very best of the English countryside throughout the seasons. The parkland offers the nature lover the chance of seeing, on their doorstep, a variety of native oak, the Spanish chestnut, one remaining elm and a birch tree which may be the oldest in England.

In midsummer in Bluebell Meadow there is nothing so pleasant than walking through the rich variety of plants and wildflowers. Many nature lovers can think of nothing so rewarding as walking amongst jagged leaves of bracken and nettle growing in the shadow of wayside oaks, while observing in the hawthorn thickets the bramble and the wild rose trailing their tenacious, prickly branches.

If all this sounds a little too lyrical in these 'technocratic' times, then so be it. What the members of the committee should be aware of is that there are people who are concerned with preserving part of the English heritage, and what finer tribute to this great nation of ours than our natural countryside.

We urge you to fight these appalling plans.

Yours faithfully

THE BRAMBLES ORNITHOLOGICAL SOCIETY
Jonathan Spalding, President,
7 Bramble Road

Dear Sir

I am writing to you regarding the proposed development of the Brambles parkland area. I take it you wish to consider opinion from all sections of the local community and the points raised in this letter represent the full membership opinion of this society.

As you know, the Brambles parkland is an open area of land close to a built-up area. We realise that Bluebell Wood will be retained but any increase in human activity will have an effect on the 'balance of nature', frightening away many bird species.

I would like to draw your attention also to the studies which have been taking place on the Brambles under the auspices of the Royal Society for the Protection of Birds. Intensive studies are taking place on the migration patterns of the Fieldfare (Turdus pilaris) a winter visitor to the British Isles when it may be seen mixing in the hedgerows with other members of the thrush family. In bird migration studies we see one of the most fascinating and, at times, controversial aspects of the feathered world and any disruption to such studies would bring great disappointment to many people.

The Society in no way wants to appear to lack sympathy for the hostel residents and we certainly do not wish our letter to be considered totally destructive. We suggest that it would be possible to site the hostel further south, increasing the distance from the wood. This would leave the Fieldfare essentially undisturbed and the important research work could continue.

We hope for an encouraging response.

Yours faithfully

No. 2 Rose Cottages
Bramble Avenue

Dear Sir or Madam

I have read in the local paper about the changes that might be happening to the Brambles. I don't want these changes to take place because I have got happy memories of this place.

I've never written anything like this before so I hope you can follow my writing because I'm not educated. I expected to end my days in peace. I don't want old men wandering down the backs of our gardens. This news has really upset me and I've had to go to the doctor with the worry of it. If my husband was alive he would be very upset about it too.

Please try to do all you can to stop this happening to our homes.

Yours truly

Gladys Plum

P.S. I can't come to your meeting because I'm having trouble with my legs.

NATIONAL ASSOCIATION FOR THE CARE AND
REHABILITATION OF OFFENDERS
Head Office: London, W12

Dear Sir

Having read in the press of the proposed plans re: *redevelop the site known as the Brambles*, this organisation would like to congratulate the Council on its forward thinking.

We are more than aware of the stigma attached to those with criminal records. We feel that the general public should rid themselves of the many false ideas associated with ex-offenders. Certainly the men who will make use of the hostel will have been disturbed, but this does not mean that they can be written off.

Having said this, we are aware that these individuals may seem odd to the local community and at times no doubt an isolated incident may give cause for concern. In the light of this, we would like to make available to you any information or service necessary to deal with the fears of the community.

We think that the residents of the hostel will respond to their new environment in a positive way. For many it will be a fresh start in life, albeit a little late, and with the help and understanding of the local community we feel that they will adapt to their new surroundings.

We appeal to all the humane and decent people of the Brambles to join us in helping these men to enjoy something of a normal existence.

Yours sincerely

Robert Martin

The name and address of this contributor has been withheld on request.

Sir

I feel bound to inform you that there is a certain group of influential residents who have conspired to use their privileged position to mount a campaign against the Council's proposals. Their purpose is to preserve the area and thereby maintain the high value of their property and land interests.

I am not suggesting for one moment that they are acting illegally, but the result of their actions might give the false impression that most of the local people (who live in rented accommodation) are against the scheme. They are creating an atmosphere of fear and hysteria amongst the elderly in particular.

I would therefore like you to mount some sort of survey to find out the people's real opinions. So many people find it difficult to write letters and they can't be bothered to attend meetings, but their views should still be sought.

Yours faithfully

TASK FOUR / THE MODIFIED PLAN

Keeping in mind the conditions laid down by the Council, make a rough drawing of the Brambles area on A4 and draw in the best arrangement of buildings and facilities that could be included in a modified plan, taking into account some of the ideas and needs of the local community and pressure groups. You must decide for yourself the priorities — not everyone can have their own way!

On a large piece of card produce a modified scaled drawing for submission to the Council. Attach to your drawing a brief report that explains the reasons for your recommended changes. Your final plan will include the best ideas from your group's drawings.

Communicating in groups

- A group is a collection of individuals deliberately formed for a specific purpose, say to play poker, while a team, say a cricket team, is a collection of individuals with a common goal that is more important to them than their individual goals.

- A meeting is a group of people who singly will do nothing and collectively decide nothing will be done.

- A meeting is a group of people who keep minutes and waste hours.

- A meeting is a gathering of people who decide when the next meeting will take place.

- A group of the unwilling, picked from the unfit to do the unnecessary.

- A camel is a horse designed by a committee.

As these definitions show, many people have a rather jaundiced view of the value of groups. However, think for a moment of the complex range of functions and interests within even quite small organisations. If no-one was allowed to speak to more than one other person at a time, how many decisions would ever get made, understood or acted upon?

Working with others in a group, whether through informal, specially formed *ad hoc* teams or informal committees, is essential as a means of gathering and disseminating information, performing tasks and reaching decisions in organisations. However, as the following activity attempts to demonstrate, working in groups is a complicated process that contains many pitfalls.

ACTIVITY

For this activity you can be either an observer or a participator. You will need two complete packs of playing cards and a large table top.

As a participator, you are in a team of three which has been given two mixed-up and incomplete packs of playing cards. Working as a team, you are to arrange both packs of cards in descending order, in four separate suits, face-up, in eight vertical lines on the table. No card must touch another. The task will be completed when you have handed to the observer a sheet of paper on which you have written the number and identity of the missing cards. The observer will ask you to continue with the task if either your answer is wrong or the cards are misplaced.

As an observer, you are to shuffle both packs of cards together, removing as many cards as you wish in preparation for the team task. Your individual task is to assess the team's performance on a copy of the table overleaf.

GROUP ACTIVITY	Team 1	Team 2	Team 3	Team 4	Team 5	Team 6
Did all the team members make an effective contribution?						
Did sufficient planning take place in preparation for the task?						
Did effective communication take place between group members?						
How do you assess it as a team performance?						
How do you assess the overall result?						
TOTAL SCORES						
Time taken in minutes and seconds						

Enter scores in the spaces provided on the basis of:

Excellent	4
Above average	3
Average	2
Below average	1
Abysmal	0

To complete the task, write brief answers to these questions.

1 In your opinion, what was the main difference between the successful and the less successful teams?
2 To what degree did strong or weak leadership figure in the teams' performances?
3 When a team's performance was hampered by the actions of individuals, what particular form did this take?
4 What role did faulty communication play in the failure of any team to complete the task satisfactorily?
5 What helpful advice would you offer to any small team which was about to embark on a similar project?

Working together

Unemployed people find that one of the things they miss most by being out of work is the social contact with their fellow employees. Perhaps if you have been unemployed, you will have experienced this sense of isolation for yourself. Similarly, one of the factors that persuades many young and not-so-young people to prematurely quit their warm beds for the classroom on cold winter mornings is the knowledge that their friends will also be at college sharing similar experiences.

Social psychologists such as Michael Argyle suggest that the need for companionship is a basic motivational drive for all human beings, and that our habits of living and working together and for playing in groups or teams is evidence of this. Indeed, membership of the work group is probably more important than many of us recognise. Not only does it give us a feeling of social and personal identity (What do I do? I'm a cashier with the Nat West in Derby, actually.), but it also impinges upon non-work activities too. For example, many employees see each other socially, or join in recreational activities which are provided out-of-hours by their employers.

The role of work as a dominating influence on our lives cannot be over-estimated, and it goes a long way in explaining why long-term unemployment is so devastating for many families. If you have any doubts about this, you might like to consider how work (or somebody's work in your family group) has contributed to your own lifestyle and life-chances *outside* the work environment.

Many organisations are so big and complex that it is difficult for employees to relate to them directly, except in a vague general sort of way. In such cases, we often identify more strongly with a smaller subgroup within the organisation, as shown in this table.

Loyalty/identification

Weak					Strong
College lecturer	Department of Education & Science	Local Education Authority	Technical College	Academic Department	Subject Team
Assembly worker	Parent company	Divisional company	Plant site	Own shift or assembly line	Nearby line workers
Chain store supervisor	Marks & Spencer	Store at which employed	Trading Department	Staff for whom responsible	Fellow supervisors

▲ *Relating to the organisation*

Some of the groups and subgroups that you have identified in the activity may have short lives or restricted functions, for instance interdepartmental working parties or safety committees. However, because of the crucial role that groups play in integrating employees within organisations, especially in the field of passing information and decision-making, it is necessary to examine their functions and characteristics in greater detail.

Group processes

In all group work there are two main components.

- Content: the subject, purpose or task for which the group has been assembled, whether it is to plan the layout of the new office or to discuss arrangements for the Christmas party.
- Process: (or dynamics) describes what is going on between the group members while the task is being performed.

Some groups operate as a succession of one-to-one contacts that are witnessed by others. For example, in a classroom when the teacher insists that only one person speaks at a time and that the student addresses the teacher rather than the other students, or in formal committee meetings where everyone 'addresses the Chair', as in parliamentary debates. Such patterns can be expressed diagrammatically like this.

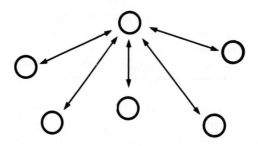

▲ *One-to-one relationships in groups*

Other groups consist of a much freer exchange of views and ideas between all members. An example of such an exchange could be a group of friends chatting in a canteen or pub. This can be shown like this.

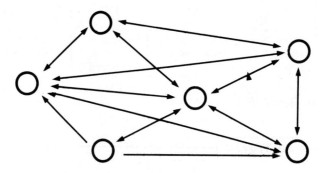

▲ *Multiple relationships in groups*

ACTIVITY

Identify both a formal (or centralised) and an informal (or decentralised) group activity in which you have taken part recently. Why were the groups organised that way? Would you have been able to communicate as effectively in any other way?

Neither style of interaction is absolutely right or wrong. It would seem silly for a group of friends chatting about their plans for the evening to talk 'through the Chair', but if the meeting consisted of a large number of self-interested groups discussing their attitudes to a proposed motorway by-pass, a free exchange of views would soon degenerate into a deafening rabble with no-one listening to anyone else. Therefore, the main factors that determine the method of communication within a group are:

- The size of the group.
- The social or business setting.
- Whether members of the group already know each other and their views.
- The time available.

Attempting to understand group processes, as we did for the first activity in this chapter, means that we must look at what actually happens to and between the members of the group while it is together. This means observing:

- The atmosphere that prevails.
- The degrees of participation or conflict between the group's members.
- Any struggle for dominance between members.
- The state of group morale.

Unfortunately, a group's task or subject often receives much more attention than its processes, which is why many groups are less effective than they should be.

ACTIVITY

Think of your class at college and your group behaviour when sitting around at break or lunch time. Now think of how your group behaves when a teacher comes into class. Does the atmosphere change? Do you become more or less talkative? Is there a change in leadership roles? Are you the same with different teachers? Jot down some notes for discussion.

None of this behaviour 'just happens'. It is the consequence of the processes going on within your group. Later on we will explore these processes, and some causes of conflict, but first let us look at roles which help or hinder group work.

Roles in groups

You may have thought that when you are working in a group you are simply being yourself and trying to get the job done. However, research undertaken by psychologists in human behaviour suggests that group members often unknowingly play one or more roles, and that these roles may assist or detract the group from achieving its objectives. Broadly, the three main roles are as follows.

Task helping roles

Task helping roles consist of the ways in which you help to get the job done, e.g., by offering or asking for information or by clarifying points made by others.

Team helping roles

Team helping roles aid the processes by which the group will achieve its task, e.g., by encouraging full participation and a constructive team spirit.

Negative roles

Negative roles are the ways in which one member sets out to frustrate the group's purpose, e.g., by talking too much, failing to contribute, or criticising others destructively.

Most meetings contain a mixture of people adopting one or more of these roles. However, we should appreciate that group members who choose to criticise ideas and proposals can be either constructive or destructive in their approach. In other words, the *way* that we present our criticisms is often more important than the literal meaning of our words.

What a performance!

John: Has everyone got their coffees? Good. Well, I asked you all round so we could put our heads together about why the team has lost every game this season. I'm afraid our performances have been pathetic.

Pat: Who needs a meeting for that? It's obvious. Four of the last practice sessions were cancelled, and we all know why!

Sally: That's it, blame me all the time. I didn't choose to have flu. I didn't ask to be sent on that course … it's just bad luck … could happen to anyone.

John: Calm down you two. No-one is suggesting anyone is to blame.

Pat: Hmph.

Mary: I doubt whether the missed practices are the main reason we did badly. Steve from the Abco team told me that they only had one full practice because of the odd shifts that they all work.

Dan: Mary's right. Abco overcame it by doing lots of individual practising — not ideal, I know, but it doesn't seem to have harmed their performance as a team. I suggest we try the same.

John: Well, what does everyone else think of Dan's suggestion?

Pat: I think it's stupid. We're supposed to be a team, and now you're telling us team practices aren't necessary.

Mary: Dan made a good point, but I also agree with Pat that we ought to try to get together whenever we can. Perhaps Wednesday evenings are the problem. Would Saturday or Sunday mornings suit anyone better?

Sally: I don't think I could get away then. I usually help my Nan at the weekends … although …

John: Any other ideas? What do you think Chad?

Chad: Uh? Oh! Yeah, I agree. Whatever you say.

ACTIVITY

Within each of the three main roles — of task helping, team helping and negative roles — there are a number of subordinate features, which researchers have identified. How many of the following did you see evidence of in *What a performance!*

Task helping roles	Generating activity Offering information Offering opinions Requesting information	Coordinating Clarifying Summarising Requesting opinions
Team helping roles	Involving/linking Encouraging Tension relieving	Responding Mediating Testing group feelings
Negative/destructive roles	Blocking Seeking recognition Seeking sympathy Clowning around	Aggression/hostility Special pleading Withdrawal

Obviously there is considerable overlap between these roles, but to some extent all must be performed if the group is to function effectively. Often members of the group switch around and adopt different roles at different times, and the skill of the chairperson is also an important ingredient in determining outcomes.

In most groups there is usually some negative behaviour. At such times it is easy to blame the main offender (X is in a bad mood today) and assume all would be well if only he/she were removed. However, an individual's obstructiveness may be a symptom of deeper problems that affect the whole group. For example, it may be because:

- Objectives have not been agreed.
- There is conflict over strategy, or the best approach to take.
- There is fear of the unknown, or of change, which more information or reassurance could overcome.

Sometimes, especially in long-established groups such as standing committees, a little negative behaviour may prove positive in the long term, if it shakes the other members out of complacent inactivity.

Group norms and cohesiveness

The bulk of our lives both in and out of work is spent in the company of relatively small groups. For those of us who have a job, the group with which we work and interact closely is called our 'primary working group'. We can easily identify the members of our primary working group because we see and work with them frequently and we are often on friendly first-name terms.

Every group develops its own 'norms'. We use the term 'norms' to describe the standards of behaviour accepted and shared by members of any particular group. Norms are in fact the 'unwritten rules' that govern our behaviour more or less continuously throughout the whole of our lives. Primary working groups are no exception to this. At work, norms may be imposed externally, for example by management, or developed informally within the group itself. The norms themselves collectively constitute the culture of the group — a concept you will be familiar with from Chapter 2.

Cohesiveness on the other hand is the sense of attraction and identification felt by each member for his or her group. These feelings, like many individual relationships, build on themselves and the closer the group becomes, the more its members will understand their goals. This makes them more effective at achieving goals, which in turn makes the group more cohesive. In the following story, you will be able to see clearly how norms and cohesiveness are closely linked.

Playing ball

The five staff in the Claims Processing Section had worked together for nearly three years. They were recognised by their supervisor as experienced and efficient, and were left very much to get on with the work as they saw fit. Each worker processed an average of twelve claims a day and no-one ever deviated by more than one or two from this average. However, since a backlog of work was beginning to develop and the staff said they couldn't work any faster while maintaining high standards, a new recruit was taken on.

Pat, the new worker, was able enough, but found his new job rather a grind and did not work particularly hard at it. After training, his output averaged only eight or nine claims a day. At first, the others in the section seemed friendly and easy-going, but within a few weeks Pat felt an increasing coolness in their attitude towards him. Although nothing was said, it was clear that his behaviour was unacceptable. Gradually Pat's output rose to twelve claims a day, and he realised that his colleagues were, after all, nice friendly people to work with.

A year later Jo was recruited to help with the continuing expansion of work. After many months of unemployment, she was determined to make a success of her new job, and threw herself into it with enthusiasm. She was surprised that the more experienced staff could only process twelve claims a day — she had no difficulty in doing fifteen — and her hard work soon earned her congratulations from the manager. Unfortunately, like Pat, Jo noticed a coolness in the attitude of her previously friendly colleagues. Again, nothing was said, but within a few weeks Jo's average output also settled down to about twelve claims a day.

This story illustrates both the strengths and weaknesses of most work groups. Cohesiveness is usually a positive and productive force, but even very cohesive groups can create their own standards and norms which may conflict with those of the organisation. Although this particular work group is described by the supervisor as efficient, the group has defined 'efficiency' as the daily processing of twelve claims per person, and processing fewer or more than this is deviant behaviour that is unacceptable to the group norm.

This kind of group behaviour at work was first observed at the Hawthorne Electrical Works near Chicago by the American researcher Elton Mayo in the early 1930s. One group of workers in the study was observed to set a standard production target for each day, and any worker who didn't reach that target was given the cold shoulder and described as a 'chiseler'. Anyone who produced too much (which was unforgivable because it threatened the men's job security) was described as a 'rate buster'. Rate busters were considered particularly contemptible and were an easy target for ridicule. But even more contemptible were the 'squealers' who ran to the bosses 'telling tales'. Squealers were just about the lowest form of life in creation: the pits. (You might like to think of equivalent words for *rate buster*, *chiseler* and *squealer*, which might be used in your own job context.) It is, however, less likely that negative behaviour will be evident in cohesive groups, as members usually like and help each other and are committed to maintaining successful outcomes. Size may be a factor in this, for the closest and most cohesive groups usually contain about five to eight members.

ACTIVITY

Lecturer 1: I just can't get through to that group. As individuals they're all fine, but as a class they just sit there in icy silence, glaring, daring you to make them crack.

Lecturer 2: Yes, it's strange. The group I've just had are on the same course. They are the same age, same qualifications, same background. Yet they're the most willing, friendly lot you could imagine. I wonder what it is that makes the two groups so different … ?

Think about your own class at college.

- Does it have a group personality, or does it consist of a lot of separate subgroups or even separate individuals?
- Can you identify any norms that exist which make your group different from others?
- Do you employ any words or phrases, or engage in any tactics, to discourage individuals from stepping outside the group's norms? What are these words and tactics?
- Now ask your teacher for his or her opinion of your group compared with similar classes he/she teaches. What conclusions can you draw?

The group in the organisation

It should be clear by now that how we behave in one group may be very different from how we behave in another. This is of interest to our employer, who is largely concerned with getting a job of work done.

COMPASSIONATE LEAVE

John worked in the Branch Accounts Section of Teknik's Head Office. Three months previously, his wife had left him, and he was looking after his nine-year-old son alone. The boy had just contracted chickenpox and John felt in need of a few days off work to nurse him and to do some housework.

John first approached his supervisor, Alan, to ask for compassionate leave. He knew that the procedure would be for Alan to gain approval from the Personnel Department, who would in turn make a recommendation to Mr Phipps, the Financial Accountant, to authorise the time-off. Alan was a much older man, a little distant from the rest of the staff, but kind and sympathetic, with a fatherly concern for his section. He promised to do what he could.

The next day John was absent. Alan, who liked everything to be done 'by the book' was a little annoyed that he had not waited for formal clearance from the boss. When John did return Alan tackled him. Had this been a particular emergency?

'No, just what we'd talked about. I needed a few days off.'

'But you could at least have waited for verbal clearance. This puts me in a bit of a spot, you taking time off without permission. Looks bad ...'

John took a deep breath. 'Actually I did know that David had authorised the absence.'

'How could you have known? Even I didn't hear until ...'

'Well, you see I know David ... er ... Mr Phipps socially. We're in the same cricket club — I'm his club captain, actually — and he's the man my wife is living with. It's all quite civilised, and I had to ring him anyway the other night, and that's when he told me that the absence would be fine ...'

From this account it is clear that John, like the rest of us, belongs to several distinct groups. He also probably relates individually to the members of these separate groups quite differently as he plays out his roles as 'family man', 'man at work' and 'cricket captain'. He may, for instance, give an impression of being a 'pipe-and-slipper-man' in the family setting, but 'one-of-the-boys' when he gets into the bar at the cricket club. Indeed, his role and Mr Phipps' role are in fact *reversed* when they move from work to a cricket club environment, and both men seem quite happy about it.

ACTIVITY

1 In the story *Compassionate Leave*, identify the two components of content and process in your analysis of what happened.

2 List at least five distinct groups to which you belong and enter the details on a copy of this table.

Identity or function of group to which you belong	Process analysis: comment on the level of conflict or cooperation and state of morale, etc.	List a few adjectives describing how you might appear to others

The adjectives in your last column may have thrown up an amazing variety of responses which on the face of it seem to be describing different people. Did your list appear something like this?

Family — moody, untidy, dreamy, selfish.
College — lazy, unpunctual, talkative.
Pub   — a good laugh, generous, a bit wild.

Some groups to which we belong are formally acknowledged and easily recognised, like the family or the work group. Others are much 'looser' and rather more difficult to define, like the gang that you meet up with before the match on Saturday or the people catching the 08.19 train from your local station. Membership of groups can be expressed by using Venn diagrams.

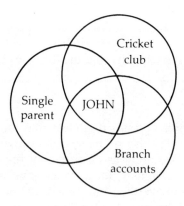

▲ *Venn diagram of John's major group activities*

If you think back to earlier chapters — on the culture of organisations and on the motivation of people at work — you will remember that employers know that it is in their interests for you to feel involved in, and committed to, the more desirable objectives of their organisation. Many go to great lengths and expense to foster a corporate spirit.

In all but the smallest organisation, subgroups soon appear. These may find difficulties in communicating easily with groups in other parts of the organisation. This is because most divisions, departments and sections take on a group personality of their own which may alienate outsiders, even if individuals within the different groups find each other compatible outside work.

Your answers to the final question may have included:

- Because we are all fairly friendly and cooperate, and people in other sections seem stand-offish and snooty.
- Because we're the only ones under thirty in the office.
- Because we're the only ones who actually want to work, and the others are just time-wasters.
- Because we all started here the same week, went through induction together, and stayed friends, even though we're now all in separate departments.

Some stresses between departments are not caused by personal or group personalities; they have more to do with the different functions of parts of the organisation and the priorities that they believe to be important. Here are some examples.

- Production and Sales Departments may be in conflict over the company's range, prices and delivery dates. Employees in each area may feel that the other department's staff simply do not understand them or appreciate their problems and needs.
- Personnel do not make or sell or count money, and may be regarded by some departments as superfluous. Their role in industrial relations disputes may cause them to be viewed with suspicion.
- Buying departments may find that both Finance and Production believe them to be redundant. They feel that they could do the job themselves much better. This can be very demoralising for specialist buyers.

Of course it isn't inevitable that different departments distrust each other, nor that they hold stereotyped images of other departments, and many employers go to a lot of trouble to ensure that they maintain close relations.

Group leadership

As we saw in Chapter 1, all organisations have a structure, usually based on functions and hierarchies. However, even quite small groups tend to acquire a structure, with members adopting different but linked roles. This can be seen clearly in family and work groups.

In most groups, a leader is formally appointed. He or she might be a supervisor of a section, a captain of a team, or a shop steward of a union. However, this 'official' leader is not necessarily the person with most authority in the eyes of other group members, as some groups may choose to have no formal leader at all.

The emergence of one person as leader may occur for several reasons.

Personality

Leaders tend to be fairly sociable and talkative and relate fluently both with individuals within the group and in group settings. They usually appear self-confident and relaxed.

Personality of other group members

Certain people prefer their leaders to show particular characteristics, which can range from generally sympathetic to vigorously aggressive. So a group which felt threatened would probably choose an aggressive member as leader, while one which valued personal relationships highly would choose a sympathetic leader.

Task for which leader is required

The qualities which make one individual excellent as leader of a negotiating team discussing pay and conditions may not make them equally effective as a regional sales manager. Many top army leaders fail to make a successful transition to peacetime political leadership.

Two American researchers, Lippitt and White, investigated the effectiveness of different styles of leadership in a youth club. Matched groups of five boys each were formed into units and asked to design, make and fly a model aeroplane. Group leaders were trained to act out three distinct leadership styles.

1 *Authoritarian*: bluntly giving instructions, with no regard for the group's wishes.
2 *Democratic*: playing close attention to the collective wishes of the group.
3 *Laissez-faire*: staying completely in the background, not intruding and leaving the boys to their own devices.

The output of each unit under the different styles of leadership was compared. Under the 'authoritarian' leader, output was high if judged in terms of speed and quality of production, but team spirit was low, the group lacked initiative and interest in the project and when it was all over they took delight in destroying the planes. The 'laissez-faire' leader produced the worst results: output of low quality and poor design; in fact output was highest when he was not around. The 'democratic' leader produced the highest morale and quality of work, but output was slightly lower than under the authoritarian leader.

Since this investigation, a number of attempts have been made to categorise the kinds of leaders in business organisations. The principal styles that have emerged are as follows.

Authoritarian

A leader who takes all decisions and simply announces them to staff, who are expected to obey without question (task-orientated behaviour or the 'tells' style).

Persuasive

A leader who takes all decisions but also seeks to persuade staff that these are the correct ones (someone who 'sells' the inevitable to subordinates).

Consultative

A leader who actively consults with, and listens to, staff before announcing any decisions, giving the group the impression that they are also part of the decision-making process.

Democratic

A leader who presents a problem to staff and creates a situation in which they can discuss and decide how to resolve it. He then carries out the decisions of the group (group-oriented behaviour).

Laissez-faire

A leader who makes no day-to-day decisions and offers no assistance to staff in coming to their own decisions. This type of leadership is often found in occupations requiring independent decision-making, such as research scientists, teachers in the classroom and salespersons.

Any of these styles of leadership may be used by someone who is appointed as a formal or task leader and, as you can see, the first three are all essentially autocratic, even though persuasive and consultative leaders do present themselves in a gentler style.

Unofficial

Often called the 'alternative' leader. Someone with no formal authority over the group, but with an instinctive ability to express the others' emotional feelings and concerns. Unofficial leaders are often given special privileges by management and sometimes form the reservoir from which future official leaders are recruited.

ACTIVITY

1 Identify several leaders whom you know, either through family, work, college or social activities. Which of the previous styles do they display?

2 From your class at college, which person would you secretly choose to represent you on the college's governing body? Of course you are not permitted to choose yourself. In the discussion that follows, it should be interesting to find out whether or not your group has a common 'unofficial' leader.

An important feature of leadership styles is the way in which information is handled. Since over 90 per cent of supervisory and management time is spent handling information in one way or another, it is more convenient to break down management styles into four categories: authoritarian, democratic, participative and laissez-faire, and present them diagrammatically.

▼ *Management styles and communication systems*

Management style	AUTHORITARIAN	DEMOCRATIC	PARTICIPATIVE	LAISSEZ-FAIRE
Diagrammatic representation				
Communication style	One-way	Two-way	Multi-way	Occasional directive from leader
Decision makers	Supervisors	Supervisors	Supervisors and subordinates together	Subordinates alone

ACTIVITY

Here are four statements representing widely different views about leadership.

● All human beings basically respond only to fear. Therefore all good leaders must insist on meting out punishment to those in the group who deserve it, in order to show others that the leader means business. I have found in my experience that threats of sackings, fines, adverse reports and the like have far more effect than any other sort of incentives. If a worker is afraid of getting the 'boot', he does the job, and does it well.

● My rule for good leadership is certainly minimum intervention in the activities of others. Most leaders say and do too much. In my opinion one should wait for others to come to you with their problems, and keep out of the way if at all possible. Interference is always fatal. Leading means waiting for others to ask for your help.

● No effective leader abdicates his superior position. He is there to make all the decisions and to see that these decisions are carried out. He is the authority and he takes all the responsibility. The followers, or workers, are there to do the work that they have been set; they are not there to say what they will do or how they will do it. Mind you, I'm quite prepared to listen to what people have to say to me, to take advice, but this is where the buck stops.

● Leadership is the ability to get the best out of people, and the way to do this is to give them as much say as possible in the performing of the task in hand. One should aim at working from within the group, attempting to allow as high a level of participation as possible. If the people working for you invest their talents and abilities in the aims of the enterprise, then they will feel that they are achieving recognition; that they belong.

1 Suggest the types of leadership implied in the statements.
2 What kinds of communication channels would you expect to find in each of the four situations?
3 In what work environment might each type of leadership style be most effective?
4 Which of the four types do you believe would be the most effective for *your* work group? Explain your reasons.

Trade unions and employers' organisations

In this section we deal briefly with the two organisations whose functions, directly or more usually indirectly, play a part in the lives of people at work. Strictly speaking, the function of trade unions and employers' groups should be covered more fully in the unit *The organisation in its environment* for students following a BTEC National course.

Some workers identify more with the trade union to which they belong than to their department or employer. We have already seen in Chapter 2 how in some industries trade unions have become the normal channel of communication between employers and their workers. Yet even unions differ greatly, and they can be classified into four main categories.

Craft unions

Craft unions represent members already skilled in a particular craft. They were among the first to develop early in the 19th century, although their roots may go back to the Middle Ages. Membership of these unions is generally in decline. Examples include the National Graphical Association (NGA) and the National Union of Scale Makers (NUSM).

Industrial unions

Industrial unions are organised on the basis of a particular industry and may include all grades and levels of workers within that industry. Examples include the National Union of Mineworkers (NUM) and the National Union of Railwaymen (NUR).

Non-manual unions

This is the most rapidly expanding sector, which reflects the growth of white collar jobs in the late 20th century. Over one-third of trade unionists are now non-manual workers. Examples include the National and Local Government Officers Association (NALGO) and the Association of Scientific, Technical and Managerial Staffs (ASTMS).

General unions

General unions impose no limit on recruitment and will accept members across occupational boundaries. They became popular in the late 19th century when workers were encouraged to move from one occupation or industry to another. Examples include the Transport and General Workers Union (TGWU) and the Associated Union of Engineering Workers: Engineering Section (AUEWE).

Most organisations have more than one trade union representing the employees' interests. This may sometimes complicate management–worker negotiations on pay and conditions; increase the number of groups with which employees identify; and lead to wasteful duplication of union resources and services. As a result, some employers are following a lead set by Japanese companies by insisting on single union representation at their workplace. This move is opposed by many unions, who believe it blurs their distinctive appeal or erodes the status of the occupations that they represent. Nonetheless, some unions have cooperated with employers in establishing single unions, although this has occasionally caused considerable disruption within the trades union movement by encouraging inter-union rivalries.

Employers may also belong to associations which represent their interests. There are about 1400 employers' organisations in the UK and their main role is to negotiate with trade unions to reach national agreements over wages and conditions. Usually they are organised on the basis of whether they operate:

- As members of a particular industry, such as the Road Hauliers Association.
- As businesses in a particular locality, such as the Chambers of Commerce.

The best known employers' organisation is the *Confederation of British Industry* (CBI). Most employers' organisations belong to the CBI, whose main role is to represent the employers' views to government and the media. The trade union national body is of course the *Trades Union Congress* (TUC), which performs for its members a similar role as the CBI.

ACTIVITY

1 Which trade unions are represented in your organisation?

2 The following is a list of the main objectives of trade unions. Rearrange them in descending order of importance, in a way that reflects what you believe to be the priorities of most members of trade unions.

- A share in the planning and control of industry.
- Full employment by resisting workplace closure.
- Job security.
- Improve standards of education, health services, and the provision of housing.
- Job satisfaction.
- Better wages, shorter hours, and longer holidays.
- Redistribution of national income and wealth.
- Defending the freedom of the individual to be in a union.
- Improve physical conditions, health, and safety of people at work.
- Income security and financial protection during sickness and unemployment.

You can find a brief comment on this activity at the end of the chapter.

Conflict in organisations

Although we can choose our own friends and acquaintances, and even escape from our family group on occasions, we are usually stuck with the people that we work with. A group which is happy with itself shares common characteristics and goals and its members enjoy a feeling of warmth and belonging. However, almost everyone meets conflict at some time at work, whether on a one-to-one or a group-to-group basis.

ACTIVITY

As an individual: is there anyone at work about whom you feel pleased or relieved when they are away? Someone who is perhaps lazy, spiteful or just plain quarrelsome? Someone who spoils what would otherwise be a happy working atmosphere? (A coded answer is desirable.)

As a member of a group: does your section or shift ever feel that it is the bad work of those idle, overpaid characters in the other group or department that is responsible for all your problems? (Be specific.)

It is always tempting for us to find an individual or a group scapegoat to blame for the frustrations we experience at work, and we might be justified in doing so, but it may not be very productive in the long run. By identifying some of the common causes of conflict in organisations we may come nearer to seeing how they can be overcome.

Causes of conflict

We can summarise the main causes of conflict as follows.

Poor communications

Poor communications may emanate from management in the form of incomplete, late or jumbled messages, or they may originate in an unreliable grapevine. While management certainly has the responsibility for ensuring effective communication, communication is a two-way process, and fault may lie with a recipient who deliberately misunderstands a message for reasons of his or her own.

Resource allocation

An individual may feel insecure about his role or status in the organisation, a feeling which can lead to jealousy and resentment. This often occurs after a reorganisation, particularly if job titles or specifications have been changed, leaving staff uncertain of their new roles.

Territory

Most of us try to create a personal space at work. However, because we do not own our 'territory', there are several ways in which it may be violated. Someone may try to occupy 'our' coat peg, for example, or our parking space or canteen place, or the office may be reorganised and a new section put into 'our' room.

Sex, race and age discrimination

No organisation is totally free of discrimination and many employees have personal experiences of harassment. Although there is legislation to discourage open sexual or racial discrimination, it may not be effective against subtler forms of harassment, conflict arising from a generation gap is difficult to overcome.

Formal and informal authority

At work, managers and supervisors represent formal authority, while an ordinary worker with a dominant personality (the 'unofficial' leader that we described earlier) may exert a different, informal authority. When the two forms of leadership are in harmony, the results may be highly beneficial, but this is not always the case.

Personality clashes

Sometimes two people have diametrically opposite personalities, or ways of looking at the world and simply find it impossible to work together.

BUYER BEWARE!

George Davis was Chief Buyer for Teknik (UK) Ltd, a manufacturer of machine tools. After a lifetime's experience he had been promoted to Head of the Buying Department and appeared on the organisation chart at the same level as the Production Manager, although his job title did not contain the word 'Manager'. George was conscious of this fact, and also that he did not have his own office like the other managers, but simply a large desk in the corner of the office that he shared with four assistant buyers and a clerk/typist.

One day, following a visit from the sales representative for Abco, Teknik's largest supplier, George noticed the rep going off to the pub with Teknik's

Production Manager, a young engineer quickly establishing a good reputation in the firm. They seemed to be laughing and joking together.

A few days later the Buying Department received an internal order requisition from the Production Department, asking them to order some components from Abco. It was not normal practice for a supplier to be specified in this way. Also the document had been left undated — which was improper — but the error was minor and the instructions perfectly clear. However, George returned the form to the Production Manager through the internal post with a sharp note saying that it could not be processed without a date and must be resubmitted.

The result was that Teknik ran out of components needed for an important rush order and wasted a week trying to obtain them. This upset a valued customer, who threatened to take his custom elsewhere, and left half the production workers idle, costing the company thousands of pounds.

ACTIVITY

You are Teknik's Managing Director. You have returned from holiday to find your machines silent and two of your senior managers at each others' throats.

1 Consider the situation that has arisen. Was it unavoidable? What are the main areas of conflict?
2 What can be done now to reduce the immediate effects of the incident and make it less likely to occur again?

Note: If you are not familiar with the duties of a Buyer in a manufacturing company, discuss this with your teacher.

Obviously where particular individuals or groups of employees are 'scapegoating' — blaming others in the organisation for all their problems — it is sensible to investigate the origins of the conflict and to uncover the root causes, rather than merely separating the warring factions. Many studies have been made of groups both competing and cooperating with each other, and a great deal of evidence about what divides and units people is now available.

Children at play

An important piece of research in this field is M. Sherif's *Group Conflict and Cooperation*. In this study he describes the adventures of a group of American schoolboys who were sent to summer camp. For the first few days they were left to settle in, form their own relationships and engage in non-competitive group activities, like setting up camp, collecting firewood, cooking, and generally sorting themselves out.

The camp was then divided into two competing groups who were instructed to engage in competitive games: races, treasure hunts, endurance tests, and so on. The good feelings of the first few days quickly disappeared and open aggression became commonplace between the two groups. At the same time, solidarity and pride within each group increased.

The researchers then set new goals to unite the two groups: activities that could only be achieved by the two groups working in harmony and close cooperation. A severed water supply and a broken food lorry created problems that could only be solved by collective action by the two groups working as a united team.

Intergroup hostility never completely disappeared, but 'us-and-them' feelings decreased noticeably, there was less scapegoating and generally a more harmonious and productive working atmosphere.

As a rule, conflict results from a clash in the objectives, interests, personalities or opinions of two parties. This may lead to three possible outcomes.

Stalemate

Stalemate is a 'lose–lose' situation where both parties become deeply entrenched in their conflict, refusing to give way, as the situation grows steadily worse. Both sides continue to suffer.

Domination

Domination is the 'win–lose' situation where one party forces the other to a grudging state of submission, and finally to defeat. This is sometimes seen in industrial relations disputes, when one side scores a resounding victory, leaving the other side broken and bitter.

Compromise

Compromise is the 'win–win' situation in which both parties emerge satisfied that they have 'won' at least something from their conflict. In fact, compromises always involve some kind of sacrifice.

Bringing about this third mutually satisfying outcome is easier said than done. It is easy for critics of your actions to argue that you have given too much away in return for very little from the opposition. Do you think that you achieved a satisfactory outcome over George Davis' conflict with the Production Manager? In that particular case, what did each side gain and lose as a result of your recommendations?

Perhaps the most important principles to bear in mind when we are involved in any form of conflict at work are:

- To recognise that every individual has needs, both as a human being and as a worker.
- To identify which of these needs they are trying to fulfil.
- To appreciate that a happy and productive working atmosphere may be encouraged and assisted — but not imposed.

Meetings

We have looked at informal groupings of people at work and the extent to which our relationships influence our effectiveness in our jobs. We have also examined the way individuals and groups cooperate within organisations. However, we have said nothing yet about meetings, and for many employees 'meetings' means 'waste of time'.

It has been estimated that a meeting of six staff, each earning £15 000 a year, costs £70 per hour. Why then, if everyone is so cynical about their value, are so many meetings held? And why are there so many strange terms used in connection with them: such as constitutions, agendas, resolutions and minutes? Surely it would be more productive if an interested group simply came together and talked things over until they reached a solution … ?

ACTIVITY

1 What is the difference between a meeting and a group of people talking things over informally?

2 List as many reasons as you can think of why meetings are held at work.

There is a considerable grey area between chatting informally with colleagues and calling a formal meeting. Busy people may say that they never stop attending meetings from dawn till dusk, even when they are queueing for lunch in the canteen or going up and down in the lift. Thus, your answer may depend on the emphasis placed on meetings and committees by your own organisation. Some of you may work for a local authority, where meetings are the cornerstone of management, or you may act as clerk or secretary to a formal committee. Some of you might be active in a trade union or a Sports and Social Club and take part in their regular meetings.

Reasons for meetings

We can roughly summarise the reasons for holding a meeting in the following way.

Statutory

You will know from *Organisation in its environment* that there is a legal obligation on most organisations, for example incorporated companies, to hold meetings of members. Other organisations, like cricket clubs or residents' associations, write it into their constitutions that regular meetings must be held, to make it less likely that the group will drift apart through apathy or get taken over by a minority faction. If you are a college student, for instance, you will be a member of the Students' Union whose members are obliged under the constitution (rules) to hold regular meetings.

Dissemination of information

Many meetings are called to offer or collect information. These may be held regularly, like sales meetings to brief reps on new product lines and receive their response to current lines, or occasionally, like a general staff meeting. A meeting is more effective than a written report because instant and direct feedback is possible, and the meeting can also be used to raise morale and improve the corporate spirit. However, as many of you who have sat through such meetings at work will know, they can also be frustrating, deeply boring, and a great time waster unless very carefully planned.

Solving problems

Meetings called to deal with specific problems are usually much less formal than the meetings described previously. They may not be called 'meetings' at all, but 'working parties' or 'task groups'. They are common in most organisations and occur whenever one person does not have the specialist knowledge to solve a problem alone and is obliged to call in experts to help. So a salesperson might consult colleagues in the production and buying departments to advise him/her on whether a customer's order can be met. The danger lies in calling too large a meeting and inviting people no matter how remote their interest in the subject is likely to be. The more people present, the longer it takes everyone to communicate with each other. A problem which four members could resolve in twenty minutes might take six people two hours, if they all want to have their say.

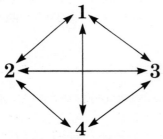

If four speakers can produce
six one-to-one relationships

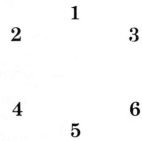

How many relationships
can six speakers produce?

Creative

Have you ever found that new ideas flow much faster when you are with a group of friends and everyone seems to stimulate each other's thoughts? This characteristic is exploited to the full in 'brainstorming' meetings, and may be used whenever the organisation wants to take a fresh look at a problem or a situation. For example, new ideas might be wanted for:

- How can we raise more money for the club?
- What shall we call the new product?
- Who will want to buy it?

≋BRAINSTORMING

Brainstorming is a technique of generating ideas within a group. Put simply, a group is given a problem to solve or asked to produce a set of ideas in response to a specific need. Members are then invited to respond by coming up with as many spontaneous ideas as possible — however silly or outrageous — within the time allowed. These ideas are written down as single words or phrases without comment. The rules for brainstorming are very simple.

- No discussion or argument of an idea is allowed.
- The group leader must stop any discussion.
- The leader can encourage the production of ideas, even if he/she has to throw in a few wild ideas of his/her own.
- All ideas, however ridiculous, should be recorded.

Although this may sound rather a strange way for a business to behave, think about how you feel about answering questions or joining in a discussion in class. Even if you do so freely, you will know that some people are very shy, fearing criticism or even ridicule from the teacher or other students. So their ideas — which may be extremely useful — do not get voiced. The brainstorming meeting removes these fears and, by allowing 'silly' ideas, encourages the possibility of finding the solution.

Let us go through a brainstorming session to see what happens. Imagine you have been given 150 used car tyres. What are you to do with them? Could a brainstorming session help. These ideas were produced by four students in ten minutes.

sell them/boat fenders/adventure playground/swings/cut them up for soles of shoes/remould them/crash barriers in road races/artificial reef in lake/buoyancy floats for boats/tree guards/car bumper protectors/weights/modern art material/assault course obstacle/motor cycle trial obstacle/aerial runway/cut up for knee and elbow pads/stage props/storage compartments/sell to leisure centre and zoos/make into trolleys/buoyancy bags for swimmers/dart board surround.

You will gather that brainstorming is an activity for the creative thinker, and creative thinkers are not initially concerned with practical problems, such as whether or not an idea will work or even whether it is sensible or not. The time for critical analysis is when the brainstorming session has finished. Then the team can weigh up each idea and discard those which they consider unsuitable. Usable ideas and suggestions then become the subject of more intensive investigation on which direct action may be taken.

The preceding pages have described four of the commonest reasons why meetings are called at work, but these do not cover all possible circumstances, and you may have direct or second-hand knowledge or experience of many different types of meeting, such as:

- The school Parent Teacher Association (PTA).
- Some neighbours in a street meeting to discuss burglaries and stealing from cars.
- The Cabinet discussing government policy.
- The tennis club discussing fund raising.

Reaching a decision

In most meetings the goal is to come to some conclusion or decision. In the same way that there are different styles of leadership, suitable for different types of groups, so there are alternative ways in which the meeting can reach its decision.

Decision by majority vote

This is the commonest method. It is usually considered fair, but may divide rather than unite the group. The Chairperson usually has the casting vote in the event of a 'draw'.

Decision by authority

After hearing everyone's views, the Chair or leader announces a decision. At best, this is a quick and efficient method, but may cause dissatisfaction if the other members resent not having a hand in the decision-making process.

Decision by consensus

The idea is that general agreement as to the best course of action will emerge naturally through discussion. If it works, this is an ideal method, as everyone feels satisfied with and committed to the eventual decision. However, it is long-winded and a single negative group member may destroy the process.

There are difficulties with all of these methods. The amount of time available for discussion, the relationships between group members, and the relative importance of the subject should determine which method is chosen in any particular circumstance. Perhaps the most important point is that everyone should know what the final decision is — whatever method is adopted. It is, however, worth noting, according to Northcote Parkinson's *Law of Triviality*, that the time a committee spends on any item on an agenda is inversely proportional to the sum of money involved. In other words, committees can spend hours discussing the most trivial issues yet allow huge sums to be spent on the nod of the head.

Who's who in the meeting?

In more formal meetings (e.g., Management of Sports Clubs) it is usual to give titles and specific roles to certain members. This is for the same reason that most organisations divide into functional specialisms — Finance, Production, Sales, Personnel — so as to avoid the duplication or neglect of certain duties, and to ensure that everyone knows his or her broad responsibilities. There is nothing sacred about the way these functions are divided and titled. It is up to each committee, when it is formed, to decide:

- Whether to give specific titles and responsibilities to certain members.
- What those titles and responsibilities should be.

Typical roles in a committee are shown below.

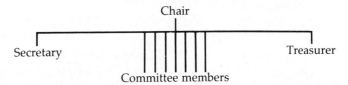

▲ *A simple committee structure*

Obviously what each holder of these titles actually does depends entirely on the type of organisation to which they belong. Take the example of Teknik (UK) Ltd *Sports Club*. It was formed to give members the chance to practise regularly and to compete with similar clubs in the area. There are 30 members, and of these 20 are happy to use the club because of its excellent facilities, but do not want to play any part in the organisation or running of events. The other ten want to be involved if possible.

At a meeting of all members, the ten interested ones volunteer for (or elect each other to) the Executive Committee of the club. This has the authority to make decisions about how the club will run, for example in arranging the fixtures and determining the level of subscriptions. Teknik's Sports Club decides to divide its responsibilities between the committee as follows.

Chair

This role may also be called Chairman, Chairwoman or Chairperson: they all mean the same thing. This is the agreed 'leader' of the group. He/she is responsible for running each meeting, for making sure that the rules in the constitution are followed (e.g., that meetings last no longer than two hours), and that when the business of the meeting is completed, everyone knows the outcome. It is helpful if the Chair possesses social skills, which earn the respect of the other members, and that he/she is not seen as bossy, indecisive or garrulous. Ideally, he/she should be able to encourage others to offer their views, then bring these ideas to a conclusion or decision that satisfies most of the group. In larger or very busy committees, he/she may be assisted by a Vice Chair.

Secretary

This is usually the hardest worked member of the committee. Like a secretary in any organisation, he/she is responsible for the administration that enables members to communicate with each other and with outside bodies; he/she is expected to know what is going on generally, and to implement decisions made by the committee. Sometimes a committee agrees that all correspondence shall go out under the secretary's name and be received by him/her. The secretary is also responsible for outlining the business to be discussed (the agenda) and recording everything which takes place (the minutes) at each meeting. Often this job is beyond the capabilities of one person and it is common for voluntary groups to have several secretaries, each with more narrowly defined duties. Teknik's Sports Club decides to appoint:

Minutes secretary

His sole job is to attend each meeting, summarise and record accurately what takes place, and write up and distribute these 'minutes' so that everyone on the committee has the same account of what took place.

Membership secretary

As the club grows, the job of recording members' names, and addresses, keeping them informed of events and collecting subscriptions may be given to a separate membership secretary.

Fixtures secretary

The committee as a whole may discuss which events it wants to take part in, but the routine administration of arranging fixtures, liaising with other clubs and organising transport or equipment would be handled by the fixtures secretary.

Social secretary

The club may feel that the social side of its existence is as important as the sporting side. Quizzes, dances and outings may all be good fun, but may involve a lot of organisation and hard work if they are to be successful.

Treasurer

He/she need not be a qualified accountant (most groups of this kind have independent auditors), but should be a competent book-keeper. Even the smallest club will have:

Income — members subscriptions, proceeds from social events, bar sales, interest on income.

Expenditure — new equipment, subsidised travel to fixtures, hire of rooms or grounds.

If the club has a bank account, the treasurer will probably hold the cheque book and be one of its signatories. Before the Annual General Meeting of all members he/she will have to prepare a report, balance sheet, and income and expenditure account, and during the year the treasurer will be expected to provide advice on financial matters to other members.

Co-opted members

Sometimes a committee may agree to 'co-opt' a person who has a particular expertise from which the rest of the committee will benefit, but who is not eligible to become an elected committee member. This person may not have full voting rights of the other members. For example, Teknik's Sports Club may co-opt a coach who is not an employee of the firm, but who is willing to assist the teams.

Thus the Executive Committee of Teknik (UK) Ltd Sports Club might look like this.

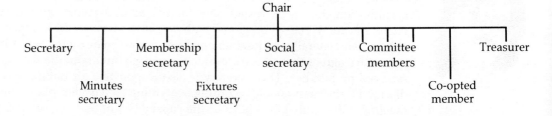

▲ *Example of a sports club committee*

Paperwork in meetings

Many committee members complain that they are swamped with paperwork, but a certain amount of written documentation is vital to inform everyone of the progress of the group. The most important documents are numbered below.

1 The calling notice

This should be sent out in advance of a proposed meeting. It is a reminder of the date, place, and time of the meeting, and can be used to invite members to indicate the topics or items that they wish to discuss. These items may then appear formally on the agenda. A calling notice might look something like this.

Reminder

SCHOOL ROAD NEIGHBOURHOOD GROUP

Just to remind you about the next meeting of our group at 8pm on Thursday 19th June at Hudson House, Poplar Road.

If you have any items you wish to see on the agenda, then please let me have them at least five clear days before the meeting.

I can tell you that Sgt Bradley will be in attendance to discuss neighbourhood watch schemes. This might be something we would all like to think about and be prepared for.

Barbara

Secretary.

If a group holds meetings at regular intervals, say every first Tuesday of the month, it is not usually necessary to send calling notices to members.

2 *The agenda*

This is a list, given or sent to members before a meeting, of topics to be discussed. Members need advance notice of items so that they can do some thinking about important points beforehand. Certain items routinely appear on agendas. Here is a typical example.

SCHOOL RD
NEIGHBOURHOOD GROUP

Executive Committee and Street Representatives' Meeting to be held at <u>8.00</u> <u>pm</u> <u>on</u> <u>Thursday</u> <u>19</u> <u>June</u> at Hudson House, Poplar Road.

<u>A G E N D A</u>

1 Apologies

2 Minutes of meeting held on Thursday 15 May.

3 Matters arising from the minutes

<u>Items for discussion</u>

4 Newsletter.

5 Annual Fete - Saturday 21st June - our stall.

6 Planning applications.

7 Homewatch - Sgt Bradley will attend tonight's meeting to discuss the forthcoming Public Meeting.

8 Any other business

9 Date of next meeting

Let us look in more detail at the items that are likely to be found on agendas.

Apologies

Most meetings start with the announcement of the names of members who have indicated (apologised) that they will be unable to attend.

Minutes of last meeting

In theory, the minutes of the committee's last meeting will be read out and members asked to agree that they represent a fair and accurate record of what took place. In practice, the minutes are usually duplicated and circulated in advance, and members invited to point out any specific objections.

Matters arising from the minutes

This item also relates to the previous meeting's minutes. It covers topics that were reported inconclusively before, and where there has now been further progress. For example, minutes of last meeting may have contained the item: '... a letter had been sent to Mr Smith, but no reply received to date'. When the Chair reaches 'Matters arising', the secretary may announce that since the last meeting a letter has been received from Mr Smith stating that he will be unable to speak at the Annual General Meeting (AGM).

The agenda should then deal with items in order of their importance, beginning with the least important (which should therefore take least discussion), working through progressively to more important ones. A helpful way to structure this process is to take items in the following order.

Matters for report or information

These will be regular pieces of information, including a statement from the treasurer of recent payments in/out of the accounts and current balance, and a summary of routine non-controversial correspondence received or sent by the secretary.

Matters for brief consideration

Short, non-involved decisions will be dealt with next. An experienced secretary will soon develop an instinct for the items that excite least interest for committee members, so their inclusion is unlikely to generate much discussion. An example might be considering which estimate from suppliers of sports equipment to accept.

Matters for detailed consideration

Under this heading go all those items that have considerable significance for the organisation, or that involve careful coordination and planning by a number of people. If, for example, an increase in subscriptions or a voluntary fund-raising event is planned, it is likely that a thorough airing will be needed.

Finally, most agendas end with two items.

AOB

Any other business. This is the chance for members to raise points that seem important but which were not listed on the agenda, possibly because they arose since it was prepared or are known only to one member. Complicated items may be held over and included on the agenda of the next meeting.

Date of next meeting

This is where the diaries come out and members argue about the best time that will least inconvenience them all.

There are no hard rules about the number of items on an agenda, but it is desirable for meetings to last no longer than two hours, which should allow sufficient time for all items to be discussed. The maximum number of agenda items is about twelve, unless a lot of the items can be dealt with quickly or 'on the nod'. Otherwise the committee may find that some have to be carried forward to the next meeting.

⌐ ACTIVITY ¬

As secretary to the Sherlock Street Youth Club, prepare a Chairman's agenda for the next meeting, which is to be held on Monday June 30. You have received the following communications. Indicate clearly where each item is placed on the agenda.

- Notice of motion: 'that a fund-raising mid-Summer's Eve dance be held.' (Named proposer and seconder).

- Letter: 'Would it be possible for our society to hire your premises for a convenient weekend in August to hold our annual exhibition.' Edgbaston Photographic Society.

- Telephone call from a member, Miss O. Korbuto: 'There has been a development regarding the hire of the gymnasium which we discussed last meeting. The local youth and recreations officer tells me we could claim a grant for this. We will have some details by the next meeting.'

- Telephone call: 'I've now received all the estimates for that alteration to the lobby and am in a position to report:' Treasurer, J. Morgan.

- Minutes of the last meeting, held at the youth club on April 24.

- Notice of motion: 'that the entrance fee be raised from 10p to 20p immediately.' (named proposer and seconder)

- Telephone call: 'I'm afraid my mother's in hospital so I will not be able to attend next week's meetings.' Julie Smith, committee member.

- Telephone call: 'Could any of your members help with our weekend cash raising for local OAP's?' Organiser, Birmingham Youth Volunteers.

---

3 Reports

In large organisations, in addition to an agenda, committee members will also receive duplicated reports supporting items on the agenda, and providing information about the decisions that are to be taken. You will already have learnt something about the uses and structures of reports from Chapter 3. Even in the case of Teknik's Sports Club, a decision about a costly spending programme might be supported by a report outlining the pros and cons of rival equipment suppliers. However, it is generally true that voluntary committees will have fewer reports attached to agendas and many will have none at all.

4 The minutes

Memories are unreliable, and one member's recollection of what took place at a meeting may be very different from another's. Minutes are essential for any committee that takes decisions and authorises people to act on them, but the ability to write good minutes is a rare skill. Many official committees — boards of directors or local authority committees — employ clerks who do not participate in the discussions, but simply concentrate on recording the decisions of others accurately and without bias. However, in most voluntary societies or clubs, the minute-taker is also a full and participating member of the committee. Different organisations use different formats for their minutes.

Resolution minutes

These are brief and record only the decision or resolution reached on each topic on the agenda. Nothing is recorded about *how* that decision was reached, whether the debate was long or bitter, or who expressed opposing opinions.

Item 5 — Christmas Dance

It was resolved that the dance be cancelled due to lack of advance ticket sales.

Resolution minutes are preferred by official bodies, which do not want to give an impression of conflict between personalities in their ranks, and hope to present a united front.

Narrative minutes

These summarise the main points of discussion, including who-said-what. They may be preferred by a voluntary committee, which comprises independently-minded individuals, that keeps few formal records other than the minutes. However, it is quite difficult for a secretary to write clear narrative minutes that are neither biased nor long-winded:

Item 5 — Christmas Dance

Colin stated that advance ticket sales had so far brought in £16 (eight tickets). He was doubtful whether the dance would ever earn sufficient to cover costs of £160 for band, disco and hire of hall. Sarah suggested that every committee member buy ten tickets themselves and undertake to try to sell them. Mike argued strongly that several members were in no position to do this and pointed out that the date clashed with the more established Beenly Bop. He suggested postponing the date and calling it a New Year Dance. Tracey stated that the band's fee would rise by £30 after Christmas and, after further discussion, a vote was taken and a majority of 8–2 opted for cancellation of the Dance due to lack of interest.

Action minutes

During a lively debate on some item on the agenda, several members may agree to do something, which they then forget as new topics take their attention. Action minutes record not only the discussions, but also the names of members delegated to take specific action.

MINUTE

Item 5 — Christmas Dance	Action by
It was suggested that the dance be cancelled due to lack of advance ticket sales. Charles suggested advertising in the local press and undertook to draft and insert a small box ad for 11 and 12 December. Pat offered to design a poster and make 20 × A3 photocopies. Sue to help put these up in local shops and windows. Des to monitor response and report back to Social Subcommittee on 15 December. Subcommittee authorised to cancel or continue with dance as they see fit at that meeting.	C.W. P.L. S.McA. D.M. Soc. Sub.

Action minutes are especially helpful where meetings are infrequent or members do not see each other regularly.

The ability to write good minutes is a valuable skill, but it is made easier if you bear in mind these simple guidelines.

Don't...

- Try to write everything down; even narrative minutes should be a brief summary.
- Show personal bias; minutes should be written in impersonal reported speech.
- Allow discussion to continue if you have 'lost the thread'; stop and ask for clarification.
- Delay writing up; if possible have minutes completed within a day or two of the meeting finishing.

Here are the minutes that were taken at the meeting of the School Road Neighbourhood Group.

Minutes of the third meeting of the executive committee of the School Road Neighbourhood Group, held at Hudson House on Thursday 19th June at 8pm.

PRESENT
Helen Grew (Chair), Barbara Fella (Secretary), Ann Williams, Des Martin, Chris Andrew, Sarah Duschesne, Nancy Donnelly, Joy Cheek, Sue Gregory, Ian Hancock, Chris Pollit.

1 APOLOGIES
None.

2 MINUTES
The minutes of the meeting held on 15th May had been circulated and were accepted as a true record.

3 MATTERS ARISING
Residential Homes for the elderly. No further progress.

Step Two Housing Project. Helen had called at 37 Ashfield Rd, but there was no reply. She had noticed through the window that there was a bed in the common room and that the furniture had deteriorated. She expressed concern that the committee had disbanded and standards had dropped.

Good Neighbour Scheme. Joy had been in touch with a social worker from social services and had been recommended to approach the Home Help supervisors. Nancy suggested getting in touch with the hospital social workers. Helen agreed to contact Maureen Webb.

40 Woodfield Rd. Helen had spoken to Steve Poole from 42, who had stated that there was noise from 40 but it was not an overwhelming problem. There was no particular pattern and it did not go on too late. Barbara would be contacting the Environmental Health Dept.

Cast iron covers. Chris A had been in touch with STWA.

4 NEWSLETTER
Not all of the newsletters had been distributed yet.

5 ANNUAL FETE
Chris P would be arranging a table. Joy had prepared a rota. Ann would be making a recruitment notice.

6 PLANNING APPLICATIONS
21 Greenhill Road. Planning permission had been refused for extensions to this property. The immediate neighbours had objected.

59 The Parade. An application had been received for a licensed restaurant and take-away. No objections were put forward by the committee.

7 HOMEWATCH

John Donaldson, the beat officer from Woodbridge Road, addressed the meeting. He explained that neighbourhood watch schemes consisted of small groups of residents with a coordinator, who would gather information and report worries. The optimum number of households varied between 7 and 200, consisting of a number of cells or one large area with several coordinators. There were sometimes difficulties in getting everyone in a cell to participate, but these problems were usually overcome. The police would provide stickers and information about reduced insurance cover. There were also video tape recordings available that could be shown at a public meeting. Barbara agreed to liaise with the police in connection with the proposed September public meeting.

8 ANY OTHER BUSINESS

Labour Party Women's Section. This group had asked SRNG to hold a meeting to discuss rape and sexual abuse. This matter would be dealt with next month.

Subscriptions. Joy requested that collections should be completed before the next meeting.

Newsletter. Barbara had spare copies if required.

List of councillors/committees. Barbara had a copy of this list.

9 DATE OF NEXT MEETING

Thursday 17th July, 8pm, Hudson House.

_____   _____
                    Chairperson   Date

ACTIVITY

1 What format has been used in the presentation of these minutes?
2 Did you notice any inconsistencies between the agenda and the contents of the minutes? What explanation is there for this?
3 Try to get hold of copies of minutes of meetings held in your own organisation and your college (Students' Union minutes?). Identify the formats used, and by sharing with others in your group, compile a set of the three general types of minutes for your notebook.

SOLUTIONS

Comment on the trade union activity on page 272
Most of the 10 million trade unionists in the UK would say that the main functions of their unions are to negotiate higher wages, shorter hours, and improved working conditions. Resisting workplace closure and promoting job security would also be high on their list of priorities.

MEMO

From __Mr Morris, Manager__

To __Chris Powell, Office Supervisor__

Subject __Staff Morale__

Internal phone __236__ Date __2/3__

I'd be pleased if you and your staff would put some ideas together about improving staff morale in the office. As you know, the recent redundancies have put us all out of sorts, but since this is now behind us I thought that we might be able to do something to cheer us all up a bit.

I don't mind how you go about this. I leave it entirely up to you and your staff, but I should be able to put my hands on about £250 to help this along. Obviously I can't allow you to spend all this on 'wining and dining', although I wouldn't object if a little went in that direction.

Any ideas and proposals would be most welcome. Please let my secretary have the details in writing by Friday of this week.

SCENARIO

You work in a small section employing about ten office staff. As office supervisor you receive this memo.

TASK ONE / BRAINSTORMING

Form into conveniently sized teams, choose a leader, and brainstorm your ideas over a 20-minute period.

TASK TWO / THE MEETING

Bring all the ideas and team members together for a general meeting. Under firm leadership, discuss the more interesting ideas before arriving at an agreed set of proposals.

TASK THREE / THE MEMO

Assuming you are the office supervisor, write a memo to the manager, under your own name, setting out your proposals as requested. You must explain in detail how the money is to be spent.

SCENARIO

A local charity, Second City Charities, has £5000 left over from its yearly outlay. It has been decided that the entire sum should be put towards one substantial project rather than scattered over several smaller ones.

The Allocations Committee is holding a meeting to decide how the money should be used. Several sponsors have put forward proposals on behalf of individuals or groups.

PRIORITIES

PROCEDURE

Five students will be chosen to act as sponsors for the five charities. The remainder of the class will be divided into small groups, each of which will organise itself into an allocating committee. All students will then spend 20 minutes preparing for their roles. This will involve:

● Each sponsor to assimilate the information contained in his or her brief, adding to it and strengthening it where necessary, developing arguments and tactics, and thinking through answers to questions that might be put by the committee.
● Each allocating committee to prepare itself by assigning duties to members, devising questions, and beginning to evaluate the various charities.

After this preparation, the meetings will begin. They will run concurrently and sponsors will move round each committee in turn.

To be sponsored

JIM JONES, severely disabled owing to a road accident several years ago, has made good progress, now holds a responsible job and feels it is time that he moved away from the hospital hostel where he has been staying. Jim's only surviving parent, his elderly mother, lives in an old people's home, so she would be unable to look after him. The doctor in charge of Jim's case feels that moving into his flat is a very necessary part of Jim's rehabilitation. The council can offer a ground floor flatlet, but it must be equipped with ramps for Jim's wheelchair, the doors must be widened, and electrical and kitchen equipment installed. The council is unable to provide this, but is happy for Second City Charities to carry out the work.

THE OLD PEOPLE at Oakleigh Flats for the Elderly need a Day Centre. The flats were built some years ago before the council recognised that the old people need not only pleasant, well-equipped flats where they can have privacy, but also a place where they can get together. Mr X, a resident in the Flats, was discovered dead from an overdose of sleeping tablets. He had been severely depressed prior to this suicide because of the loneliness and isolation that he felt day after day in his flat. The Council are willing to allow one of the flats now vacant to be converted into a Day Centre, but have not got the money to pay for the conversion and the provision of the necessary equipment. Social workers concerned with the flats say the Day Centre would make all the difference to the residents and could even prevent a tragedy such as Mr X's.

(continued)

ASSESSMENT

The sponsors will be assessed for:

● The clarity and vigour with which they present their case.
● The promptness and intelligence with which they respond to questions.
● Their ability to use non-verbal communication (eye contact, gestures, facial expressions, etc.) to aid their case.

The committee members will be assessed for:

● The efficiency with which their meeting is organised.
● The relevance, sense, clarity and promptness of their questioning, and their readiness to put supplementary questions to unsatisfactory answers.
● Their ability to argue logically and constructively and to identify strengths and weaknesses in the cases presented.

PRIORITIES

continued

3 **ON THE HIGHFIELDS ESTATE,** a group of high-rise blocks of flats, several children have recently had to be taken into care because they were battered or in danger of being battered. Mothers living in the flats find it very frustrating to be shut up day with small, very active children. There is no suitable place for small children to play without supervision; this means their mothers must stay with them whenever the children go outside. Stresses are thus put on both mothers and children. The Council would have no objection to an adventure playground being set up on a vacant piece of Council land near the flats. However, they cannot pay for fencing off and equipping the playground.

For £5000 a sturdy fence could be erected and a reasonable number of swings, climbing frames and other equipment could be purchased. The local residents are enthusiastic and are willing to carry out most of the work of setting up the playground themselves, as long as Second City Charities provides the capital for the initial outlay. They are now talking about organising a rota amongst the mums living in the flats, so that children playing there could have constant supervision.

4 **THE BRUMMINGHAM MATERNITY HOSPITAL** has no oxygen monitoring machine in its intensive care unit. Because of this, the oxygen content in the blood of newborn infants in the unit has to be monitored by blood tests taken throughout the day. Doctors at the hospital point out that this method is chancy. At least 100 premature babies in Britain are permanently blinded when blood oxygen content rises too high during treatment. Some may even die. A machine that monitors oxygen content continuously could prevent this. The hospital is the only one in this area still without such a monitoring machine. An appeal to the Local Health Authority this year was turned down, since funds must be allocated to what the Authority regards as more urgent needs. The Friends of the hospital have asked Second City Charities for £5000, saying that they will find the means to match this sum and thus provide the estimated £10000 needed for the machine.

5 **A HOSTEL IN EAST BRUMMINGHAM** has had great success in the rehabilitation of ex-prisoners. Many of these people have no homes to return to when they leave prison. Because they find it difficult to readjust to life 'outside' and because they have no family or friends to give them help during a difficult period, they often return to crime and end up back in prison. The Brummingham Hostel has a high success rate. Over the past 7 years, only two hostel 'graduates' have had subsequent brushes with the law. Most are now established in steady jobs, several have married, and many are outspoken in their praise for the hostel's work. The waiting list for hostel places is long and growing longer. A small extension providing three more places could be erected for £5000 but, since the hostel is privately run, they must look elsewhere than to the Council for money. They believe that they can present a strong case to Second City Charities, along the lines that the extension might well make the difference between rehabilitation and re-imprisonment for three men now, and many more in the future.

DISMISSAL?

Micron Tools plc owns several factories which manufacture components and small tools for the local metal bashing industries. They survived — in fact prospered — through a period of recession by being flexible and earning a good reputation for supplying high-quality goods with a quick delivery service for orders placed at short notice. Micron's Derby works employ over 100 workers, 30 of them delivery drivers.

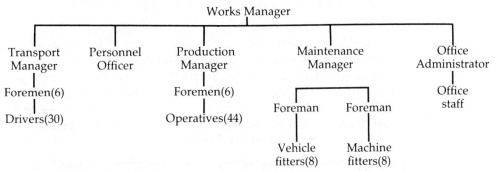

Micron Tools — structure

For the past 18 months the factory has been operating a 24-hour day, 7-day week, so that most employees, except the managers, work shifts. Micron (Derby) is a friendly place to work except for the presence of one of the delivery drivers, Simon Hanks. He has been with the firm for five years, has always been an active trade union member, and is shop steward of the drivers' union branch. The Transport Manager describes Simon as 'militant', anti-management and not above using intimidation to keep his members in line. Though articulate and intelligent, he is regarded warily by management as a source of trouble. The other drivers respect the success he has had in obtaining high pay and good conditions of service, although he has few close friends. Other workers sometimes grumble that drivers get more than their fair share simply by making the most noise.

Last Sunday afternoon three of the drivers were caught leaving the factory without clocking out, an offence for which the company rules specify dismissal. One of the drivers was Simon Hanks. On Monday the following conversation took place at a meeting between:

Eric Palmer, *Works Manager*
James Dunbar, *Production Manager*
Jennifer Smythe, *Personnel officer*
John Lees, *Transport Foreman*

Eric: Jenny, first of all, what's the legal position here? Are we within the law if we dismiss the drivers for this offence?

Jennifer: On the face of it, yes. The rule is clearly stated in the rule book and a copy is given to every employee when he joins us. We are within our rights, provided that rule has always been applied in the past. But if we've allowed the rule to lapse, we could face a case of unfair dismissal.

(continued)

DISMISSAL? continued

Eric: Well I don't remember a case like this coming up for at least five years, but if one had I'm pretty sure we'd have applied the rule. After all, we can't just have people wandering off the site whenever they fancy it. How do we maintain a service to customers if we never know how many drivers are available? Anyway, they're paid to be here, not down the pub or at home digging the garden.

Jennifer: Yes Mr Palmer, but the point is, have all previous cases been reported, or do the foremen sometimes turn a blind eye to it? John, can you help us here?

John: Well, that's a tricky one, can't really swear to it, know what I mean? I mean, I'd never let them do it, but they're a slippery lot, some of those drivers, and you never know, some of the foremen may just turn a blind eye on the odd occasion. I mean, things are always slack on Sundays, duty drivers just sit around playing cards most of the day anyway. I suppose one or two foremen just might … Only to keep the drivers sweet of course, get them on your side, so they'll work over a bit at other times.

James: Hmmph. But does all that make any difference now? Surely this is our chance to take a firm stand and not let the drivers get away with it this time — show them who's boss! I've got good men under me who have always worked hard and played straight, but now say it pays to be militant and bloody-minded, because management always gives in. If we don't look out, they'll all have that attitude.

John: Oh I agree, I agree. Those drivers are just in it for what they can squeeze out of us. They don't give a damn about the rest of the company. Only last week, one claimed he had a puncture right outside the gate. I swear he let the tyre down himself and just wanted to sit in the canteen and get paid for it, know what I mean? We foremen are getting fed up of having our authority undermined all the time, and management never backs us up, never. We must stand firm and sack them this time, or they'll think they can do what they like.

Jennifer: That's all very well, but you know what Hanks will say, don't you? That he's been victimised because he stands up for the rights of his members, and management are just out to get rid of him. I wouldn't put him past taking us to court for unfair dismissal, and we could have a fight — to say nothing of a strike — on our hands if he does.

Eric: Not only that, we could face a walk-out from the drivers at our other factories — you know how these drivers stick together. Whatever the legal rights and wrongs of a full blown strike, it would severely damage both our trading profits and our reputation. The Managing Director would never stand for it.

James: Sorry, but I think that's a short-sighted view. We owe it to everyone here — and the majority are on our side — to stand firm against this bunch of reds. They're just out to ruin Microns.

Eric: Well, we'll have to adjourn now while I sort out another matter. We'll reconvene at 2 o'clock and then a decision will have to be made — do we sack them or don't we?

TASK ONE / THE QUESTIONS

It is the lunch hour before the reconvened meeting and you are reflecting on what has taken place.

1 Taking each of the main participants, what is each one trying to get out of this situation?

2 Who is trying to influence whom, and in what direction?

3 What examples of task-helping, team-helping and negative roles are being displayed?

4 What styles of formal or informal leadership are in evidence? (You must also take into account the people who did not take part in this meeting, as well as those who did.)

TASK TWO / THE MEETING

Form groups of six and assume the roles of the five participants of the meeting, plus a secretary, then continue the afternoon meeting until you reach a conclusion. The secretary is to take notes.

TASK THREE / THE MINUTES AND SHORT REPORT

Take five photocopies of the secretary's notes, then all participants:

- Prepare narrative minutes of the two meetings.
- From these minutes, produce a short formal report, which is to be sent by you as the Works Manager to the Managing Director of Micron Tools, describing the situation that has arisen, the action that you are taking, and the possible implications for the parent company.

Who's best for the job?

Despite increasing automation, robotised factories and hi-tech offices, the most important resource possessed by most organisations is still their *human* labour force. However, the employer who spends months in research and careful consideration before investing in new equipment, may recruit a switchboard operator on the strength of only a ten minute interview. Yet that employee will provide the first — and maybe the only — impression that most callers gain of the organisation, and while most equipment comes under guarantee or on approval, staff, once employed, can be very difficult to get rid of.

Identifying an organisation's needs

In recent years, organisations have become more determined than ever to improve efficiency and productivity. Decisions to replace an employee who has left, or to recruit a new member of the workforce, are now taken only after careful assessment of the need for an extra pair of hands. This process involves analysing the work that is not being adequately dealt with by existing resources, and by producing a **job description** for the new post. In doing this, it is possible to discover not only whether there is enough work to justify a full-time employee (a part-time one may suffice), but also what particular demands the job will make on the employee recruited to undertake it. As part of this process it is usual to consider:

- The title of the job to be created.
- The identification of the section or site in which the job is located.
- The duties required to be undertaken.
- The physical, intellectual and social demands that it will make.
- Any unusual or exceptional requirements not already specified.

Having listed the demands of the job and decided that either a full- or part-time, permanent, temporary or casual employee is needed, it is necessary now to specify the qualities that will be looked for in an ideal applicant. These qualities are then included on a **job specification** for the new post. The range of factors to be considered for this include:

Physical What does the job demand by way of health, physique, eyesight, strength? Could a disabled person do it?

Intelligence Does the job require average or above average levels of intelligence?

Aptitude Does the job require any special abilities or skills?

Education and attainment What level of education, training and experience is desirable?

Disposition and circumstances Does the job call for any personality characteristics such as self-reliance or sociability? Is it desirable to employ someone who lives close to the premises?

Pay, conditions and prospects What rewards will have to be offered to meet agreed conditions or to ensure that the post will be attractive enough to suit applicants?

Here is a simplified job description and a job specification for the post of night watchman at Ebenezer Jones (Precious Metals) Ltd. Once these descriptions are produced they are normally held and kept up to date by Personnel for future use.

ANALYSING THE JOB (JOB DESCRIPTION)

	REQUIREMENTS	QUALIFICATIONS
HEALTH AND PHYSIQUE	GOOD GENERAL HEALTH. GOOD EYESIGHT AND HEARING. CAPABLE OF WALKING DISTANCES. GOOD BUILD. 5 FOOT 6INS AND OVER.	BAD EYESIGHT. BAD HEARING. BAD HEALTH.
GENERAL INTELLIGENCE	AVERAGE. ABLE TO UNDERSTAND AND REMEMBER SIMPLE ORDERS.	HIGHLY QUALIFIED.
APTITUDE	RELIABILITY AND HONESTY. SKILL AT WRITING SIMPLE NOTES. USE OF TELEPHONE. DRIVING LICENCE.	CRIMINAL HISTORY UNRELIABILITY. NO DRIVING LICENCE
ATTAINMENTS	PREVIOUS EXPERIENCE ESSENTIAL IMPECCABLE REFENCES RE: HONESTY. USED TO NIGHTWORK.	NO EXPERIENCE.
PERSONALITY	A BALANCED PERSONALITY CAPABLE OF WORKING CONFIDENTLY ALONE.	EXTRAVERSION MENTAL ILLNESS.
PROSPECTS, PAY AND CONDITIONS	£85 PER WEEK. FOUR WEEKS PAID HOLIDAY. OVERTIME. 40 HRS SATURDAY WORK. PENSION. SICK PAY. GOOD CONDITIONS.	REFUSAL TO WORK OVERTIME.

DESCRIBING THE PERSON (JOB SPECIFICATION)

JOB TITLE	NIGHT WATCHMAN.
JOB LOCATION	WORKS MAINGATE OFFICE. PATROLLING WORKS TWO BUILDINGS. THREE FLOORS. OUTBUILDINGS. WORKS YARD. OCCASIONAL DRIVING.
PHYSICAL BACKGROUND	MUCH WALKING. NO LIFTING. WALKING UP AND DOWN STAIRS. COLD ROOMS. OUTSIDE WEATHER.
DUTIES	REPORTS TO WORKS MANAGER FOR INSTRUCTIONS. LOCKING AND CHECKING DOORS. OVERALL SECURITY. TEL. EMERGENCY SERVICES. SWITCHING LIGHTS. CLEARING SNOW. CHECKING PARKING OF VEHICLES.
SOCIAL FACTORS	WORKING MAINLY ALONE.
COMMENTS	ON RARE OCCASIONS EXPECTED TO DRIVE V.I.P's TO AIRPORT AND STATION.

Having decided to recruit a new employee, an organisation must now advertise the vacancy, and that cannot be approached in a haphazard manner. There are clearly decisions that have to be made about how this is to be done.

You probably chose (b), (c) or (e). But would you have chosen the same media if you were an engineering business seeking to employ a full-time mechanic? Making the best decision about how and where to search for staff can be difficult and expensive in time and money if an unsuitable medium is chosen.

Advertising vacant posts

Trial and error, as well as more careful study of the labour market, have led firms to advertise for new staff in a number of predictable ways, as described below.

In-house advertisement on notice-boards or by circular memo

There may be staff who feel they're doing a second-choice job or who fancy a change, and by advertising among existing staff, it avoids creating resentment that outsiders are being given priority.

Notifying job centres or private sector employment bureaux

These agencies 'refer' suitably qualified or experienced job-seekers to employers, sometimes for a fee.

Local newspapers and radio stations

Where the local labour market is likely to include suitable applicants, this is a good way of reaching both those who are currently out of work, and others who may want to change their jobs.

National newspapers and specialist journals

Where the labour market in the organisation's locality is unlikely to include suitable applicants, a wider field can be reached through national newspapers and a deeper field through specialist publications.

Putting up a sign in the window

This is a very cheap method, but in recent years 'vacancy' boards outside factories have become a folk memory. Again, it assumes that suitable applicants for any job are likely to pass by.

Headhunting

Private agencies exist to advise firms on the appointment of key personnel. These agencies maintain informal links with promising or successful people in particular sectors of commerce and industry. When a company approaches them with a need for staff, the headhunter will consider the profiles of the people he knows (or knows of) and approach a suitable person to fill the vacancy. Headhunters are paid a commission when they 'deliver' a new member of staff, but the system is not generally liked because it leads to allegations that staff are being 'poached' by rival companies.

ACTIVITY

Assume you are Personnel Director for Intransit UK, a delivery firm based in the commercial heart of Manchester. How would you recruit staff for these vacancies?

1 Local van delivery driver.
2 Odd-job person: part-time, 15 hours per week.
3 Salesperson with experience of selling within the haulage industry. Territory will be NE England (Northumberland, Durham, Tyne and Wear, North Yorkshire, Cleveland).
4 Chief Accountant, with experience of computer operation and programming and systems analysis.

Having chosen an appropriate medium, it is also important how we phrase an advertisement to attract the desirable number of applicants. For example, asking for a 'Person for office work ...' might result in 160 applicants, many of whom will be unsuitable, while on the other hand specifying a 'Person to operate Pegasus accounting system on IBM PC. Must be aged 23–28, 2 A Levels, AAT qualified, experienced in using this package, and with at least 5 years employment in the international contract cleaning industry' is so detailed that it may attract no replies at all. It is therefore important for job adverts to have the following characteristics.

- *Precision*: exactly what job is available and at which location?
- *Target group*: what characteristics, including experience and qualifications, is the successful applicant likely to have?
- *Specification*: what will he/she be required to do 'in post'?
- *Benefits*: sick schemes, salary, company canteen, car, perks?
- *Reply arrangements*: by letter? By form and CV? To whom? By what date?

But we still have to take great care in the actual wording of our advertisement.

ACTIVITY

> *Strong, fit white lad required for warehouse duties ...*
>
> *Dolly Girl Friday needed to cherish and obey harassed but handsome male executive in return for luxury office and generous clothes allowance ...*

Why would we be unlikely to see either of these advertisements in today's papers? Make a list of other legal restrictions placed on employers when recruiting staff.

Does your list include the following Acts?

Sex Discrimination Act 1975 **Race Relations Act 1976** **Disabled Persons Act 1958**	These Acts make it illegal — with certain specified exceptions — to discriminate against applicants on the grounds of their sex, race or disability.
Rehabilitation of Offenders Act	This Act makes it illegal to discriminate against an ex-offender after a period of time has elapsed since sentencing and the sentence is deemed to be 'spent'.
Employment Acts 1980 and 1982	These guarantee the rights of employees to be members of trade unions — with some exceptions — and cover such matters as the existence of closed-shops and single union agreements.
Health and Safety at Work Act 1974 **Shops, Offices and Railway Premises Act 1963**	These Acts restrict the recruitment of additional staff if their appointment is likely to lead to premises becoming unsuitable because of overcrowding or inadequate heating.

There are of course many more laws that directly affect the employment of staff. These laws relate to the payment of wages, dismissal, hours worked, time off and contracts of employment.

The applicant's response

The next problem faced by employers is how to ask the applicants to respond to the advertisement. Should they:

- Complete a standard application form?
- Write a letter of application?
- Apply by telephone?
- Call in person?

ACTIVITY

1 Which method is likely to be the easiest for most applicants?
2 Which method is likely to be most difficult for applicants?
3 Which method will create the greatest difficulty for the employer?
4 Which is the easiest method for the employer to deal with?

The method that a company chooses to adopt in the selection of staff is usually based on their needs and experiences. So, if they have in the past experienced difficulty in finding staff, asking applicants to ring will ensure that no-one is put off by the effort needed to reply to the advert. Similarly, if a job requires no reading or writing skills, there is no point in insisting that candidates make written applications, particularly if that might put off some otherwise suitable people.

This does not mean that asking applicants to call in person is always ideal. It is of course true that a face-to-face encounter is necessary before anyone can be appointed because of the importance of non-verbal communication in making judgements about their potential (see Chapter 3). Nonetheless, dealing with a queue of applicants can be time-consuming, and turning down unsuccessful candidates in the flesh can be depressing for everybody (which is why rejections are often delivered in the post). So it is probably better to control or restrict application-in-person by making it the second stage following an initial method, such as the completion of an application form.

Whether a letter (supported by a CV) or an application form is to be preferred depends on the number of replies anticipated, the time available to read them, and the regularity with which similar posts are advertised. A small business, only occasionally seeking new staff, will not find it worthwhile to produce a standardised form. However, a big company with many people doing broadly similar jobs will find it saves a lot of time by having standard job application forms. If they then receive many applications for a single post, comparing the relative strengths of candidates is easily done by looking for key points in clearly identified sections of each form.

Sometimes, whenever a large company is looking for an exceptional candidate with flair and originality, the standard application form is dispensed with and candidates are asked to reply by letter in order to show off their individual characteristics. Usually such letters will be supported by a CV, an example of which can be found on page 99.

Having sorted through the applications received, and rejected some on the grounds of qualifications, age, experience, or just sloppy presentation, most employers draw up a short list of candidates to interview. Some of the rejected applicants might be people who would be excellent in the job, but who do not fulfil some predetermined criteria for suitability (for example, they may be above an upper age limit). References are now taken up. References are private statements made about the candidate by a person of standing, experience and integrity, who has known the applicant well for some time. Typically, existing employers, headteachers or senior figures in the community are asked to provide them. References are meant to be honest and independent assessments of the candidate, but are often so vague as to be of little value. At the same time as references are sought, the employer also writes to everybody on the short list, inviting them to attend for interview.

Reference for **TRACEY HUME**

Application for the post of **ASSISTANT SHOP MANAGER**

A most attractive young lady with good dress sense who is always willing to do one a good turn. She works very hard in my shop and is very courteous to the customers, who are always commenting on her lovely smile and nice hands. I have worked with Tracey for about two years and I have found her very easy to get along with. I hope she gets the job she deserves.

Signed T. Shaw   Status Shop Manager   Date 3 March.

299

The interview

Ideally, recruitment interviews should be two-way exchanges of information and ideas. They should provide applicants with opportunities to learn more about the organisation and employers opportunities to learn more about applicants. The employer, as well as finding out more information, hopes to discover whether an applicant will 'fit in' to the organisation. But are interviews really effective as a way of selecting the right person for the right job?

> Many years ago a researcher had twelve sales managers interview 57 candidates for a selling job, and rate them according to preference. There was very little agreement, and one candidate was ranked first by one of the managers and 57th by another!

The most difficult problem to overcome in selection interviews is the 'Halo and Horns' effect. The interviewer sees a candidate of attractive appearance with a refined accent. He/she may assume that he is intelligent, reliable, personable and hard working. In a word, the candidate is given a 'halo'. Another candidate, say with a strong regional accent, a partially shaved head, and a tattoo bearing the motto DEATH across his knuckles, might be thought to be unreliable and uncouth (because he has 'horns'). The 'right' appearance and manner usually varies according to the job under consideration, and many experiments have been conducted in which volunteers are shown photographs or videos of different individuals, plus a list of jobs, and asked to fit face to job. Even those who consider themselves unprejudiced tend to hold clear but biased views about the 'type' of person that holds certain jobs. This tendency we have for creating misleading but convenient easy-to-understand images of people is known as 'stereotyping'.

Most of us are also, quite unconsciously, influenced by what are called 'idiosyncratic rule systems'. These are the generalisations and prejudices used to ascribe personality characteristics to people, based on some observed physical features, such as:

'... red-haired people are quick tempered ...'
'... fat people are jolly ...'
'... people with receding chins are weak and indecisive ...'
'... people with small eyes set close together can't be trusted ...'

Panelists at interviews are no less influenced by idiosyncratic rule systems, and sometimes even a name or a manner of speaking reminds an interviewer of someone he knows already, which may prejudice his view of a candidate's suitability. Studies also indicate that judgements tend to be made within the first minute or two of an interview. It appears that the remaining 30 or 45 minutes are spent searching for evidence to back up the original decision. It is amazing that on the basis of just a few minutes of subjective assessment, a candidate may be appointed to a very important position — however this does seem to be what actually happens. (For a more detailed consideration of the organisation of interviews, see Chapter 4.)

Shrinking the halos and horns

There have been many attempts to make interviewing more objective. A five-point plant, offered by Munro Fraser in *Employment Interviewing*, sets out five qualities that could be looked for in a potential employee.

1 *Immediate impact* on other people, such as fellow workers and customers, of the individual's appearance, speech, manner, health and general fitness.
2 *Qualifications and experience* (knowledge and skills), particularly in the area of general education, vocational training and work experience.
3 *Mental ability and alertness*. What would the candidate be capable of achieving if given the opportunity?
4 *Motivation*. Does the candidate give an impression of having drive and enthusiasm and a determination to get the job done?
5 *Emotional adjustment*. Does the candidate seem able to cope with stress and work pressures? How will he/she get on with other people?

These qualities are each divided into five grades, ranging from A to E, and then assessed in terms of the characteristic displayed by the candidate. Used for reference at the interview, a profile is built up. At the end of the interviewing period, the relative merits of all the profiles are then discussed by the panel and form an important ingredient of the decision-making process. Of course, assessments can only be based on value judgements about the 'weight' of each quality and the existence of that quality in a candidate. For example, *immediate impact* might be a more important quality for salespersons to possess than office workers. Here is an example of a five-point plan.

After discussion, tick appropriate column

Confidential Name of candidate	E Well below average	D Below average	C Average	B Above average	A Well above average
First impression					
Qualifications					
Abilities					
Motivation					
Adjustment					

▲ *The Munro Fraser five-point plan*

Some organisations question whether anything useful can be learned at a recruitment interview, and rely heavily on attainment or ability tests. These tests attempt to measure levels of intelligence and personality and whether the candidate has an aptitude in say number, verbal, artistic or mechanical skills. Indeed, some universities and colleges offer places to candidates solely on the basis of their written applications, references and examination results. However, selection interviews remain best at assessing social and interpersonal factors, such as whether the candidate gives an impression of being 'one of us' or perhaps has the 'right sort of attitudes that we are looking for in this company'. Whether you think the interview method is equally fair to all applicants is a topic you might like to discuss further.

Promoting efficiency: management services

It has been estimated that one-quarter of the work in a typical office is unnecessary in that it duplicates work already done elsewhere, perhaps by a computer or another section. Even that which is not duplicated is often so uninteresting or uncongenial that it is only performed at 60 per cent efficiency. However, by reorganising work to eliminate unnecessary operations and by combining several essential operations to provide more interesting jobs, both motivation and productivity can be increased for the benefit of employers and their staff. As line managers are ill-equipped to do this job themselves, a relatively new function has emerged in many medium-to-large organisations: the Management Services Department.

Management services consist of all those services which help management to plan, control and improve the activities of an organisation. The title, status and responsibilities within which it operates vary between organisations, but this might be a typical arrangement.

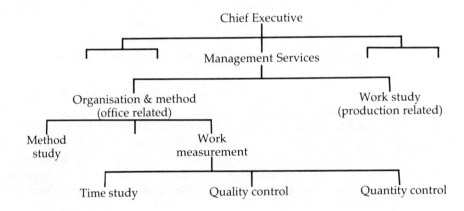

▲ *The Management Service Department*

The people employed in the Management Services Department are usually concerned with:

- Defining the problems which exist.
- Examining the methods by which work is done.
- Examining how staff spend their time.
- Examining the implications and applications of new equipment.
- Advising management on the organisation's structure and possible reorganisation.
- Advising on office design and layout.

This is a wide brief, so management services is often divided into two broad areas.

Method study

This is the study of all steps in existing and proposed procedures, including all aids employed to carry them out, with the aim of improving efficiency and reducing costs.

Work measurement

This follows a method study. If we assume that the 'method' by which a job is done is satisfactory, what follows is the analysis and measurement of the human effort required to perform specified tasks at a defined level.

We will now look at these two aspects of management services in more detail, and in particular their application to office jobs.

Method study

This you will remember is the study of the way a job is done, so the first stage in the work of the management services investigation team is to conduct a survey of existing methods. The purpose of the survey is to determine whether the organisation is likely to benefit sufficiently to justify the application of a full work study. Although there have been many instances of spectacular savings in terms of staffing levels, time saved, and document storage reductions, usually the benefits are more modest. If a point is reached where the savings are less than the cost of the method study, plus the disruption it will create and possible staff resentment, then it is not worth proceeding. If the potential improvements outweigh the disadvantages, then a full study will be carried out.

ACTIVITY

Jot down one or two 'problems' in your employing organisation with which you are familiar and which might be improved if subjected to method study. For example, do you find yourself under-occupied on some days of the week and rushed off your feet on other days? Or are documents delayed in their passage through the system, waiting for several people to process them, resulting in delays and bad customer service?

The survey

These are the steps you might take in the execution of a survey.

Select

Select the subject to study. Choose a problem with a likely solution, discuss your terms of reference with the manager concerned and agree how much time and money can be spent in considering a solution.

Inform

Inform the staff concerned. Tell them why the study is being carried out and reassure them that it is not intended to be used as an opportunity to dismiss any existing post holder.

Record

Record the relevant facts. This might be by observing people at work and by interviewing them, perhaps using a questionnaire. The results are then recorded on a process chart.

Examine

Examine the information collected. This is usually done in a methodical way, subjecting the data to six questions.

1 WHAT is done?
2 WHERE is it done?
3 WHEN is it done?
4 WHY is it done?
5 HOW is it done?
6 WHO does it?

Develop

Develop ideas for improvement. This includes the human as well as the organisational implications of any changes. This may result in the amalgamation or reordering of the sequence of tasks, the elimination of duplication, the re-design of forms or the ordering of new equipment.

Implement

Implement the recommendations.

Monitor and maintain

Monitor and maintain the new system. The managers of the department in which the new system is located are responsible for its operation, but organisation and method officers may be called upon to advise on installation or operation when the system is introduced.

Process charts

These are used in method study as a graphic means of representing work systems or processes. Writing down long-hand all the clerical procedures involved in, say, dealing with an invoice from the time it arrives in the post to its filing away is tedious and time-consuming. It is also more difficult to analyse the job in this wordy form. So process charts use accepted symbols to represent either:

- *What the person is doing*, in which case it is logged on a man-type chart, or
- *What is being done to documents*, in which case it is logged on a material-type chart.

▼ *Process chart symbols*

Symbols	Stage	Man-type chart (example)	Material-type chart (example)
○	OPERATION	Clerk records data on document.	Document is prepared.
☐	INSPECTION	Clerk reads document.	Document is checked.
▷	TRANSPORT	Clerk walks to filing cabinet.	Document is passed to new section.
D	DELAY OR TEMPORARY STORAGE	Clerk waits for reply to letter.	Document waits in in-tray.
▽	STORAGE	Clerk files documents.	Document is filed.

Just as flow charts are used as an aid to computer programming, so process charts are used in method studies as an aid to the identification and analysis of procedures. This is an example of a man-type process chart.

Job: Check water in car radiator

Note: Based on the assumptions that the bonnet catch is located inside the car, that the water level does not need topping-up, and that the driver starts outside car and finishes sitting inside.

2 metres	⇨	To car door
	◯	Open car door
	◯	Pull bonnet catch
	◯	Close car door
3 metres	⇨	Walk to front of car
	◯	Lift and secure bonnet
	◯	Remove radiator cap
	☐	Inspect water level
	◯	Replace radiator cap
	◯	Close bonnet
3 metres	⇨	Walk to car door
	◯	Open door
	◯	Get into car

Summary

◯	=	operations 9
⇨	=	travels 3
☐	=	inspection 1

ACTIVITY

1 Compile a detailed process chart listing all your activities from waking up to leaving your house in the morning. It is not enough simply to record: get up, get dressed, have breakfast, leave house. Remember, the aim is to see whether you can economise on unnecessary journeys or activities, so a detailed chart is required. Exchange charts with a friend to see whether you can identify any time- or energy-saving alternatives to those of your present arrangements.

2 Imagine that you are the organisation and method officer for your section at work. Using the stages in method study surveys listed previously, plan your own work study of the existing processes in your office. Try to represent your observations using a process chart.

Work measurement

This is the analysis and measurement of human effort and movement required to perform specified tasks at a defined level. Most work done in offices is measurable in terms of the number of items dealt with during an hour, day or week. For example, typing, machine operations, filing and reprography, and even jobs which cannot easily be assessed, such as telephone calls and dealing with enquiries, may have the total time spent on them measured, to demonstrate how best to allocate different tasks to a number of staff over a given period. Work measurement therefore studies:

- *How often or how long*: the *time* that each job takes.
- *How much or how many*: the output or *quantity* of work done.
- *How well*: the *quality* of work done.

Time study

This may be a study of the time taken to type one letter or to deal with one customer. To avoid the threatening and demoralising need to stand over an individual with a stop-watch, it is often done on an 'averaging' basis. Here, batches of work of average difficulty are given to several staff on several occasions and the average time taken for completion is calculated. Time study has more applications in manual than in clerical or administrative jobs, mainly due to difficulties in:

Applying it to mental processes   How long does it take to deal with a difficult client?

Applying it to variable operations   It is difficult to determine how long an 'average' piece of typing or an 'average' telephone call is.

Relating the time taken with the accuracy of the finished job   There is little point in emphasising speed at the expense of quality.

Quantity control

This process measures whether someone is producing what is thought to be a reasonable amount of work. This might be the number of claims or orders processed in a day or the number of clients interviewed. It only has limited applications to office jobs due to a variety of factors that affect output.

ACTIVITY

Two typists share an office. At the end of the day it is discovered that one has typed seven pieces of work, the other twenty-one. List reasons why this may have occurred.

Your list might include factors such as:

- Type of typewriter or word processor.
- Length of each piece of work.
- Complexity of each piece of work.
- Legibility (or audibility) of the original.
- Interruptions (one typist may sit nearer the telephone than another).
- Whether carbon copies were required.
- Whether work flowed smoothly (was one typist left idle for part of the day?).

Nevertheless, quantity control may sometimes be useful for establishing staffing levels when applied to sections or departments, rather than to individuals.

Quality control

In industry, quality control is an activity by which samples from batches of goods being produced are vigorously tested to ensure that they meet the required standard. In recent years many British firms have tightened up their standards to match the high standards of quality control of imported goods. However, notions of 'quality' in office work are different and consist principally of a need for accuracy and freedom from avoidable errors. But what is the best way of achieving this? As with the work of the police in their fight against crime, there are two main approaches.

Prevention of errors

If typists continually produce messy work, which is full of mistakes, it may be possible to improve the situation by seeking an answer to the following questions.

- Are the errors caused by misleading information from outside sources? Put simply, if the manager mis-spells the client's name in his draft, can the typist be expected to spell it correctly?
- Are the staff capable of, and adequately trained for, the tasks expected of them?
- Does loss of concentration result from boredom at the monotony of the job or from environmental defects such as a stuffy over-heated room?

- Have unreasonable deadlines or an excessive work load caused tiredness?
- Have supervisors ever established acceptable standards of quality and attempted to ensure that they are met?

Finding answers to these questions will indicate ways in which quality can be improved.

Detection and correction of errors

Human error can never be completely eliminated, but early detection should reduce its consequences. Unfortunately, comprehensive checks of everyone's work are impracticable, as they are either:

Expensive In effect each job is being done twice, once by the original employee and then by the checker, or

Unsatisfying Both boring for the checker and demoralising for the person who did the original job, knowing that he/she is not trusted to do it properly.

However, it is often possible to build 'automatic' checks into a system, which reduce the need for individuals to check each other's work. For example:

- Double entry book-keeping (recording every transaction in two ledgers).
- Validity checks programmed into a computer.
- 'Dictionary' programmes in word processors to correct spelling errors.

Work measurement is more usually applied to manual jobs. The method most commonly used in offices is known as 'activity sampling'

Activity sampling

This process measures the proportion of time spent on different categories of work, which is then recorded by ticking or drawing lines across an activity chart.

NAME   SECTION   POSITION   DATE

Description of job	7 am	8 am	9 am	10 am	11 am	12 noon	1 pm	2 pm	3 pm	4 pm	5 pm	6 pm	
Personal													
Telephone calls													
Interruptions													
	STARTING TIME		FINISHING TIME		LUNCH BREAK			TOTAL		TOTAL			

▲ *An example of an all-purpose activity chart for office use*

307

What happens is that an employee is asked to complete the chart (or diary) daily, recording the time spent on each activity. The all-purpose chart has an advantage in that it can be tailored to suit different time scales and activities in a wide range of office jobs. The purpose of these charts is to:

- Estimate how often a certain job is done or a machine used by each individual.
- Estimate the total amount of time spent on certain jobs.
- Assist in replanning the working day to reduce wasted time or money. For example, charts may indicate that most telephone calls are made in the morning, and reorganisation of the work load would allow them to be made in the cheaper afternoon period.
- Expose the need to delegate certain tasks from busy staff to less busy colleagues. They will also reveal any job descriptions that are out of date.

The limitation of activity charts is the difficulty in recording accurately how long people spent on separate tasks. In your own job, you probably find yourself doing several tasks at the same time, maybe answering telephone enquiries while trying to draft a letter or check a form, and having a chat with your boss about next month's figures. How could this be recorded on the chart? It is also easy to forget to complete it until the end of the day or week, by which time details of how people divided up their day or week will have been forgotten. Finally, it is not unknown for staff who have a particular grievance or demand to use the chart to highlight it. For instance, they may want their 'own' telephone and so record a high rate of telephone usage. Fortunately, these limitations are well known to management services staff, who are expert in interpreting results.

ACTIVITY

Compile a multiple activity time chart, based on the previous example, to cover a typical day's work. What difficulties have you experienced? Compare your chart and the difficulties experienced with others in your group. What sorts of jobs do you think these charts are best suited for?

The development of microprocessors is giving a new dimension to the activity sampling branch of work measurement. Computerised workstations take away from employees the chore of manually recording their jobs and the time they spend on them. For example, in the bus industry, new 'intelligent' ticket-issuing machines with their own microchip will record where a bus is at any particular time and the number of tickets issued. The information enables managers to respond quickly to changes in levels of demand.

Many offices are also introducing computerised workstations, as we saw in Chapter 5. Here, too, the computer can log tasks and alert managers to congestion, delay or under-utilisation. However, there is more than a feel of 'Big Brother' to all this, as in the case of an employee on a day-release course, whose computer reported her to head office for never doing any work on Wednesdays — the day when she was away at college!

ACTIVITY

Your office or section is about to introduce activity sampling, either manual or electronic. Draft a memo to all staff informing them that this is to happen. Explain the advantages of the process, both for the organisation and for the employees themselves.

Improving job satisfaction

Unfortunately, boring and monotonous jobs exist in every organisation, and managers, eager to apply motivational theories to their workforce, are often at a loss to know how they can instil a sense of motivation and commitment into those staff engaged on routine and repetitive tasks. However, much can be done to make most jobs less dissatisfying and quite a bit can be done to make them positively more satisfying.

Job rotation

An office may contain several clerks of the same grade doing equivalent but different jobs, such as cashier work, wages, sales, ledger and purchase ledger. Instead of leaving the same individuals on the same jobs for the indefinite future, they can all be trained on all the jobs and 'rotated' between them at, say, six-monthly intervals. The organisation benefits by having a better trained workforce who can substitute for each other, and the workers may find this relieves the monotony of a single-task job.

However, there are negative points. Job rotation may be resented by staff who find it unsettling to be moved around. Also many comparable jobs carry widely differing status amongst those doing them, and leaving the more popular jobs may increase, rather than reduce, ill-feeling. Job rotation does not guarantee satisfaction. In other words, while it may relieve dissatisfaction amongst those doing monotonous jobs, it can rarely improve motivation and job satisfaction.

Job enlargement

This is the attempt to increase each worker's job in content and variety. Let us see how this could be applied to a Purchasing Section containing four clerks.

- One checks 'goods-received' notes from the firm's four depots and marries them to orders.
- Another checks invoices that come in and marries them to the appropriate 'goods-delivered' note and order.
- A third deals with credit notes and queries.
- The fourth posts the purchases to the ledger and authorises payment.

This is *process-based* organisation, with each clerk involved in only a small part of the total job. If the section were reorganised on a *geographic basis*, each clerk would deal with *all* the purchasing processes and documentation for just one depot, resulting in each having an enlarged job.

Job enlargement has been applied to car assembly lines where the monotony of doing just one small job repeatedly can lead to declining quality and poor morale. Manufacturers such as Volvo have tried allowing small teams to assemble a whole car, which appears to increase pride in the quality of the work. It is also being applied to office work. As employers install computerised workstations, it becomes possible to liberate staff from a narrow group of tasks to enable them to follow a transaction from start to finish.

Job enlargement offers scope for individual initiative, for pride in seeing a job through from beginning to end, and for taking responsibility for the end-product. However, there is a risk if the system is not sensitively applied. Some workers might feel that they are still doing boring jobs: in fact doing more of them! This method of organising work is described as 'horizontal loading', which means there is greater width, but not necessarily greater depth, in the range of work tasks.

Job enrichment

The aim is to make the job more important to the worker by enabling him to take decisions about how it is to be done and to take responsibility for its success or failure.

This may be achieved through 'vertical loading', or deepening the worker's commitment to a much greater degree than before. Here is an example.

MOTAMART

Motamart employed sales reps to sell motoring accessories, mainly to petrol stations. Basic pay and conditions were good, and a generous commission was available if a certain level of sales was reached. Yet despite this, staff turnover was high and morale poor. The firm set out to discover why.

Each rep was given a 'patch' and a list of known outlets, each of which had to be called on once a week. He also had a product price list from which customers made their orders. When interviewed about how they saw the job, a typical comment was:

'We're just postmen, calling week after week on the same garages, sticking the same bit of paper under their noses and waiting while they choose the same stock they've taken for the past five years. Commission targets are a joke — don't know anyone who's ever reached them ...'

The firm organised a series of training courses about their product range. The topics covered included which lines were most profitable, a 'profile' of typical customers for different products, and information about the garages that bought them. Reps learned that only 10 per cent of the outlets accounted for over 80 per cent of sales and they acquired greater understanding of the type of person visiting, say, a motorway or inner city petrol station. They were relieved of the obligation to make weekly calls on all garages and encouraged instead to allocate their own time in whatever way they thought would be most profitable. They were also given discretion to organise discounts and special offers where they thought these would promote profitable sales. Commission was linked to profitability rather than volume of sales.

The results of all this were dramatic. The firm's profits rose sharply and staff turnover fell. The reps agreed that they found the new regime far more satisfying:

'At last we're being credited with having a bit of intelligence and using it.'

Motivation and job satisfaction are not easy to 'switch on', but may sometimes be improved by:

- Thoughtful management and supervision, which encourage and extend the individual rather than restrict him.
- Company reorganisation or restructuring, which may facilitate job enrichment.
- Developing team work, to increase the feeling of belonging.
- Setting identifiable and achievable targets for workers and then rewarding them when they achieve them.

ACTIVITY

Identify some routine office tasks with which you are familiar. Describe ways in which either job rotation, job enrichment or job enlargement could be applied to these tasks and predict the effects of such changes on the individual worker and the whole organisation.

Motivation

If organisations are genuinely anxious to get the best from their workpeople, it is sensible for them to consider exactly what it is that leads particular people to take particular jobs. If organisations can ensure that their objectives are closely matched to employee needs, the results should be more satisfying for both employer and employee.

Why do people work?

Why did you take a job, or why are you planning to look for one when you leave college? Probably your immediate answer is *money*, and certainly few of us would do our jobs if we were not paid. But is this the only reason? Imagine some future society where everyone received the same wages irrespective of whether they emptied dustbins, worked as brain surgeons, or lay in bed all day staring at the ceiling. Would you really choose to do the latter? Perhaps for the next 50 years … ? It is worth recalling that when people are interviewed after a huge pools win they sometimes announce: 'No, I won't give up my job. I want to carry on just the same …'. This is because although everyone enjoys weekends and holidays because they provide a complete change from going to work, many people have other needs that only their jobs can satisfy easily.

ACTIVITY

List the reasons why people might choose to work rather than spend the rest of their lives 'at leisure', even when there is no financial advantage to be gained. Consider people with jobs different from your own: an MP, a veterinary nurse, a cross-continental lorry driver, a self-made millionaire. Did they have the same reasons as you for choosing their jobs?

Did your ideas include any of the following points?

Social contact

For people who live alone or in an isolated area or who have heavy domestic pressures, going out to work may be the main opportunity to avoid being house-bound and to give them the chance to widen their social horizons. This factor will even affect the choice of job that someone is prepared to take. For example, not many of us would wish to be a lighthouse keeper or a night watchman, and a secretary may accept reduced pay and less interesting work to move to a large, friendly typing pool, rather than endure the more lonely life of a personal assistant to one boss.

Job satisfaction

This is also known as 'self-expression', 'vocation' or 'the need to exploit one's natural talents'. If you really enjoy caring for sick animals, or gain deep satisfaction from successfully selling something or making things, you may have few opportunities of satisfying these needs in your everyday social life (short of stoning the cat, then giving it first-aid!). The best way of satisfying them is to find someone who will employ you to do so.

Challenge

The satisfaction here is in tackling and solving problems that others may have regarded as impossible. Think of the Chairmen of some of our nationalised industries. Many come from higher paid jobs in private industry, and receive few thanks from government, consumers or their own industry. So why do they take on the job? Possibly they do so to prove to themselves that they alone are able to take on the challenge and win through.

Power

This is the desire to lead, to change, or to dominate. Politicians work unsocial hours and receive little gratitude, but may believe their position confers on them the authority to change the world around them.

Prestige

Certain jobs are thought to hold status or glamour, regardless of their pay or intrinsic satisfaction, such as some media jobs and those involving travel.

Social norms

To be the only person without a job when all one's friends work, is a lonely, demeaning and isolating experience.

Self-advancement

Some people consciously decide to work for someone else for a number of years solely to give them the expertise and contacts that they will need to benefit themselves in the future.

Obviously, it is unlikely that any of us in work would fit neatly into just one of these simple categories, as we probably experience changing proportions of each factor as we progress through our working lives. If we take the single but important category of job satisfaction and plot it against an average working life in Britain, we can get an idea of this.

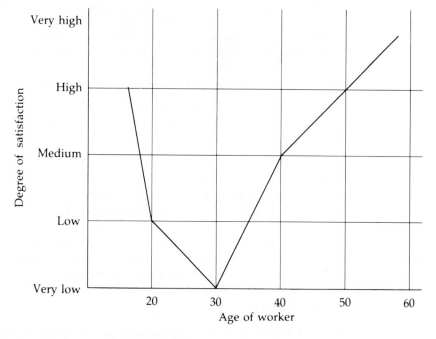

▲ *Changes in employee job satisfaction*

As you can see, when young people leave school, they have high expectations about their first job. Possibly the shock of long hours and the absence of glamour brings them down to earth with a jolt, perhaps with the realisation that 'work' is a lot tougher than they imagined — including having to go to college! This results in increasing dissatisfaction and a tendency to change jobs, which is the usual way in which the level of job satisfaction is measured. This tendency to change jobs continues, though at a decreased rate, until the age of about 30, after which working habits, along with personal life styles, become more stable. Middle age brings even greater stability, when most workers' levels of job satisfaction reach a peak. Why do you think older workers are less inclined to change jobs?

Attitudes and work output

If a person is happy in his job, and at least some of the previous 'needs' are being satisfied, he is likely to work with energy and enthusiasm to improve his output. If he is unhappy, bored or frustrated, the quality of his work will probably reflect this. However, this relationship between attitude and output is complex and may also be affected by:

Nature of the job

Although all jobs are likely to be done better if they are done by someone who enjoys their work, the difference may not be too significant where the work is routine, mechanical and unskilled. However, in work which is creative, or where success depends on relationships with others, the demotivated employee may be more of a liability than an asset to his employer (e.g., an unhappy sales rep or a teacher).

Employee's personality

Conscientious individuals will work steadily, even if they do not enjoy their jobs, and may be more productive than a highly motivated but disorganised and inefficient colleague.

Work groups

Work groups set their own norms or acceptable standards of performance and behaviour. It is very difficult for an individual working in a team to 'swim against the tide' by working to a significantly higher or lower standard than the rest of the group. The influence of the work group on the individual is discussed in more detail in Chapter 4.

Meeting human needs at work

It should be clear by now that it is in everyone's interests to have a satisfied, highly motivated workforce. The employee gains by spending around one-quarter of his life doing something he enjoys, while the employer gains by getting higher productivity from his motivated staff. But how can the well-intentioned employer obtain this level of commitment and enthusiasm while there remain boring and disagreeable jobs to be done? Most use a range of techniques, which can be broadly categorised under the headings 'carrots' and 'sticks'.

- *Carrots* are the inducements offered to employees, including pay rises, flexitime, luncheon vouchers or cheap canteen meals, a company car, cheap loans, sports and social clubs, pension and training schemes.
- *Sticks*, on the other hand, are the punishments that employers can inflict, including any demotion, redundancy, compulsory transfers, or withholding performance-related pay.

However, no external incentive or threat is ever as powerful as our own inner motive for doing a job well. Motivation was once described as 'the stirring from within', while incentives are the 'danglings from without'.

ACTIVITY

On a copy of this chart, record the more important carrots and sticks offered by your firm or college.

Carrots	Sticks
1	1
2	2
3	3
4	4
5	5
6	6

Occupational psychology

One of the by-products of the explosion of interest in psychology has been its application to the world of work. Two occupational psychologists have had a considerable impact upon management thinking. They are Abraham Maslow and Frederick Herzberg.

Abraham Maslow

Maslow, in *Towards a Psychology of Being* (1968), saw individuals as having certain needs, which they are constantly trying to satisfy. These needs are like a pyramid, in that different people have reached different levels or stages, but that we are all, according to Maslow, trying to climb to the next level. He represented this scale of escalating needs, which he called a 'hierarchy of needs, like this'.

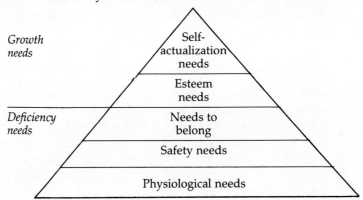

314

Maslow thought that deficiency needs must first be satisfied if we are to progress to growth needs at the apex of the pyramid.

In what sense can we understand these five terms, and what relevance have they in terms of going to work?

Physiological needs

By this Maslow meant needs that are basic to our continuing existence, such as nutrition, clothing and shelter. Not until these needs have been met, will we aspire to the next level. We would find it difficult to concentrate on doing our job well if we did not know where our next meal was coming from or where we would sleep at night. Employers meet these needs by paying an adequate wage.

Safety needs

This is the need to be safe from danger and threats. It includes the need to be assured of a continuing standard of living, an orderly life, and emotional as much as physical security. If we live under constant threat of redundancy or transfer to another part of the country, this need for security will seem more important than the job itself.

Belonging needs

Once these first two needs have been satisfied, Maslow argued, we will become concerned with our social groups. As social animals, we have a need to be liked or at least accepted by others, including our work colleagues. There again, few people can devote themselves wholeheartedly to their work tasks if they feel isolated or alienated from those around them.

Esteem needs

Everyone likes to feel of value. This is the search for self-respect and self-confidence and to feel that we are making a visible and acknowledged contribution to the organisation. Some of us try to satisfy this need by seeking promotion, an office of our own, or bigger car. For others it can be achieved through a simple 'Thank you' from a supervisor.

Self-actualisation needs

This is the top of the pyramid, which is reached only when the previous needs have been satisfied. Many of us never get there. We are too busy trying to survive. In fact, getting there is not nearly as important as the *struggle* to get there. It is the inner drive to realise one's full potential, whether through creative work, as with an artist or actor, or by selling 'fridges to Eskimos', or some equivalently challenging job in our organisation.

Not everyone agrees with Maslow's theories. One researcher, Clayton Alderfer, in *Existence, relatedness, and growth* (1972), proposed a simpler model based on only three factors that are *not* arranged in a hierarchy. He argued that Maslow was wrong in thinking that we have to satisfy lower needs before we can progress to higher needs. Alderfer believes that needs exist independently of each other, and we may need to experience all or any of them at any time. This is known as the ERG theory.

E = *Existence*: physiological and safety needs.
R = *Relatedness*: the need for satisfying social relationships.
G = *Growth*: the need to develop one's own potential.

Whether Maslow or Alderfer is preferred, more enlightened managers accept that businesses cannot function effectively unless employees' basic needs are met, in order that they can devote all their energies to the job itself.

ACTIVITY

1 What steps does your organisation take that could be said to satisfy self-actualisation or growth needs?
2 What inexpensive steps *could* they take that they are not taking already?

Frederick Herzberg

In his book, *Work and the Nature of Man* (1966), Herzberg looked at factors that might motivate people at work. He interviewed 200 accountants and engineers about how they felt about their jobs by asking them two questions about a range of factors which are of importance to people at work, ranging from pay and conditions to job security and personal recognition. The questions were:

1 Which of these leads you to experience most dissatisfaction with your job?
2 Which of these provides you with most satisfaction?

To Herzberg's surprise, the factors that the employees regarded as satisfying were not the opposite of those they found dissatisfying. This led him to the theory that there are two main groups of factors affecting motivation at work. He called them 'hygiene factors' and 'motivators'.

Hygiene factors

By hygiene factors, Herzberg was not referring simply to matters affecting health. Instead, he uses the term to describe employment conditions which, when they are unsatisfactory, make people feel very dissatisfied with their jobs, but which — even when they are very good — do not positively improve their sense of job satisfaction. In doing this Herzberg used the word 'hygiene' as an analogy. He likened these factors to hygiene in a hospital. Good hygiene can prevent the spread of infection (dissatisfaction), but cannot in itself cure a patient (satisfy him). For example, working in a dirty, draughty, cramped office can lower morale and increase general dissatisfaction. But does anyone wake up on Monday morning buoyed up by the prospect of spending the coming week in a warm, luxurious office with panoramic views and deep pile carpets?

The principal hygiene factors are:

- Organisational policies, practices and rules: people frequently complain about policies and rules they dislike but rarely notice when they are satisfactory.
- Style of supervision and management.
- Pay, pensions and related benefits.
- Interpersonal and social relationships at work.
- Working conditions and environment.

Problems relating to these factors can usually be recognised fairly easily by management and steps can be taken to solve them, but any beneficial effects are quickly taken for granted.

ACTIVITY

Apply Herzberg's concept of hygiene factors to your own workplace or to college. You should identify not only the obvious causes of current dissatisfaction, but things which are taken for granted, even though they may be highly satisfactory.

Hygiene factors	Examples of current dissatisfaction	Examples of 'taken for granted' advantages
Organisational policies Supervision Pay and related benefits Social relationships Working conditions		

Motivators

By the term 'motivators', Herzberg meant those factors that have a positive and long-lasting effect. They are usually associated closely with the job itself, and when present, tend to motivate workers to produce better work because of improved morale. They include:

- A sense of achievement: satisfaction derived from work well done.
- Recognition of effort and achievement by superiors.
- The work itself, which should ideally be challenging, rewarding and socially acceptable.
- Levels of personal responsibility.
- Actual or promised promotion.

Unlike hygiene factors, motivators can be very difficult for even well-intentioned management to introduce, especially where the job is routine and unskilled.

ACTIVITY

Take a copy of this questionnaire and conduct a survey amongst a representative sample of working men and women. In a short written report based on your findings, draw attention to those findings that throw light on what you identify as hygiene factors and motivators. What conclusions can you draw?

EMPLOYEE OPINION SURVEY

Directions — Indicate your answer by filling in circle.

	YES	NO	STATEMENT
1	○	○	Male.
2	○	○	I am 21 years of age or over.
3	○	○	I have worked for this firm less than a year.
4	○	○	I have worked for this firm for more than five years.
5	○	○	On the whole, working conditions are good.
6	○	○	More staff meetings are needed.
7	○	○	My work performance is usually discussed with me.
8	○	○	There is too much favouritism in this firm.
9	○	○	Generally, my co-workers are friendly and easy to get along with.
10	○	○	Morale in this firm is poor.
11	○	○	On the whole, I would say this firm is a leader in most respects.
12	○	○	My training in this firm has not been adequate.
13	○	○	My supervisor is friendly and easy to get on with.
14	○	○	Advancement depends more upon whom you know than merit.
15	○	○	All employees work well together.
16	○	○	Information about our fringe benefit schemes is inadequate.
17	○	○	Work is distributed fairly.
18	○	○	My supervisor does not show enough interest in the people he works with.
19	○	○	I feel free to express my own ideas and suggestions.
20	○	○	My supervisor changes his decisions a lot.
21	○	○	Career opportunities for women are good in this company.
22	○	○	I don't like to tell people that I work for this company.
23	○	○	I would definitely recommend my job to my best friend if I were leaving and he was capable of doing it.

How managers see themselves

It should be clear by now that managers in organisations have a strong interest in ensuring that their workers are as happy and highly motivated as possible, as this will encourage them to devote all their energy and commitment to their jobs. Yet, in the past, as now, managers have held widely differing views on how to get the maximum output from their workers.

Pre-scientific management

Before the industrial revolution, in a basically rural society, most work units were small and there was little competition for jobs. Workpeople and their families rarely moved around and many jobs were held for life, or even for generations, within the same family group.

The progress of industrialisation brought recognition of the need to organise production processes more efficiently. This efficiency was achieved by allowing workers to specialise in the jobs that they could do best, a process which later became known as the *division of labour*.

Scientific management

The growth of large, labour-intensive industries in the 19th century led to a re-evaluation of the role of the manager. This was mainly because competition was getting more intense and labour more expensive as the newly formed trade unions began flexing their muscles in their bid to improve conditions and wage levels. Parliament, too, was demanding an improvement in working conditions with its *Factories Acts*. Clearly, in this competitive atmosphere management had to get its act together or risk closure. The term 'scientific management' has been coined to describe the process whereby the activity we call work is put under the microscope and studied objectively with a view to making it more efficient.

Frederick Taylor was chief engineer at the Midvale Steel Company in Philadelphia and supervised the shovelling of iron ore around the site. He observed how wasteful the 'initiative and incentive' theory of management was, with many labourers using unsuitable tools and techniques to do their work. In 1911 he published *The Principles of Scientific Management* in which he outlined his theories on management's role in production processes. He suggested:

- Observing each operation and breaking it down into separate elements: this was the beginning of what we now call work study.
- Recognising managerial responsibility to plan work and devise the best method by which it should be done.
- Selecting and training all employees in the light of skills identified.

Taylor was highly successful in terms of raising productivity and his recognition of the importance of training and work study is still accepted, but he was also criticised for his attitudes to labour, which appeared to treat workpeople as human machines.

ACTIVITY

In one of his 'scientific' observations, Taylor observed that workers shovelling coke did so with a range of shovels that held loads of $3\frac{1}{2}$ lb up to a maximum of 38 lb. He wondered 'surely there must be an ideal shovel load, not too light and not too heavy, that could move coke efficiently?' After a series of tests, Taylor proved that the ideal load per shovel was $21\frac{1}{2}$ lb, and that workers with shovels designed to carry that weight produced the highest output. What would Taylor's advice be to the designers of shovels for shifting cotton waste, iron ore, lead ingots? (Solution on page 322 — but do not look until you have figured it out.)

The human relations school   (The Hawthorne experiments)

An early writer who greatly influenced this school of thought was Elton Mayo. Mayo was a psychologist who conducted experiments in the early 1930s at the Western Electric Company's (WEC) Hawthorne plant in Chicago, where over 30 000 employees assembled telephone equipment. WEC was a caring employer that was trying to reduce dissatisfaction and increase productivity by improving working conditions. A group of women workers were chosen for one experiment into the effects of changes in the length of the working day and rest breaks. Throughout the experiment an observer sat with the women, keeping them informed on what was being done and noting their views and complaints. The women worked a standard 48 hour week, including Saturdays, with no tea breaks.

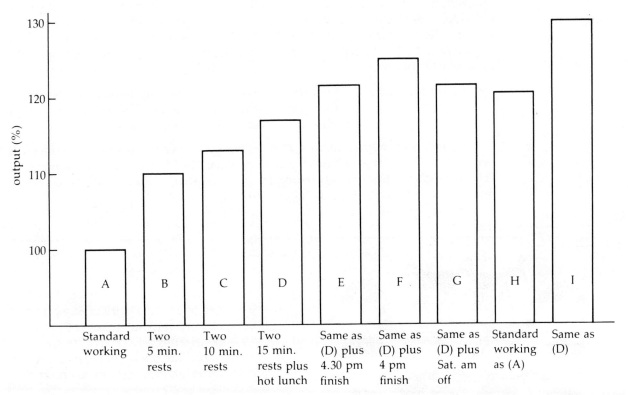

▲ *Selected results from one of Mayo's experiments*

As you can see in the chart, productivity increased with each change in working conditions, even when the length of the working time was reduced. This high output was maintained even when all improvements were withdrawn and the women returned to a 48 hour week (H).

This unexpected phenomenon led Mayo to question Taylor's theories on management, which had stressed the importance of analysing tasks in raising productivity. Eventually he concluded that it was the interest shown in the girls and their work which had affected them far more than the actual changes made in processes or conditions. Today, we call the influence experimenters have on changing the behaviour of the people that they are observing the *Hawthorne effect*. Put simply, Mayo believed that:

- People are motivated by more than just pay and conditions.
- The need for recognition and a sense of belonging are very important.
- Attitudes towards work are strongly influenced by the group that one belongs to, since work is very often a group activity.

A further experiment carried out by Mayo is described on page 264.

Participative school

Writing in the 1930s, Chester Barnard, in *The Function of the Executive*, argued that motivation is an unstable and unreliable force in the workplace, varying between individuals and groups at different times. He suggested that it was management's responsibility to bring individuals together in a cooperative relationship within the organisation and to persuade them to cooperate more willingly. He identified potential for conflict between:

organisational objectives — which seek to maximise profits and minimise costs, and which seek to achieve acceptance of the rest of the workgroup within an agreeable working environment.

Barnard saw management's role as bringing these two objectives together by persuading the parties of their common aims: that both share an interest in the organisation's health and prosperity. He believed that workers could be convinced of this by being offered a share in decision-making.

'X' and 'Y' managers

After the Second World War, textbooks on managing people at work began to appear in large numbers. One such book was Douglas McGregor's *The Human Side of Management*, which suggested that management styles fall into two broad categories: those managers who believe in *Theory X* and those who believe in *Theory Y*.

Theory X

This manager believes most people dislike work and will avoid it where possible, that they dislike responsibility, lack ambition and prefer to be told what to do. Such managers think that employees have to be forced and threatened with punishment before they will make an effort.

Theory Y

This manager believes that physical and mental effort at work is natural, that workers not only accept but seek responsibility if committed to the organisation's objectives, and that most are capable of more creativity and ingenuity than they are given credit for.

According to McGregor, an organisation run by X style managers tends to be traditional and authoritarian. It often employs a large proportion of unskilled workers doing routine jobs. It is more usually prevalent in periods of recession and high unemployment. On the other hand, Y style organisations are more likely to be young, expanding and employ mainly highly skilled staff.

McGregor's theory is sometimes criticised for being an over-simplified generalisation. Most organisations employ a mixture of managers, exhibiting both X and Y characteristics, and the same manager may reveal both X and Y tendencies, depending upon whom he is trying to manage. Although the Y style is often presumed to be the 'right' one, these characteristics do not necessarily lead to a popular and effective manager. If the individual is not very self-confident and able, he may appear weak and indecisive, in contrast with an X manager who gives an impression of effective control and competence, especially in a panic situation.

Functions of the manager

> Management is tasks. Management is a discipline.
> But management is also people.
>
> *Peter Drucker 1979*

ACTIVITY

Jot down a list of the tasks that are performed by your head of department or by another manager you know of at work. Compare these tasks with those performed by the following people. Allowing for the different nature of the end-products, are there any broad similarities in the work they all do which suggest common features in the function of management?

- A pub landlord
- A college lecturer
- A parent
- A football team captain

Would you describe any of these as being supervisors rather than managers? What is the difference between the two titles?

Hopefully your discussion will have given you a clearer idea of the range of duties and responsibilities that are involved in management and supervision. Broadly speaking, the functions of a manager are to:

- *Communicate* — with other managers, subordinates, suppliers and customers.
- *Plan* — what to do (aims and objectives).
  — how to do it (strategies for implementation).
  — when to do it (judging demand and timing).
- *Organise* — people, money, worktasks, plant, equipment and materials.
- *Coordinate* — across several subgroups or teams.
- *Lead and direct* — facilitate the implementation of policy decisions.
- *Make decisions* — and accept full responsibility for their consequences.

The duties of supervisors, however, while involving some of these activities, are principally concerned with the implementation of management strategy, by ensuring that the targets and standards specified by managers are achieved by those staff under the supervisors' control. You will of course learn a great deal more about supervision and management when you are studying for your BTEC Higher Certificate.

Perhaps we can finish this chapter on an everyday story of management.

The buck stops here

Kathy has been the sole receptionist-cum-typist at Coldfish Garage for the past four years. Although she refuses to do overtime and weekend work, she works at a steady pace and maintains a high standard of personal service for the customers. She is paid £88.50 basic per week, but has no formal business qualifications. Following extensive improvements and enlargement, Coldfish Garage employs 20-year-old Janice, the daughter of the chief mechanic, to work alongside Kathy in an extended office. Janice is very keen, has a BTEC National Diploma, and hopes to continue her studies up to BTEC Higher level. She is also willing to work overtime and seems to be learning the job fast from Kathy.

Six months later, Kathy sees Janice's pay packet and realises that Janice is getting about £10 more a week than she is. Kathy also learns through the grapevine that there is talk about promoting Janice to office supervisor — in fact that she has already been offered the job in preparation for further office expansion. Both women have an almighty row and demand to see the manager the next day.

ACTIVITY

1 As a manager, prepare a strategy for dealing with this problem.
2 Conduct the interviews as a role play. Kathy and Janice will have thought about their own roles and how they intend to present themselves to the manager.

SOLUTIONS

Solution to Taylor's shovel puzzle on page 318. Shovels should be designed to a size capable of carrying a single load of 21½ lb. So the capacity of a shovel for shifting cotton waste would be huge compared with that of a shovel for lead ingots.

THE HOT SEAT

SCENARIO

An important post is available at Janes Office Furniture (Manufacturing) Ltd. You and your management colleagues have first to complete certain tasks before you are ready to fill the post.

BACKGROUND INFORMATION

The company requires a person who has had some experience in selling office furniture and supplies and in dealing with customer-led enquiries for personalised office refurbishments. The company employs 190 staff, mostly production workers.

This person will:

- Lead a sales team of five, all engaged in the same sort of work.
- Report in writing to the Managing Director each month.
- Liaise with the works Production Manager on a day to day basis, particularly with respect to special orders.
- Travel abroad for the company, visiting customers, usually about four times a year, mainly in Europe but occasionally in the USA.
- Have some technical background and be willing to learn new ideas in the field of office technology and furniture design.
- Have the confidence to train a team in selling techniques.
- Have had some selling experience in office furniture or allied field.
- Be able to communicate.

Address of company: 114 Hollyhead Road, Skeffington, SW3 1EJ. *Manager*: Mr Burton.

TASK ONE / THE ADVERTISEMENT

Draw up the wording and produce an interesting design for a suitable display advertisement for the post at Janes Office Furniture. You may invent certain details as you see fit, but you must remain reasonably faithful to some of the company's needs. When completed, you will need to:

- List the reasons for your choice of what is included.
- Say why you left out certain details.
- Suggest where you would place the advertisement.
- Find out how much it will cost.
- Suggest alternative ways to advertise the post.

TASK TWO / JOB DESCRIPTIONS

Draw up a suitable job description and job specification for the post being advertised. You will need to use your initiative in the inclusion of some information.

The interviews . . .

The interviews. You now have to make a decision about whether to be an interviewee or an interviewer.

TASK THREE / PREPARING FOR THE INTERVIEW

As an interviewee   You are to role play one of the following candidates. You need to familiarise yourself with the details as presented and prepare yourself for a convincing performance. Anticipate what questions you might be asked and how you should deal with them. What questions are you going to ask?

As an interviewer   As a member of an interviewing panel you must read the short-listed application details carefully. When you have prepared five general questions to put to *all* candidates and two specific questions for *each* candidate, you are ready to start the interviews. Use an assessment guide based on Munro Fraser's five-point plan. You are to role play one of the following:
- Managing Director
- Personnel Director
- Works Manager
- Sales/Office Manager

TASK FOUR / THE INTERVIEWS

The conduct of the interviews is the responsibility of the interviewing panel. The interviewees can expect to be informed of the procedures by the Chairperson of the panel. It is usual to conduct each job interview in private, or at least out of hearing range of the other applicants. The interviews may be recorded or observed.

TASK FIVE/THE AFTERMATH

In the discussion to follow, the panel will name the successful candidate and give reasons for its decision. The panel will also be invited to explain why it rejected the other candidates. Non-panelists are expected to make a vigorous contribution.

APPLICATION DETAILS FOR DIANE McNALLY

AGE	27
NATIONALITY	Irish.
ADDRESS	36 Layton-Hall Road, Garston, Liverpool.
STATUS	Ms. One girl child aged four.
PRESENT OCCUPATION	Unemployed.
PREVIOUS EMPLOYMENT	Two years full-time primary school teacher, Liverpool. Two years sales advisor with Ambrose Educational Equipment Ltd. Lately Joint Sales Director of Office Wholesalers Co. until voluntary liquidation.
EDUCATION	Sacred Heart Convent, County Cork. School Leaving Certificate. Rollaston College, Derby. Certificate of Education. At present studying for Open University degree in politics.
INTERESTS/HOBBIES	Reading, swimming, eating out, politics.
PERSONAL DETAILS	Rheumatic fever at 14. Left teaching following severe nervous breakdown.

Reasons for application

Before my previous company went into voluntary liquidation I was personally responsible for leading and organising a sales staff of twenty-three. We were a highly profitable company and our annual turnover was increasing to the point where our American owners saw fit to withdraw from their European markets. You can see from my record that I have had fairly extensive experience in selling and I am confident to take executive decisions. I believe in teamwork and in decision-sharing.

Reference for Diane McNally

My relationship with Diane is based on our Joint Directorships in Office Wholesalers Co. and our mutual interest in local politics, where Diane is our leading strategist. When the company went into voluntary liquidation I was conscious of a promising career being cast aside. She was in charge of a substantial and successful sales team, which made her redundancy even more tragic. She was, more than anybody, responsible for a significant increase in orders during her term of employment.

In purely technical terms, she is extremely knowledgeable and competent in her work. She has fine leadership qualities and she is more than capable of welding a dynamic sales team to promote your products.

Trevor Hurst
Director (retired)

APPLICATION DETAILS FOR STEPHEN GARDINER

AGE	33
NATIONALITY	British.
ADDRESS	c/o 14–18 St Mungo Avenue, Dunfermline, Scotland.
STATUS	Widower. Wife recently died tragically. Four children, two boys and two girls. Presently living with mother. Plans to remarry shortly.
PRESENT OCCUPATION	Salesman and sales team leader with major office supplies company.
PREVIOUS EMPLOYMENT	Ten years in British Army from Cadet to Colour Sergeant. Active service in Germany and Northern Ireland. Wounded and decorated. Recommended for Commission. Four years team leader in sales team for medium sized medical equipment suppliers.
EDUCATION	Robert Burns Junior School. Clydebank Secondary School, Glasgow. Army Cadet Training School. Driving and Vehicle Mechanics qualifications in Army.
INTERESTS/HOBBIES	Football, mountaineering, darts, fishing, qualified amateur football referee.
PERSONAL DETAILS	Usual childhood illnesses. Served six months' prison sentence on wounding charge following release from Army.

Reasons for application

I am at the moment responsible for a medium sized team working north and south of the border. I believe I can say without undue modesty that we are a successful team and that we are maintaining our success despite the recent recession in manufacturing industries. I urge you to judge me on my results.

The reason that I am applying to your firm is because I want to live in that part of the country because my future wife has relatives there and I want to give my kids a better start in life by bringing them up in a more prosperous part of the country.

Reference for Stephen Gardiner

Mr Gardiner is one of our success stories. He is an extremely successful sales leader and is personally responsible for mounting and spear-heading our initiatives in England. He is also an extremely nice man. He can give and take orders and is regarded quite highly by his team workers and by the management board.
I understand that he has mentioned his prison sentence on his application form. This is the sort of man he is; incredibly honest, even when he needn't be.
I wish him great success, even though this means our loss.

Hamish Johnson
Chairman

APPLICATION DETAILS FOR WINSTON J. GLADSTONE

AGE	26
NATIONALITY	British.
ADDRESS	32 Station Road, Hall Green, Birmingham.
STATUS	Married. Two children. Boys aged five and two.
PRESENT OCCUPATION	Senior Sales Officer, Jason Wholesalers Ltd, Solihull, West Midlands.
PREVIOUS EMPLOYMENT	Time served apprenticeship in relevant industry. Two years foremanship and junior management positions. Joined sales staff and progressed to senior position. Presently in part control of sales staff of 25.
EDUCATION	Junior Boys School, Spanish Town, Jamaica. Northfield Comprehensive School, Birmingham. Three 'O' Levels, including English. Matthew Boulton Technical College. City and Guilds qualifications in Furniture Design and Construction. Now studying Economics and Law at 'A' Level.
INTERESTS/HOBBIES	All sports. Table tennis tournament player. Voluntary helper at local Youth Club.
PERSONAL DETAILS	No serious illnesses. Leading figure in Black religious movement. Unsuccessful attempt to gain councillor status in local government elections.

Reasons for application

If you are willing to give me a chance in this job, I can guarantee that I will work hard for you. I've had some good experience in selling of late and I am eager to expand my wings and take on a new challenge.

You will see from my history that I'm basically a practical man and I pride myself on my technical knowledge of the goods I sell — I always think that selling is basically about knowing the product inside out. I've also been used to supervising people in teams and I believe that this is valuable experience.

Reference for Winston Gladstone

There are only three things that matter about any employee.

1 Is he/she capable?
2 Is he/she reliable?
3 Can he/she work well with other people?

As far as Winston is concerned, the answer to all these questions is a resounding YES. I would stake my reputation on this man's future success.

John H. Kavanagh
Director

APPLICATION DETAILS FOR GARY SWAN

AGE	23
NATIONALITY	British.
ADDRESS	49 Grove Road, Bidford-on-Avon, Warwickshire.
STATUS	Single.
PRESENT OCCUPATION	Council refuse Collection. (Temporary appointment.)
PREVIOUS EMPLOYMENT	None, except for casual work.
EDUCATION	King Edwards Grammar School, Stratford-on-Avon. Three 'A' Levels. Warwick University. First Class degree in Business Accountancy. London Business School. Diploma in Personnel Management and Sales and Marketing.
INTERESTS/HOBBIES	Travelling and map-reading, meeting people, rambling.
PERSONAL DETAILS	Childhood bouts of minor epilepsy. No attack for five years. Slight speech defect, but receiving therapy.

Reasons for application

You can see from my educational details that my life's ambition has always been directed towards business management. My qualifications in this area are fairly good, and all I ask is to be given the opportunity to put theory into practice. It is perfectly true that I am fairly young and I lack practical experience in sales and shop-floor production skills, but I can bring to the job a fresh and open approach that an older person may not be prepared to give.

If you think that I am not quite old enough or not experienced enough, I am willing to be employed on a short-term employment contract. Then you can see what I am capable of and yet retain the option of dismissing me if I am unsuitable. I do hope that you can see a way to open the door for me.

Reference for Gary Swan

It gives me great great pleasure to recommend this young man for a responsible position in your company. As an undergraduate he was quite outstanding and ranks as best student in his year. In his submitted written work he made striking and original contributions at a high theoretical level and must be considered potential high asset material. He did have some small problem with his speech in oral seminars, but I understand that he is receiving successful therapy for this. I most earnestly recommend him.

Ewan Macalister
Professor in Accountancy,
Warwick

APPLICATION DETAILS FOR EDITH CAUSER

AGE	43
NATIONALITY	American. Naturalised British.
ADDRESS	Flat 11a, Windermere Court, Putney, London.
STATUS	Single.
PRESENT OCCUPATION	Sales Executive, Mandoline Cosmetics Ltd, Hammersmith, London.
PREVIOUS EMPLOYMENT	Twenty years continuous employment in sales management in junior and executive positions in USA and UK in various industries, including cosmetics, furniture, printing, ladies fashions, etc. (a total of ten companies).
EDUCATION	Baltimore High School for Young Ladies. High School Certificate. College for Business Ladies, New York State. Diploma in Business and Professional Studies, Class Alpha.
INTERESTS/HOBBIES	Long-distance driving, free-fall parachuting, gliding, Museums of Art and History, French and Spanish cooking, reading dictionaries.
PERSONAL DETAILS	Candidate did not complete this section. Reason unknown.

Reasons for application

If you are looking for a fairly competent sales leader with a fairly average sales growth potential, then I am definitely *not* the person for you. If you want a zippy, winner-take-all, 18-hours-a-day work-a-holic who doesn't give up on anything and who hates losers, then you should consider my application seriously.

I am a career person and to be successful in my job is important to me. I like to lead and I have the confidence and ability to organise a sales team into a successful unit. If a market does exist for your products, then we will sell them easily. If the markets do not exist, we will find a way to create them.

Reference for Edith Causer

There is little I can tell you about Edith that you wouldn't discover within five minutes of meeting her. She is the most confident person I have ever met; so confident that she can, inadvertently, give a wrong impression of being over-bearing. But she is, in fact, underneath it all, kindness itself, and has the very special quality of bringing out the best in everybody. I would hate to lose her.

John H. May
Managing Director,
Mandoline Cosmetics

Anonymous note received in yesterday's post:

Why don't you ask Miss Causer why she wants to leave Mandoline Cosmetics?
Why don't you ask her about Charles Grey?

TRUDY'S TROUBLE

Trudy Payne had been very pleased when she was promoted to section head of Purchase Ledger Records six months ago. In the two years she had spent at Harcourt Cosmetics since leaving university, Trudy had moved around most of the different departments, gaining experience of all aspects of the business, but this was her first position with any real authority and she was determined to make a success of it.

At first everything had gone smoothly. The work of the section was straightforward and routine and most of the staff had been there several years and could do the work in their sleep. It was a busy section, and Trudy was proud that she had been able to negotiate for a new clerk to join them to relieve pressure on the others. Purchase Ledger Records was one of the last sections in the company to retain a wholly manual records system. Harcourt Cosmetics was slowly, and sometimes painfully, being computerised, and for the past 18 months there had been talk of when PLR would join the new system and the kinds of changes that might ensue. Trudy wasn't worried. In fact she was looking forward to the challenge of managing the changeover.

	Trudy					
	Rita	Liz	Helen		Neil	Tracey
Age	38	34	35	23	22	16
Service	6 yrs	4 yrs	7 yrs	2 yrs	1 yr	4 mths

▲ *The Purchase Ledger Records Section: personnel details*

Purchase Ledger Records was based at Harcourt's head office. When one of the eight depots wanted to buy materials, they raised their own order and sent a copy to PLR. Here it was filed, pending arrival of a copy delivery note, which was compared with, then 'married' to the order. Suppliers sent invoices direct to PLR, where they were compared with and attached to order and delivery notes and sent to Accounts for payment. Complications arose when the three documents did not agree, and each clerk had a number of 'queries in progress' requiring credit notes or referral back to the works manager of a depot for clarification. It was fiddly work, with limited opportunity for job satisfaction, and Trudy often wondered how the longer-serving clerks could survive doing the same thing year after year. However, each clerk except Tracey had their 'own' depots and seemed to have built up good relationships with the storekeepers and works managers with whom they were in regular contact.

For her first few months in the job Trudy had been welcomed and given a lot of help by her new section. However, during the past two or three months, the atmosphere seemed to have soured. Perhaps it had started about the time when — honeymoon period over — she became aware of a certain inflexibility, particularly from the three women. Sometimes they seemed to have their own set of unwritten rules, which dictated exactly how often, and on what terms, they would assist each other and share jobs when the need arose. At other times they would pass queries to Trudy to resolve even when they were perfectly able to sort them out themselves. This attitude puzzled Trudy, who thought problem-solving was the most interesting and rewarding aspect of the job and who had tried to involve the team in seeing problems through to their solution.

Tracey, who was in her first job, seemed willing enough when told exactly what to do and watched over while she did it, but she showed little interest or initiative and only perked up when given the opportunity to leave the office on some errand, which always took her past her friends in another part of the building. Neil was the exception. Although very quiet and self-contained, he did at least show more intelligence and initiative than the others, and was proving himself the most efficient at getting through the work. Because of his willingness to accept additional responsibility, Trudy found herself involving him more and more in the complex cases and, indeed, relying on him as her main support.

At first Trudy thought she might just be imagining a decline in morale. However, it was becoming obvious that occasional absenteeism from all the section was increasing and the excuses given — dentist, bad cold, period pains, headaches — did not always ring true. Despite the arrival of Tracey, a backlog of work was building up and the number of unresolved queries was also increasing. Previously the three women at least had been on friendly terms, often going out together at lunchtime, but now no-one seemed to have anything to say to each other, except the occasional bitchy remark passed about whoever was not in the room at the time.

Trudy was worried. She had studied all the theories about motivation, morale and conflict at work for her business studies degree. It had seemed so easy in theory, and she had been looking forward to being a good manager in practice. Now it all seemed to be going wrong ...

What do you think?

1 With reference to the theories of at least one management thinker, identify some reasons why morale in the Purchase Ledger Records Section seems to be in decline. Which of these reasons do you think is the most significant?
2 As section head, what would you now do to try to make the team more effective?
3 Discuss ways in which (a) job rotation, (b) job enlargement, (c) job enrichment could be applied to the work of this section. What would be the likely effect of such changes on the individuals in the team and on the organisation?

More about organisations

How organisations grow

In Chapter 1 we took a general look at organisations in society, and particularly at the way in which organisational structures affect the working relationships of management and staff. We are now ready to advance our knowledge of organisations by exploring the role that they play in a wider economic and social context. A reasonable starting point for this is to ask ourselves why organisations exist at all.

There are at least six basic reasons. Organisations provide:

- *Greater efficiency*

  Efficiency is increased because workers are able to specialise in particular skills and become proficient. This 'division of labour' increases production to a point that far exceeds the productive capacities of individuals who choose to operate outside an organisational structure. There are some urgent forms of human activity that could not be accomplished in time without group effort, such as harvesting and preparing for the Olympic Games.

- *An enlargement of individual activities*

  Organisations are not only more efficient than individuals working alone, they also happen to be the only way in which a modern society can provide most of the goods and services it requires. It is not possible for unorganised groups of individuals to build cars, aeroplanes, run a railway, or even bake bread (where does the oven and power source come from?), let alone put men on the moon — and get them back again!

- *Needs and wants*

  Only organisations can fulfil society's growing needs and wants. As we get more goods and services, so we want even more, and it is only within efficient organisations that we can produce enough to meet our demands at prices that we can afford to pay.

- *Centres of power and influence*

  Organisations provide an opportunity and a focal point for the exercise of power and influence. National and local governments, pressure groups, trade unions, multinational and nationalised industries, all carry political or economic clout that far exceeds the sum total of power that could be exerted by their individual members. 'Unity is strength' is a phrase that only makes sense in an organisational context.

- *Centres of knowledge and expertise*

  Organisations are able to accumulate and conserve the knowledge and skills they acquire much more effectively than individuals working alone. They are also able to record and store information in sophisticated retrieval systems that can be called upon more and more as the business expands. It would simply be impossible to collect income tax, run a hospital, or distribute welfare benefits without a formal organisational structure.

- *Satisfying social needs*

  As we discussed in Chapter 1, organised work usually provides a whole range of human contacts, including the opportunity to make new friends, join clubs and societies, and generally provide a forum in which we can share our interests and worries, often with like-minded fellow workers. For some people, an organisation like the workplace is the *only* place where they can derive a sense of purpose and meaning from their lives.

All organisations are subject to influences and constraints that affect the way they operate, develop and change. Some of these are imposed from outside.

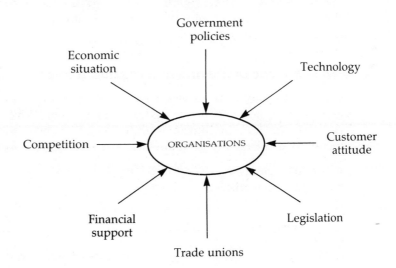

▲ *External influences*

Others are generated from within:

- Management policies and procedure
- Research and development
- Communication systems
- Physical resources
- Cash flow

As well as these constraints, every organisation has at its disposal the four major resources that you learned about in your other studies. These are:

- Land
- Capital
- Labour
- Enterprise

We can bring together these constraints and resources in a diagram.

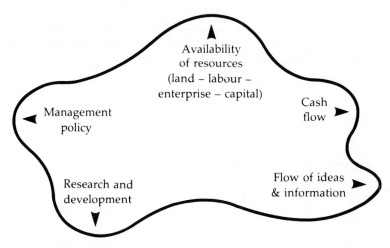

▲ *Pressures that determine the organisation's shape and structure*

The organisation's ability to manage its resources, and respond flexibly within its constraints, affects how successfully it develops. Growth can take several forms: in turnover, in production, in product range and in locations, but an increase in orders may not necessarily generate, nor be resolved by, an increase in the numbers of employees. We will look in turn at some of the structural and physical problems generated when an organisation changes in size.

The shape of the growing organisation

One of the problems experienced by all growing organisations is the creation or expansion of non-productive middle management. While most mangers would argue that they are anything but non-productive, it has been said that only two levels in the hierarchy of a large organisation have any real value. These are:

- Top management   — who decide WHAT to do
- Bottom line workers — who DO it.

ACTIVITY
Without cheating (by looking back to Chapter 1), state which levels in the hierarchy have been left out. To what extent do you agree or disagree with this view?

Obviously it is not practical for organisations such as the Gas Board, Jaguar Motors or a holiday tour company to employ thousands of clerks, engineers and drivers who are directly accountable to a few senior managers. The span of control would be so large that no-one could be effectively managed. However, many expanding organisations whose growth is not closely planned or monitored, suffer from a tendency for their hierarchies to grow vertically (for the chain of command to lengthen) in a way that may not benefit the organisation as a whole.

SUREPARTS LTD

Sureparts Ltd supplies car accessories to petrol stations and DIY stores throughout the UK. Three years ago they employed 720 sales reps, managed by 82 middle managers under a Sales Director, as shown in the following structure.

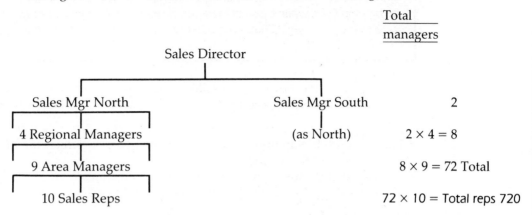

	Total managers
Sales Director	
Sales Mgr North Sales Mgr South	2
4 Regional Managers (as North)	$2 \times 4 = 8$
9 Area Managers	$8 \times 9 = 72$ Total
10 Sales Reps	$72 \times 10 =$ Total reps 720

It became clear that Sureparts' potential sales justified doubling the number of reps to 1440. Rather than doubling the span of control of each Area Manager to an unwieldy 20, the company's management hierarchy was completely restructured.

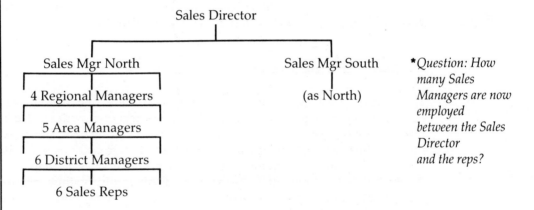

Sales Director

Sales Mgr North   Sales Mgr South

4 Regional Managers   (as North)

5 Area Managers

6 District Managers

6 Sales Reps

Question: How many Sales Managers are now employed between the Sales Director and the reps?

Within a year, the problems with the new structure became apparent. Both the reps and their managers complained about the time it took for requests, instructions and recommendations to travel up and down the hierarchy. The Accountant started to peer closely at the increased salary bill and demand for company cars, and asked searching questions about associated increases in sales …

Eventually, following advice from a management consultant, the sales team was again restructured.

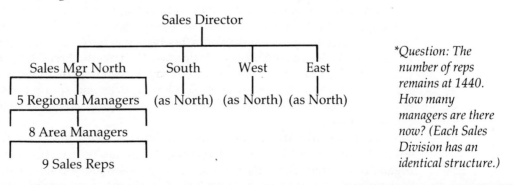

Sales Director

Sales Mgr North   South   West   East

5 Regional Managers   (as North) (as North) (as North)

8 Area Managers

9 Sales Reps

Question: The number of reps remains at 1440. How many managers are there now? (Each Sales Division has an identical structure.)

* The answers to these two questions can be found on page 359.

It may well be that Sureparts' decision was influenced by the fact that managers are relatively and absolutely more expensive to employ than those whom they manage.

ACTIVITY

Rank Xerox estimated that a manager's salary makes up only one-third of his overall cost to his employer, while those of lower grade employees represent only half of their total cost to the employer. What is the other two-thirds of the cost of a manager made up from?

As well as the obvious costs, like company cars, expenses, pensions, National Insurance contributions, non-statutory sick pay and holiday entitlement, did you include:

- The space each employee's workstation occupies, on which the employer may pay rent of about £200 a square metre?
- The heat, light, paper and telephone calls he consumes?
- The mess he makes, which the cleaners are paid to clear away?

Thus the savings available to a growing company like Sureparts through reorganising its management structure become clear. However, it is important not to forget that the consequences of changing the length of the chain of command, or the width of the span of control, affect more than just the organisation's wage bill. This point was dealt with on pages 12 and 13. Can you anticipate what problems Sureparts management will have to deal with? Check back to Chapter 1 if you're not sure.

Some causes and effects of growth

This section develops some of the ideas that were first introduced in Chapter 1. However, in the diagrammatic summary of the effect of growth on structure on page 25, it was assumed that growth arose from organisational success. This need not always be the case. Businesses do not grow just because of increased turnover, they may instead decide to diversify by introducing new products or services, perhaps in areas of activity in which they have not before been engaged. Alternatively, they may be worried about the market penetration that one of their rivals is achieving, and make a takeover bid. In either case, growth in the organisation will occur, leading eventually to a more complex structure.

At one time, such acquisition or amalgamation was thought to be very sensible. It explains the growth of the giant motor vehicle manufacturing corporations, of which British Leyland is an obvious example. The advantages of bulk buying, standardised vehicle parts, corporate advertising and a spread of products across the market for vehicles, were thought vastly to outweigh any disadvantages of inefficiency from which these huge structures might suffer.

Today, the climate of expert opinion has changed. Now, small-scale business units are argued to be more efficient, and some experts consider their widespread introduction to be inevitable. For example, in his book *Up the Organisation*, Robert Townsend advises someone whose business has grown too large to 'break it up into autonomous parts', and Tom Lloyd in *Dinosaur and Co* says it will happen anyway in this high-tech age, as dissatisfied employees take their bright ideas and set up their own small-scale enterprises, seeking the financial and personal rewards which the giant multinationals cannot provide.

The key word today is **autonomy**. This means giving line managers the maximum amount of freedom to do their own thing in the interests of the business. Writers on organisations argue that this will increase motivation and job satisfaction at lower levels in the organisation. However, the people in positions of power are not usually willing to let go of all their power that easily, and as a result continue to exercise control, often by setting financial budgets or other targets within which their subordinates must work.

Divisional structures

A widely followed formula for permitting greater autonomy within a large corporate structure, whilst keeping overall control in the hands of senior management, is the divisional structure. In this type of organisation, there is a small headquarters which oversees the activities of a number of divisions, each of which is responsible for a limited range of the total organisational output. Each division is more or less free-standing and has its own management structure, probably similar to that of the headquarters unit. Sometimes divisions are called by that name, although a common practice is to set up a range of subsidiary companies instead, each company being controlled by a holding company, which is similar to the headquarters operation.

Supporters say that this method enables the headquarters unit to monitor much more carefully which parts of the organisation are meeting their targets, and which are not. Divisions that are not performing satisfactorily can then be 'floated off', perhaps in the form of management buy-outs, which you will have studied in the *Organisation in its Environment* unit. In such a case the management of the division, or of the subsidiary company, buy the equity in their company from the headquarters or parent company. An example of a divisional structure follows.

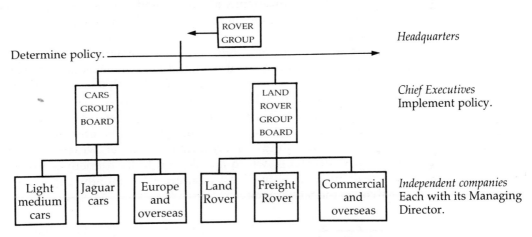

▲ *Part of a simplified divisional structure of Rover Group*

Organisations in crisis

The divisional structure is typical of the solutions which organisations have devised to deal with various problems that beset them during their evolution. A few modern writers on organisations argue that such changes only occur as a result of a crisis, in much the way that Personnel Departments might emerge after something has gone badly wrong with industrial relations, staff turnover or in-house training. The crises are thought to occur in a predictable order.

Crisis one: Who's in charge?

After an initial burst in which a business is carried along by the exuberance of its founder employees, conflicts of ideas and purpose arise. Direction is needed, and a controlling figure is seen to be the answer.

Crisis two: We're being smothered!

The controlling figure directs the organisation, but other people feel that they are not being given enough authority of their own. Decisions referred up take too long to come back down again. The solution is to delegate some of the controller's authority.

Crisis three: We've been here before!

With authority delegated, confusing and contradictory policies and decisions become commonplace. Everyone agrees that there should be an agreed system for dealing with certain typical problems and situations. Exhaustive procedural rules are drawn up and meetings follow meetings.

Crisis four: There's too much bloody red tape!

Doing things 'by the book' means that other people have to be kept informed, and agreed systems adhered to. This takes time and may mean missed opportunities. Communication chains need to be shortened, so structures such as the divisional model or a matrix are implemented.

Crisis five: Not again!

Once more there's uncertainty about role and direction — the difference is that this state of affairs is no longer thought to be undesirable by some of the new breed of writers on organisations.

Instead of preaching uniformity and stability, there is recognition by this small heretical group of writers that organisations will never achieve a state of equilibrium in which each part is in balance with itself and with its market environment. Rather than recommending off-the-shelf solutions for the organisation's problems, some management thinkers argue that the effectiveness of a network is inversely proportional to its formality, which seems to suggest that tightly structured, stable organisations might be the *least* efficient forms of organisations. Other writers call for 'loosely coupled', short-lived structures, which are allowed to flash briefly across the corporate heaven before dying in an orgy of restructuring a few months later. This truly is *Crisis five* — anarchy in the boardroom!

ACTIVITY

Jot down some of the more serious problems that your organisation is facing at the moment — if necessary ask your colleagues at work for some suggestions. If you don't work, then ask your college lecturer about some of the problems he/she identifies at college, but make sure you have a big sheet of paper.

- Are any of them serious enough to be called a crisis?
- Can you plot them according to the sequence of crises given previously?
- What outcomes do you predict?

Relocating the growing organisation

We have looked at some of the problems faced by evolving organisations. These problems affect the organisation's hierarchy and the way in which tasks and responsibilities are allocated. However, both growth or contraction may create more immediate and practical problems for management. One issue is where to locate an organisation that can no longer function satisfactorily in its existing premises.

Planning for a change in location is a complex management problem. Unfortunately, any decision is likely to prove expensive and a firm may be forced into adopting a negative 'least worst' solution. The following are some of the major factors that have to be taken into account.

Labour

Even in periods of high unemployment, lost staff may be difficult and expensive to replace. People with necessary skills are not always available locally and training the unskilled takes time and money. As well as the obvious costs, the organisation may suffer from reduced efficiency while inexperienced newcomers are learning their jobs. If the move is fairly local, many existing staff may remain, but feel demotivated due to the extra travelling time or reduced shopping facilities. This may show itself by staff taking more uncertified days off than they normally would.

Amenities

Most people do not live only for their work. Relocation involves taking account of more than the new premises alone. Availability and cost of local housing (especially in the South-east), public transport, shops, recreational and social facilities are all important if the move is to be made acceptable. Staff with growing families may also have to think seriously about the disruption to their children's schooling and job prospects.

Transport

We do not like commuting and not everyone owns a car. These facts must be borne in mind before we are likely to be tempted by the apparently cheap rent and rates in many rural locations. Every organisation must consider the extent to which customers need to visit their premises. For example, there would be little point in locating a Job Centre or Building Society branch office miles from where people live. On the other hand, it is possible to be too close to transport if noise from motorways, trains or low flying aircraft distracts staff from their work.

Associated industries

Access to suppliers and markets is less important for service industries, especially where computers can facilitate communication. However, it may still be sensible for manufacturing industries to group near their suppliers, their sources of materials or their subcontractors, in order to reduce costs in time and deliveries.

Politics

Central and local governments usually have reasons for wishing to promote or discourage moves to particular locations, typically into the depressed regions of the country (e.g., Tyneside) and away from high-cost areas such as London and the 'home counties'. By showing flexibility towards relocating, an organisation may gain substantial benefits in terms of reduced rent/rates and cheap loans. The dangers in embracing such a package too uncritically are that the hidden costs (e.g., staff demotivation, disruption of production, reduction in efficiency) of an unsuitable move may outweigh the benefits, and that a policy change may lead to a sudden move away from, say, promoting the development of green-field sites, in favour of inner city rejuvenation.

Economics

Occasionally managers are attracted to change for its own sake, in the hope that it will provide a miracle cure for a declining or mismanaged industry. Relocation is never a cheap option and the frequently under-estimated 'hidden' costs may take some time to identify and years to overcome.

We can now sum up the problems associated with company relocation in the form of a diagram.

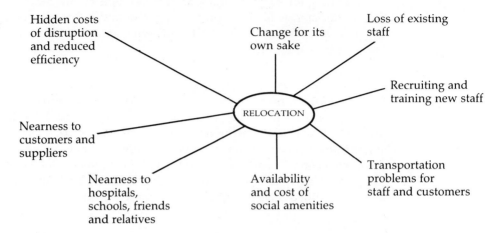

▲ *Some problems of relocation*

INTERNATIONAL FREIGHT ≋

International Freight is a company dealing with the storage, removal and delivery of bulky goods within the UK and overseas, for both domestic and commercial customers, most of them based in the West Midlands. For the past thirty years the office has been housed in an old-fashioned, multi-corridored, four-storey building in a narrow, noisy one-way street in the centre of Birmingham. The fleet of 16 transporters and 10 vans are garaged in the goods storage depot, a large but shabby ex-bus garage, in a busy residential suburb six miles south-west of the city centre. One hundred and fifty staff are employed, most of them clerical workers and a few specialists in export procedures. The drivers, storekeepers and one clerk are based at the depot.

The volume of International Freight's business is expanding, although this is a volatile business where competition is intense. An optimistic forecast is that space requirements will increase by 10 per cent per annum for the next five years and that the number of vehicles required double over the same period. The managers are also conscious that their antiquated assortment of personal computers will not cope with the expanding business, which needs comprehensive reorganisation.

The lease on the office building expires in three years and the owners have advised that they intend to demolish and redevelop the site. The managers of International Freight are now considering several alternative locations.

(a) Keeping the storage depot and renting more modern office accommodation in central Birmingham.
(b) Moving everyone to a purpose-built factory unit in the heart of a large industrial estate under 'Spaghetti Junction', five miles north of the city.
(c) Moving everyone to a converted manor house, with outbuildings and extensive grounds, in a peaceful rural setting a few miles from Redditch new town, which is 18 miles south of Birmingham on the M42.

ACTIVITY

1 Present a case for and against each proposal, taking account of each of the factors mentioned previously in the text.
2 Have you any alternative suggestions to help the firm cope with its enforced move?

Reorganising the office

Although most organisations relocate only occasionally, an internal move within a building (or a merging or a breaking-up of sections, or a change imposed by technological installations) is fairly frequent and usually calls for a re-design of the office layout. As with wholesale relocation, the re-design of an office layout is influenced by several variables. It is important to note that a badly-planned office affects performance by:

● Reducing efficiency through poor workflow and communications.
● Reducing motivation and creating dissatisfaction if working conditions are poor.

Therefore, when planning a new layout for any type of office the following need to be taken into account.

Efficiency factors

Furniture and equipment should be intelligently positioned to facilitate the flow of data between individuals and sections, taking account of planned growth or contraction in particular areas of work.

Legal factors

Legislation affects office design and layout, particularly through the Health and Safety at Work Act and the Offices, Shops and Railway Premises Act. It may seem very efficient to pack 50 staff into a room measuring 7 m × 6 m, in terms of close communication and reduced movement, but it is also unlawful under legislation, which demands a minimum of 3.7 square metres per person.

Ergonomic factors

Ergonomics is … 'that aspect of technology concerned with the application of biological and engineering data to problems relating to the mutual adjustment of men and machines'. Put simply, ergonomics describes the way in which staff perform in relation to the job, given differently designed furniture, equipment or workstations. So an ergonomically-designed car is one in which all controls are comfortably accessible, while an ergonomic workstation is one at which the worker is able to reach telephone, VDU and desk-drawers with minimum strain or wasted effort.

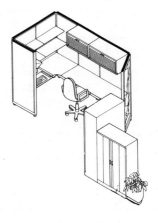
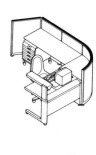

▶ *Ergonomically-designed desk units*

Personnel factors

Although not strictly a design factor, it is important for staff to feel comfortable with any proposed change in their environment. It is by no means certain that all staff will welcome changes — even moving to brand new, lavishly equipped premises. So, to avoid problems, management should:

- Keep staff informed throughout the planning stages.
- Invite staff to make suggestions of their own and to participate in the decision-making processes.
- Take time to explain why the changes are necessary.
- Try to avoid marrying-up incompatible personnel.

Reorganisation?

Auntie Katies Candy Shops Ltd manufacture a variety of confectionery lines, some with a highly seasonal demand. These are distributed to shops throughout the UK via a network of sales representatives. There is a small but growing demand for export sales.

The Sales Administration Department employs 20 full-time staff, plus up to 50 part-time casual staff to help at busy periods like Easter and Christmas. They process orders sent in by the reps, organise delivery and provide a contact for customers unable to reach their rep directly. The work is often hectic and the staff are often asked to work under pressure in a noisy atmosphere.

The department occupies three small rooms, one dealing with business in the North and Export territories (6 staff), another with the Midlands (8 staff) and the third with the South (6 staff). There is nowhere for the reps to sit if they call in to the office — opinions are divided over whether this is a good or a bad thing!

As part of a general office reorganisation, the company is considering what to do with the Sales Administration Department. There seem to be three main options.

- *Option one* — Move into a single, larger room with enough extra desks to accommodate the reps and casual staff.

- *Option two* — Move into the main Administrative Office, which already houses about 40 clerks and typists from Accounts, Buying and Records.

- *Option three* — Stay in the existing rooms, but possibly reorganise the division of the work.

ACTIVITY

Assume that you are the Sales Manager. The Sales Director wants you to write a report, with a recommendation for one of the three options, to be submitted to the next board meeting. What factors will you have to consider before recommending any changes? Make out a list.

The points you considered for your report should have included:

- Whether change of *any* kind is necessary or desirable, or simply being suggested for its own sake.

- The cost of each of the proposed moves, including any of the 'hidden' costs mentioned earlier in the chapter.
- The staff's attitude to any changes. Is there rivalry between the three sections or with the Administration Office, or will sex or age differences affect their ability to work together under different circumstances?
- Projections about how the work will be done in the future. Is Sales Administration likely to be centralised or computerised? Will staff be expected to retrain in new skills?
- Projections about the volume and flow of work. Is there to be an expansion of exports or introduction of new seasonal lines?
- Projections about whether staff numbers will expand or contract.
- Statutory requirements which may limit the number of employees in each room, depending on fire escapes and floor area. Are there any other factors to take into account?
- The nature of the work itself. Is it very noisy? Are the staff handling confidential material or conducting private interviews? Does it involve cash handling? Must access be given to the general public?

Designing an office layout

Broadly speaking, the designer of an office layout, faced with adequate space, chooses from one of three alternatives.

Closed/cellular offices

Each confined room is dedicated to a single function, say, for typing or costing or sales administration. Typically there are fewer than eight to ten staff occupying each room. This was the traditional way of arranging offices and often still applies where the structure of the building prevents larger rooms or where the nature of the work makes privacy, security or the restriction of noise desirable.

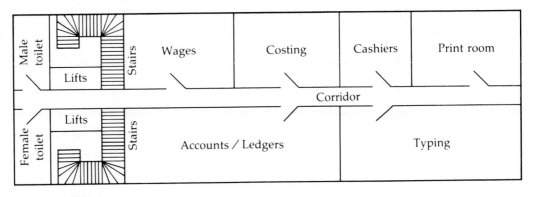

▲ *A traditional cellular office building*

Open-plan offices

These are nothing more than multifunctional spaces. In a very small organisation, the total number of staff in a room may be no greater than in a cellular office; the difference is that the occupants will be of different statuses and doing different jobs.

The original open-plan offices became popular in the USA in the 1920s when architectural developments made it practical to build large undivided floor areas. At that time, the motivation to change office design was largely economic. By switching to open-plan layouts, a firm could reduce its space requirements by one-quarter, or alternatively achieve 20 per cent more use from its existing space. With office rentals escalating, this remains a powerful justification for the change. Unfortunately, these early open-plan offices were more reminiscent of the school gym at exam time than the offices that we know today! Endless rows of desks containing staff from all functions of the organisation showed little regard for confidentiality or natural work teams. If you saw the film *9 till 5* you will know the sort of office arrangement being described.

The more flexible use of space offered by open-plan layout, together with economies of heating, lighting, office rental and easier and faster communications may be offset by some disadvantages. These include greater noise, increased distraction, loss of privacy and confidentiality, and the difficulties of achieving universally accepted levels of heat, light and ventilation.

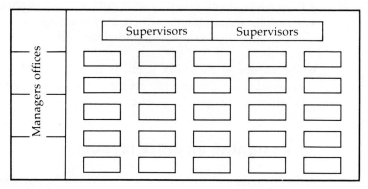

▲ *Open-plan offices*

Landscaped offices

To overcome these disadvantages, a system developed in Germany, called a 'Bureaulandscaft', was introduced into the UK in the 1950s. This attempts to 'landscape' the large open office space through strategic grouping of desks, filing cabinets, office furniture and low screens.

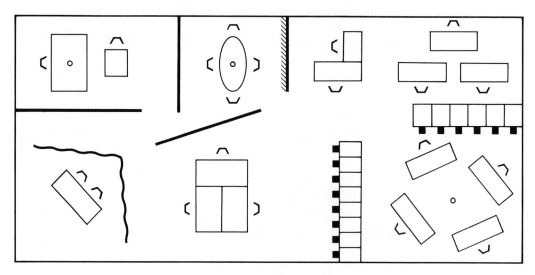

▶ *Landscaped offices*

Landscaping enables staff to relate to their own work group or section, and even light and ventilation may be adapted to the requirements of each area. Noisy sections may be placed in a corner and the sound from their telephones or machines partially absorbed by filing cabinets or rows of potted plants. Ideally, landscaping should apply to *all* staff, not only the junior clerks, if the benefits of integration and good communications are to be enjoyed. However, like all compromise solutions, there is a price to pay: the landscaped office is expensive to design and equip and much more extravagant of space than 'traditional' open-planning.

ACTIVITY

In the previous activity you were asked to think about the factors that might lead to re-designing Auntie Katies Sales Administration offices. Jot down the advantages and disadvantages to the company of switching to a 'traditional' open-plan layout. Include in your answer your analysis of how the switch might influence human relationships and communications.

From the pre-industrial office to the electronic office

To a great extent, it is the reorganisation of work and systems, and changing shifts in the pattern of work in offices, that have led to changing designs of office layout. Thirty years ago, the typical office contained people talking, both 'face to face' and on the telephone, writing, filing and typing. It is much the same today. What has changed in that time, however, is the number of staff who use keyboards as part of their normal working day.

At one time, only trained typists and secretaries used a keyboard and their job consisted almost entirely of copying work generated by others. Now almost any job in an office, at any level, may require you to be 'keyboard literate'.

ACTIVITY

List six non-secretarial jobs that make regular use of keyboarding skills for purposes other than typing.

Your list could have included, amongst many others:

Travel Agent
Accountant/Book-keeper
Directory Enquiries
Librarian
Doctor
Designer

These changes have affected the way in which work is carried out and information is processed in offices. Three distinct evolutionary stages have been identified, each with its own style of management and relationships between staff and their customers.

Pre-industrial office

This still exists in most small or professional offices. Here, output depends largely on the performance of individuals, rather than on their equipment or the systematic organisation of their work. The office probably contains information-processing equipment such as telephones, photocopiers and dictating machines, but there is little conscious effort to get the most efficient and productive use from them. Employees are expected to learn their jobs and to do whatever is required, and varied personal styles of work contribute to, rather than detract from, the success of the operation. Emphasis is placed on loyalty, understanding and mutual respect.

Pre-industrial organisation may work well in a small and fairly simple office. However, it is inefficient for larger or more complex operations where greater coordination is required. If work load increases, the office may simply recruit more staff or demand more from existing staff without changing its basic organisation. This is likely only to impose greater strain on existing processes, and to lead to a decline in efficiency and breakdown in morale.

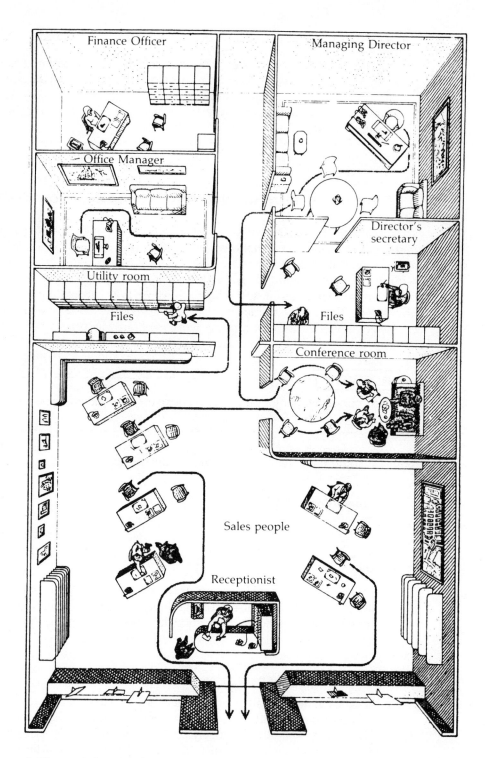

▲ *The pre-industrial office*

Industrial office

The industrial-age office attempts to resolve problems brought about through growth by applying Taylor's principles of scientific management (see page 318) to information processing. The result is essentially a production line, using process-based organisation.

Work moves from desk-to-desk, or from section-to-section, with each worker receiving documents in a particular form, performing a few simple tasks, then passing them on to the next worker in the chain. There is little scope for initiative, nor for working substantially faster or better than other members of the 'production line'.

Industrial offices are most often found in organisations that handle a large volume of similar transactions, for example in headquarters offices of banks and insurance companies. An attempt will have been made in such offices to analyse and plan work to facilitate the speed and efficiency of its processing. Unfortunately, such repetitive work leads to a high error rate, and because few workers have an overall understanding of the job, mistakes may multiply. Customers with complex queries may have difficulty in finding anyone who understands and can resolve their problems.

Information-age office

Despite the recognition of these limitations, before the 1970s there was little that the large service organisations could do to improve the situation. Since then, information technology has made it possible for one individual to handle all the processes for a fairly small number of accounts rather than handle just one process for a much larger number. In the information-age office, each worker is provided with a terminal linked to a main computer, which maintains a data base on all customers. The worker has access to all records relating to each customer and can correct or update these records as required. Because there is no delay in the processing of amendments, all other users of the system have up-to-date information at all times.

Such a system benefits both the customer — in terms of improved quality of service — and the employee who has a more interesting and satisfying job. Although the system has in some cases produced redundancies, in other organisations an improved level of service and increased number of customers have led in turn to increased staff levels.

You will find that this subject has been more thoroughly explored in Chapter 5.

ACTIVITY

Draw up a short questionnaire to help you find out in which of the three types of offices most of the students on your course are employed. Obviously you can't expect any office to be *wholly* one of the three types described, rather it is likely to be nearer one of them than another. You will have to think carefully about the wording of your questions. For example, you will need to know about:

- The size and function of the office.
- The existence of a data base, and use of computers.
- Links with customers' homes and field offices.
- The level of repetitive functions and production-line processing.
- Records processing and up-date facilities.

In a short report, present your findings in a visually interesting way to show the extent to which the three types of offices are represented. You can find advice on how to compile questionnaires and write reports in Chapter 3.

Health and safety at work

Another factor that has led to re-designing of office processes and premises has been increased government pressure for safe, healthy working environments. Before the 19th century, responsibility for the health and safety of employees was only a moral duty for an employer. During the industrialisation of Britain, piecemeal legislation emerged, usually in response to published reports which gave hostile accounts of working conditions in industry or on the treatment of working women and children. Sometimes legislation to improve safety was introduced only after a serious accident had led to the death and injury of literally hundreds of people, for example after an avoidable coal-mining disaster or the sinking of the 'unsinkable' *Titanic* (which led to more lifeboats and safer sea routes).

All this health and safety legislation, including all the *Factories Acts*, were consolidated into the *Health and Safety at Work Act* (HASAWA), an 'enabling' Act that applied laws already passed to *all* persons at work. This new Act included five million workers not previously covered, in particular those in medical, educational, leisure and transport premises, and visitors to businesses. Today, the principal legislation affecting office employees is:

Health and Safety at Work Act	1974
Offices, Shops and Railway Premises Act	1963
Fire Precautions Act	1971
Employers' Liability (Compulsory Insurance) Act	1969

The responsibility for ensuring that working conditions are healthy and safe is a shared one.

- *Employers* — They must provide a safe and healthy environment for all workers and others who live nearby or who are passing through.
- *Employees* — They must follow safe working practices and take reasonable care of themselves and others.
- *Manufacturers* — They must provide goods that are safe and adequately tasted.
- *Contractors* — They must avoid risks to the health and safety of users or operators of equipment that they instal.
- *Landlords* — The owners of premises also carry a responsibility for its safety.

ACTIVITY

You are the newly appointed Safety Officer, and your boss has asked for an inspection and report on health and safety conditions in your workplace. (If this isn't possible, you may be asked by your lecturer to conduct a similar survey in the college.) Select several specific areas to investigate, for example fire escape procedures and heating and ventilation, and prepare a report for management on what you have discovered and on improvements that may be required to comply with legislation, some details of which are listed on page 352.

You will of course ask your boss for permission and time to conduct your investigation before you begin, and you may need to research into existing procedures and documentation. You will find advice on report writing in Chapter 3.

Health and safety in the office

Although we normally associate death and injury at work with people in factories and in the construction industry (by far the most dangerous occupation), we are apt to under-estimate the hazards that are present in the most up-to-date and well-designed office. According to a 1984 report published by the *Association of Professional, Executive, Clerical and Computer Staff (APEX)* on office technology, the introduction of new technology has serious health and safety implications for employees. Many employees pointed to visual display units as a major cause of eye strain, headache, migraine, neck and backache, fatigue and increased irritability. In fact, 26 per cent of those surveyed had noted an increase in employees wearing spectacles. More information on this interesting report can be found in Chapter 3.

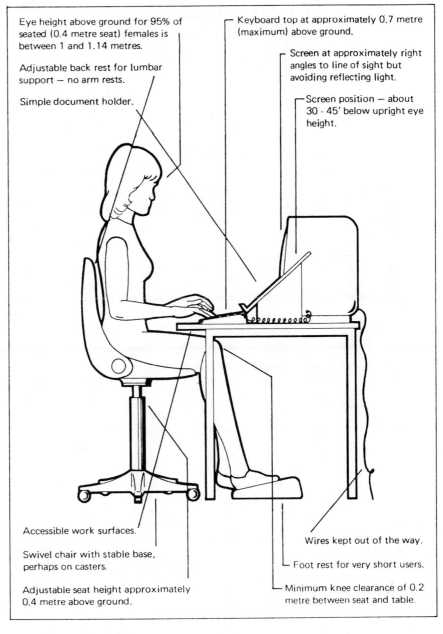

▲ *Good workstation principles*

In more recent years, there has been increasing concern amongst medical experts about an industrial disease called 'tenosynovitis' (Teno for short), which seems to be very fond of office workers. These extracts are taken from an article published in *Office Secretary* (June 1986).

RSI –

Occupational hazard of the office

By Penny Comerford

What is the latest health concern among the working population? AIDS, you may guess, smoking related diseases or obesity? According to many sufferers and researchers in this country and abroad, the most insidious, disabling and unrecognised condition among predominantly female office workers is Repetitive Strain Injury (RSI). This term, coined in Australia, covers a multitude of musculo-skeletal injuries which are uncomfortable at one end of the scale, totally incapacitating at the other. Its prime sufferers, say the Australians, are women using typewriters, keyboards, or even the telephone constantly. Cases over there have increased tenfold since 1978, doubled since 1980 and the incidence had spurred government departments into research and action.

So what is RSI? It is a generic term for a soft tissue disorder, mainly in the arms and hands, caused by the overloading of particular muscle groups from quick repetitive action and hav-ing to maintain a constrained posture. Tendons, muscles and joints become inflamed and sore and as the movement is repeated, the inflammation becomes permanent, the tissues break down and scar and become damaged in the same way as if you had bruised your arm and someone kept hitting it, never giving it a chance to heal.

It is not a new condition, cases have been around for years, particularly in industry where packing or assembly have to be done repeatedly, but it is the advent of new equipment and expectations of more and more speed and efficiency by employers, that has brought the problem into the modern office. People who use electronic typewriters, word processors or computer keyboards are most susceptible, possibly because they work up frightening speeds, are not sitting properly and do not take sufficient breaks in betweeen work stages. Symptoms range from tingling in the fingers to pain in the knuckles wrists and elbows accompanied by swelling. It comes on quickly after starting to type and only disappears after a night's rest.

Unfortunately, this is not a problem which once recognised can be cured and forgotten, for much controversy surrounds RSI.

The first is one of definition. You may have heard the terms, "typist's cramp", "scrivener's palsy," "washerwomans' wrist", "tennis elbow", or more contemporarily, "data processors disease." Chances are that these labels refer to one condition, tenosynovitis, an inflammation of the tendon sheaths in the fingers, wrists and elbows. These sheaths provide lubrication for the tendons inside, allowing them to move freely and painlessly. Nerves are also affected and carry the pain all the way through the arm. It begains usually with tenderness, numbness and sometimes a crackling sound in the wrist. Movements of the hand or arm become restricted and painful, you can't grip and pain sometimes spreads to the shoulders. In extreme cases, tasks like turning taps, dres-

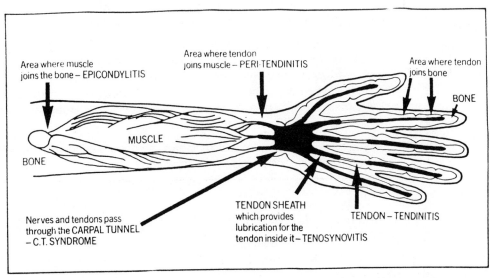

Area where muscle joins the bone – EPICONDYLITIS

Area where tendon joins muscle – PERI-TENDINITIS

Area where tendon joins bone

BONE

MUSCLE

BONE

Nerves and tendons pass through the CARPAL TUNNEL – C.T. SYNDROME

TENDON SHEATH which provides lubrication for the tendon inside it – TENOSYNOVITIS

TENDON – TENDINITIS

sing, washing up, sewing, and opening jars and packets, become practically impossible.

Tenosynovitis, once diagnosed, is recognised as an industrial disease by the DHSS and technically sufferers can claim compensation. At present around 2000 people get compensation for teno every year, but many sufferers and trade unions feel that these are the tip of the iceberg and there are many others who either do not claim or do not get claims recognised.

Another problem is that teno is only one form of RSI. Others include: carpal tunnel syndrome causing tingling, numbness and weakness in the hands; tendinitis causing inflamed tendons which are locked into their sheaths so fingers, hands or arms can't be moved easily; and peritendinitis which is the inflammation of the muscle tendon junction and surrounding tissue, producing swelling and pain in the forearm. None of the other forms of RSI are claimable.

Assessing the extent of the problem is not easy.

The fact that it is mainly women who suffer from RSI, has encouraged employers and even doctors to be sceptical. Some call it "skivitis," hysteria, mass malingering. Most of the sufferers we spoke to had had opposition from their employers, if not their doctors and most of them had lost their jobs through the condition, never being able to type or use a keyboard again. Some of these girls were barely in their twenties, others were experienced secretaries who only got teno when they were expected to work ridiculously fast with little change of position. This was less likely to happen in the days of mechanical typewriters.

The sad thing is that there is no real cure for RSI. The symptoms are only alleviated by rest and in severe cases even this takes some time. Fingers and arms may need to be splinted, phsiotherapy given and the sufferers must not resume typing. Drugs such as pain killers and cortisone injections are not very satisfactory.

A secretary who can't type and a computer operator who can't touch the keyboard is no good to an employer, so the inevitable end result is loss of

Teno is an inflammation of the tendon sheaths in the hand, wrist and arms

the job – training and experience go down the drain, financial difficulties arise, whole careers have to be replanned.

Prevention is the only hope for the future and this cannot come about properly until the problem is widely recognised. Ergonomic design of seats and tables so that operators can get the least tiring and strenuous posture is helpful, but there need to be supervisors to train others in the best ways of sitting and working. Seat height, back support height and angle should be adjustable for different people and the feet should be firmly on the floor so that the weight is not taken by the backs of thighs. Elbows should be held at the level of work height with forearm horizontal and upper arms hanging freely at the sides. If you hold your wrist extended in the same position for long periods, you will probably suffer. Using an elbow rest or lowering the keyboard height is a good idea.

ACTIVITY

1 According to the article, what causes teno and repetitive strain injury? Why do you think that the incidence of these diseases is on the increase?

2 Some employers and doctors question the existence of teno by referring to it as 'skivitis', 'hysteria' or 'malingering' on the part of women workers.
(a) Why do you think women workers are seen in this light?
(b) Explain whether you believe that there is any truth in these attitudes?
(c) Are there other medical conditions or any other social situations in which women workers are seen in this light? Explain.

3 Can you think of any way in which management intervention can help either to eliminate or reduce the effects of this condition?

Enforcement of health and safety laws

The *Health and Safety at Work Act* established a Health and Safety Commission to draw up regulations and codes of practice, and to employ inspectors to visit working premises with powers to:

- *Prohibit certain practices* Inspectors can issue a 'Prohibition Notice' on the person in control of activities that involve a serious risk of personal injury. The notice usually contains a list of activities that must stop at once, or say within 21 days, in which time what is wrong must be put right.

- *Improve unsatisfactory practices* An inspector can issue an 'Improvement Notice' if he finds that a person is breaking the safety laws. Either an employee or an employer is given a time period in which to remedy the situation. An employer might appeal against an Improvement Notice at an industrial tribunal that has the power to modify or cancel unreasonable demands made by the inspector.

- *Prosecute and fine offenders* If an employer chooses to ignore either a Prohibition or an Improvement Notice, he risks up to two years' imprisonment and/or unlimited fines in the law courts.

Here are a few examples of recommendations and obligations relating to health and safety in the office. Where Acts of Parliament impose legal obligations, the following codes apply:

(a) Office, Shops and Railway Premises Act.
(b) Health and Safety at Work Act.
(c) Local Government Fire Regulations, or Fire Precautions Act.

Structural
Provision of adequate lighting, especially over machines (a).
Reasonable ventilation and control over temperature. Minimum temperature is 16 °C (61 °F) (a).
Carpets or other floor covering to be in good repair (a).
All exit doors to open outwards (c).
Alternative emergency exits to be provided and kept unlocked during working hours (c).
Corridor doors to be self-closing (c).

Equipment
Should comply with Department of Trade safety standards.
Furniture should be of fire-resistant material.

Ergonomically designed chairs should be supplied for workers who have to maintain a fixed posture, e.g., typists and keyboard operators.

File storage should not exceed two metres in height unless fixed safety ladders are integral with the filing unit.

Noise-absorbing mats should be provided for noisy machines on desks, e.g., typewriters.

No-one may be required to lift or carry loads that may cause injury (a).

Furniture and layout

A limit is imposed on the number of people in a room: 7.7 square metres per person (a).

Gangways and exits must be kept clear of furniture (c).

Trailing electric leads are forbidden (b), and wired-up desks should be fixed to the floor.

Noisy machines should be localised and kept some distance from other staff.

Management controls and emergency arrangements

Fireproof storage for inflammable materials, e.g., duplicating fluid, must be provided (b).

Fire-fighting equipment must be provided and may be periodically inspected (c).

Instructions to be followed in the event of fire must be prominently displayed (c).

Easily accessible first-aid equipment must be provided, and staff trained in first-aid (a).

Accident reports must be made out following serious mishap (a).

Smoking should be forbidden or restricted to named areas.

Cloakrooms should be provided for hanging outdoor clothing (a).

Security checks to be made on suspicious incoming packages.

Alarms must be tested regularly and staff must be aware of escape routine (a).

ACTIVITY

You are the safety officer, and you have just received the following list from your Safety Committee. Identify whether any relevant Acts have been transgressed, and suggest what action could be taken in each case for the office to conform to the law.

1 The new metal filing cabinets have corners so sharp that a clerk has twice cut his hand when trying to shut them.
2 The keys for the fire escape door are only available by going to the office manager.
3 The area around the typing section of the open-plan office is very noisy.
3 The wheeled trolley used to move heavy stocks of stationery is so high that, when loaded up, it is difficult for the person pushing it to see where he is going.
5 No fire drill has been held for over a year, and most employees are not aware what they should do in case of fire.
6 Staff sitting near the south-facing picture windows complain that they get very hot because of reflected heat from the sun.

Change in the commercial environment

No-one can have failed to see the changes that have taken place in the world of work. In the UK in 1986 there were just over 27 million people in the labour force, although of these about 3.25 million were unemployed. As you can see in the following chart, the working population *and* the unemployed population have been increasing between 1973 and 1986. You will also notice that between 1983 and 1986, the number of people employed has increased by about one million, although many of these new jobs have been in part-time work. Projections of the civilian labour force, running up to the end of the century, also indicate that the number of people in work will continue to rise, although this does not necessarily mean that the number of people unemployed will decline.

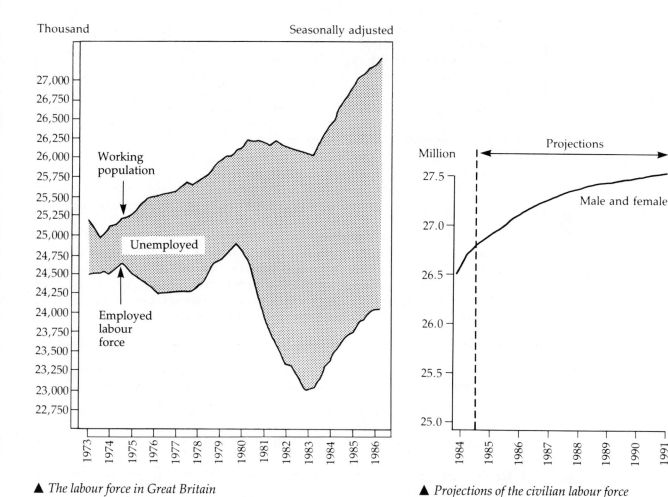

▲ *The labour force in Great Britain*

▲ *Projections of the civilian labour force (Department of Employment)*

It is largely in the service industries that most job creation is taking place. In the 30 years between 1955 and 1984, the service sector has grown from 45 to 65 per cent, as shown in this diagram from the White Paper *Employment: The Challenge for the Nation*.

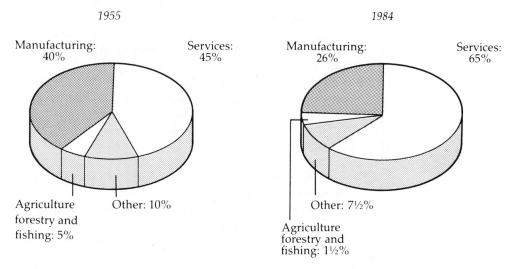

▲ *Changing pattern of employment in the UK*

These sectoral changes have been matched by an occupational shift from blue collar to white collar jobs. In the five years between 1979 and 1984, there has been a relentless growth in the demand for jobs associated with information technology, and even within manufacturing industry a much higher proportion of people are in non-manual occupations, particularly scientific, technological and professional ones.

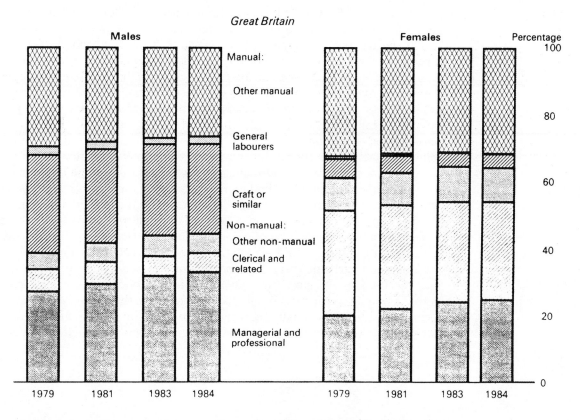

▲ *People in employment — by occupation and sex (Department of Employment)*

355

It appears that employment will continue to decline in traditional manufacturing industries and, while growth of the service industries may slow down in the 1990s, as Information Technology is applied ever more widely, the services sector should continue to be the major employer of both men and women. However, what will the broader effects of the new technology be — particularly on working conditions? Let us look at the case of Sinclair Research Ltd, which was producing personal and business computers in 1982/83 and had a turnover of approximately one million pounds per employee.

At the time, Sir Clive Sinclair did not actually produce anything himself. He used subcontractors, who were themselves capital-intensive rather than labour-intensive, which means they employed lots of machinery but few people. Although the later fortunes of Sir Clive were not too successful, the implication of the success of his early enterprise for the businesses of the future suggests that success will depend on a few highly creative individuals who are capable of managing and organising the work of others across a wide spectrum, rather than on the efforts of traditional producers who operate in inflexible factory units on industrial estates. New businesses will have no need for expensive bureaucracy. At one time automation used to imply a degree of inflexibility, but the new machines can reset themselves for new tasks at the whim of senior managers. Why should managers spend several hours a day dictating letters so that secretaries can spend several more hours typing them, when word processors, filled with 'stock' letters, can produce faultless personalised copies in a fraction of the time?

In the past, there was an elite of talented or privileged individuals who had the most interesting jobs, while the rest of us laboured in manual or clerical work to support them. It seemed that there would always be a need for people to type, keep books, mind machines and fetch and carry. Information entrepreneurs need less help. One individual may receive, classify, store, retrieve and transmit goods and services across the world without human assistance. While many of us view this prospect pessimistically, new techniques can allow small enterprises to pull the mat from under established companies. Let's look at one such possibility that was reported in a local paper.

The robots are here!

The manufacture of window frames and similar types of building carpentry is a mechanised operation in which expensive machines make batches of standard parts. This standardised product cannot be matched for price by a small producer without the machines.

But a new generation of machines is coming! A *robot woodworker* is not only more efficient than the traditional machine, it is able to reset itself to make an enormous variety of components.

The case for standardised mass production then disappears, and a small company, say a local builder or a timber merchant, can make any shape or size of frame to order on just one machine. So while jobs disappear in manufacturing, local builders may take on architects, designers or draughtspersons, specifically to exploit the machine's potential. The most successful firm becomes the one with the most flair and imagination in adapting the technology to respond to the demand created for cheaper, more flexible carpentry and wood products.

Another example has been the upsurge in 'Instant Print' shops, which have brought offset litho printing and high quality photocopying onto the High Street. They may have taken some work away from established printers, but they have also created a brand new market for inexpensive short-run colour printing and reproduction.

ACTIVITY

In the story *The robots are here!*

1 What are the long-term consequences for employment trends if this type of workplace technology becomes commonplace?
2 If you were the manager of a company about to instal a robot woodworker, how would you further exploit the machine's potential, assuming that your company is a major supplier of window frames?
3 Can you identify any other small-scale business enterprises that have been established in the last ten years, mainly as a result of more efficient technology?

The vanishing office

Where then will a new generation of workers find jobs? After all, if you work from a terminal linked to your organisation's main data base, there may be no reason why you should physically inhabit the same building. Commuting is tiring, expensive and time-consuming. Why spend three hours a day and several hundred pounds a year travelling to your employer's premises to do a job that you could do just as effectively in your spare bedroom? There could be other advantages too, for employers as well as employees. The expense of renting and equipping office space would reduce dramatically and the feasibility of 'opening' for much longer hours would improve if staff found that alternative working times suited their domestic arrangements. With electronic mail, operations could easily continue around the clock. Such futuristic working arrangements are not pipe dreams, they are already here.

- F International is a software consultancy firm with several hundred employees — many with young families — who work from home on computer terminals. Only about 30 staff travel into the firm's token headquarters at Berkhamsted. Most staff are freelance and never set foot from one year to the next on their employer's premises.

- At the executive end of the housing market, builders are beginning to realise that electronic links to the office make houses in remote locations much more saleable. A few years ago, a luxury development in the Cotswold village of Hook Norton was not selling well. The builders blamed the remote geographical region, problems with commuting and the long-delayed M40 extension. They approached Telecom, who installed two phone lines to each house, one for ordinary calls and Prestel, the other connected to a communicating workstation called Tonto — a unit combining a computer with a phone via a built-in modem. Tonto can access the Telecom Gold electronic mail service, and Prestel if necessary. The final installation in each house was a Merlin facsimile transmitter, allowing documents and diagrams to be sent and received electronically. The executive buyer now had full office facilities without leaving his or her front door.

However, not everyone wants to work from home, amidst crying babies and unwashed dishes! Most modern houses are particularly limited in terms of space and privacy. Work is also for most people an important part of their social and cultural life, providing relationships and stimuli that are important and satisfying — a point already made in Chapter 8. As many sales representatives have discovered to their cost, working alone can create problems in maintaining a high level of personal enthusiasm and motivation. One solution has been the neighbourhood work centres where neighbours — probably all working for different companies but with similar technical and human needs — spend their days in an independent local 'office' sharing information-processing equipment.

What will be the effect of such changes on the backbone of the organisation: the bureaucrats and middle managers? It appears that office automation takes place through a series of phases.

- *Phase one*   In the 1970s most organisations acquired computers which remained physically remote from most staff, hidden in specially furnished and air-conditioned suites, guarded and manned by the 'Computer Department', whose jargon and jealously guarded expertise was incomprehensible to most workers.

- *Phase two*   By the early 1980s the spread of terminals — and the demystification of many computer operations — had started to make equipment and procedures accessible to non-specialists.

- *Phase three*   This phase saw inter-communicating personal computers servicing boardrooms, factories and overseas branch offices, with information flowing sideways as well as up and down the hierarchy.

- *Phase four*   A future phase, when universal office machines make all employees 'information independent'. This creates doubt as to what will be left for managers to manage, once instant access to company information is available company-wide.

Resistance to change

We have looked at management in previous chapters: at the different techniques that may be appropriate to different situations or types of worker. In order to manage change effectively, it is useful to identify the factors that generate resistance to it.

Security

As explored by Maslow (page 314), the desire for security is a basic need that we all share, both within and outside the workplace. If proposed changes are seen to be undermining job security, they will almost certainly be opposed, and it is this resistance that is often the root cause of long-term industrial disputes.

Status and esteem

Status and esteem needs, as identified by Maslow, may also be threatened by change. This threat is felt not only by workers in high-status positions, such as supervisors and managers, but also by those who feel that their worth and self-esteem are being undermined by new technology and reorganisation. Skilled industrial craft workers and office workers who handle complex administrative documentation can be badly affected.

Economic

Similarly, a change seen as leading to lower wages or a higher cost of living will always be opposed and may also result in organised resistance and strike action with trade union support.

Personal

Some changes are seen as reducing the freedom of the individual to do their job in their own way, or increasing the extent to which he/she is supervised or 'spied on'. Do you remember the fierce opposition of lorry drivers to tachographs (spies in the cab), which record road speeds and driving hours?

Social

The change may be seen as an attempt to break up long-established and cohesive work groups and to isolate staff from their fellow workers and friends.

Of course, identification of such factors does not make them disappear, but it may enable managers to provide reassurance if the fears appear to be groundless or exaggerated.

ACTIVITY

There is about to be a major reorganisation of your workplace, which will include the relocation of staff and resources within the same building, the breaking up and reformation of work teams, and the introduction of labour-saving technology.

1 Working in a small group or 'think tank', draw up a step-by-step guide that could be adopted by your management team, which offers advice on the best way to communicate their proposals to the staff.
2 Suggest if there are likely to be any further staff needs to be satisfied, in addition to new equipment or structural changes, before the proposals can be put into full effect.
3 There are likely to be many pointed questions asked by staff.
  (a) Draw up a list of six subjects that you believe will worry staff most of all.
  (b) Jot down a few ideas or responses for each subject on your list that the management team will find helpful in the formulation of their replies.

SOLUTIONS

The answers to the questions on page 335 are 290 and 184 respectively.

SCENARIO

Perlambulatory Insurance, whose headquarters are at 10 The Parade, Swindon S5 1ED, is committed to a major reorganisation. The three main threads of its restructuring plans are:

- A switch to computerised data base, involving the passing back of all paper records to a 'fail-safe' system only.
- A change from selling insurance on a door-to-door basis by Perlambulatory's own reps, to direct sales to the public from shop premises in main shopping precincts.
- The incorporating of home and vehicle security advice, supplies and installation into Perlambulatory's activities.

IMPLICATIONS

- The existing company structure will be radically overhauled, involving redundancies and closure of existing offices. The existing pattern of HQ, four regional offices and the ten district offices in each region are to be replaced with 60 combined shop/office premises to be called *Protection-For-All Centres*. Each shop will report directly to an enlarged HQ operation, where records will be kept by type of account, rather than by each region as before.

The revised structure, including that of the typical branch shop/office will be as follows:

▼ Proposed structure of Perlambulatory Insurance

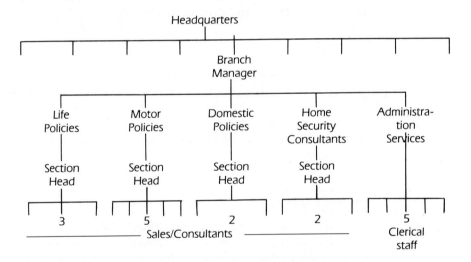

- It has been decided that about half the existing door-to-door sales representatives are to be retained: they will be offered jobs in the new *Protection-For-All-Centres*. The rest will be made redundant. However, some may wish to reapply for jobs as Home Security Consultants. Some training will be given for this.

- About two-thirds of the existing regional and district office staff will be made redundant. The remainder will be offered jobs in either the *Protection-For-All Centres* or in the enlarged HQ.

TASKS

1 Draft a letter that can be used as a standard letter to be sent to all existing sales reps who are to be made redundant. Try to compensate for the effect of this bad news.

2 Draft a memo to be sent to all the office staff selected to be retained. It should seek to boost morale and, at the same time, request volunteers to move to headquarters.

3 Design the layout for a typical *Protection-For-All Centre* from the floor plans supplied by a local estate agent, and provide a provisional list of the main items of equipment and furniture that are required.

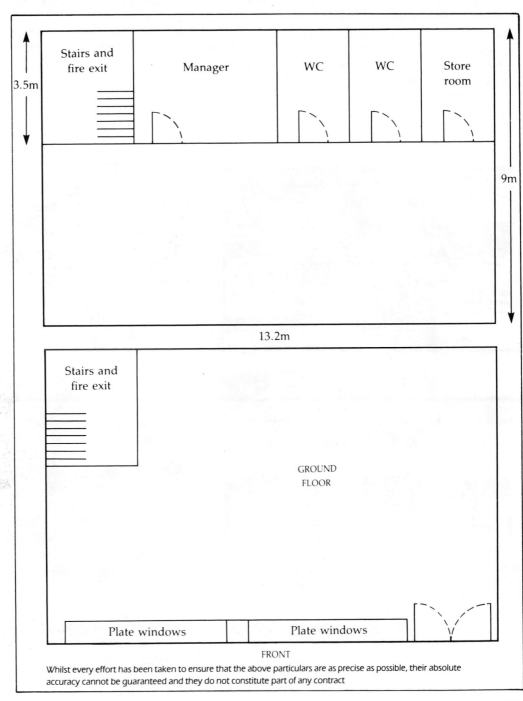

WORK

A Japanese firm specialising in the production of computer software, most of which is to be exported by road to Common Market countries, is to build or occupy a new factory in Britain. The company intends to employ about 250 full-time and the same number of part-time workers, some of whom will receive in-company training in the new production techniques. After a thorough investigation, the company's management team has to come to a decision about which of the two alternative sites to select:

- An existing purpose-built factory on the outskirts of Liverpool.
- A new factory, which is to be built in a largely rural area in the 'computer belt' region near to the M4, 50 miles west of London.

1 Discuss the advantages and disadvantages to the company of each site in relation to:
   (a) the recruitment of staff and likely staff turnover
   (b) transport facilities.
2 Contrast the availability of jobs and the chances of remaining unemployed in the two regions.
3 Suggest a few reasons why most unemployed people are unwilling to move to more prosperous parts of the country.
4 What evidence is there in these statistics that supports the view that Britain is a 'country of two halves'?

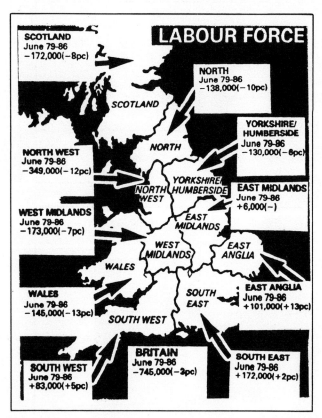

▲ *Government statistics showing the gain and loss of jobs between 1976–86*

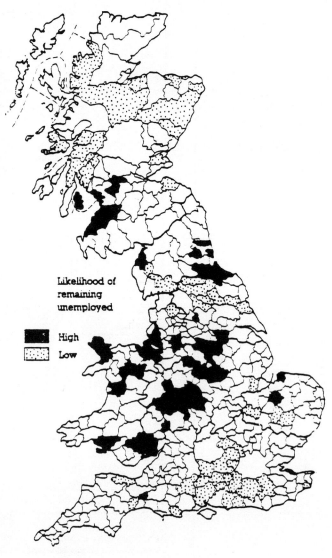

362

ROYAL SOCIETY FOR THE PREVENTION OF ACCIDENTS

Dear Safety Officer

We are becoming greatly concerned by the increasing number of accidents occurring in offices. Last year in Britain over 5000 office workers were seriously injured and many thousands more sustained less serious injuries that required medical attention.

WE INTEND TO SEE THIS NUMBER REDUCED AND WE NEED YOUR HELP TO DO IT.

We believe that the first step is to raise safety awareness, by drawing attention to the dangers that are ever-present in any working environment. Our research suggests that many office workers simply do not believe that *their* office is a source of danger.

Therefore we are asking you to conduct a survey of your colleagues to test their safety awareness, and we have drawn up the following questionnaire to help you with this task.

When you have conducted your safety survey, we recommend that you present your findings to your safety committee *and* management team, who may then decide to introduce more effective safety campaigns if these are indicated.

Thank you for your attention

Yours sincerely

SAFETY SURVEY

1. Do you know the nearest escape route in case of emergency?
2. Where is your nearest fire alarm located?
3. What should you do if you discover a fire?
4. Where is your nearest fire extinguisher?
5. Where is your assembly point when you are out of the building?
6. If you are injured at work, what should you do?
7. Do you need to report an accident that results in minor injury?
8. Where is your nearest first-aid box?
9. Who is the person in charge of the first-aid box?
10. If you operate machinery, is it maintained regularly?
11. Are your filing cabinets fitted with anti-tilt devices, or a label advising opening one drawer at a time?
12. If you have to store materials above your normal reach, are step ladders provided for you?
13. Do you know how to lift weights correctly?
14. Do you store your flammable liquids and materials in a suitable container? (Typewriter fluids and correction thinners.)
15. Do you always switch off or disconnect electric machines and appliances when you have finished work for that day?

SCENARIO

As office Safety Officer, you receive this document from the Royal Society for the Prevention of Accidents (ROSPA).

TASK ONE / THE SURVEY

Conduct your survey on as large a group as possible, preferably within your own office.

You will need to think about how you intend to record their responses.

TASK TWO / THE REPORT

Draw up a report on the basis of your findings. Your Safety Committee might find it helpful if the more important findings are presented graphically.

FOLDABOX LTD

For the past six years Helen and Barry Richardson had owned a small business that supplied cardboard cartons and containers, mostly to local dairies, cosmetics and confectionery manufacturers. Their reputation for quality and prompt delivery was good and turnover was increasing rapidly. It was a straightforward business: the design and printing of the card was done 'out', while Foldabox and its staff of 18 cut and assembled the cartons and packed them ready for delivery to customers.

Helen was in charge of sales. Using contacts from a previous job, she travelled around seeking new orders, while two clerks took orders by telephone. Barry was responsible for administration, handling book-keeping, basic accounts, stock control and staffing matters.

Following an approach from a large national company interested in placing a very substantial regular order, the Richardsons decided that it was time to take the plunge and expand their business. They obtained an £85 000 loan from an investment bank, plus a £15 000 short-term loan from their local bank. A large factory unit was acquired in a new inner city industrial estate, about five miles from their existing suburban workshop, and new equipment was installed that enabled them to do their own printing and increase the size, range and quality of their cartons. Amidst a fanfare of publicity in the local press, they recruited another 44 operators, an accountant, a printing manager, two clerks and two sales reps. The senior foreman was promoted to assembly manager and several of the most experienced operators were made supervisors.

However, only three months after the move, it was apparent that problems over and above normal 'teething troubles' were affecting the business.

- Two of the newly promoted supervisors resigned, saying they were 'craftsmen, not bloody troubleshooters' and that they could not cope with the additional responsibility.
- The system did not seem able to cope with the extra wages administration and on one or two occasions it was touch and go whether pay packets would be ready on time.
- The new printing manager and the assembly manager had an argument over quality and the latter handed in his notice.
- Occasional absenteeism and sick leave seemed far higher than previously.
- The Richardsons observed that the atmosphere at work was strained. The place seemed to be full of strangers and no-one appeared to recognise them. If an operator was asked how he was getting on, he never knew his production target, nor whom to consult with any problems.
- After a hectic day sorting out the slow progress of an order, Helen noticed a group of operators sitting around, apparently with nothing to do. On being asked why, one replied in a bored manner that he thought 'they had run out of card'.
- Several orders for last month were not ready by delivery date and one of the oldest customers warned he might take his business elsewhere.

1 Using brainstorming techniques, list all the possible factors that may have influenced the present state of the company.

2 Divide your brainstorming ideas into two lists: those that are fundamental to the underlying problems and those that are temporary 'hiccups' which will sort themselves out naturally.

3 Role play a meeting between Helen, Barry and their senior managers (you may choose whom to include) and spend about 20 minutes discussing the situation and devising a plan of action.

4 On the basis of these discussions, write a brief report from Barry to the managers summarising the situation and outlining the strategy to be adopted.

Index

absorbed actions 238–239
activity sampling 306–307
advertising 239, 296–297
agenda 282–283
Alderfer, C 315
appraisals 162–163
Argyle, M 71, 258
argument 218–223
attitudes 313–314
authority 13, 156–157
autocratic 268, 270

bar charts 127, 226–227
Barnard, C 320
bar codes 180
brainstorming 277–278

calling notices 281
circulars 94–96
cohesiveness 263
communication
    barriers 69–74
    business related 45–50
    culture related 45–46, 51
    electronic 180–184
    entropic/redundancy 66–68
    feedback loops 49
    formal/informal 46
    handling problems 140–142,
       154–155, 170–173
    importance of 41–43
    improving 74
    in groups 257–261
    meaning of 56–57
    mechanistic approach 56–57
    process 57–66
    relation to structures 12, 52–55
committee structures 279–280
computers 201–202, 204, 207–209
    keyboards 178–179
    memory 186
    networks 181, 183, 199–200,
       205–206
    passwords 184
    printers 183
    spreadsheets 189
    storage 184–188
conclusions, in reports 119
control 198–199
control, span of 12
Cork, K 48
corporate image 239–240
counselling 164–167
curriculum vitae 99, 299

Data Protection Act 187–188
desk-top publishing 196–197
disciplinary procedures 171, 291–293
discrimination 298
division of labour 318
duplicating 195–196

employee participation 34
employers' organisations 271–272
employment 353–355, 362
employment law 298
entropy 66–68
envelopes 82, 88
ergonomics 341

facsimile transmission 183
feedback 49–50
files 184–185
findings, in reports 117
five-point plan 301
flexitime 77
flipcharts 236–237
flow diagrams 176–177, 232
forms, application for job 99, 125
    design 123–124
    report 112
Frazer, M 301

Goldsmith and Clutterbuck 54
grapevines 157–158
graphs 225–228
groups
    in organisations 265–267
    leadership 268–270

groups – *cont.*
  norms 263–264
  process 259–261
  roles 261–263

Harvey-Jones 139
Hawthorne effect 319
headhunting 297
health and safety 247, 349–351, 363
Health and Safety at Work Act 134, 298, 347–348, 352–353
Herzberg, F 316–317
histograms 227–228
house magazines 45
Hunt, 25–26
hygiene factors 316–317

ideograms 59
induction 35–37, 151
ink duplicators 195–196
inputs 178–179
interviewing 159–161, 300–302, 324–330

jargon 62
job applications 97–101
job descriptions 294–296
job satisfaction 134, 309–317
  enlargement 309
  enrichment 309–310
  rotation 309
job specifications 295

Keyboards 178–179

Laser pens 179–180
leadership 268–270
leakage 145
letters
  advertising 94–96
  circulars 94–96
  construction 81–82, 90–91
  job applications 97–101
  layout 84–88
  letterheads 82–84
  standard 96
  tone 92–94

management
  development of 318–321
  function 321–322
  styles 268–270
management services 302–303
maps 230
Maslow, A 314–315
matrices 231–232
matrix structures 31, 39
Mayo, E 264, 319
McGregor, D 320–321
meaning, creation of 56–57
media 242–246
meetings
  agenda 282–284
  calling notices 281
  minutes 284–287
  official roles 278–280
  reaching decisions 278
  types 276–277
memoranda 104–107, 110–111
messages
  conception 58
  encoding 58
  decoding 62
  interpretation 65
  transmission 60–62
method study 303–305
microfilm 184
minutes, types of
  action 285
  narrative 285
  resolution 285
models 233
Morris, D 143, 149
motivation 311–314, 317
Munro Frazer 301

networks 181, 183, 199–200, 205–206
non-verbal communication 143–144, 154–155, 168–169
  accents 153
  appearance 150–152
  eye contact 146–147
  facial expression 148
  gesture 144–146
  orientation 149
  paralinguistics 152–154
  posture 150
  proximity 149–150
  touch 150

norms 263–264
offset duplicators 126
office, the
    design 343–345
    development 345–347, 357–358
    organisation 199–200, 341–343
oral communication 122–123,
    140–142
organisations
    communication in 45–55
    culture 45, 51–52
    definition 7, 11
    divisions 9, 11, 12, 15, 337
    effects of size 25–27
    functions 332–333
    growth 334–337
    influences 333–334
    internal conflict 272–275,
        337–338, 358–359
outputs 191–198
overhead projectors 237

passwords 184
perception 71
performance monitoring 50
personnel function 137–140
persuading 210–211
pie diagrams 229
pictograms 228
phonograms 59
photocopiers 196
posters 73–74
presentations 211–218, 224–239
press releases 244–246
procedures (in reports) 117
process charts 304–305
promotions 239–241
project teams 30

quality control 306–307
quantity control 306
questionnaires 125–127

race relations 298
recruitment 296–299
recommendations (in reports) 119

redundancy 66–68
reference, terms of 117
references for jobs 299
relationships in organisation
    259–260
    line 13–14
    staff 14
relocation 338–341
reorganisation 342–343
reports 107–123, 127–128
    informal 110–112, 117
    long formal 119–120
    oral 122–123
    presentation 127–128
    short formal 113–119
responsibility 13
resistance to change 358–359
Robinson, W 42

Self image 43
selection procedures 294–302
scalar principle 13
Sherif, M 274–275
Sinclair, C 356
slide projections 237
slogans 241
specialisation
    by function 8–9
    coordination 9
spirit duplication 195
spreadsheets 189
storage 184–188
stress 133–136
summarizing 101–103
systems analysis 175
systems 175–178
System X 182

Taylor, F 318
telephones 192–193
teletex 104, 183
telex 103–104
tenosynovitis 350–351
theory X and theory Y 320–321
time study 305–306
trademarks 241
trade unions 271–272

typewriters 193–194

venn diagrams 233
Viewdata 183
visual aids 236–238
voice systems 179

wages 189–190
weeding 185
whiteboards 236–237
word processing 194–195
work measurement 305–308